Praise for *True Compass*

A *USA Today* Bestselling Book of the Year

The *Boston Sunday Globe* Best Nonfiction Book of the Year

"A passionate, partisan, poignant, punch-pulling portrait."

—*Pittsburgh Post Gazette*

"Upbeat, gossipy, and often uproariously funny, as was its author . . . Fans of politics and fans of Ted Kennedy will enjoy this book for its sweep, its readability, and its characters, as fascinating as they were famous. Those who view the Kennedy saga with disgust, disdain, and they might admit, a tinge of envy will find little evasiveness here . . . [He] compiled a roster of legislative achievements unequaled in the history of the U.S. Senate. How he did it informs the lively narrative . . . In TRUE COMPASS, the author found his voice . . . Just as he enjoyed his life, Ted Kennedy enjoys the telling of it, with all of its and his faults."

—*San Francisco Chronicle*

"Long the runner-up, Teddy has made a final, persuasive case for why he may actually be his family's greatest torchbearer."

—*TIME*

"Touching . . . This is a book that all but the most toxic Kennedy critic could love . . . Following a candid first chapter on dealing with the diagnosis of his brain tumor last summer, Kennedy writes evocatively of the years just before World War II that split his family forever . . . Later, there is much substance about his political life. His accounts are richly detailed . . . The youngest Kennedy reveals his own fears . . . [and] reminisces warmly about most of the figures in his public life."

—*Boston Sunday Globe*

"Weaving the history of the twentieth century with his family's tales of triumph and tragedy, this readable memoir is fresh, bittersweet, and is absent the score-settling of most politicians."

—*Chicago Tribune*

"This is really the first time we get the story of the Kennedys from the inside . . . at the inter-dynamics of a family that dominated our consciousness and our country . . . it's a portrait of himself that is so much more reflective and honest that we normally get from politicians."

—Doris Kearns Goodwin

"Filled with colorful tales of his siblings and inside-the-Beltway detail . . . a thoughtful, intermittently gut-wrenching read."

—*Entertainment Weekly*

"Offers rich detail on his relationships with his father, siblings, and children that round out a portrait of a man who lived the most public of lives and yet remained something of a mystery . . . Provides new details about a life in America's famous political family and covers a remarkable career . . . A rare look at life from the inside of a storied American family."

—*New York Times*

"Never mind that you've probably heard a lot of these stories before, TRUE COMPASS leaves the impression of a complicated, passionate man who spent most of his life dealing with a legacy he never sought . . . no one will fail to appreciate the expansive, beloved personality on exhibit here."

—*O, The Oprah Magazine*

"Revealing . . . one of the best biographies/memoirs I have ever read . . . you must read it . . . You will never forget it; you won't put it down."

—Larry King

"Compelling . . . TRUE COMPASS really is a sensation . . . Infused through it all is a sadness and vitality that are Kennedy trademarks, all the more poignant because this is the only memoir a Kennedy brother will ever write . . . But no recitation of Ted Kennedy episodes amply represents the depths of emotion displayed in this volume."

—Bloomberg News

"Kennedy writes in these pages with searching candor about the losses, joys, and lapses of his life; the love and closeness of his family; the solace he found in sailing and the sea; his complex relationships with political allies and rivals. His conversational gifts as a storyteller and his sense of humor—so often remarked on by his friends—shine through here, as does his old-school sense of public service and his hard-won knowledge. In these pages Mr. Kennedy draws some telling portraits of other politicians . . . Later in this volume, Mr. Kennedy addresses his own failings and regrets."

—Michiko Kakutani, *New York Times*

"A lively guide to Kennedy's life . . . a revelatory account of his storied life and career . . . The highs and lows of his extraordinary life are chronicled in this enjoyable work . . . Since people will no longer have the chance to sit with Mr. Kennedy on the porch of his home in his beloved Hyannisport overlooking the ocean as he sips hot tea and tells yarns, reading TRUE COMPASS is the next best thing."

—*Washington Times*

"Offers a full recounting of Kennedy's many legislative victories . . . spiced throughout with the self-deprecating stories for which Kennedy was famous."

—*New York Daily News*

"Memoirs true to the life of an enjoyer . . . a book whose clarity of recollection and expression entitles it to share in the lineage established by America's first great memoir of public life—*The Autobiography of U.S. Grant* . . . [Kennedy's] natural gifts as a storyteller and as a sharp, painterly observer shine through every page . . . [what is] remarkable about this memoir is its capacious and generous spirit . . . a portrait of his extraordinary family, as well as an account of his own eventful life."

—*Los Angeles Times*

"With incomparable wit and candor, Kennedy offers up his perspectives on Senate colleagues, presidents past, and most of all himself . . . Deeply affecting on the subjects of grief, his battle with brain cancer, and his devotion to his family, sailing, and the Senate."

—*People*

"The Kennedy who emerged from his brother's shadow to become one of America's greatest senators appears vividly in this posthumous memoir . . . The book is a self-deprecating and, at times, painfully honest account of a life marked by repeated tragedy . . . it is an odyssey that has to be read to be believed. So much of it is so familiar . . . Yet it comes across as fresh."

—*Financial Times* (U.S. Edition)

"A memoir of triumph and tragedy . . . A great deal of this book consists of anecdotes, of memorable figures, as well as friends, whom Kennedy encountered during his long career . . . Reading these stories is almost as enjoyable as it must have been to hear them when Kennedy kicked back after hours—not without moments of grating obliviousness, but generally with the kind of curiosity and appreciation of human folly . . . the book's lasting historical value, though, lies in its brief but trenchant insider descriptions of political battles during the long period of conservative domination that commenced with the election of Ronald Reagan . . . Kennedy's memoirs, which have become his final political statement, are a testament to his resolve and persistence. But they also bring a jolt of recognition of all that has vanished with him."

—*Philadelphia Inquirer*

"Of course, the recent death of Senator Kennedy adds an extra layer of poignancy, but this would be a welcome addition to the political memoir bookshelf under any circumstances . . . despite the firm line he draws in the sand about discussing his personal life, Kennedy's tone of contrition is sincere. When he was a child, Kennedy's father told him, 'You can have a serious life or a nonserious life.' He chose the former, and at the end, seems genuinely grateful not just for what that life gave him, but what it enabled him to do for others."

—*Publishers Weekly* (starred review)

"An absorbing tour of the Kennedy backlot . . . Kennedy's recollections of his first exposure to national politics are fresh, vivid, and surprising . . . Insiders will also relish some delicious gossip, a hilarious portrait of Reagan's White House, vignettes of Beaverbrook, Brezhnev, and Clinton."

—*Guardian*

"When you read TRUE COMPASS, it is almost like sitting down with Ted Kennedy right by your side and letting him tell you his story . . . I learned so many things about the senator that I did not know . . . This is a very moving memoir . . . you will see his love for his family and politics . . . you will even find yourself laughing at times."

—BestsellersWorld.com

"Kennedy's voice emerges powerfully here . . . Readers get a vivid sense, for example, of the anguish he felt when his brothers were killed . . . as an up-close look at what happens when the history of a family is intertwined with the history of a country, this is high-interest primary source material."

—*Booklist*

"A remarkable book . . . tells of the things that mattered to him, from his Catholic faith to the love of his family to the peace he found sailing. The abundance of personal recollection makes him more real than I think any previous account of his life managed to do."

—Adam Clymer, DailyBeast.com

"It's extremely engrossing, and it's fascinating to hear the senator speak in his own voice about his dramatic life."

—ReadersDigest.com

"A revelation for its intimate view of his formative years . . . written in his characteristically upbeat humor . . . For political junkies, there is a news story on nearly every page of this book."

—PoliticsDaily.com

"The memoir reads like a modern American history lesson, as Kennedy traces his life's story from his childhood days in England before World War II, when his father was the American ambassador, to his diagnosis with brain cancer in 2007—and all the notable political events in between . . . Kennedy enjoys both the highs and lows of his political career."

—TheHill.com

True Compass

To Kara
Maine
'98.
Ted K.

EDWARD M. KENNEDY

a memoir

True Compass

TWELVE

NEW YORK   BOSTON

Twelve
Hachette Book Group
237 Park Avenue
New York, NY 10017
www.HachetteBookGroup.com

Twelve is an imprint of Grand Central Publishing.
The Twelve name and logo are trademarks of Hachette Book Group, Inc.

The publisher is not responsible for websites (or their content) that are not owned by the publisher.

Printed in the United States of America

Originally published in hardcover by Twelve.

First Trade Edition: April 2011
10 9 8 7 6 5 4 3 2 1

ISBN: 978-0-446-53926-5 (pbk.)
LCCN: 2009931859

For Vicki, my true compass on this voyage.

"My bounty is as boundless as the sea,
My love as deep . . . for both are infinite."
—William Shakespeare

I lay on the bowsprit, facing astern, with the water foaming into
    spume under me, the masts with every sail white in the
    moonlight, towering high above me.
I became drunk with the beauty and singing rhythm of it, and
    for a moment I lost myself—actually lost my life.
I was set free!
I dissolved in the sea, became white sails and flying spray,
    became beauty and rhythm, became moonlight and the ship
    and the high dim-starred sky!
I belonged, without past or future, within peace and unity and a
    wild joy, within something greater than my own life, or the
    life of Man, to Life itself!
To God, if you want to put it that way.

               —Eugene O'Neill, *Long Day's Journey into Night*

Contents

True Compass

PROLOGUE

The Torch
2008

It was on the sunny spring day of Tuesday, May 20, 2008, that I emerged from a medicated drowsiness in a Boston hospital bed and looked up into the face of a doctor who explained to me in a somber way that I was about to die, and that I had best begin getting my affairs in order and preparing my friends and family for the end.

As I lay in that hospital bed, my friends and neighbors on Cape Cod were just then getting their boats ready for the summer cruises and races. I intended to be among them, as usual. The Boston Red Sox were a good bet to defend their world championship. There was a presidential primary campaign in progress. My Senate colleagues were pushing forward on our legislative agenda. I had work to do.

No. As much as I respect the medical profession, my demise did not fit into my plans.

I was hardly "in denial" that I faced a grave and shocking threat to my life. The first symptoms of what would prove to be a malignant brain tumor had struck me three days earlier. They'd descended on me as I padded toward the kitchen of the Hyannis Port house that has been the center of my life and happiness for most of my seventy-six years. I was intent on nothing more than taking Sunny and Splash, my much-loved Portuguese water dogs, for their morning walk. My wife, Vicki, and I had just been chatting and having our morning coffee in the sunroom.

Life seemed especially good at that moment. The sixteen years of my marriage to Vicki had been good ones. Her acute understanding and love of *me* had made her my indispensable partner in my life. We shared countless joyful hours aboard my antique wooden schooner *Mya*, including nights of sailing along the coast, guided by the stars. Vicki had given me such a sense of stability and tranquillity that I had almost begun to think of life in those terms—stable and tranquil. But never boring. Certainly not with this funny, passionate, fiercely loyal, and loving woman.

Vicki and I had enjoyed an especially exhilarating winter and early spring. On January 27, thrilled and inspired by Barack Obama and the hope he embodied, I took the podium at American University in Washington to endorse his quest for the presidency. The best hopes of the past and present converged around me. My niece Caroline Kennedy stood at my back, alongside my own son Patrick and the candidate himself. The crowd roared its approval for my message. And I felt myself lifted—with a renewed optimism for my country, and by the unexpected notes of an old bugle, calling me once again to the campaign trail. Other years, other hustings, other adventures swept out of the past. "It is time again for a new generation of leadership," I declared to the cheering crowd in front of us, as another voice echoed down the corridors of my memory: *Let the word go forth from this time and place, to friend and foe alike, that the torch has been passed to a new generation of Americans . . .*

I felt joyous and exuberant through the inevitable exhaustion of the Democratic primary campaign, as I had felt in Wyoming and West Virginia in 1960 for Jack, and in Indiana and California in 1968 for Bobby. "No one said we couldn't have a little fun!" I shouted to a Latino crowd in San Antonio before belting out "Ay Jalisco No Te Rajes" in my version of Spanish. I had so much fun that I sang it again in Laredo. By mid-May, Obama had won the crucial North Carolina primary and had taken the lead in committed delegates. Some commentators were declaring the race already over. I certainly intended to keep on campaigning for him through the late spring and summer, but there was time to steal away for a few sails on Nantucket Sound.

On May 16 I took part in a ceremony at a favorite historic site of mine, the New Bedford Whaling National Historical Park, where I joined Massachusetts congressman Barney Frank and others to cut the ribbon at the Corson Maritime Learning Center. Barney and I had secured appropriations for repairs and other improvements to the building after it was damaged in a 1997 fire. I felt especially good that day, and threw away my prepared remarks to speak from my heart about my love for New Bedford, and the sea, and for the connection to our history that the park represented. Vicki told me afterward that Barbara Souliotis, our dear friend and the longtime chief of staff of my Boston office, who was sitting beside her, turned and whispered, "He's really *on* today!" I certainly felt "on." Change was in the air. And tomorrow, Vicki and I would enjoy our first sail of the year.

But that next morning, everything changed.

I had just meandered through the living room and had come within two steps of the grand piano that my mother, Rose, used to play for the family more than half a century ago as we gathered for dinner. Sometimes Jack, young and thin in his customary rumpled pullover, would stand at about the spot where I passed just then, and sing a solo to Mother's accompaniment.

Suddenly I felt disoriented. I moved toward the door leading to the porch, where several spacious chairs face the lovely prospect that I've known since childhood: a view to Nantucket Sound and the several masted boats at anchor in the nearby harbor. "Well," I told myself, "I'll just go outside and get some fresh air."

I didn't make it outside. Everything seemed hazy. I walked past the front door and into the dining room, where I lowered myself into a chair. That's the last thing I remember until I awoke in the hospital.

I learned later that I'd been discovered almost at once by Judy

Campbell, our household assistant. Judy called out for Vicki, who was still in the sunroom, waiting for me to return. When Vicki saw me, she ran to my side and instructed Judy to call 911, and then my physician in Boston, Dr. Larry Ronan. As she waited for the local rescue team to arrive, Vicki wedged herself into the chair beside me and cradled my head. I was not aware of it then, but she held me tenderly, kissing my cheek and patting me and whispering, "You're going to be okay."

It took just four minutes for the first responder to arrive. He was a Hyannis police officer who told Vicki, "I was an army medic," to which my wife blurted, "Oh, thank God! Come in!" The paramedics arrived about half a minute later. No one knew how to diagnose me. They suspected a stroke. They prepared me for transportation—this took some time—and took me to the Cape Cod Hospital, where I was deeply sedated while they performed initial tests. Vicki was in constant contact with my doctors in Boston, who were in turn in contact with the Cape Cod team. The Boston doctors dispatched a medevac helicopter to transport me to Massachusetts General Hospital. In fairly short order, I was airlifted to the hospital in Boston. Vicki, meanwhile, continued to focus on the necessary tasks. Sitting in the car while I was being readied, before we even left home, she phoned as many members of our combined families as she could reach. "The second I called 911," she explained to me later, "I knew that this was going to be on the news, and I didn't want everyone close to us to find out that way." To every family member who asked Vicki, "Should we come?" she replied, "Yes. Yes. You've got to come." Then, as the chopper hurtled through the air on its half-hour flight to the hospital, Vicki hitched a ride there with the Hyannis fire chief, Harold Brunelle, who is a good friend of ours. She continued calling family members all the way to Boston.

I came out of sedation in the late afternoon. It took me a while to realize where I was; I had no memory of anything after sitting down in my dining room in Hyannis Port. It soon became clear I was in a hospital room, and I was happy to see Vicki's large hazel eyes studying me with obvious love and anxiety. The immediate cause of my collapse had been a generalized seizure brought on by the deeper affliction. Every muscle in my body had contracted severely, and I was in extreme pain.

The children poured into the room that evening. I savored their embraces, and we ordered in chowder from Legal Seafood and watched the Red Sox game on TV.

A biopsy the following Monday confirmed that I had a brain tumor—a malignant glioma in my left parietal lobe. Vicki and I privately were told that the prognosis was bleak—a few months at most.

I respect the seriousness of death—I've had many occasions to meditate on its intrusions. But I wasn't willing to accept the doctor's prognosis for two reasons.

The first was my own obstinate will to carry on in the face of adversity, one of the many habits of discipline that my father instilled in me and all of my brothers and sisters. We were taught never to give up, never to passively accept fate, but to exhaust every last ounce of will and hope in the face of any challenge. This was almost certainly the teaching that led our eldest brother, Joe Jr., to volunteer for a highly dangerous flying assignment near the end of World War II, one that in fact cost him his life. It fueled Jack's determination to stay alive as he floated in the Pacific after his patrol torpedo boat was rammed and sunk by the Japanese. And I am convinced that it accounted for the life force and cheerful resolve of our beloved sister Rosemary, who pursued laughter, games, travel, and social affairs well after it became clear that nature had placed severe limits on her intellectual capacity.

The second was the way the message was delivered. Frankly, it made me furious. I am a realist, and I have heard bad news in my life. I don't expect or need to be treated with kid gloves. But I do believe in hope. And I believe that approaching adversity with a positive attitude at least gives you a chance for success. Approaching it with a defeatist attitude predestines the outcome: defeat. And a defeatist's attitude is just not in my DNA. Anyway, I'd heard this brand of doom speak before. As hard as it was to hear the news about my own illness, it was nothing compared to the body blows I'd suffered when two of my children had been diagnosed with particularly lethal forms of cancer. When Teddy Jr., then twelve, discovered the lump below his knee that turned out to be bone cancer back in 1973, our doctors warned us that very few people survived this form of the disease. We were determined that Teddy would be an exception. His leg had to be amputated and he endured two years of the most painful, taxing medication and therapy. But as I write this, Teddy is a happily married forty-seven-year old businessman and lawyer, and the father of two beautiful children. And then in 2002 my daughter Kara was diagnosed with "inoperable" lung cancer. She faced slim odds of survival, the doctor told us. As with Teddy, the family refused to accept this prognosis. We were told that every doctor we would consult would say the same thing, and I recall saying, "Fine. I just want to hear every one of them say it." But when I brought together a group of experts in the kind of cancer Kara had, they didn't all say the same thing. She did have an operation and aggressive chemotherapy and radiation. My wife, or I, or both of us, accompanied her to her chemotherapy treatments. I prayed for Kara, as I had for Teddy Jr., and frequently attended daily mass. Kara responded to my exhortations to have faith in herself. Today, nearly seven years later as I write this, Kara is a healthy, vibrant, active mother of two who is flourishing. And so, fortified with experience and our faith, Vicki and I decided once again to fight. I would live on for as long as I could. And in electing to live on, I would offer myself as an example to those struggling with the unacceptable news that there is no hope.

Vicki and I began to develop a plan of action. "Let's just take it one step at a time," we told one another.

The first step was to sail. Sailing, for me, has always been a metaphor for life. But on Wednesday, May 22, the day I left Massachusetts General, as Vicki, the dogs, and I stepped aboard *Mya*, docked and waiting for us at the pier in Hyannis Port, our sail was more than a metaphor: it was an *affirmation* of life. *Mya* cut smartly through the sparkling waters of Nantucket Sound under a brisk wind—the same waters on which Jack had taught me to sail more than sixty-five years earlier. Everything seemed back to normal, except for the crowd of cameramen and reporters who awaited us onshore.

The culminating event of my hiatus on the Cape was the annual Figawi regatta on Memorial Day. In this spectacular season-opening race, some three thousand sailors in two-hundred-odd boats of all sizes compete in various divisions in a race from Hyannis to Nantucket and then, two days later, back again. Vicki and I, Teddy Jr. and his wife, Kiki, and our usual crew of good friends had won our division on the race back from Nantucket to Hyannis the previous year. I'd itched for the chance to defend my title, even after the symptoms struck; but my wise first mate was understandably hesitant. But when the weather report predicted clear skies and a strong southwest breeze for the almost due north race course back from Nantucket to Hyannis—perfect conditions for a schooner like *Mya*—Vicki smiled at me and said, "Let's do it." It was a glorious day. For the sake of the historical record, I will note that *Mya* finished second, with a crew that included Vicki, daughter Caroline, daughter-in-law Kiki, sons Teddy Jr. and Patrick, and our old friend Senator Christopher Dodd of Connecticut.

While we were sailing and digesting the news, we had asked our dear friend Dr. Larry Horowitz to line up a team of doctors to consult with us. Larry Horowitz is a Yale Medical School graduate and my former chief of staff, who had also served as staff director of my Senate subcommittee on health in the late 1970s. Larry immediately tapped into his vast network of contacts, and began feeding us advice on doctors as well as state-of-the-art medical centers. He brought them all together for a meeting in Boston.

I welcomed the doctors who had assembled from around the country to advise us. "I want to thank you all for coming," I told them. "I want to approach this in a way that makes sense. I want to be prudently aggressive. And I want this process to be helpful to others. If I can show that there is hope for me, perhaps I can give hope to all those who face this kind of disease. I want to do that. I want to give people hope." By the end of the meeting, we had decided on a plan for surgery, followed by chemotherapy and radiation. Unlike some cancers, mine would be treated like a chronic disease, requiring continued treatment after the initial phase that Vicki referred to as "shock and awe."

We headed to Duke Medical Center in Durham, North Carolina, for surgery a couple of days later. Vicki recalls that I was on the phone nearly the entire trip, asking my Senate colleagues on the committee I chaired to help shepherd through some particular pieces of legislation that were important to me. I asked Barbara Mikulski, the able senior senator from Maryland, to take the lead on the higher education bill. To Chris Dodd I turned over the work on mental health parity. I conferred with Speaker of the House Nancy Pelosi on some of the issues that we were working on with the House. I didn't want to leave unfinished work on the table. My personal affairs were in order, and I suffered neither dread nor anxiety. I intended to beat this thing for as long as I could. But it didn't hurt to have all my bases covered, just in case.

The surgery accomplished everything the doctors had hoped. And as Vicki and I headed happily home to Hyannis Port a week later, we began planning our steps toward a secret goal that she and I had agreed upon the very day we committed to the surgery: if everything went as expected, we would travel to the Democratic National Convention in Denver and I would address the delegates.

Being able to speak at the Democratic convention in August, as I had done at so many conventions past, became my mission and stayed in the forefront of my mind during my radiation and chemotherapy treatments that summer, as Vicki and I made the round trip by car from Hyannis Port to Boston five days a week for six weeks. The timetable was in our favor: radiation would end in July, and we'd been told that I could expect to regain much of my energy after that. The convention was to be at the end of August. It made for an ideal goal. I have always been a person who schedules his time, and I always try to be on time. Having open-ended free time makes me restless. I suppose you could say that preparing for the convention was also part of my recuperation that summer.

And so I embarked on a summer of rehabilitation, sailing, and planning to rejoin my fellow Democrats at the moment of their great celebration. I sailed nearly every day. Teddy Jr. delighted me by setting up his office in Jack's old house, nearly next door to us, and moving in along with Kiki and their children, Kiley and Teddy III. Kara and her two children, Grace and Max, also spent most of the summer on the Cape. Patrick was there a lot, as much as the congressional schedule allowed. Curran Raclin, Vicki's son and my stepson whom I had helped raise since he was nine, was working in Boston and often just drove down for dinner. Caroline Raclin, the newly minted Wesleyan graduate, was a frequent visitor. My sister Jean even rented a house in Hyannis Port for a while. And of course Eunice and Ethel and lots of nieces and nephews were already there. I decided that I was finally going to indulge my passion for Four Seas, the legendary ice cream that is freshly made on Cape Cod only in the summer. I may be the only patient in the history of Massachusetts General who went through both chemotherapy and radiation and *gained* weight!

I soon began work on my convention speech, asking my longtime friend and old speechwriter Bob Shrum to come talk to Vicki and me. I knew essentially what I wanted to say at the outset, and Bob and Vicki and I have a synergistic way of working together.

As the summer lengthened, I felt my strength returning, just as the doctors had predicted. Still, there was no medical guarantee that I'd be able to follow through on my hope. We decided to keep this project a secret, but of course speculation eventually mounted that I *might* attend the convention.

We flew to Denver on Sunday, August 24, the day before the convention opened, in a chartered jet. With us were my internist Larry Ronan and some close friends and family members. Inside the private apartment in Denver that we had rented, my aides and I began a run-through of my speech on a teleprompter. After a minute or two I held up my hand. "You know, I really don't feel well," I said. I felt a sharp pain in my side and we didn't know what it was. I was taken to a hospital, where I was surrounded by three doctors, all of them, coincidentally, named Larry, which would have been funny if I hadn't been in so much pain.

Unbelievably, after making it through brain surgery, radiation, and chemotherapy and meeting my goal of being ready and able to address the delegates in Denver, I had been struck, out of the blue and for the first time in my life, with a kidney stone. As the doctors prepared to administer a very powerful pain medication, my wife, who is usually unflappable in a crisis, burst into tears. "If you give him pain medicine, then you will have made the decision for him about speaking tonight. You can't take away his ability to make this decision for himself. He's worked too hard for this night." After doing a back-of-the-envelope calculation on how long the medication would stay in my bloodstream, the doctors assured her that it would be out of my system in time for me to speak, though, as they later told us, they did not think I would be feeling up to speaking in any event.

Now doctors from all over Denver had begun to descend on my room, Larrys and non-Larrys alike. A neurologist arrived, and a urologist, and several other -ologists. I welcomed them all, of course; but Vicki's preoccupation (and mine) was not diagnosis, it was the danger of overmedication and overpowering sleep well past my schedule for appearing at the Pepsi Center.

We were not vigilant enough. A nurse gave me more pain medication when no one was looking. The doctor had not yet changed the orders in the chart to reflect our private conversations. Vicki, shall we say, remonstrated with her. Yet there it was, the sleep-inducing drug, coursing anew through my system. How long before it would lift?

"What do you think?" I asked Vicki drowsily.

"You can just go out and wave," she replied. "Just go out there with the family and wave."

But I had not come all the way to Denver just to wave.

We worked on a compromise: Shrum cut my prepared remarks down to about four lines, in case my deep drowsiness persisted. Then, assuming the best—which by now was not as good as I'd hoped—he cut the original in half. That would be the version I would give if I was strong and awake enough to speak at any length at all.

The convention's opening gavel was scheduled for 6 p.m. At around 4:30, I awoke and told Vicki, "I probably ought to get up now and see if I can walk and not fall flat on my face." I made it from my bed to the end of the room. "I think I'll go back to sleep now," I said.

I didn't sleep long. We would have to leave for the center no later than 6:30 if we had any hope of being on time. I had not had the chance to rehearse my remarks on the teleprompter and had not seen the text in two days. Nor would I again until I spoke it. We showered and dressed at the hospital. Someone was combing my hair as the aides stared at their wristwatches; someone else was wrapping my hand in an Ace bandage, to conceal the intravenous line still implanted there.

Larry Horowitz was on the phone with the Pepsi Center. They needed to know which version of the speech if any to put in the teleprompter. I said the original one that I had rehearsed at the Cape, but Vicki and Larry persuaded me that Shrum's abbreviated version was probably a better idea.

"Let's go," I said. The three Larrys—Ronan, Horowitz, and Larry Allen, a wonderful young doctor we had met when I had surgery at Duke who had coincidentally moved to Denver—escorted us to a waiting van. Vicki and I sat in the middle seats, between the driver and the doctors. We sped off toward a convention hall I'd never been in, and a stage whose contours I did not know, to give a version of a speech that I had never seen. Even the full speech had become the stuff of distant memory.

I can handle this, I kept telling myself. *I can handle this.*

My niece Caroline Kennedy gave a beautiful and heartwarming introduction. After a spectacular film produced by Mark Herzog and Ken Burns, we heard the announcer's voice: "Ladies and gentlemen, Senator Edward Kennedy." This was it. Showtime.

My wife walked with me out onstage and to the podium, held my face, and kissed me. And then she went to sit with the rest of our family. I could feel myself start to settle down.

And so on Monday evening, August 25, 2008, I fulfilled my personal dream that would never die. "It is so wonderful to be here," I declared to the cheering delegates. "Nothing, nothing was going to keep me away from this special gathering tonight."

I acknowledged the friends and family members in the hall: the people who had stood with me through the successes and setbacks, the victories and defeats, over the decades. I then made a vow that I would be on the floor of the United States Senate in January 2009 to continue the cause of my life—affordable health care as a fundamental right.

"There is a new wave of change all around us, and if we set our compass true, we will reach our destination—not merely victory for our party, but renewal for our nation."

As I approached my conclusion, the final phrases of my speech demanded a high note—a bugle call. They were a conjoining of John F. Kennedy's words and my own. I took a breath and gathered my strength, as Jack's words and mine converged:

"And this November, the torch will be passed again to a new generation of Americans.

"And so with Barack Obama—for you and for me, for our country and for our cause—the work begins anew, the hope rises again, and the dream lives on."

It is that passing of the torch and that living dream that have inspired me to write this memoir. For several years, long before the prospects for my longevity had abruptly come into question, I had been building an archive of my memories, both personal and political, through an oral history project at the University of Virginia. I also had more than fifty years of personal notes and diaries that I kept. I'd supposed that they would be useful in an account of my life.

As I grappled with the dire implications of my illness, I realized that my own life has always been inseparable from that of my family. When I sit at the front porch of our Cape house, in the sunshine and sea-freshened air, I think of them often: my parents and my brothers and sisters, all departed now save for Jean and myself. And each alive and vibrant in my memory. I remember how each of us, distinct and autonomous from one another though we were, melded wholeheartedly into a family, a self-contained universe of love and deepest truths that could not be comprehended by the outside world.

My story is their story, and theirs is mine. And so it shall be in these pages.

PART ONE

Family

CHAPTER ONE

Safe Harbor
1941

The bridle paths on Cape Cod are mostly old cranberry roads. Deep underground, clear waters help feed a vast aquifer system. The wet, peaty terrain is among the best in the nation for cranberry-growing, and as I look at it from the air, flying home after a week in Washington, this fertile swath of land can resemble a pink-and-green patchwork quilt in harvest season.

I rode on horseback along those peaceful bridle paths with my father when I was a small boy, on summer mornings in 1941, just months before America entered World War II. My father wore flannel shirts and scuffed horseman's boots on those rides, and looked about like any other fellow on Cape Cod who liked to ride horses.

A year and a half earlier, in another place, I had seen my father in different attire, different circumstances: wearing a tall black hat and black cutaway coat, and getting in and out of limousines with important-looking men, many of them with bushy white mustaches, who wore similar black clothes and serious expressions. The Kennedy family was in London, where my father was ambassador to the Court of St. James's. I was seven then, and understood dimly that a big war was happening, and that it might come to London soon, and that my dad was working very hard to prevent this. He could not prevent it, and we all came back home. Now

America was on the brink of war. I understood that my two eldest brothers were thinking about enlisting.

I understood these things, and yet they were abstractions, fleeting elements in the half-real, half-dreamed universe of a small boy's mind. None of us, perhaps excepting my father, could anticipate what the war would mean to us: the terrible sacrifices it would exact within our family. Not even my father could imagine the centrality of the Kennedys in the postwar world: the struggles of Jack, and then Bobby, and then to some degree myself, to build upon our country's military victory with victories for social justice and democracy.

The plaid-shirted figure on horseback in front of me on those morning rides was not—and never would be to me—primarily an American diplomat, or financial titan, or motion picture producer, or source of exotic legend. He was my father.

Such was the perspective of the boy on the trailing horse.

From my vantage point as the youngest of the nine Kennedy children, my family did not so much live in the world as comprise the world. Though I have long since outgrown that simplistic view, I have never questioned its emotional truth. We depended upon one another. We savored food and music and laughter with one another. We learned from and taught one another. We worshipped with one another. We loved one another. We were mutually loyal, even as we were mutually competitive, with an intensity that owed more to joy than to an urge for dominance. These values flowed into us on the energies of Joseph and Rose Kennedy. They helped us form bonds among one another, and to develop personalities based on those bonds, to an extent that remains to this day underappreciated by the chroniclers of my family. They sustain me still. They lie at the heart of the story I wish to tell.

I was nine years old in that summer of 1941, the final summer of the familiar world into which I was born. I was not clear why we had all come back home from England, but I was happy that we had. I was too young to fully understand that my father had resigned his ambassadorship. I was

certainly too young to comprehend that he'd resigned because he had of-
fended some people in England by saying that the British might not be
capable of fighting a war against Germany. It would have been news to me
that Dad had displeased President Roosevelt with these same remarks. Or
that when he was away from the Cape house that summer, in New York
and Washington, he was trying to persuade other people to join his effort
at keeping America out of the war. Or that, despite their differences, Joseph
Kennedy continued to support Franklin Roosevelt as president.

I just knew that on weekends, he and I would ride horseback together
on the Cape, and that was all I really cared to know.

It's hardly surprising that these facets of my father's life were unknow-
able to me as a child. If my father were alive today, there are things I
would like to ask him—about his relationship with FDR and his government service—but I've rarely investigated the myths surrounding him.
Perhaps other sons and daughters of towering personalities might find it
familiar: his presence within the family eclipsed nearly everything else
about him. In some persistent region of my mind, Joseph P. Kennedy
remains to me, eternally and solely, *my dad.* Just as I remain the ninth and
youngest child of all the Kennedys.

Dad was always an early riser. At around six o'clock, I'd blink awake
to a rap on my bedroom door on the second floor of our house at Hyannis
Port, followed by, "You can come riding if you are downstairs in five minutes!" He meant exactly that. If I were late, he would be gone. I was seldom late.

Dad always bought his horses in Ireland, big Irish hunters that were
strong and calm. Most times it was just the two of us, and I savored these
chances to have him all to myself. Bobby was never interested in riding.
Jack liked it, but he sometimes suffered asthma attacks afterward, and
concluded that he was allergic to horses. Joe Jr. loved to ride, but he tended
to gallop off on his own.

My father's horse was named Swifty. I rode Blue Boy, an old and gentle
animal that all my brothers had ridden in years past. If it was harvest season,

the cranberry-hauling pickup trucks would ramble along the roads and keep the vines at bay, and Dad and I could ride side by side. After the trucks left, the vines would quickly overtake the road again, and we'd ride single file. Sometimes in high summer they grew so fast that my father assigned me the task of clearing them away again, and this gave me the chance to plunge into one of those clear, chilly ponds for a quick swim. Other times, at low tide, I'd drop behind to gather up some of the clams that had ridden in on the waves: succulent Northern quahogs and sweet surf clams.

My father was a complicated man, and during our rides I came to know different sides of him. His temperament was never hard to discern. If he was in a cheerful mood, he would talk freely in his high, Boston-pitched staccato, and our conversations could be rich and animated: how well (or not) I was performing at school or at sports, a book he wanted me to read. If he was preoccupied, he'd be introspective and mute, his reddish hair aglow and his rimless glasses glinting in the morning light, with only the clop-clop of our horses to break the silence. Most typically, Dad liked to wax philosophical, thinking out loud about the family.

"The summer of 1941 was the last one that our family would ever have together," my mother has written.* Is that literally true? Were all eleven of the famously in-motion Kennedys ever together under the Cape house roof that year? I can't recall, but Mother usually had her facts straight. In any case, I can look back and see all of them as they might well have been on a given weekend morning, each one distinct yet a part of the whole; absorbed in the moment, wondrously alive.

Their familiar bedlam would be pouring through the windows as Dad and I returned from our ride, me still tingling from the chill morning air and my father's coveted companionship, avid for breakfast, imitating his stride. We would hear their raucous, contending voices and laughter, their

---

* Quoted passages are from *Times to Remember* by Rose Kennedy, and my father's letters, published in *Hostage to Fortune*, edited by Amanda Smith. See the bibliography for elaboration.

high-spirited insults and their tramping on the stairs, as telephones rang, dogs barked, radios blared, and some passing virtuoso banged out a few notes on the living room piano en route to somewhere else. A visitor once recalled being startled by "so many young people . . . who looked alike when they grinned and managed to keep the atmosphere in the house at a fever pitch." Well, that was our family.

Joe Jr., rugged and magnetic, might have been locked in an early-morning duel of wits with Jack—these two were archcompetitors in a family of competitors. If Jack managed to outdo him at chess or in one of the word games he loved, "Categories" maybe, Joe tended to retaliate with a little friendly muscle. But as competitive as they were with each other, they were unbeatable when united: in 1938, the two of them crewed together to win the intercollegiate sailing championships on the waters off Annapolis.

I looked up to my older brothers. "Hero worship" wouldn't be too far off the mark. As long as I can remember, I wanted a boat so I could sail the way they did. They were my earliest sailing instructors, and they encouraged me more than they even knew. I did my first solo sailing under their watchful eyes. "You can go as far as that boat anchored over there, Teddy, then sail back to us . . . Stay inside the breakwater . . . Let me see you tack . . . Now gybe . . ."

I remember one July at the Cape when the cook had baked a big beautiful birthday cake for Joe, slathered with chocolate frosting. Joe loved chocolate frosting, so he sneaked into the kitchen while the cake was cooling, scraped all the frosting off the surface and sides, and sculpted it into a little pile on the side of the platter so that he could eat it all when the cake was cut. Jack was watching this. As soon as Joe left the kitchen, Jack charged in, scooped up the pile with one hand, and raced outdoors. Joe heard the commotion and lit out in pursuit. He chased Jack all the way to the end of the breakwater, where Jack dodged and ducked around a small navigation beacon, trying to balance the pile of warm chocolate in his hand, while Joe tried to trap him. Jack was rescued by Eddie Moore, Dad's secretary, before Joe could close in.

We competed in every conceivable way: at touch football, at sailing, at skipping rocks, and seeing whose seashell could float the farthest out to sea. We competed at games of wit and information and debate. We competed for attention at the dinner table, which meant a good deal of boning up: entry stakes for those conversations amounted to a substantial mastery of the topic under discussion. It is no accident that copious research and preparation have defined my methods as a senator: I will not champion a bill or a cause, no matter how complex, until I have understood it well enough to satisfy the standards my father set for table talk.

Competition, of course, is the route to achievement in America. As I think back to my three brothers, and about what they had accomplished before I was even out of my childhood, it sometimes has occurred to me that my entire life has been a constant state of catching up.

By "catching up," I mean with my own life and with the members of my family. I don't mean that I felt envious of any of them; I loved and respected every single one. I mean that they set an extraordinarily high standard for living a life in general, and in particular in public service. So from the very beginning I started really behind the eight-ball. My brothers and sisters were already on a very fast track. I was the ninth of nine.

There was no question of catching up to Joe Jr. in that summer of 1941. At twenty-six, he had already started to prepare himself for a career in politics. He had attended Harvard and the London School of Economics, and had served as a delegate to the 1940 Democratic National Convention in Chicago. There, he showed his independent streak by backing James A. Farley for the nomination against an unprecedented third run by Franklin D. Roosevelt, whom Joe Sr. continued to support despite their complicated relationship.

Dad respected his son's decision. He respected all our decisions that were not frivolous. His scrupulous neutrality regarding our life choices stands counter to one of the more persistent myths about the Kennedy family: that our father had somehow "designated" all his sons for office at the highest levels of government, starting with the presidency for Joe. This is simply not the case. My eldest brother's political ambitions were entirely his own, as was another ambition that ran even more sharply against our father's grain.

In agreement with Dad, Joe had made anti-interventionist arguments in his two years at Harvard Law School. But now, convinced of America's inevitable involvement in the war, Joe had dropped out of law school and put his political plans on hold to join the navy as an aviator.

Less than a year earlier, in October 1940, in a national radio address endorsing Franklin Roosevelt for reelection and at the same time pleading for American neutrality in the war, Joseph Kennedy Sr. had reminded his listeners, "My wife and I have given nine hostages to fortune. Our children and your children are more important than anything else in the world." Yet he uttered not a murmur of protest at his eldest son's decision, nor at Jack's that same summer.

Joe would commence training in the fall and earn his wings the following year. Then he would be sent off to England, and from there to the British coastal skies, headed for Europe, and then on to eternity.

In an essay for a privately printed book of reminiscences about Joe, which he edited, Jack wrote, "Joe did many things well, but I have always felt that he achieved his greatest success as the oldest brother. Very early in life he acquired a sense of responsibility towards his brothers and sisters, and I do not think that he ever forgot it." Joe, too, saw the family as his world, and Jack understood this.

Jack also saw our eldest brother as something of a puzzle. "I suppose I knew Joe as well as anyone," he wrote in that essay, "and yet, I sometimes wonder whether I ever knew him. He had always a slight detachment from things around him—a wall of reserve which few people ever succeeded in penetrating."

Jack, twenty-four that summer, might well have been describing himself. I cannot deny that he had qualities that made him enigmatic to some. He read more books than any of us, and perhaps the ideas in them drew his attention inward. I served in Washington—all too briefly—with Jack in the early 1960s, when he was president and I was a senator. In this sense we were adults together, and colleagues at the pinnacle of public service. Yet I always looked up to Jack. He was more than a revered older brother to me. He was almost a second father. In fact, he was my godfather, a role he had requested in a letter to our mother, written from Choate in 1932, shortly before I was born. "Can I be Godfather to the baby?" he asked. Rose Kennedy gladly consented. She held to the theory that godparents should play active roles in guiding younger children. Nearly fifteen years in age separated us, which meant that my childhood self saw him as a grown-up, and that perception never really changed, bolstered by his godfatherly enthusiasm.

Jack claimed a broad mandate. Delighted that my arrival was February 22, the birthday of our first president, he waged an unsuccessful campaign for me to be named George Washington Kennedy. He invented wondrous games for us from the simplest objects on the seashore. Scallop shells became "floaties," or tiny racing yachts. Sometimes Jack and I would play "football" without a football. I would run a pass pattern as if I were the receiver and he the quarterback. But instead of throwing a pigskin, Jack would bat a softball on a line into my outstretched hands with the accuracy of Sammy Baugh of the Washington Redskins. Later he taught me to sail. He was my mentor, protector, wise counsel, and constant friend.

Jack was bedeviled by health challenges for all of his life, but he refused to let illness slow him down for long. He was resilient enough to play junior varsity football at Harvard, work as a ranch hand in Arizona, and sail competitively in Hyannis Port and elsewhere. He was fearless enough to tear around Europe in his own convertible in 1937; and, amid the tensions of 1939, to explore the Soviet Union, the Balkan countries, parts of the Middle East, Czechoslovakia, and Germany, returning to London on September 1, the day Germany invaded Poland. The book that resulted from these travels—an expansion of his Harvard senior honors thesis and titled *Why England Slept*—was published in 1940 and became a best-seller.

Jack would occasionally send us "mementos" of his travels, and some of these were rather exotic. During one of his Arizona visits, my brother decided that his Doberman pinscher was getting to be a nuisance, so he crated the dog up and shipped him back to the family in Hyannis Port, with special instructions for me to look after him. A delivery truck brought the dog to our house from the railroad station. A note fixed to the crate read, "My name is Moe and I don't bite." When I looked at Moe through the slats, I was glad for that news, because Moe was one big, muscular dog.

I opened the crate. Moe bounded out of the cage, gave me a glancing nip, knocked me over, and bounded full speed down the lawn. He circled a bit and then made for the McKelvey house next door. Johnny McKelvey, a boy a little younger than me, was standing in his yard, his eyes riveted on Moe. Moe bore in on Johnny and sent him flying like a tenpin in a bowling alley. Johnny started to bawl. His nanny came rushing out of the house and screamed, "Get up, Johnny! Get up! Your mother doesn't want you to ruin those nice new pants! You're getting a grass stain on them!" Johnny couldn't stop howling. Moe, meanwhile, was having a hell of a good time. He came charging back up to our house, tongue and tail waving. The delivery truck man, a true profile in courage, crouched, spread his arms, and somehow managed to grab him. Dad had been monitoring all this, and had reached an executive decision. "Put him back in that crate and ship him back!" he ordered me. I was happy to oblige; it gave me a rare chance to tease Jack. I wrote him a note back on the crate: "This dog that doesn't bite just jumped out of his cage and bit me. Teddy."

My eldest sister, Rosemary, was twenty-three in 1941. Luminously pretty and round-faced, with a widow's peak, dark brows, and a great smile that dimpled her cheeks, Rosemary was the one sibling with whom all the others were unfailingly gentle. Her affliction, diagnosed as mental retardation, left her struggling to comprehend things as quickly and as clearly as other people. She was a sweet and loving human being.

Rosemary enriched the humanity of all of us. Our sister Eunice seemed always to be near her, helping her through simple childhood games such as dodgeball, inviting her along and giving her assignments in sailing races. As she grew into adolescence, Rosemary knew she could count on Jack or Joe to escort her to dances at the Yacht Club at the Cape, or to the Stork Club in New York. I looked out for her too, when I could, though I was fourteen years younger—she was my godmother, after all. Dad wrote affectionate letters to her from abroad, and Mother actually altered her own handwriting from the swirling "fine Spencerian hand" on which she'd prided herself, to a simpler style that imitated typographical print, so that Rosemary would have less trouble following it.

But in the fall of that year, our father, concerned that Rosemary's condition would pose insurmountable dangers to her as an adult woman in the world, listened to doctors who assured him that a new form of neurosurgery would greatly benefit her and improve her quality of life. The doctors were wrong, the surgery further injured Rosie, and my parents were devastated. I, of course, knew and understood nothing of what had happened. Rosemary spent her remaining sixty-three years mostly in comfortable supervision at her home in a Catholic community in Wisconsin. Over the years, through her regular visits to Eunice's home or her summer days on Cape Cod or wintertime in Florida or Thanksgiving at Jean's, Rosemary remained a loving and inspirational presence in our family, not just for her siblings, but for the next generations too.

If Kathleen happened to be at the Cape with us, there'd be a touch of stardust in the house. Kathleen, twenty-one in 1941, had already made a glittering debut into London society before the king and queen in 1938, the year Dad arrived there as ambassador—a debut that she shared with Rosemary. Admirers of all ages and nationalities trailed in "Kick's" wake. She'd returned to America and completed two years at Finch College in Manhattan. She spent a good deal of time on the Cape that summer, before signing on as a reporter and reviewer at the *Washington Times-Herald*.

The war soon spoke to Kick's sense of duty, as it had to that of Joe Jr. and Jack. In 1943 she would put aside her reporter's notebook and mink coat and recross the Atlantic to London to join the grim, vital mission of the American Red Cross.

Eunice, lanky, athletic, and intense at twenty, might have been trooping up to the house from the tennis court after an early-morning match with a friend, a barrette clinging to her tousled hair. "Keep up your tennis and your golf," Dad instructed her from London in 1940. "I am still going to make a champion out of you." A champion she became: tennis player, swim team captain, and superb competitive sailor, winning many races at the Cape in those years. Eunice's famous drive, which she applied to good works in her adult life, may have been prompted in part by a wish to emulate Joe Jr. and Jack. She remarked in later years, "To us they were marvelous creatures, practically god-like, and we yearned to please them and be acceptable."

Pat might have been curled on a sofa in her robe and bobby sox, flipping through a copy of *Variety* or *Photoplay* as Dad and I headed into the house. She was seventeen in 1941, and dreamed quietly of the Hollywood glamour world that she would one day be a part of. She agreed with Kick and Eunice that in Joe Jr. and Jack the family had its own bright stars. "To us they were heroes, young gods," she once reminisced, echoing her sister.

Our father's career as a movie studio investor and producer in the 1920s and '30s inspired her. After directing and acting in several plays at Rosemont, Pat became a world traveler and travel writer, a producer for the beloved singer Kate Smith, and, in time, part of the Hollywood scene herself. She married the British screen actor Peter Lawford in 1954.

Pat always had a good eye for detail. In a 1946 diary entry, she gently lampooned Winston Churchill, who stayed at our Palm Beach house while in America to receive an honorary degree from the University of Miami: "We hadn't been in the house long before Winston appeared downstairs with an enormous cigar, bare-footed in his dressing gown, complaining as to whether quarter to ten meant quarter to or past. Mrs. C. calmed him [and] he went upstairs."

Multilayered, deeply religious, Bobby was loving and warm beneath his famously aggressive exterior. He was a collector of stamps in those early days, small and shy, a stubborn struggler in the classroom and on the playing fields. A resolute youthful reader of "serious" books: *The Crisis*, *The Hurricane*, and *Men Against the Sea* in one stretch of 1939. A year before that, he'd composed an essay about himself, probably for a school assignment:

> I am thirteen years old, and about five feet two inches tall. I have got a lot of freckles. I have hazel eyes, and blond hair which is plenty hard to keep down because I have many licks, and so much of it. I am not very fat, but fat enough. . . .
>
> I have a pretty good character on the whole, but my temper is not too good. I am not jelous of any one, I have a very loud voice, and talk alot, but sometimes my talk is not very interesting.

My tablemate at breakfast—at a small separate table a short distance from the big family one—would likely be my sister Jean, the closest of the children to me in age. This arrangement did not necessarily thrill Jean. She was thirteen then, and yearned to be included among the older siblings privileged enough to sit with Mom and Dad. So did I, if truth be told, but the rules were the rules. Occasionally another sister would take pity on Jean and say, "I'll switch with you." No one ever said that to *me*.

My family's future ambassador to Ireland was a tender and shy little girl. She looked to Joe Jr., her godfather, for special attention among the elders, and Joe provided it. After the loss of him, it was Jean, in a wide-brimmed white hat and floral dress, who in 1945 would christen the destroyer USS *Joseph Kennedy Jr.* It was Jean who would introduce her Manhattanville College roommate Ethel Skakel, lively and prankish at seventeen, to the twenty-year-old Bobby, and then subtly steer the two toward one another until Bobby "got it" and married Ethel in 1950.

Also at the Big House, as we called it, and nearly as much "family" as we nine children, would be the Gargan kids—Joey, Mary Jo, and Ann. These were the children of Joseph F. and Agnes Fitzgerald Gargan, my mother's sister. After Agnes's death in 1936, my parents took the small trio into the Kennedy household for summers and school vacations. Joey was eleven in 1941, two years older than me, but he was my constant chum. Dad and Mother took good care of them and saw that they were interwoven into the family's fabric.

The small figure who held us all together might have been arriving at the house just as Dad and I were. She'd have stepped out of the blue two-door coupe that she drove to and from morning mass at St. Francis Xavier Church despite barely being able to see over the top of the steering wheel. Unlike the rest of us, my mother would have been dressed in a way befitting respectable society, in a tilted broad-brimmed straw hat and floral dress, her earrings and pearls in place, a small purse held tightly in her two gloved hands.

Both of my parents were deeply religious, and the family prayed together daily and attended mass together at least weekly. Yet it is Rose Kennedy, mainly, to whom I owe the gift of faith as the foundation of my life. It is a core factor in my understanding of who I am.

My own center of belief, as I matured and grew curious about these things, moved toward the great Gospel of Matthew, chapter 25 especially, in which he calls us to care for the least of these among us, and feed the hungry, clothe the naked, give drink to the thirsty, welcome the stranger, visit the imprisoned. It's enormously significant to me that the only description in the Bible about salvation is tied to one's willingness to act on behalf of one's fellow human beings. The ones who will be deprived of salvation—the sinners—are those who've turned away from their fellow man. People responsive to the great human condition, and who've tried to alleviate its misery—these will be the ones who join Christ in Paradise.

To me, this perspective on my faith has almost literally been a life-saver. It has given me strength and purpose during the greatest challenges I have faced, the roughest roads I've traveled.

Mother was also our Pied Piper into the world of knowledge and ideas. She led us on educational outings to museums and concerts, to Concord and Bunker Hill and the Old North Church, rattling out improvised math challenges to us along the way. ("What is two plus two, subtract three, then add two?!") She was our unflagging grammarian and standard-bearer of decorous speech. Woe unto those of us who neglected to use "whom" after a preposition! Once Mother wrote to me, "I noticed you are quoted as using the word 'ass' in several expressions. I do not think you should use that word. I am sure you realize it really does not look very well in print." I was forty years old and a senator when she sent that one. It still hangs on my Senate office wall. Still later, she nailed me again: "I just saw a story in which you said: 'If I was president.' You should have said, 'If I were president' . . . which is correct because it is a condition contrary to fact."

She was moderator of our topical dinner table conversations, the topics—geography one night, the front-page headlines the next—announced in advance on cards that she wrote out and pinned to a billboard near the dining room. She was the disciplinarian of all our headstrong impulses, and was sometimes strict: spankings and whacks with a coat hanger were in her arsenal, as were banishments to the closet. On one such expedition, I stood in the darkness feeling sorry for myself, until I realized I was not alone: Jean was standing beside me, serving out her own time for some infraction of the rules.

But Mother was also the tender index-card archivist of the small moments, the letters, notes, and remarks that were the lifeblood of our family. "Having barrels of fun," I once cable-grammed her from the Riviera. "Send money for more barrels." She kept that one, and hundreds like it.

Through all of this, the house on Marchant Avenue in Hyannis Port was the Kennedys' safe harbor. My father liked to say that "home holds no fear for me." We understood what he meant. We knew that we could always always come home, that we could make mistakes, get defeated, but when all was said and done, we would be respected and appreciated at home. Dad himself had no fear because he knew in his heart that he was working hard for the family; he was doing everything he possibly could to show us how to lead constructive lives. But at the end of the day, it was up to each of us to carry out what he'd taught us. This was the abiding philosophy at the Cape house. And so it remains today for Vicki and myself, and everyone in the family who comes to stay with us.

We were just incredibly close, all of us, through all our younger years and after. And even though the Cape house was our base, and you'd think we would be restless to get away from it now and then, explore other places, that was not the case. Our whole lives were centered in this one place. We didn't really go out to other places to play. We didn't go off to other kinds of events. It was all here, all here: all the playing, all the enjoyment, all the fun.

For me, it still is. And always shall be.

The original structure was built in 1902 and known then as the Malcolm Cottage. My father rented it in 1926, while his growing family still lived in Brookline, Massachusetts. Dad bought the cottage and enlarged it two years later, as a summer retreat. My own earliest memories of "home" revolve around the house in Bronxville, New York, where I lived most of the time in my early years; but in 1941, Dad closed the Bronxville house down. In the decades that followed, as fate and fortune scattered us to far-flung cities and ports of call, it was the Hyannis Port house, paradoxically, that grew in its stature as our center.

It was the place from where I strode proudly on summer days into the surrounding neighborhood of graceful houses, with their pitched cedar roofs and shutters and gardens bursting with flowers, to pursue my career as a wage earner. I delivered newspapers and sweated and struggled behind those old manual lawn mowers to supplement my allowance of ten cents a week, eventually raised to a quarter.

It was the place where we could and did play practical jokes on one another, and on our dear mother, who was always a most satisfying victim. My favorite running prank was to find a pair of Jack's shoes, the dirtier the better, and place them smack dab on the polished top of Mother's grand piano. This would drive her absolutely crazy. She'd always come in and spot the shoes as if it were for the first time, and start in on Jack—didn't he know where to put his shoes? Didn't he know the piano was not the place for them? This joke, and Mother's clockwork response, continued while Jack was president, Bobby was attorney general, and I was a senator.

Even Jack's presidency didn't buy him much slack around the Cape house. Not many weeks after his inauguration, he was a bit fatigued as he joined the rest of us for our usual weekend at Hyannis Port. He slept in late on Sunday morning in his old first-floor bedroom—until he heard the footsteps of our father ascending the stairs after the eleven o'clock mass at St. Francis Xavier Church. Realizing that he was just seconds from being caught and scolded for missing mass, the president of the United States threw himself out of bed, yanked on a pair of pants, sneaked out of the door, hightailed it toward the garage, and scrambled over our neighbor Rodger Currie's fence to safety.

Just a few final random memories, now, of life in that sanctuary in those sweet summers before the war:

In the evening before dinner we'd gather in the living room, where my mother would play the piano. She played with great delicacy and finesse. She'd come downstairs at 6:30 and seat herself at the keyboard, and she'd play until the family had formed. Then she'd stop and the conversation would begin.

Once in a while Jack would drift into the room from vigorous games out of doors after changing into a clean shirt, an absolute requirement in my parents' home. When a lull softened the general din, he might nod to Mother, and then begin to sing, alone, to her accompaniment. My brother had a fine voice—a fact that very few people know. One of his favorite tunes was "September Song." Jack could imitate the gravelly voice of Walter Huston, who'd made it famous on Broadway, and still project the ballad's aching tenderness.

And the days dwindle down
To a precious few
September
November . . .

Sometimes Jack would sing that song directly to me.

At dinner, we would often sit down to platters heaped with clams and lobsters. We were not assigned seats, but Mother and Dad always sat in the same places. We each had a napkin, and that napkin was expected to last the entire week. If it suffered any stains—which of course is what napkins are designed to do—too bad. One a week. I had two or three important roles in our summer dinners. It was my special task to head down to the shore with two buckets and return with enough salt water to cook the shellfish. Another chore was to bring home fresh water from the pump at the golf course. Two of Dad's mealtime passions were good tomatoes and fresh water. Finally, if our dessert was ice cream, it would be ice cream that I had churned, by turning a handle for about forty-five minutes, over a bucket of ice. I was one of the few fellows who could claim that ice cream made me physically fit!

Our noisy dinner table always bore the foods of the seasons. When the corn was in, we had corn on the cob. And then we had corn pudding, and then we had cornbread. Every meal seemed made of corn. And when the blueberries came in, everything was blueberry: blueberry pie, and blueberry shortcake, and blueberry muffins. The same with the strawberries. And of course the cranberries.

But whatever dishes were set before us, the one "menu" item that never varied was conversation. After grace, ideas and information would start to flow. The spirit was generally upbeat but always informative.

Only rarely did the talk grow heated, and even then it had its comic side. I recall one mealtime when Joe Jr., who had recently traveled in Russia, began to wax enthusiastic over what he'd seen there. Joe was reliably his father's son when it came to economics and politics, but he'd been more than a little naive in his reaction to the way the Soviets described their system. "You know, there's something interesting about that communism over there," he declared to our father. "This idea of 'each according to their need, each according to their ability' . . ." That was as far as he got. Dad set his knife and fork down. "When you sell your *car*, and sell your *boat*, and sell your *horse*, you can talk to me about that," he exploded at Joe, "but otherwise *I don't want to hear any more about it in this house!*" And boom! up he got, and out the door he went. The kicker was that as my poor brother sat there openmouthed, my mother said to him, "Joe, you shouldn't upset your father."

After dinner, toward sunset, my father liked to retire to his porch on the second floor and sit in the corner by the window that looks out into the harbor and the lantern that was there. He would read into the late evening. But he'd also keep a lookout for his younger children as we trudged home from one last sail or game of tennis or flashlight tag. If you were "it," and if you shone a flashlight on a hiding child, they were out. Jack continued playing flashlight tag with the younger children as president.

A variation of flashlight tag, which we also played into adulthood, was a game we called Murder. We'd play with all the kids and adults and use the whole house at the Cape. Someone was "it," and if they tagged you, you were dead, but then you became the Murderer. The goal was to hide from the Murderer so that you were the last person not tagged. One night, Congressman Jack Kennedy was the second to last person tagged and he couldn't find the last person, who had crawled in Mother's hat box shelf. That person was Lem Billings, Jack's loyal lifelong friend whom he'd met at Choate. Since they couldn't find him, Jack proposed that everyone go to a movie. When we all came back two hours later, we found Lem still in that closet, covered with sweat and still waiting to be caught.

As children, we'd have to be home from our games by the time the streetlights came on, and of course as the summer days got shorter the lights came on earlier and earlier. If any of us arrived late, we'd pick up the gaze of Dad's steely blue eyes at about thirty yards, and then whatever excuses we'd invented would melt by the time we got to the door. Dad could see everything that was happening from that chair in that room. Everything in the world, it sometimes seemed.

Down in the basement was a small movie theater, with projector and screen, that Dad had installed. Through his Hollywood connections he could get new movies before they were released to the theaters. We saw the Walt Disney feature cartoons like *Dumbo* and *Snow White*. Dad knew Walt Disney, who gave him several of his paintings, renderings of his cartoon characters. For a long time we had those paintings on a wall of our house in McLean, Virginia.

Later we'd watch adventure films: *Four Feathers*, the 1939 film about a young British officer who has to disprove his reputation as a coward during the invasion of North Africa. I think it is one of the great movies of all time, along with *Call of the Wild* and *Captains Courageous*. I loved the latter movie so much, in fact, that when Vicki and I adopted a new puppy recently, we named him Captains Courageous. I loved movies about the sea, and about men at war.

Later on, Dad would screen some romantic movies—but at the moment when the lead characters would start holding hands, he'd call out, "Teddy! It's time for you to go to bed!" Jean wasn't much luckier. Just as they got to the embracing and kissing stage, she'd hear that voice of his: "Jean, you've got to go up to bed!"

The cranberry fields are smaller now than they were in 1941—as is every childhood image when seen through a grown-up's eyes. But my favorite boyhood vista from our porch in Hyannis Port has not diminished. This is the shoreline, where the shallow waters of Nantucket Sound lap peacefully, then draw back toward the open sea. Tied up on the beach, in my memory, its flat stern bobbing in the surf, is a little boat.

When I was six, Joe and Jack began teaching me to sail in that little boat. They introduced me to the wind and the tides and the currents, and my life on the sea was under way.

The boats grew larger over my lifetime, and I ventured farther and farther from shore. I sailed alone, I sailed with my own family, I sailed in regattas, I sailed with political leaders and celebrities who were my guests. I've sailed with just about anyone I could get onto the boat with me. I took up painting, first with acrylics and later with oils, to pass time with Jack when he was recuperating from back surgery in the 1950s, and then again while I was recuperating from an injury in the 1960s, and most of my canvases have been of sailing boats, including my cherished antique wooden schooner *Mya*, and of the sea, and of harbors, safe harbors.

CHAPTER TWO

No Crying in This House
1932–1938

Hyannis Port is my true home, but it was not my first home. At the time of my birth on February 22, 1932, the family spent summers and early autumns in Hyannis Port, and then headed to Bronxville, New York, for winters. The colonnaded house there stood in the village's leafy Sagamore Park neighborhood. Its three stories and twenty rooms occupied a crest of land, its red-tiled roof catching the sun above a thick scattering of tall old trees. We lived there in winter for six years after I was born.

Dad had accumulated most of his fortune by then. He had traded brilliantly in the stock market, and invested with his typical acuity in the still young Hollywood movie industry. In 1928, my father had greatly increased his wealth by buying and consolidating two small movie-related businesses into Radio-Keith-Orpheum—RKO. He'd protected that fortune by phasing out of the market several months before the crash in October of 1929.

The New York suburbs were new territory for the Kennedys. It is Boston, of course, that holds the deep transplanted roots of my family in the New World, on both sides. The Irish famine drove my great-grandfather Patrick across the ocean to the city in the 1840s; and within a decade, Thomas Fitzgerald and several members of his large family made a similar pilgrimage. My parents' marriage in October 1914 united the Boston Kennedys and the Boston Fitzgeralds, and the couple settled in a trim little house on Beals Street in Brookline. The house still stands. It was where Jack, Kathleen, and Rosemary were born—assisted by Dr. Frederick Good, who presided at the births of all of us. (Joe Jr., the first, arrived in a summer house in Hull, Massachusetts, in 1915.) Dad moved the family to a larger house in Brookline, where Eunice, Pat, and Bobby were delivered. The expanding family made an even larger house necessary, and Dad's expanding wealth made it possible. After the move to Bronxville, though, my mother insisted that one bond with her origins remain unbroken: any children still to come would be born in her native city—never mind the intervening two hundred miles. In 1927 she returned to her beloved Boston for the birth of Jean. And in early 1932, at the age of forty-one, my mother returned to Boston again for my birth at St. Margaret's Hospital.

My mother saved many mementos of my birth, as she did for all the children. One of them I still have hanging in my Senate office: a framed card that bears an illustration of the White House. The card apparently accompanied a floral bouquet. Across its surface, in faded ink, is the handwriting of my mother: "Perishable flowers." The card is signed by President Herbert Hoover. There is a stamp mark of postage due, a rather humorous souvenir from the man who presided over the Great Depression.

I was born Edward Moore Kennedy, after my father's longtime personal secretary, confidant, and close family friend. Eddie Moore had been an assistant to three Boston mayors, including John F. "Honey Fitz" Fitzgerald, my mother's legendary father. My dad cherished Eddie's convivial soul and his immersion in the Boston Irish political culture. This was the same Eddie Moore who rescued Jack, the chocolate frosting thief, from our brother Joe down at the Cape.

When I was confirmed at twelve years old, a saint found his way into my name. We confirmation boys were told that we could keep our own middle names or add a saint's name to the one we already had. The boys ahead of me in the line all had middle names like Michael or John or James.

When it came my turn, the bishop asked me mine, and I said, "Moore." He said, "No, your middle name." I said, "It's Moore." The bishop said, "Oh. Thomas More." I didn't want to hold up the line and call any further attention to myself, so I said, "Yes." In that way, my name became Edward Thomas Moore Kennedy. Given that Saint Thomas More is the patron saint of politicians, I'm rather happy to have him in there.

Even as a small boy, I missed the ocean during the months away from Hyannis Port, but the Bronxville house, built around 1920 and sadly torn down in the 1950s, held many pleasures of its own. A curving third-floor balcony rested on top of three Ionic columns, and a smaller balcony below it stretched above the front entrance. Inside, amid the master rooms, were such modern wonders as shower baths, an oil-burning hot water heater, and a number of enclosed porches. The basement held a billiard table, and the garage was big enough for five cars.

The part of the house that most interested me, though, was a large, dimly lit room up on the third floor. Inside it, my brothers presided over an elaborate, always-growing electric train system. Joe Jr. and Jack had begun the collection, with Lionel cars and tracks supplied by Dad. Control shifted to Jack and Bobby as time went on and the routes grew more intricate. When Jack began his travels, Bobby became chief engineer.

My brothers could make you believe that running those trains was a mission of vital importance. But then they could give you that feeling with anything they were up to. They certainly convinced me. As soon as I was old enough to climb the stairs to the train room, I sat for hours watching the action with envy and fascination. I itched to get my own hands on the levers that made those engines race and the signals flash and the whistles shriek. But the train room was my brothers' kingdom, and they were always happy to remind me who was in charge.

Their message stuck. Just a few years ago, well over half a century on, I was visiting the Wyeth family at their home in Brandywine. Jamie Wyeth showed us into the room where his family kept its own model train system. Without warning I was catapulted back across the decades to that third-floor room in Bronxville, and in my memory I could hear Bobby's excited chatter above the sound of his engine and its cars on the track. And we were all startled by a loud voice that shook the Wyeths' room: "DON'T TOUCH THE TRAINS!"

It was me, imitating Bobby.

Bobby's voice, and those of the others in my family, echo through my early memories of Bronxville as they do through the house in Hyannis Port. My father's voice is paramount. He was never abusive, never wounding toward any of his children, but he had a way of letting us know exactly what he expected of us. Once, when I was thirteen or fourteen years old, Dad called me into his room for a chat. I must have done something that prompted the conversation, but I don't remember what it was. But he used phrases so concise and vivid that I can remember them word for word nearly sixty-five years later: "You can have a serious life or a nonserious life, Teddy. I'll still love you whichever choice you make. But if you decide to have a nonserious life, I won't have much time for you. You make up your mind. There are too many children here who are doing things that are interesting for me to do much with you."

I went back to my room with his words replaying in my mind. It didn't take me long to decide which kind of life I wanted to lead.

Another powerful ethic that Dad taught us was to respect the privacy of others and to ignore whatever disrespect of privacy might come our way. I learned this particular lesson at a birthday party for myself in about 1946. My sister Kathleen had organized it, and brought a lot of my friends to the house to play games. At some point in the afternoon I wandered upstairs—to use the bathroom, I think. I passed a bedroom and heard a boy's voice. I looked in and saw Lafay Paige, one of the young party guests, talking on the phone, to one of his parents, I guess. His back was partly turned, and he couldn't see me.

Lafay was saying, "I hope this party gets over pretty quick because it's really dull and we're not having much fun at all. It's really drab, so will you come and get me?" I stood there sort of paralyzed and embarrassed that the boy felt my party was dull.

Then I heard footsteps behind me. My father had just walked out of the master bedroom and spotted me listening to the telephone conversation. He quietly told me to come back with him into his bedroom. I thought maybe he was going to console me, but he had another topic entirely on his mind. He said, "Teddy, let me give you some advice. Follow it, and you'll be much happier for the rest of your life.

"Never listen to a phone call that isn't meant for you. Never read a letter that isn't meant for you. Never pay attention to a comment that isn't meant for you. Never violate people's privacy. You will save yourself a great deal of anguish. You might not understand this now, but you will later on."

Well, he was absolutely prophetic in what he said. It is advice that I followed again and again, and its use has extended well beyond phone conversations and letters. I've learned to turn my attention away from all sorts of things that can cause anguish: for instance, the books, the magazine pieces, the newspaper stories that carry malicious gossip or opinions about me or my family. I just stopped hearing it after a while. And I have been happier for it. I would recommend Dad's advice to anybody.

No observation by Joseph Kennedy Sr. had as much lasting influence as a similar dictum: "There'll be no crying in this house."

The "house" he had in mind, I am certain, was the House of Kennedy. He repeated this admonition to all of us, and he pronounced it with the force of moral law, and all of us absorbed its import and molded our behavior to honor it. "There will be no crying in this house." To understand the profound authority of this charge to us is to understand much about my family.

We have wept only rarely in public. We have accepted the scrutiny and the criticism as the legitimate consequences of prominence in a highly self-aware society. With exceedingly few exceptions, we have refused to complain against the speculation, gossip, and slander.

Some have viewed our refusal as excessive reticence, even as tacit admission of the innuendo at hand. In my view, it is neither. At least for me, it's the continuing assent to Joseph Kennedy's dictum: "There will be no crying in this house."

I associate Bronxville with late autumn and winter. And largeness. Everything within our gates seemed so large back then—including my siblings, from my littlest-kid perspective. The three-story white house and its surrounding trees appeared to reach into the clouds. My sisters have told me they had the same sensation. A driveway bordered by shrubbery arced downward along the terraced lawn until it reached the street. Jack taught me to ride a bicycle through the swirls of autumn leaves on that driveway, and it was fun, except for the sudden stops. Jack and Bobby would helpfully push me along as the bike gained momentum and barreled down the drive, until it was brought to a halt—say, by a tree—and I went tumbling over the bars into a heap. "That's very natural!" Jack would assure me as the two of them raced down the hill to pick me up. I was never quite convinced.

Neighborhood children liked to romp into our yard for games of football and tag, and sledding in the winter. Sometimes an emissary from the larger world—Hollywood, the Catholic Church—showed up at our house. President Roosevelt arranged for Dad to escort Eugenio Cardinal Pacelli to several sites around the country when Pacelli visited the United States in 1936, not long before he headed back to Rome and his eventual coronation as Pope Pius XII. One of his last stops was at our house. I remember crawling up onto his lap. I was fascinated by his long robe and scarlet skullcap, and his long aristocratic nose. We still have the couch where he sat, and the plaque that Mother put on it.

The dinner table conversations at Bronxville were as lively as at the Cape. But it was here that Jack found a way to invest mealtimes with even more challenge and intrigue. He invented a new game. The pawn was the platter of roast beef. Jack's goal was to get served from it before the rest of us children. He knew that the platter always went to Dad first, and then to Mother. But which way would it travel after that?—to the left, or to the right? The question was important because whoever got served first was treated to a thick, juicy slab of beef, and the last person served had to settle for end scraps. Jack's guess on any given night determined which side of the table he'd choose to seat himself. He liked to say in later years that the reason he was so thin was that he always chose wrong.

Every space around the big house was a potential source for adventure. Our roof looked to Joe and Jack as if it might be ideal for launching a parachutist. So they made up a parachute from sheets and ropes. For the test run, they were generous enough to invite the son of the chauffeur to share the adventure. They helped him on with the straps, and then they helped him off the roof. Luckily, he only suffered an ankle sprain, but it was a pretty bad one.

Yet quiet moments there were—and even these were rich in stimulation. I can still see Bobby frowning into a magnifying glass as he bent his small frame over his stamp collection, which included contributions from President Roosevelt. Sometimes we brothers would sprawl on the floor absorbed in practice maneuvers with the cast-iron soldiers that our father collected for us as Christmas presents from countries all over the world, their brilliant hand-painted uniforms rendered in precise detail. As we lined them up in battle formation, our mother would often bustle in, bearing maps and information about their countries of origin.

Mother would make learning opportunities, too, from the dolls Dad bought in the countries he visited. These were spectacular dolls, always dressed in ceremonial costumes, accurate in detail. They were heavy, and sometimes a foot or so high. Mother would sit with the girls and the dolls and get them to think about the cultures they came from: How are the Polish dolls dressed, and why? What about the Lithuanians? What can their dress tell you about the people?

Mother delighted in her acquaintences with Catholic bishops and cardinals and, later, popes, but she enjoyed social circles less ecclesiastical as well: during the 1930s she was named the best-dressed woman in public life by a poll of fashion designers. And she became a familiar figure in international ports of call: after seventeen years of birthing and nurturing her nine children, Rose Kennedy in her forties resumed her girlhood penchant for travel, making several trips to Europe and to her beloved Paris in particular. Dad would arrange to be at home with us when Mother was rekindling her love of European art, languages, and cities.

Our parents escorted us on frequent excursions beyond the house and grounds. A Sunday ritual, after church, was our two-car caravan into Manhattan for a family luncheon at a Longchamps, that bygone chain of art deco restaurants with their stained glass and murals and heaping plates of delicious food. Then we'd all head over to Radio City for a movie. Jack must have loved those outings; he often brought Jackie to Longchamps for dinner in the early days of their marriage.

A reminder that the outside world was a lot less secure than our own occurred when I was five, shortly after I was enrolled at a kindergarten off Pondfield Road in the Bronx. The school was only a five-minute car ride from our house, and one fine autumn afternoon I decided to impress my parents with my independence by walking home through the crunchy fallen leaves. My mother wasn't expecting this, and when she drove to the school and didn't find me, she grew terrified. The famous Lindbergh baby kidnapping and killing had occurred shortly after my birth, and parents across the nation were still haunted by it. My parents knew the Lindberghs and had observed their pain firsthand. And so instead of congratulating me on my adventure when I strutted through the door, my mother reasoned with me via a coat hanger, and then banished me to the closet.

But the outside world also held wonder, especially when my father was along. He took me to a ball game at Yankee Stadium once when I was about seven. We had box seats, but Dad apparently found these a little too remote from the action, and boosted me over the wall onto the playing field during batting practice. The ushers smiled at us and touched their caps. We strolled around and I drank in all the huge famous men in pinstripes firing baseballs at one another, and was just turning my attention back to the hot-dog vendor roaming the seats when I heard Dad say, "Teddy, come over here." He was standing beside a big grinning moon-faced man in a business suit. "Teddy, this is Babe Ruth," Dad said, "the greatest baseball player of our time." Ruth had been retired for a couple years, but I knew who he was. Honey Fitz had told me about cheering the Babe when he played for the Red Sox before 1920, and my grandfather was an organizing member of the Royal Rooters. Now I'd have something to tell Grampa.

Ruth reached down a huge paw and grabbed my hand. I can't remember what I said to him, but to this day, meeting Babe Ruth remains the strongest memory I have of being awestruck by someone. I was tongue-tied.

A household as teeming with children as ours required some reinforcements for the parents. I recall a couple of governesses in particular, one of them a legend within the extended Kennedy family, the other not quite so beloved.

The less-than-adored caretaker was an Irishwoman we called Kico, who sometimes let our rambunctiousness get the better of her. I can still hear the nighttime *thump . . . thump . . . thump* of poor Bobby's forehead as Kico banged it against a wall in an effort to discipline him. Bobby's famous hardheadedness served him well in these moments. Kico did not last long at the Kennedy house.

The legendary governess was Luella Hennessey (later Donovan), who was in our lives for forty years, assisted at the births of twenty-three Kennedy children, lavished tender care upon my father after he suffered his stroke in 1961, helped nurse me back to health after my airplane crash in 1964, and was a particular favorite of Jack's. In 1963, President Kennedy coaxed the hardworking Luella to expand her horizons by enrolling at Boston College to get her college degree. He died before she received her bachelor of science diploma, but she endearingly remarked, "The president said he would come to my graduation if I got my degree. I guess he'll know I'm getting it."

Our expanding household, as I noted earlier, was an important reason that Dad found it necessary for us to leave Boston. But there were other reasons—reasons I did not suspect as a child; reasons that had to do with the outside world from which he tried to shield us until we were ready for it. Much of what he knew about the world did not please Joe Kennedy, and some of it quite rightly infuriated him.

The Boston of my dad's young manhood remained in certain ways as it had been since the mid-nineteenth century: two cities, in effect, mutually hostile and resentful. One was the silk-stocking Boston of old, landed Yankee power and influence; Beacon Hill; Harvard; the bankers and captains of industry. The other city consisted of the teeming storefronts and docksides. This was the Boston of immigrants' working-class descendants. These were mostly Irish, but included Italians and Portuguese.

The Irish Catholics had established a small middle class, which overlapped with a strong and tightly knit political class. Mayor and Congressman "Honey Fitz" was an exemplar of the latter. My dad's own father, Patrick Joseph, lived in both. He was the soft-spoken owner of three saloons and a liquor-importing business, a bank founder and president, a real estate promoter, and a leader of East Boston's Democratic Party, serving four terms as a state representative. He was a regular presence at community events, known for his gentlemanly manner and political influence. P.J. and his perceptive wife, Mary, hoped their son would move upward in the world through the classic Irish route of politics.

Dad had his own ideas. He thrived academically, at Boston Latin School and then Harvard. In 1914, he blocked the hostile takeover of his father's neighborhood bank and became, at age twenty-five, the state's youngest bank president, ultimately becoming one of the financial masterminds of his generation. Dad immersed himself in the intricacies of buying and selling stock. In 1934, when the U.S. Congress created the Securities and Exchange Commission to protect investors from insider trading, President Roosevelt appointed him chairman of the new regulatory agency. He was the right man for the job precisely because he knew how the system worked.

Yet even as he marched through one invisible barricade after another, Dad always understood that he was never *completely* accepted as an equal by the old Yankee stock. He would always be an "Irish Catholic" first, and an individual second. "I was born here. My parents were born here. What the hell do I have to do to be called an American?" he blurted after yet one more paper referred to him as an "Irishman." In 1922 he was turned down for membership in a country club on Boston's South Shore, and years later complained that the Protestant elite would not have accepted his daughters as debutantes. He bought the home in Hyannis Port only after realizing he could not gain entry into a more exclusive neighborhood, and even many families in Hyannis Port greeted him coldly. His conviction that "Boston was no place to bring up Irish Catholic children," as he declared to a reporter, was the impetus for the family's self-exile from the city.

Dad could convey strength and inspiration precisely at those moments when he might seem, at a glance, to be stern and unbending. One example among many has lodged in my memory, perhaps because it involves an early encounter with the sea. We must jump ahead in time for a few moments, from Bronxville of the 1930s to Hyannis Port in the summer of 1943, when I was eleven. The war across the sea cast its long shadow—a half-terrifying, half-enthralling shadow for a boy—even into our little coastal village. Car owners were instructed to paint their headlights half black. All of the drapes in the Cape house were black, to keep any light from shore from reflecting off our tankers and troopships that were moving up and down the coastline.

And yet for a Hyannis Port boy, these were almost make-believe precautions, hardly more urgent than storybook drama. The true object of my epic dreams was the timeless, shimmering water that lay before my eyes each summer day.

For some months, I'd been allowed to explore Nantucket Sound in that sixteen-foot sloop, the *One More*. But I had another adventure in mind, and I was finally successful in getting Dad's permission.

I wanted to take the boat around Point Gammon, at the tip of Great Island, some two miles out on Nantucket Sound, and then to the mouth of the Bass River, five miles east: a short distance for an experienced sailor, an uncertain voyage for an eleven-year-old boy. Adding to the adventure was the understanding that I would be out on the boat overnight.

My "crew" on that voyage, as on so many voyages of my boyhood, was Joey Gargan, then an old salt of thirteen. It was a rainy day, but we boarded the little open boat anyway, clutching paper bags with our sandwiches inside. It rained and rained, but we pressed ahead through the choppy water. The "Big House" disappeared into the fog behind us. Squinting against the wind and the salt spray, we made it around the point and on to the river mouth, and anchored the boat near shore. Still it rained and it rained, and it was cold, and the day crept along, and it rained, and it was cold.

We found ourselves trapped. Our overnight adventure no longer looked so enticing, but we had neither the strength nor expertise to get the boat back home. We spent a frigid night huddled inside that boat, hardly sleeping. A gray morning dawned. Wet and hungry, we left the boat at anchor and swam to the shore. Then we trudged until we found a gas station, from where we called up the house. Dave, our chauffeur, answered the phone. I groaned, "You've got to come down and get us. It's been bad. It rained all night. My sandwiches are wet, and I'm cold. Oh, I'm so cold."

Dave came down and picked us up and drove us back to the house. Just as we arrived, we met my father getting ready to go out for his morning horseback ride. He said, "Teddy? I thought you were going for your little cruise."

I said, "I did, Dad. But it was cold! It rained. It was bad, it was cold!"

"Where's the boat?" he asked. I said, "It's anchored at Bass River. We'll go back and get it later. But now I'm going upstairs to get warm, and get breakfast, and rest, and get some sleep. I'm so cold and wet." But my father said, "Dave, take Teddy and Joey back to the boat. Teddy, if you leave with the boat, you come back with the boat."

So the car turned around and off we went, me boo-hooing all the way. If there was anybody in the world who felt sorry for themselves that morning, it was me. But we arrived back at Bass River, and suddenly the sun came up, and a breeze came on up, and the sails on the boat came up, and the warmth came on out, and Joey and I had just a terrific sail that day.

In the long hours and days and years, my father has been there to turn me around and send me back to do what is necessary. To come back with the boat. I can envision him now, striding toward me, looking me straight in the eye, his handshake firm, his laugh wholehearted. I grew up eager not to disappoint him, determined never to meet any challenge in a half-hearted way, ultimately confident that if he knew I had done my best, he would—even if things turned out badly—give me what amounted to his benediction:

"After you have done your best, then the hell with it."

My father knew whereof he spoke. By the dawn of the 1940s he had already done his best, on the world stage, and failed—failed to forestall the most devastating war in history.

In February 1938, within days of my sixth birthday, Joseph Kennedy sailed for London to take up his duties as President Roosevelt's newly appointed ambassador to the Court of St. James's. History shows that Roosevelt, whose campaign Dad had vigorously supported, had conferred the appointment despite my father's lack of diplomatic experience in hopes that Dad could negotiate an important British-American trade agreement, and that his famous bluntness would give the administration an unvarnished pipeline into Britain's responses toward Nazi Germany.

On March 12 of that year, Adolf Hitler lit the fuse that would in time dash everyone's hopes for peace and detonate the second global war of the century, by sending his storm troopers across the German border to occupy Austria, in direct violation of the Versailles Treaty.

Three days earlier, the happy insularity of my early childhood ended. Along with my mother, the other four younger siblings, Miss Dunne, and Luella Hennessey, I marched up the gangplank of the USS *Washington* to join Dad in London. (Joe Jr. and Jack remained at Harvard.) This would be my first time on the open sea. More important, the voyage would mark a transition in my understanding of the world, at a moment in history when the world was careening nearly beyond all understanding.

CHAPTER THREE

Wartime London
1938–1939

My first ocean voyage opened up many facts about the sea that I'd never before suspected. One such fact was that it could make you seasick. Our six-day crossing from New York Harbor to London took us through the North Atlantic at the height of the winter storm season, and my stomach felt every one of the thirty-foot waves that daily lifted and rolled our ship. I loved the water, but this was more water than I really wanted.

The American ambassador's residence then was 14 Prince's Gate, on Kensington Road across from Hyde Park. I later learned that this four-story Victorian building had once been the London home of the banker J. P. Morgan. I was more interested, at the time, in the Indian chief in full headdress sculpted above the main entrance.

Kathleen, Rosemary, Bobby, and I lived at No. 14 with our parents, while Eunice, Pat, and Jean boarded at a nearby convent. Our bedrooms were on the third floor. "Bedroom" hardly does them justice. Luella Hennessey later recalled mine as being almost as big as a schoolroom. She noted the twin beds, the big fireplace, a desk, a dresser, a chest of drawers, a chaise lounge, and a breakfast table with two chairs. A caged elevator got us to the main floor and back. I loved to race ahead of everyone else and push its activating button and hear the machinery start to clank.

At age six, I could tell that Dad was on an extremely important mission in London, but its nature was a mystery. Important visitors came to our residence: the king and queen of Great Britain, for instance.

It took more than a year, but George VI and Queen Elizabeth paid a call on Ambassador Kennedy in May 1939. We children were fixed up, cleaned up, and gussied up for this occasion. I seem to recall being told that they were the most important people in the world, and that this was the most important event that was ever going to happen.

My involvement in it all was rather brief. I have blurry memories of the king in a scarlet tunic, his chest covered with braids and medals. And I remember that I practiced for hours to perfect my bow. Bobby and I later met Princess Elizabeth and Princess Margaret at Windsor Castle. We danced with each other. I doubt that any of us children made a huge impression on any other.

The London press and public seemed taken with us. Everyone was curious about my dad, of course—what news and assurances this new ambassador might bring from America to a nation bracing for a massive Nazi assault, and how sympathetic this Irish Catholic would prove to British interests. I knew nothing of all this; just that a lot of adults with serious expressions wanted to talk to him. As for my sisters, Bobby, and me, we submitted to scrubbing and hair-combing, marched out to watch the Changing of the Guard, and smiled. My mother certainly never forgot the "spontaneous outpouring of human warmth," as she put it. She later wrote, "I almost began to feel that we had been adopted, as a family, by the whole British people."

Life in London held its dangers. I found this out when a zebra decided to have me for lunch. He'd made a good start on my arm before a rescuer managed to get his mouth open.

It happened during ceremonies reopening the Royal Children's Zoo in Regent's Park. The great British biologist Julian Huxley himself handed me the shears to cut the ribbon as the photographers pressed in, Bobby and Jean watched (representing little children everywhere, I suppose), and nice British ladies beamed.

I cut the ribbon and handed the shears back, and then a zebra in a nearby cage caught my eye. I'd never before seen a real zebra. He looked friendly. I wandered over and reached through the bars to hand him a peanut. In the next instant he had my arm in his mouth all the way up to my elbow.

I screamed. The more I pulled away, the deeper the zebra's teeth took hold. Luckily I had a thick coat on, and a jacket underneath it, and a shirt underneath the jacket, so the animal wasn't able to bite deeply into my flesh. Still, he wouldn't let go. I screamed and pulled and hauled, and the zebra kept angling for a better fix. Some guards came running and tried to help, but they didn't quite have the drill down on how to extract an arm from a zebra's mouth. So someone summoned a very special zebra keeper— that's how I thought of him, anyway—and he arrived and snapped a whip across the zebra's tailbone, and the animal sort of gagged and let me go.

I wasn't seriously injured, but I did cause an incredible commotion that took a bit away from the occasion. There was Julian Huxley, and the nice ladies, and the pretty ribbon, and all the cookies and crackers, and all the little cups of juice that we were going to have—and suddenly there was this kid screaming at the top of his lungs that he was getting eaten by a zebra. And the kid happened to be the ambassador's son.

I recall all the grown-ups in the vicinity calling out to me to "keep a stiff upper lip." It wasn't my upper lip that I was concerned about.

My sisters performed their ceremonial roles with a great deal more poise. Rosemary, then nineteen, and Kick, eighteen, made their social debuts just weeks after we arrived. The setting was Buckingham Palace, where they were to be presented to the queen, and the event required end-less drilling and preparation. My mother took them across the Channel to Paris on several weekends to select gowns for their debuts and the long string of social events that would follow.

The evening arrived, and when their names were called Kathleen and Rosemary made their march together in their shimmering white gowns from the antechamber up the red carpet toward the queen. My sisters curtsied perfectly. Kick danced especially brilliantly through all of the debutante balls that season, the Kennedy ball included, and her smiling beauty attracted partners from the British Isles, Europe, and Russia.

For Bobby and me, the pageantry grew familiar in time, along with the peculiar diesel smell of London's streets and the accents and the left-side driving. The demands of schoolwork took hold; and, for me at least, a certain loneliness as well.

The Gibbs School on Sloane Street near the square inaugurated my long and somewhat unhappy years of school life in Britain and then America: an endless succession of institutions, each of which had its own rules, cliques, standards and punishment systems (I was to become something of an expert in punishment systems), and obstacles to being liked. I liked to be liked, and up until my school years I'd taken my likability for granted. After all, I was the youngest, used to being doted on by everyone. I am by nature and disposition a happy person. I like to laugh and have people laugh with me. If my siblings found themselves in trouble with Dad, they would sometimes send me into his room ahead of them to "soften him up" before the reckoning began.

The world of strangers proved different.

Bobby and I were driven to Gibbs in an embassy car at first, but before long we were confident enough to make our way by bus and Underground.

Bobby was thirteen then, older than most of the Gibbs boys. He had little trouble with the curriculum. I was younger than most, and had trouble with the curriculum and with everything else. I struggled to learn my lessons; I struggled to learn cricket. When I broke the rules, I was invited into the headmaster's office, where he made me hold my palms up and then whacked them with a ruler until they were bright red.

One rule that I'd learned from my parents was the need for politeness, especially given my high visibility as a diplomat's son. And so when a young British schoolmate named Cecil took to pounding on me every day, I handled the problem with perfect tact. I politely secured my father's permission before flattening Cecil.

The loneliness I felt was obvious to those around me. Bobby tried to keep me company, but he'd joined a circle of friends his age. Dad spent as much time with me as he could—an amazing amount, given the obligations that preoccupied him. He came to my cricket games at school. He invited me with him on morning horseback rides along the centuries-old Rotten Row in Hyde Park, or at the lovely stables in Roehampton. In the evenings, before leaving the house with Mother for a dinner or the theater, he would come into my bedroom and read to me, sometimes for forty-five minutes or an hour.

I couldn't then fathom, of course, the burdens on his mind as he shared those moments with me. Only as a grown man myself, after the London days had passed into a bygone era and I began to look through its history and our family's archives, did I begin to understand my father's anguished role in prewar diplomacy: his passionate wish for American neutrality; his belief that neither America nor Britain was prepared militarily to engage Hitler's forces; the streams of letters he was writing back to President Roosevelt, senators, and journalists analyzing the international situation; and the speeches he delivered, blunt to the point of provoking outrage, that led to the foreshortening of his diplomatic career.

Nor could I have suspected that, even as he poured out those unvarnished dispatches and speeches, Dad was dooming a possibility for himself that he must have known about and desired. The 1940 presidential campaign in America lay not far ahead. Franklin Roosevelt had already served two terms, and no president had ever served more. No one then knew for sure whether he would try to break the precedent—but, as I learned much later, my father's name was among those being prominently circulated as his successor.

I never asked my father about these things. I've often wished I had. But they belonged, like other elements of his life, to a part of him that existed beyond our personal relationship. In my family, we did not press one another beyond these boundaries. Nor did we discuss with one another or the world the details of private behavior. It was a matter of respect.

The Munich Conference of September 1938 (which he did not attend) had given my father some hope that war might be averted. His friend and ally, the British prime minister, Neville Chamberlain, along with the French prime minister, yielded to Adolf Hitler's demand to occupy the Sudetenland, part of the famous "appeasement" strategy that in hindsight was catastrophic. German troops invaded Czechoslovakia the following March, and the frenzy of futile diplomacy intensified.

As this latest barrier to peace was falling, our family journeyed from London to Rome to witness the coronation of Eugenio Cardinal Pacelli as Pope Pius XII. Dad was President Roosevelt's representative to the ceremony. We viewed the ceremony from the front row of a stand in a portico outside St. Peter's Basilica on Sunday, March 12, 1939. I later learned that the Kennedy entourage had created a minor diplomatic crisis for the Vatican: official delegations were limited to seven persons, and our group, including the governess, numbered eleven (Joe Jr. was in Spain). But the problem was handled in the usual suave Roman manner: new seats were added, and everything was just fine.

On the following day, Dad had an audience with the new pope, and on Wednesday, March 15, I received my First Holy Communion from the pope himself at the Vatican. I wore a blue suit and had a white rosette on my left arm. As he blessed me, he said, "I hope you always be good and pious as you are today." It caused a great deal of a stir in some circles—a seven-year-old American boy given his First Communion by the pope, who himself was giving that honor for the first time as pope and to a non-Italian to boot. But it was among the greatest moments of my life. I received a beautiful rosary blessed by the pontiff on that occasion, which I later gave to my stepdaughter Caroline Raclin on the day of her First Holy Communion some sixty-odd years later.

Our last family interlude of prewar leisure was a monthlong holiday in a villa Dad rented at Cannes, on the French Riviera. Joe and Jack were on hand, and they gave me some sailing lessons and also taught me how to dive, using a cliff above the Mediterranean at the Eden Roc as the instruction site. That I had not yet learned how to swim well did not strike them as relevant to the exercise—one or the other would fish me out after I hit the water. All three of us kept this activity a secret from our father.

Our interlude was cut short on August 24. Germany and the Soviet Union informed the world that they had signed a mutual nonaggression agreement. The implications were massive. Poland in particular appeared to lie in the path of destruction.

Dad left for London as soon as he heard the news. After meeting with a shattered Chamberlain, he contacted Mother and told her that she and we children must leave Europe.

Our mother needed no convincing. The dread of a Luftwaffe assault over London had been running rampant since spring, when air raid drills grew common. Bobby and I witnessed the city's preparations for civil defense on our way to school and back: the sandbags, the barrage balloons, the scaffolding for gun emplacements. We'd participated in air raid drills, joining the flow of schoolchildren into bunkers, strapping on foul-smelling gas masks. We returned to classes clutching emergency rations. I have the strangest and most vivid memory of seeing human blood on the streets. Given that the bombing of London would not commence for a year, when I was safely out of the country, this memory is all but inexplicable—unless it was blood from an accident or an incident that I had seen. Perhaps my "memory" is of a dream, fueled by the growing terror I saw and heard and felt every day.

Whatever it was, the blood of Europe began to flow soon enough. On September 1, Germany invaded Poland. Two days later, Britain gave up the pretense and declared war on Germany, along with France. My parents, Joe Jr., Jack, and Kathleen sat in the Strangers Gallery in the House of Commons that Sunday afternoon to listen to Neville Chamberlain issue the declaration that broke his heart, and to speeches in support of the declaration. Afterward, hysteria seized the city. Keepers killed all the poisonous

snakes in the London Zoo, lest they be freed to slither about the city when
their cages were shattered by Nazi bombs. That night the city was blacked
out and air raid warnings sounded throughout London, but no attacks
came.

On September 5, President Roosevelt issued a proclamation of American neutrality.

Poland surrendered on September 27. By the end of 1939, artillery
duels were erupting along the Western front.

By this time, most of the Kennedys were back in the United States.
Dad took precautions in booking several of us on two different ships, not
wishing to lose all of us in a torpedo attack by one of the U-boats that now
prowled the North Atlantic's depths. Joe sailed several days later on the
Mauretania, surrounded by a convoy, and Jack flew westward aboard the
new Pan American airship the *Yankee Clipper*. The two of them reentered
Harvard; Joe began making preparations for the Democratic convention
in Chicago the following summer. Dad and Rosemary remained in England. Rosemary was enrolled at a Montessori school in Hertfordshire, well
away from the bombers' likely targets: a school where she was showing
signs of learning improvement. My father continued his duties and began
planning for a December visit to the States, where he would meet with
Roosevelt and then celebrate Christmas with us in Palm Beach.

Kathleen, who loved London, and who would soon return, described
our final night at No. 14 in a brief essay, "Lamps in a Blackout." She lamented the absence of "the scintillating signs of Piccadilly and Leicester
Square . . . the gaily-lit nightclubs. . . . But yet the moon shines through
and one can see new beauties in the silent, deserted city of London."

She described vignettes of our family's fumbling attempts to cope
with the blackout regulations:

Young Ted ripped the black curtain . . . to prevent the last ray of
light from shining through. Within five minutes three air-raid wardens called to complain of great streaks of light shining through the

window. . . . Jean sprained her ankle in falling downstairs. Joe returned from an exploring trip with a very swollen eye. No one believed his story of walking into a lamp post, until we read in the next morning's paper, of hundreds bumping into trees, falling on the curb and being hit by autos. . . . Thus, now one hears [the] tap, tap, tap, not of machine guns, but of umbrellas and canes as Londoners feel their way homeward.

She concluded:

May England soon have her midnights changed to mid-day with lights of victory and until then may the moon and stars and brilliant lamps of courage and faith shine gloriously in the blackout!

I lacked my sister's eloquence and perception of what was happening. But I missed my father, worried about him, and wrote to him from Bronxville:

Dear Daddy,

It snowd on Friday and give my love to Rose I hope not many bombs have drop near you sir james come on Sunday. we have bot some pansies flowers and I am takeing care of them. my reading is beter in school

love Teddy

CHAPTER FOUR

Boarding School Boy
1940–1950

Back home in America at the end of 1939, I began my preparatory school years on a note of great expectation. Yet these did not prove to be happy, joyous years.

I was very young, nearly always younger than my grade level. And nearly always a stranger: counting kindergarten at Pondfield and Gibbs in London, I attended ten schools between 1937 and 1950, nine of them before high school. That kind of transience was not a recipe for academic success. In those years, as the family shuttled seasonally between Hyannis Port and Palm Beach, I was essentially without a central home as well, although Cape Cod felt most like one. My father met with Roosevelt in Washington on December 8, 1939. We all celebrated a Christmas reunion at the Palm Beach house, and not long afterward my father sailed back to London. In January 1940 we all began to fan out.

Pat, Eunice, and Jean returned to their pre-London schools. Kathleen, almost twenty-one now, completed her studies at Finch College in New York. Early in 1941 she took her writing talents to the *Washington Times-Herald*, working as a research assistant before she was promoted to reviewing plays and movies. In the spring, Rosemary flew home from England, in the care of Dad's close friends Edward and Mary Moore.

Joe Jr., who'd served as an informal secretary to Dad in London after graduating Harvard in 1938, enrolled in Harvard Law School. Jack graduated cum laude from Harvard in June, the season in which *Why England Slept* was published. He enrolled in the fall at the Stanford Graduate School of Business, and in the spring he traveled through South America, meeting up with Mother and Eunice in Rio de Janeiro.

Mother enrolled Bobby at Portsmouth Priory, a school run by Benedictine monks in Portsmouth, Rhode Island. I initially stayed with Mother, but when she moved from Palm Beach to Bronxville with the seasons, I did too. In the second grade alone, I attended three different schools, with three different curriculums, with three different peer groups and sets of friends to make.

By the spring of my third-grade year, Mother thought that a short-term stint in boarding school was the best option for me, and she tried to ease the pain of separation by having me go to the same school as Bobby. If we both were at Portsmouth Priory, she reasoned, he could look after me, and I wouldn't be so lonely. And anyway, we would all be together on Cape Cod in the summer.

The Benedictines were happy to accommodate Mother's wishes, but there was a bit of a complication: Portsmouth Priory started in the seventh grade; it had no elementary school. No problem, said Mother. Bobby, a fourteen-year-old eighth grader, would be there to look after me, and after all, she was planning to keep me at Priory just until the end of the school year. Unfortunately, "just until the end of the school year," even if it's just two or three months, can be a very long time.

I entered the seventh grade at Portsmouth Priory in the spring of 1941 when I was barely nine years old, boarding and competing with boys who were four years older than me. It was a recipe for disaster.

My time at Portsmouth Priory was not an education; it was a battle. I took French, which I'd studied a little at Gibbs. On my first exam, I got a 13. I went to math class but the work was incomprehensible to me, and so was Latin.

My classmates did not befriend me. Once in a while, if I was really lucky, someone would take me out for a sail on a boat. But I was rarely chosen to go. I was rarely picked to be on any of the teams during that period, because I was so young. Bobby was there, of course, but, being a regular teenage boy, he already had his own group of friends and was generally involved with them. A few of my classmates proved as cruel as only children can be.

I'd brought my pet turtle to school with me, and in those hours of loneliness I played with him. But after a few weeks, my turtle died. I took him outside and dug a hole in the frozen ground outside my dormitory where I buried him and said a few prayers, giving him my own nine-year-old version of a funeral. Then I went back inside, found my cubicle—our dormitory rooms were cubicles with open ceilings—and crawled into bed and cried myself to sleep. At some point during the night, I was awakened by a strange sound from the hallway. *Thump. Thump. Thump.* And then laughter. I didn't know what it was until the next morning, when I awoke to find my dead pet turtle in my bed. Some of the students must have spotted me burying him. That night, they dug him up and tossed the shell with his lifeless body back and forth down the hall. *Thump. Thump. Thump.* And then they put him between my sheets. I buried him again that morning.

Bobby didn't think that family solidarity required him to be my protector. One day I got into a fight with a boy named Plowden. He was a head taller than me, and soon had the better of me, twisting my arm up between my shoulder blades. Bobby came walking past, and I shouted to him, "We're fighting because he says the Plowdens are better than the Kennedys!"

Bobby walked on. As he left me behind, he called back, "You have to learn to fight your own battles in life."

I didn't learn much else at Portsmouth Priory. I certainly didn't improve my spelling. "Dear Daddy, We are down in cap-card," I wrote to my father around this time, "mother has gone to jacks graduain. joe is here. The weather is very dad. Would you get the kings autograph for me I will send you an other lettor soon."

In the summer of 1941, Cape Cod was for me an oasis of stability and family love. Joe and Jack helped me with my sailing when they were there. My sisters and Mother doted on me. Bobby paid more attention to me than he had at Priory. And I basically was able to be a carefree nine-year-old boy, riding my bike, swimming, and perfecting my sailing.

In September 1941, Mother sent me to Riverdale Country School for Boys in the Bronx. All three of my older brothers had gone to Riverdale. They had been day students, but since the family was no longer headquartered in the house in Bronxville, I was a boarder. And the happiness of my Cape Cod summer did not take long to evaporate.

If Portsmouth Priory taught me about the cruelty of children, then Riverdale taught me about the cruelty of adults. And it was not the kind of cruelty that could easily be erased by the happy days of summer. Our dorm master was an abuser. He lived in the residence hall with us, in loco parentis if you will, and violated every trust that our parents had placed in him. He specialized in terror and humiliation. In evenings, at "lights out" time, R., as I will refer to him, would summon a rotating group of boys to his room, have them stand in a circle, and lead them in a matching-word game. He might say "shoe," and someone would respond with "leather." He'd say "heel," and someone would say "sole." Then he might say "shoe-lace," and if you couldn't think of a matching word, you'd have to take off an article of clothing. Since the boys were in pajamas, they didn't have too many articles of clothing to take off. Soon they were naked and subjected to R.'s "inspection." No boy was spared the humiliation.

R. had enlisted two senior boys, Argentines, as accomplices who would sometimes help him lead the word game. They added a cruel twist by shouting out words in Spanish. But the young boarders at Riverdale didn't know any Spanish. The humiliation arrived even sooner.

I could not believe this was happening. There were whispers that R. also took a private interest in some boys and would send the Argentines to round them up. I spent many terror-filled nights under my bunk, hiding lest I too become one of those victims. I kept telling myself that this would pass. That I would get through this nightmare. That my brothers had survived boarding school and I would too. *It's going to be okay*, I told myself. I had to believe that.

I have a particular memory of that horrible time that I can see in my mind as vividly as if it happened five minutes ago. There was a path on the grounds at Riverdale that led along a ridge, where the ground fell away quite steeply. Quite a way down, another path ran along the top of a bluff above the Hudson River. One fall afternoon, I was walking the upper path. I looked down and saw a little boy, maybe even younger than I was, walking fast and half running along the lower path. He carried a suitcase and his teddy bear. R. was hurrying after him. The boy was trying to run away, but the older man caught him. "Where do you think you're going, young man?" he shouted. The poor little boy was weeping and clutching his teddy bear and his suitcase. R. ripped the teddy bear from the boy's arms and threw it on the ground. Then he yanked away the suitcase and with one of the most evil expressions I have ever seen, he opened the suitcase and emptied all of the boy's belongings down the hill. Then he dragged the sobbing child back to the dormitory. I couldn't stop staring at the clothes strewn everywhere and the teddy bear still lying on the ground.

The dorm master was eventually caught and fired. But his activities were all hushed up; nothing was ever said to the parents.

As for the Argentine accomplices, I saw one of them ten years later. I was in the army, doing basic training at Fort Dix, New Jersey. Two buddies and I were in a New York bar on a weekend pass, having a drink. I looked at the man standing next to me at the bar. It was one of the Argentines. I said to him, "I know you from Riverdale. This bar isn't big enough for both of us." He took a look at me and my friends and walked out.

Just a few years ago, as I write this, I was at a social event in Palm Beach, chatting with a lot of people. I saw a man approach and said to myself, "Who is he? I know him from somewhere." Then it hit me: he was the other Argentine. When he came up to me and put out his hand, I turned my back on him.

I was saved from the worst of R.'s terror by two things. First, Mother wanted my sister Jean and me to be near her during the winter months, so she took both of us out of boarding school and had us attend day school while we lived with her in Palm Beach. While this plan of switching schools for just the winter term was not exactly conducive to keeping and making friends or to doing well in school, it saved me from R.'s abusive games during that winter. I was too ashamed to tell my mother what had happened, but I was thankful to be safe at home with her.

The second thing that saved me was whooping cough. When the winter came to an end, I went back to Riverdale, where the terror began all over again. Perhaps it was the stress, but I got sick, very sick, with pneumonia and whooping cough. And again, I was able to return to the safe and loving arms of my mother.

Whooping cough was serious business back then, before the pertussis vaccine was widely available. Children often died after days or weeks of sustained coughing and gasping for breath. It nearly killed me when, accompanied by a case of pneumonia, it struck me in 1942.

When I first fell ill, I was rushed from school to a New York City hospital for emergency treatment, after which Mother brought me up to Cape Cod to recuperate. This was the first time since infancy that I really had my mother to myself, and the first time I enjoyed such close attention from her, and I basked in it. We took long walks on the nearly deserted beach together—it was spring, and the crowds hadn't yet descended on the town—and in the evenings she would read to me: books on science, history, geography, and the occasional adventure from Jack London or Sir Walter Scott. I still remember those terrible dogfights in London's *White Fang*. I couldn't sleep after I heard them read. And the elaborate prose of *Ivanhoe*, those chivalric images and cadences.

But more than any specific activity, it was my mother's constant tenderness and attention that I cherished. When the original bout of whooping cough was nearly over, I went out in the rain and suffered a recurrence of the pneumonia, and Mother patiently nursed me back to health again. As sick as I was, those days were a tonic for me. And they cemented a special bond between my mother and me that survived until her death at the age of 104.

Dave Powers, one of President Kennedy's closest friends and aides, long remembered and wrote about an incident that happened when I was about sixteen. Dave was having breakfast at the Cape house with us and listening to me excitedly tell Dad about my plans to compete in the Edgartown regatta that weekend. Mother walked into the room in time to hear some of this. She reminded me that she expected me to make my annual visit to a religious retreat north of Boston, which was happening that same weekend. Without so much as furrowing my eyebrows, I immediately replied—as Dave recalled—"Yes, Mother, I'll be ready to go."

My father was watching this exchange as well. He supported my mother, disciplinarian that he was. But after observing the exchange, he volunteered that I could drive his car to the retreat. Since no one ever was allowed to drive Dad's car, the message was unmistakable. *I know this is hard for you, Teddy. I know you want to compete in the regatta. But you're doing the right thing by honoring and obeying your mother.* I've never forgotten that day. And as much as I'm sure I would have loved the regatta, I doubt I would have remembered it any more than the one the year before or the year after.

Friends have asked me, over the years, whether I felt anger toward my parents for this exacting discipline, and for launching me off to these nomadic boarding schools at such an early age. My answer is that no, I did not, and do not. For one thing, I was taught not to complain. That was one of the rules that Dad lived by, and thus one that we all lived by. *"Kennedys never complain!"* For another, sending children away to school was simply what many parents did in those days. I knew lots of other children in circumstances similar to mine. Some suffered, but suffering is a given in life. Most, I think, grew up to be good parents themselves and to enjoy prosperous lives.

Besides that, I never once doubted my parents' love. Dad could be stern, but he not only loved us; he showed us all a deep respect. He always kissed us when we came home. Not many fathers kissed their children back then. And even as grown men, we kissed our father on the cheek when greeting him or saying goodbye. I continue that tradition with my own sons.

Now, I don't mean to imply that Dad was a pushover. I was reminded of the limits of his indulgence—and of his insistence on self-discipline—at age eleven, when I was about to leave home for yet another boarding school: Fessenden, I believe. Dad sat me down for his traditional pep talk. At the end of it, he said, "Well, now, Ted, you may go down to the cupboard in the pantry and help yourself to a piece of my butter crunch."

Everyone in the family knew that Katie Lynch's Butter Crunch was my favorite treat. It was a taste I shared with my sister Rosemary—and with Dad. I raced into the pantry and helped myself to much more than one piece. My pockets were bulging with as much butter crunch as I could jam into them. My newly bulky profile proved suspicious to my eagle-eyed father. He insisted on looking in my pockets, where he found them chock-full of what amounted to two complete boxes of the candy. He exploded. And I was sent off to school without so much as a taste of Katie Lynch's Butter Crunch.

Confrontations (as opposed to competition) were actually quite rare in our household, and they almost never occurred between any of the brothers and sisters. This was no accident. Dad raised us to cooperate, not to quarrel. This may sound like a tall order for any parent, but our father made it work. First, he respected us, and in that way he showed us how to respect him and one another. He used a tactical ploy as well: he would draw any sign of tension away from us and toward himself. Mother did not always understand this, and would worry when one of us argued with

Dad. He would explain to her, "As long as they're not fighting with each other, as long as their disagreements are with others and not among themselves, I can deal with it. I can't deal with the fact that they're differing or fighting with each other."

Another important factor in our harmony was that, as strange as it might seem, Dad and Mother never fought. My niece Caroline Kennedy tells of asking Mother once, "Did you and Grampa ever fight?"

Mother said, "Oh, no, dear. No, Grampa and I never fought."

Caroline said, "Well, how did you handle your differences?"

Mother replied, "I would always just say, 'Yes, dear,' and then I'd go to Paris."

It was about three years until Dad and I clashed again, but it was a beaut. This time I was the aggrieved party, or I thought I was, and the upshot was that I decided to run away from home. The provocation was something silly. My parents had promised that I could go on the boat, and then they withdrew their promise. That was my perception, anyway. The more I reminded them of the promise, the more unreasonable they grew—in my view. I was an adolescent now, and so I was mortally wounded. "I'm going to run away," I announced. I stormed out of the house and got into one of the cars and started driving. I drove west, toward the Cape Cod Canal, as I remember. Just before I crossed the Cape Cod Canal bridge, the landmark that would officially take me "off-Cape," I stopped and found a telephone and called home. My intent, or so I told myself, was to reiterate to my parents that I was running away.

Jack, who was visiting the Cape house, and not Dad, answered—to my great fortune. "I'm running away from home!" I repeated to him. "I'm tired of it all. This is it. I'm finished. I'm out of here."

Jack subtly took charge of the situation. He didn't try to persuade me that our parents may have had a point. Instead, he said, "Well, Teddy, before you run away, why don't you meet me at the Midtown Theater?" This was a movie house in Hyannis.

Pride made me hold out in grim silence.

"There's a war picture on," Jack said. "Come and watch a war picture with me."

He really knew how to get me. Watching a war picture with a hero of World War II. Who was my brother. It was all over, and we both knew it, but I needed to salvage a little dignity. I pretended to think about it.

"Well," I said. "All right."

I turned around and headed for Hyannis, where I met my brother at the movies. At the end of the war picture, as we were walking out, Jack turned to me and said, "It's getting late, Teddy. Why don't you come home with me and get a good night's sleep and run away in the morning."

"I'm not sure about that," I said.

"That's the right thing to do, Teddy. Otherwise you're going to have to find some other place to sleep tonight," he said.

That convinced me, even though the truth is that I didn't need too much convincing by then.

When we got home and I went to sleep, Jack found our father and said, "I think you ought to let up on Teddy."

Early the next morning, Dad knocked on my bedroom door and said, "Teddy, do you want to go riding?" I said, "Sure, Dad." And all was forgotten.

Jack's easy mastery of a crisis, and his way of making an adolescent boy feel like a worthy person whose feelings mattered—these formed another aspect of my wish to "catch up." It wasn't entirely about matching my brothers' accomplishments. It was about conducting myself like them as well.

When Dad was still in England, he was never far from my thoughts. Looking over old and poorly spelled letters, I find myself making many assurances that I was living up to his wishes: "We had a Halloween party lost week. Afterwards I got dressed up like a ghost and went all the way down the road I didn't scare because you said not to scare anyone because they may have a weak heart."

Dad never wanted us to flaunt our wealth. Thus I was not allowed to even have a bicycle until the majority of boys among my friends had received theirs. Later on, I was not allowed to have a car until most of my friends owned one. My brothers and sisters had to obey the same rule. At the time, we felt a little sorry for ourselves. We never complained, of course. And years later, we all looked back and understood how important this rule was to our development. The underlying principle was that we were always to distinguish ourselves through achievement, not mere flamboyance.

I didn't write as often as Dad would have liked. "You and Bobby are the worst correspondents I have in the family," he chided me in September 1940. German bombs were falling on London by then, and Dad's life, like everyone else's in the city, was in danger. It was typical of him to tell me about the bombing in a casual, man-to-man sort of way, as if I were his intrepid chum who just happened to be on the other side of the ocean:

> I don't know whether you would have very much excitement during these raids. I am sure, of course, you wouldn't be scared, but if you heard all these guns firing every night and the bombs bursting you might get a little fidgety. . . . I hope when you grow up you will dedicate your life to trying to make people happy instead of making them miserable as this war does today.
> Well, old boy, write me some letters and I want you to know I miss seeing you a lot, for after all, you are my pal, aren't you?
> Love
> Dad

With Bobby, who was fourteen then, Dad was more candid:

> I thought you might be interested to get my opinion as to the present situation here. There is . . . a very definite feeling that within the next forty-eight or seventy-two hours Germany will try an invasion. There are evidences that they have accumulated a number of barges and ships to move their forces all along the French Coast.

There is also an indication that their guns, which they are firing from the French Coast . . . will [produce] the sort of rainbow effect over the channel that they will send their fleet under for protection. . . .

The whole problem will finally be dropped in the lap of the United States, because as the manufacturing facilities here are destroyed . . . we in the United States will have to furnish more supplies . . . within a very few months we will have the settling of the whole matter right in our own hands.

The "settling of the whole matter" implied almost certain U.S. involvement in the European war. Far from my awareness and even Bobby's, Dad's desire to keep America neutral and his pessimism about Britain's capacity to defeat Germany was costing him the goodwill of the British government and people. His stormy relationship with Franklin Roosevelt was likewise reaching a breaking point. As correspondence was to reveal years afterward, Roosevelt had long considered Joseph Kennedy "dangerous" because of his bluntness and penchant for harsh public criticism, but valued his skill as a negotiator and his keen ear for information.

My childhood self suspected none of these intrigues. But the upshot of them rang clear as a bell to me. I excitedly wrote this letter to Dad, shortly after receiving some good news in the autumn of 1940:

Dear Daddy, I was so glad when you told me today that you were coming home soon. I had my bicycle painted blue and silver, and fixed up, so now I don't need a new one. I hope it didn't cost too much. Are you lonesome at wall hall? How is Rose and Stevens and Mr. Begley? Is he as nice now as he used to be? Does Stevens go fishing anymore? He was awfully nice to take me when I was at wall hall. Are there any fogs now? Or any air raids? Write us again. Love, from Teddy.

My father returned to America from London for the last time as ambassador on October 26, 1940. Letters and diaries show that he was ambivalent about supporting Franklin Roosevelt for a third term, and preoccupied with resentments about what he saw as a falling away of trust and support from his chief. He poured out his frustrations directly to FDR over dinner at the White House the day after he arrived back home. Yet the next night, less than a week before the election, Dad put all this aside and spoke to the nation as a patriot. Paying for his own airtime, Joe Kennedy delivered an address over 114 radio stations of the Columbia Broadcasting Network urging Americans to reelect their president. He saved his most heartfelt argument—the famous "hostages to fortune" passage—for the last.

FDR won reelection. On December 1, Dad announced his intention to resign as ambassador to the Court of St. James's within a week. He was never again to serve in public life.

In the spring of 1941, I entered the Palm Beach Private School, not far from my parents' Florida house. I was nine then, and was placed in the fourth grade. School life quickly returned to normal for me: my teacher, Mrs. Cochrane, wrote on my first report card, "No foundation for fourth grade." But I liked her, and slowly my grades improved.

Following that glorious summer at the Cape in 1941, the summer of cranberry bogs and horseback riding with my dad, I resumed a pattern that would hold for the next four years: shifting from school to school, south to north and back again, as I followed the sun with my parents.

I put in three stints at the Fessenden School, a forty-one-acre campus in West Newton ten miles west of Boston, in the fall of 1942 and the spring of 1943, and then again in the fall of 1944. I distinguished myself during my first tour at Fessenden by getting paddled fifteen times. I've always joked that my father must have been the inspiration for Federal Express. When the headmaster wrote the parents at the beginning of the year to ask whether to paddle their sons or dock them days from their vacation if they misbehaved, my father's approval to have me paddled seemed to arrive by 10:30 the next morning. I had no resentment about being paddled. It was delivered by Mr. Giles, an elderly instructor who'd lost a leg in the First World War, and although it stung immediately, it didn't hurt so much after a few minutes. Anyway, I deserved it every time. Walking on the roof, for instance, with some of my friends, with water bombs—water inside the fold of a little paper—and dropping them three stories down onto members of the faculty. Not a wise thing to do. Or we would put strips of tape between our cubicles to trip the night watchman and make him fall down. That was not a good thing to do either. These boyhood pranks, more than anything else, were my way of trying to fit in and be one of the guys.

My most incredible escapade was with two brothers who went on to distinguished careers, and they are still good friends of mine. But at Fessenden they had a sort of an outlaw streak. We all did.

One night we thought it would be a good idea to lower one of them down on a rope from the roof to the faculty room window, so the boy could climb through, locate the student files, and find out our grades. I thought that was a good idea myself. So we lowered one of the boys down. Just as he got inside, it began to rain. One of the teachers was trapped outdoors and got rained on. He headed for the faculty room to get his umbrella. The boy heard footsteps and scampered into the closet. The teacher opened the closet door to get his umbrella, and there he was. That was nearly the end for the brothers. They came within a whisker of getting expelled. Luckily for Fessenden, they were allowed to stay and graduate. The last I heard, the brothers had contributed a boatload to the school.

Far from these hijinks in Massachusetts, the war that Dad had tried to keep at bay from his country and his children exploded onto American territory on December 7, 1941. World War II proceeded to draw several of Joseph Kennedy's "hostages to fortune" into its maw.

Joe was the first. He earned his navy aviator wings in May 1942 at the Jacksonville Naval Air Station. My father was on hand to pin them on him.

Jack followed our brother a few weeks later. He had faced numerous health challenges growing up, and he was concerned that he wouldn't be allowed into the military. And in fact he had failed the army physical, mostly because of his torturously bad back.

But he would not give up. He threw himself into a rigorous exercise program. Then he prevailed on Dad to help get him in. After some behind-the-scenes prodding by Dad's friend and former naval attaché in London, Admiral Alan Goodrich Kirk, Jack passed a second physical and joined the navy as an ensign two months before Pearl Harbor. He served in the Office of Naval Intelligence in Washington, where he socialized with Kick and her friends. In January 1942 he was sent to a South Carolina ONI office, then spent some time recuperating from illnesses in naval hospitals before reporting to the midshipman's school in Chicago in July.

Kick soon put aside the glittering Washington life that suited her so naturally. In July 1943 she resigned her newspaper position and returned to a now devastated London, where she was handed a gas mask and took up the grimy demands of volunteer work for the American Red Cross.

Bobby was chafing to enter the service as soon as he came of age. He followed the war's news intently in that summer of 1941. He would turn seventeen in November of the following year and become eligible to enroll in a training program for the navy.

The summers at the Cape changed as the war went on, with so many of my brothers and sisters absent, and sometimes one or the other of my parents as well. I sailed alone and with Joey Gargan, exhilarated by the freedom and sense of power in my little sloop, at the safe fringes of an ocean where U-boats preyed upon convoys of ships.

The war reached its midpoint in 1943, and that was the moment when Jack was nearly killed and emerged a hero.

Jack got himself assigned to the Solomon Islands in the Pacific theater and arrived as the twenty-six-year-old commander of a patrol torpedo boat, an extremely dangerous assignment that he'd virtually demanded.

PTs were small, often badly built, lightly armed craft deployed to prowl combat-zone waters at night in search of Japanese destroyers and cruisers. Jack's boat was numbered 109.

On August 2, as part of a squad of fifteen such craft sent to intercept a Japanese convoy off the island of New Georgia, PT 109 was rammed by an enemy destroyer and sliced in half. Two of the thirteen-man crew were killed. My brother exhorted the survivors to swim toward a flyspeck island, personally towing the badly burned engineer for five hours by clamping the man's lifeboat straps in his mouth. Jack then swam back out into the ocean to try and signal a passing boat, though he'd been without sleep for a day and a half. Unsuccessful, he swam back to his men half unconscious. The ordeal continued for a week, with Jack directing swims to larger islands. The men went days without water. The navy assumed that all of them had been killed, and in fact held a funeral service for them on the small island of Tulagi a few days after the encounter. On August 9, the party made contact with a New Zealanders' camp on Cross Island via a message Jack had scraped into a coconut shell. (That coconut is now in the John F. Kennedy Library in Boston.) The message made it to an American base, which sent a PT to rescue the men.

I didn't even know my brother was lost and presumed dead until I learned he had been found. Along with my sister and some friends, I rode my bicycle over to the News Shop in Hyannis Port one balmy August night to get the papers for our parents. We stared at the big headlines that confronted us, along with a drawing of a PT boat. We raced home, yelling that our brother was a hero. Dad heard us out, and then told us he had been notified several days earlier that Jack was missing. He'd remained hopeful, he said, and had decided not to worry us with the news.

On furlough the following year, Jack playfully let me share the aura of his "hero" image—which he himself never took seriously. Tanned and rawboned and flashing his great smile, he showed up at the family residence in Palm Beach with his service buddy Paul "Red" Fay Jr. When I ventured inside his room to awaken him on that first morning, he hugged me, then dug some war souvenirs out of his duffel bag and gave them to me: native swords and clubs from the South Pacific.

Then he appointed me courier in a make-believe PT mission. He ordered me to awaken "Red" Fay, down the hall, with the message, "This is PT 109 to Captain Fay, over." I gladly ran off. Red sent me back to Jack's room with, "Romeo Echo Delta A-okay. What is our first mission this morning?" This went on for a while, and the jargon got a little too military for me to understand—but those two found it a great joke. And I was in the clouds.

Better still, Jack escorted me on board an actual PT boat. He was stationed at a shakedown center in Miami Beach, and before sunrise one morning he rousted me out of bed to come along with him. I couldn't believe it. I was barely twelve years old, and my hero brother was going to take me aboard a ship with him. What I didn't know at the time was that civilians, especially little kid civilians like me, weren't really supposed to be aboard navy vessels and certainly weren't supposed to go out to sea on them. But my brother knew how much it would mean to me and all the crew enjoyed being co-conspirators in our adventure.

As we boarded the boat and headed for open water, I had a huge smile plastered across my face until I got drenched by a torpedo-like squirt of tobacco juice from the mouth of the biggest sailor I'd ever seen. It splattered my shirt and hands. The crew loved it, and Jack showed me no mercy whatsoever. After I got over the initial shock, I thought it was pretty funny too. I prowled the coastal waters for a couple of hours that day with my brother and his crew, and I've treasured the memory my entire life.

Jack's back problems prevented him from returning to active duty, but while in a naval hospital, he was awarded four more medals. He was released in October 1944.

* * *

If my brother gave me an imaginative glimpse into World War II that year, another colorful relative whisked me back into the brass-band exuberance of my Boston Irish political roots.

Fessenden was near enough to the city that on autumn Sundays I could board a train on the Boston & Albany Railroad line in West Newton and roll along the few short miles to South Station in the heart of town. From there I would walk up Beacon Hill to the old Bellevue Hotel. Standing as it did next to the State House with its golden dome, the Bellevue is properly remembered as "a political Grand Central Station." I would wait in the lobby until I was summoned up to the suite of the stationmaster, one of Boston's greatest politicians: my maternal grandfather, John Francis Fitzgerald. Honey Fitz.

He was eighty then. He was the son of an Irish immigrant family who made it to the top: a Massachusetts state senator from 1892 to 1894, a U.S. representative (1895–1901), and twice mayor of Boston (1906–08 and 1910–14). But those offices hardly begin to describe how much Grampa meant to Boston, and vice versa.

Pay a visit sometime to Franklin Park Zoo, that wonderful seventy-acre site down in Jamaica Plain and Roxbury. It's one of the oldest zoos in the hemisphere now, built in 1913. That zoo was developed by Grampa.

He played a key part in the shaping of Fenway Park, which was finished in 1912. This was back in the glory years when the Red Sox won six pennants and five World Series from 1903 through 1918. Honey Fitz was right in the middle of it all—a passionate Red Sox fan. He formed the team's first pep club, the Royal Rooters, along with his pal Mike "Nuf Ced" McGreevey, a bartender with a walrus mustache. Every Opening Day, the two of them would put on their silk top hats and cutaway coats, hoist a few frothy pints at the bar, light up their cigars, and then go strutting at the head of a parade through the city to the ballpark, waving their red umbrellas and belting out songs, while a brass band behind them oom-pa-pa'd. Grampa was short and stout, and he had a big, sweet tenor voice. If things were going badly for the Sox, either Grampa or "Nuf Ced" was likely to begin bawling from the stands the words to the sentimental waltz "Tessie," which became the team's unlikely lucky song:

Tessie, you make me feel so badly,
Why don't you turn around?
Tessie, you know I love you madly,
Babe, my heart weighs about a pound.
Don't blame me if I ever doubt you,
You know I couldn't live without you.
Tessie, you are the only, only, only.

"Tessie" may sound a little quaint to today's ears, but Grampa's rendition of it was good enough to cause the great Pittsburgh shortstop Honus Wagner to commit two errors in a single inning during a World Series game.

Honey Fitz provided and lit the first civic Christmas tree in the United States, on Boston Common, back in 1912. New Yorkers sometimes like to claim credit for the first public tree, in Madison Square Garden, but an expert researcher named Caroline Kennedy did some digging and figured out that Grampa's tree went up fully thirty minutes before the one in New York.

He was a life force, and that force fueled the life of the city. Many of his ideas came from his travels in European countries. He'd take note of the dynamic civic features in all the European capitals, and he'd say, "There's no reason that Boston can't have these, just like these other great cities!" So he adapted them to Boston. And then his innovations were adapted in other cities across the country.

Grampa loved people. And the people he came in contact with felt his warmth and returned it. I think Grampa wished he could get to know every single person in town.

There's no question that I inherited this joy of people from him. I inherited the whole way I approach politics. Being in a crowd, looking into new faces, shaking hands, laughing, swapping stories, singing some of the old songs—I love it all.

Still, Honey Fitz's love of people exceeded anything I've ever seen. He used to board the passenger train at North Station and ride it up the Atlantic coast to Old Orchard Beach in Maine, a distance of about a hundred miles. The trip would take two hours and ten minutes. Once there, he'd board the next train back to Boston. These trains left at intervals of about an hour in those days, and Honey Fitz would take them all, at intervals of about five days. He'd stagger his departures and returns so that each time he would catch a different crowd of commuters. And what would he do on those journeys? Why, he'd walk up and down the aisles of the passenger cars the whole time, tipping his hat and shaking the hands of the people on board. Grampa respected working people, and it's largely because of him that my brothers and I respected and fought for them as well. Grampa would lean down and start chatting with some fellow puffing a stogie and squinting at the racing form, learn his name and opinions, and by the time the train pulled into Old Orchard Beach, Honey Fitz would have fifty or seventy-five new friends. And then he'd get on the train heading back, with a new group of strangers, and do it all over again.

Of course, even a man of Honey Fitz Fitzgerald's energy needed a little downtime now and then. And so on weekends he would march into the lobby of his favorite hotel, find himself a comfortable easy chair, and wait for the people to come to him. Someone would walk through the main door, and he'd jump up and bound over to them with his hand outstretched. He would do this all day long. When I was about sixteen, I remember driving Grampa to the Breakers Hotel in Palm Beach. Grampa's idea of fun was to sit in the lobby and wait to meet new people. He would tip the hotel desk clerk to ring the bell when guests checked in— once if they were from Massachusetts; twice if they were from Boston. When the bell rang twice, up would go Grampa, introducing himself to the strangers. "I'm John F. Fitzgerald. You're from Boston, aren't you?" By the end of the day, he would have gotten himself invited to lunch and dinner and would have had the time of his life. I'd pick him up at 10 p.m., and he was overflowing with stories about his great day. Grampa loved to laugh. He would get tickled by his own stories. One of his favorites was a tad off-color. But nobody ever realized that it was off-color, because Grampa could never get to the punch line without falling into a laughing fit so severe he could barely breathe, let alone finish the joke. The joke involved the name of a lovely little seacoast town about twenty miles southeast of Boston, named Scituate. Well, I can't reconstruct Grampa's joke completely, but the punch line involves a slight scatological mispronunciation of the town's name, so that it comes out—well, *you* know. Grampa would always try his best to make it through. But as he got close, he'd begin to chuckle, and then fight for breath, and his eyes would squeeze shut and fill with tears, and his face would turn red, and he'd fish his handkerchief out of his breast pocket. And everybody else in the room would be laughing and choking along with him, not knowing really why they were doing it. They were all just captured by Grampa's sense of fun. It was so infectious.

In 1943, Honey Fitz was just seven years from his passing in 1950, but his mind was still sharp and his political sense acute. On those autumnal Sundays of 1943, I had this marvelous legend all to myself. He took a special interest in me, for Lord only knows what reasons. In my later grade school years, he and I grew very close. While my older siblings would be off at different places and doing different things, Grampa Fitzgerald and I would be together, traveling around Boston.

Entering his suite at the Bellevue, the first thing I'd see would be what looked like a moving newspaper, with short legs. Grampa liked to keep informed, and he'd have torn-up editions of all the Boston papers scattered around the floor. In those days the newspapers published several editions, with updated news all day long, and Grampa read all of them from cover to cover. The items that interested him he would pin to his lapels and other parts of his clothing. (When he visited at the Cape, he'd have us kids constantly on the run to the village for the latest editions.) I believe Mother's habit of adorning the bulletin board near our dining table with topical items came directly from this.

He'd unpin himself—mostly—and take me downstairs to lunch in the hotel restaurant. I'd have to hustle to keep up with this plump, dapper old man with the twinkling blue eyes. We'd enter through the kitchen. This gave Grampa the chance to introduce me (once again, in most cases) to all the cooks and waitresses. At the table, I could hardly wait to order my mashed potatoes and meat, but as soon as we sat down, a crush of Bostonians would descend upon us, and Grampa would greet each one and make introductions again. Often my ice cream would be melted before I had a chance to spoon it. Then we'd hurry out of the hotel—Grampa scooping up the newer editions of the papers in the lobby—and he would lead me on one of his enchanted walking tours of Boston.

He'd take me to Milk Street and tell me, "It's called Milk Street because that was where the cows used to walk down and wait at the Commons." And Water Street: "Because of the well that was there." And then down to where the ships came in. And then we'd walk over past Paul Revere's house, and he'd talk about Paul Revere.

Along the way, he would tell me about the Irish experience in Boston. He'd talk about the discrimination against the Irish that he'd seen, and would show me the signs he'd collected: "No Irish Need Apply." I still have some of those signs in my house. Then he would take me down Beacon Street and Tremont Street and show me the glass windows that dated to American Revolution time. He'd talk about the difference in the Boston social classes illustrated by Boston Common, and the Public Garden. The Common, he'd explain, was were where the British soldiers trained. And where the cattle used to graze. The Garden was funded by, and largely enjoyed by, the wealthy people, though it was open to the public.

Finally we'd get to the Old North Church, where Grampa would spot the rector. The two of them would cross Salem Street and cock their chairs back opposite the church, so they could look at the steeple. They'd begin to talk, oblivious to the people walking by. They would talk about the architecture, and about the church, and about what was happening in the North End. Grampa would give me some money to go buy cannolis. At last the time would come when he would say goodbye to the rector, and continue our little tour, and finally bring me back to Park Street. I'd get on the train to get back to Fessenden.

Grampa had a good pal, a fellow named Clem Norton, who seemed to spend his whole life reading books at the Athenaeum on Beacon Street. Sometimes Grampa would go and fetch Norton. "*Nawton!*" he'd say, in that Boston accent of his. "Let's go and watch the boys row over at Hawva'd!" Norton would say, "Fine!" and put down his book. They'd go over to the Charles River and watch the college boys row. Grampa would call out, "*Who's that Number Two, Nawton?*" "Number Two, that's Hallowell's boy! State Street Bank! Hallowell! State Street Bank!" "*Who's that Number One up there?*" "That's a Lowell!" "*Is that Ralph Lowell's son?*" "Yes, he's up at the First Bank of Boston!" And on it would go. And then my grandfather, ever the politician, would head over to State Street Bank, for example, and wait outside until closing time, when Mr. Hallowell left the building. He'd rush up to the banker and say, "Mr. Hallowell, Mr. Hallowell, I'm John F. Fitzgerald, the former mayor of Boston." I doubt that Hallowell was pleased to see him. But then Honey Fitz would say, "I saw your boy row over at Hawva'd today. Number Two. Beautiful stroke. Beautiful stroke." And in a beautiful stroke of political genius, Grampa would have won over the Brahmin banker. And of course, that was exactly what he had in mind the whole time.

My memories of this good, grand old man have restored hope in me when things have been darkest in my life. He was a constant in my life during the difficult, nomadic years of boarding school. His simple bequest to me has been more precious than any fortune. Love life, and believe in it.

In September 1943, the newly commissioned naval pilot Joseph Kennedy Jr. made a dashing farewell visit to the family at Hyannis Port. I came over from school for the occasion. With permission, he flew his PB4Y Liberator up from Florida to the Cape, where he landed and shook hands all round and said goodbye. He took off again, and this was the last glimpse we were to have of Joe. Soon he was in England, where he would complete twenty-five combat missions, and then, in August 1944, volunteer for one more.

Bobby and I became quite close that autumn. He was attending Milton Academy just south of Boston, playing football and studying as he kept his attention focused on the war and international politics. In October, still six weeks shy of eighteen, he enlisted in the naval reserve as an apprentice seaman, restricted from active duty until the following year.

We spent several weekends together at the Cape house that fall, usually just the two of us, though sometimes Lem Billings would come along. We'd drive to Hyannis Port after dusk and comb the deserted streets for a lonely open grocery store where we could buy some staples. Dad closed the house down when the weather turned cold, so we would sleep in the little apartment above the garage, bundled up against the frosty nights. Before turning in, we'd walk along the shore. Our talk would be typical of any two brothers—plans for the future, our schools, girls. I relished his company. He was still quiet, inner-directed, deeply devout. But the self-deprecating humor that would mark him as a grown man was beginning to emerge. And he was always interested in what was going on in my life. Those chilly weekends at the Cape cast a quiet spell on both of us, I think, that is hard to describe.

I do recall one preoccupation of Bobby's around that time. I'm convinced that his anguish over it led directly to one of the most famous Catholic doctrinal disputes of the late 1940s and early '50s, a dispute that still has resonance today. I believe, though I cannot be certain, that Bobby's concern resulted, over time, in the excommunication of a popular Boston priest, and to a major shift in Catholic teaching regarding the possibility of salvation for non-Catholics.

Bobby was among many students attracted to the Thursday evening lectures given by Father Leonard Feeney, a priest, Jesuitical scholar, and a colorful, mesmerizing advocate of traditional doctrine. In the mid-1940s Father Feeney had become convinced that Catholicism as practiced in America was defective. In particular, the Church had gone lax on a tenet that Feeney believed to be a pillar of the faith: that salvation for people outside the Catholic Church was impossible.

This implied consignment of millions of worthy souls to Purgatory troubled Bobby, and he talked to me about it as we walked along the beach. He discussed it with our father one weekend at the Cape house. I well remember the conversation.

Dad could not believe that Bobby had heard Father Feeney correctly. "But," he said, "if you feel strongly that you did, I'm going to go into the other room and call Richard. Maybe he'll want you to go up to Boston and see him."

"Richard" was Richard Cardinal Cushing. Dad and the cardinal enjoyed a long and profound friendship. I remember the cardinal coming to visit at the Cape. He and Dad liked to go out on the *Marlin*, dad's motorboat, with a pitcher of chowder and another pitcher of daiquiris, and talk theology and world issues while they cruised.

Bobby said he felt strongly indeed. Bang! Dad called up "Richard" and arranged for Bobby to visit him. The cardinal, as nonplussed as Dad, sent some of his people over to hear Father Feeney's Thursday evening lecture. When he found that my brother was right, Cushing banned Feeney from speaking there; Feeney refused to obey the order, and in September 1949 the archdiocese formally condemned the priest's teaching and suspended him from his duties. In February 1952, Father Feeney was excommunicated.

Bobby wasn't the only critic of Father Feeney, of course, but he was among the first to achieve results. Nor did his principled gesture end with the banishment of Feeney. Reinforced by Cardinal Cushing's discussions with the papal hierarchy in Rome, it became an animating impulse of the Second Ecumenical Council of the Vatican, which opened under Pope John XXIII in 1962.

It was in August 1944 that I had my first encounter with tragedy. Our family, Mother especially, was already digesting some unsettling news: in May, Kick, at twenty-four, informed us from London that she'd married her beau of six years, a British lord named William Cavendish. Cavendish was an Anglican—a Protestant—and as deeply as Mother loved Kick, she could not at first reconcile her daughter's decision with her own strict Catholic tenets about marrying and agreeing to raise your children within the faith.

This situation was still fresh in our minds as several of us idled away the pleasant Sunday afternoon of August 13, in the sunroom of the Cape house. Our little family group included Mother, Jack, Joey Gargan and me, and Jean and Eunice, and also a young European friend of Eunice's, Peggy Edgerton Byrd, who was about eighteen. We were listening to a recording of Bing Crosby singing the number one tune of that year, "I'll Be Seeing You," when a strange dark car pulled into the front driving circle and stopped. Two naval chaplains got out, walked up the steps to the porch, and knocked on the screen door. Mother looked up from the Sunday paper she'd been reading in a tiny rocking chair that only she could fit into. As she received the clerics, we could hear a few words: "missing—lost." All of us froze.

The chaplains asked to speak to Mr. Kennedy. Mother turned and rushed upstairs, where Dad lay napping. Moments later the two of them came back down. They took the clergymen into another room and talked briefly. When they emerged, Dad's face was twisted. He got the words out that confirmed what we already suspected. Joe Jr. was dead.

After completing his required twenty-five combat missions and earning the right to return home, Joe had volunteered for a mission so dangerous that some members of his ground crew pleaded with him not to go. Along with a copilot, he was to take off in an experimental drone loaded with high explosives and pilot it on a trajectory toward a target in Germany. Over the English Channel, the two young Americans were to eject themselves, parachute into the sea, and let a radio beam guide the craft, by then a loaded weapon, to its target. Something had gone wrong. Perhaps the radio beam itself had ignited a tiny spark. Whatever the cause, the drone had exploded into a fireball just minutes before the two pilots were due to bail out.

I recall that suddenly the sunroom was awash in tears. Mother, my sisters, our guest, myself—everybody was crying; some wailed. Dad turned himself around and stumbled back up the stairs; he did not want us to witness his own dissolution into sobs.

This went on for about fifteen minutes. And then Jack spoke up.

"Joe wouldn't want us sitting here crying," my brother said. "He would want us to go sailing. Let's go sailing. Teddy, Joey, get the sails. We're going sailing."

And that was what we did. We went sailing.

My countless hours upon the sea have mostly been happy ones. This was the first of the many times when taking the tiller has steered me away from nearly unendurable grief across the healing waters on the long, hard course toward renewal and hope.

Joe was posthumously awarded the Navy Cross, the Distinguished Flying Cross, and the Air Medal. In 1946, the navy commissioned a destroyer in his name. None of that mattered to my father. I don't think Dad ever fully recovered from the death of his eldest son.

Three weeks after those men visited the house with the tragic news about Joe came the news of a second crushing loss. Billy Cavendish had been shot dead by a German bullet in Belgium. Kathleen, who had returned to be with our family after Joe's death, was shopping with Eunice in New York when a messenger found her and told her she must go back to the Waldorf-Astoria, where Dad had a suite.

Kathleen and Billy had been married four months, and had spent only a month together before Cavendish was called to the front.

* * *

My prep school education moved along in its checkerboard fashion, and then stabilized. In 1945, the year of the Allied victory in World War II, I was enrolled at Cranwell, in western Massachusetts. There, I kept getting into fights with my roommate, a fellow named Francis Aloysius O'Hara. The punishment for misbehavior at Cranwell was memorizing and reciting long prayers. O'Hara had a photographic memory and could learn the prayers in no time. I had to struggle for hours with them.

Then the following year I finally was matched up with a school where I felt at home, and stayed a while: Milton Academy, where I spent my four high school years.

Mentally and physically, I began my transformation from boy to young man at Milton. My grades improved, spurred by my blooming interests in civic affairs, debate, and public speaking. For the first time, I thought of a career in public service. And I started to convert the chubbiness that I'd carried since childhood into muscle. I began to go out with girls at Milton. Nancy Burley was perhaps my first sweetheart—she attended the nearby Milton Academy Girls School. We went to dances together for about three years.

I had not quite outgrown my love of pranks while at Milton. I had an outside tutor for chemistry, an extraordinary teacher in the local community named Dr. Nervais, a Belgian. He turned out students who won all sorts of national awards. None of them, I must report, came from my crowd.

We were more absorbed in playing practical jokes on Dr. Nervais. Among his teachings was that a liquid substance, when vaporized, would weigh exactly the same if it were passed through a sealed pipe, then exposed to cold water on the pipe's other end until it cooled to room temperature. "You vill see," he'd say in his studious Belgian cadences, "that ven it comes through, it vill veigh the same as ven we started—exactly two and a half grams." Except it never did. "Well, it isn't the same," one of us would muse. "It's heavier over here." And Dr. Nervais would patiently repeat the experiment: "Vell, ve vill do the situation again."

I can't remember how he found out about the magnets in the drawer on the cooling side of the table. I should not have even been a part of that prank. But it seemed very funny at the time. Dr. Nervais was actually quite a good sport about the whole thing. He was an excellent teacher and obviously knew a lot about how to handle silly adolescent boys. But I still can't figure out valences.

I joined several of Milton's teams: wrestling, then track, and ultimately football. Milton had a famous wrestling coach named Louie Andrews. Louie's squads didn't lose a meet in twelve years. They used to beat even Andover and Exeter, two hot teams. Louie's approach was simple and inspirational. He wanted you to be the best, and you didn't want to disappoint him.

I must thank Bobby, as in so many things, for connecting me with Louie. Before he graduated, my brother went to the coach and said, "Teddy is coming. Shape him up." Which he did. I learned balance, I learned how to use my legs and feet, and I learned muscle-building and aggressiveness. All these were to come in handy sooner than I could have predicted.

The Milton years were like a bright dawn to me after the cheerlessness of my early boarding school years. My knowledge increased more rapidly in Milton's classrooms than at any other place of learning, perhaps including Harvard. Even the summers away from school, at the Cape, were especially glorious.

Joey Gargan and I were sailing on August 15, 1945, when we heard a deafening volley of explosions erupting from Hyannis Port. Fireworks. We headed for shore, and learned that World War II was over—Japan had announced its surrender, following that of Germany the previous May. A parade was organized, and Joey and I found ourselves in a convertible filled with happy relatives and friends, driven past the dancing, cheering crowds lining Hyannis's streets by Lieutenant Jack Kennedy.

I began sailing in earnest during those years. I had loved the sea even before I could name it, but now I began to take full command of my nautical skills and plunged into competitive racing. I raced Wianno Juniors with Joey and then Wianno Seniors, sometimes with Jack and sometimes with local friends such as Dickie Rounds. I did well and soon began to place second and third and even first. Sailboat racing is an indescribably joyous thrill. It combines the adrenaline edge of competition with the exuberance of simply being on the water, the boat leaning sidelong into the waves as its sails take the wind and convert it to velocity. I learned all the winds; I learned the tides and currents; I learned the movement of the boat through the sea; I learned to judge my location on the water by the distant cliffs and lighthouses and rooftops onshore. Those were the sparkling summers when the sea transformed itself into a home for me, a charmed universe that I could enter in any season, any weather, and find comfort, transcendence.

As I hit the books at Milton in November of 1946, Jack distinguished himself again by getting elected to Congress at age twenty-nine. Jack's initial interest in elective office registered as a mild surprise in our family. He had never to my knowledge talked about political ambitions. The last I'd heard, he was thinking about a career in journalism. He'd written articles for the *Chicago Herald-American* and the International News Service after his injuries in the Pacific. In the months after the war ended, he kept writing as a stringer for those outlets, covering stories in Ohio, London, Potsdam, and other places, and also did work for the United Fund in Boston.

Not even Dad saw this coming. Jack later credited those dinnertime political conversations, steered by our father, as stimulating his interest in the field, but as Jack saw it, Dad didn't think he had the stamina for politics. He weighed 120 pounds after the first of three operations on his war-injured back. He still felt and showed the effects of the malaria he'd contracted in the Pacific, and of the synthetic drug known as atabrine that was used to treat the disease, which tended to discolor the skin. The igniting spark, as we later learned, seems to have been a speech—the first public speech Jack gave. He delivered it to a Boston American Legion audience in

August 1945, on his return to the United States from his reportage in Europe. It covered the wartime fates of Britain, Ireland, and Germany—"Victor, Neutral and Vanquished," as his title had it. The speech was a big success, to Jack's surprise, as were several others he gave not long afterward. The following year, James Michael Curley resigned his congressional seat to run for a fourth term as mayor of Boston. Jack, at loose ends and not sure of what to do with his life, decided to run for Curley's vacant 11th Congressional District seat. He won.

I was sleeping one early morning at Milton in the middle of May 1948 when I heard the door to my cubicle open. I opened my eyes to see the headmaster, Mr. Norris, peering at me. I immediately suspected that something bad had happened.

This time it was Kick. A small chartered plane in which she was flying had crashed in the south of France. Killed along with her was the man she wanted to marry, the Irish-born Lord Peter Wentworth FitzWilliam. The two had been flying to the Riviera and on to Paris where Dad awaited them. Kick was twenty-eight.

Even though it was spring, I remember that morning as exceptionally cold and dark. I waited alone for a long time before Jack arrived to pick me up and take me to Hyannis Port.

My mother was right when she observed in her memoir, "It has been said that time heals all wounds. I don't agree. The wounds remain. Time—the mind, protecting its sanity—covers them with some scar tissue and the pain lessens, but it is never gone."

Bobby graduated from Harvard that spring and set sail with a friend on the *Queen Mary* for a tour of Europe and the Middle East. Two years later he married Ethel Skakel, and they began to raise up a large new brood of Kennedys.

Jack remained a larger-than-life presence. The Edgartown regatta had been an annual chance for us to race together. One July not long after Jack's reelection to Congress, I entered the race with Joe Gargan as my partner. As the weekend approached, Jack decided that he wanted to sail too. He telephoned me at the Cape house to advise me of his intentions, but told me not to wait for him if he got there late. But of course Joe and I wanted him with us, and so on the day of the race we sailed our boat around and around the Edgartown harbor until it was almost time for the race to start. It was an overcast day, and suddenly out of the mist there appeared a single-engine plane, descending rapidly over Edgartown. The plane flew over our boat. We looked up and saw Jack grinning and waving down at us. He zoomed for shore and touched down on a grassy field at the edge of town.

A huge crowd milled around the pier, and twenty boats in each of two classes were tacking back and forth, their crews getting ready for the start. Joe and I realized that even if Jack could worm his way through the humanity, he would not have the proper racing identification, an official red tag, in his billfold. (He rarely even carried a billfold.) We began to appreciate how far-fetched his impulsive scheme had been. Still, he'd just flown over our heads, and so there was nothing to do but wait.

We didn't wait long. About six minutes after he touched down, a taxicab screeched to a halt at the edge of the pier and Jack jumped out, wearing a blue suit and tie and clutching his briefcase. He sliced his way through the mob of people toward the end of the pier and I steered the boat into the wind and alongside the pier for a quick pickup. An official started to yell, "Hey! You can't just pick people up here!" but Jack barged past him and leapt onto the boat. Just then the gun went off marking the start of the race. The three of us quickly pushed off, set the sails, and headed out to the starting line. Jack made a quick change belowdeck into clothes more appropriate for sailing, and I handed the tiller to my brother. We were late, but we were on our way.

It was a long course and a drizzly, misty day, and we had trouble seeing the other boats. But even with our late start, we managed a first in our division. Jack had taken a different route from all the other boats and there had been a wind shift that we were able to take advantage of before

any of the other racers. What a thrill! There was a lot of cheer aboard
Victura that afternoon. On the way into Edgartown harbor, Jack got
drenched by a passing motorboat, but he quickly dried himself off and
changed back into his blue suit. Pretty soon we saw his little single-engine
plane flying over us again, en route back to Washington. He disappeared
into the mist.

I said farewell to Milton in May 1950 and launched out with Joey
Gargan on a summer trip through Europe. My letters home show that I
complained of "paying an outrageous bill" and getting caught stealing
ashtrays in Sorrento, eating cornflakes in Florence, upsetting a canoe on
Lake Como, visiting Hitler's Eagle's Nest at Berchtesgaden, and contemplating the Nazi death camp at Dachau.

Harvard awaited me in the fall. I felt ready for it.

CHAPTER FIVE

The Harvard Screwup
1950–1958

The Harvard I entered in the fall of 1950 was in many ways the timeless Harvard of my father's and brothers' eras: a grand old national treasure of tree-scattered greens and yards and ancient redbrick buildings. Legendary professors such as Samuel Eliot Morison and John Kenneth Galbraith hurried to classrooms filled with intense young "gentlemen scholars" in their Harris Tweed jackets, their pipes tucked into their breast pockets. There were the final clubs, and parties.

Harvard was familiar to me from my many autumnal visits with the family to watch Jack and Bobby play football. I'd even visited Joe Jr. there once when he was in law school, and was amazed by how messy his room was. I savored an unfamiliar feeling—adultness—as I unpacked my suitcases in Room C-31 of the low-slung Wigglesworth dormitories that stretch along the southern edge of Harvard Yard. But I was still a kid in many ways—still *the* kid in the family. I looked forward to a rosy, uncomplicated existence as a Harvard man: good fellowship with new friends, stimulating contact with great professors, and playing football. As it turned out, my existence at Harvard was much more complicated than I had hoped.

I started off lucky, with a great roommate: a slim, sandy-haired boy named Dudley Richards. I'd casually known Dudley from summers in

Hyannis Port. He and his older brother Ross were good sailors. Ross had sailed against Bobby and given him all my brother could handle.

Dudley's passion was ice skating, and by his early teen years he was a top Olympic prospect. But at sixteen he'd seemingly shattered that dream: diving into water that was shallower than he realized, he'd suffered a broken neck. He recovered, but only after two years of intensive physical therapy, during which time he did not skate at all.

By the end of freshman year, Dudley's hard work had paid off and he'd gained the rank of number two amateur skater in the nation. Our friendship continued after Harvard, and I cheered him from afar as he went on to win some Olympic bronze and silver medals. In January 1961, Dudley shared a gold medal in the pairs at the U.S. Championships with the young skating star he intended to marry, Maribel Owen. Tragically, they both were killed, along with the entire U.S. skating team, in a plane crash on the way to the World Figure Skating Championships in Prague in February 1961.

I drove to Cambridge in my mother's old blue coupe in that fall of 1950. As soon as I was able to buy a snazzy Pontiac of my own, I got a special horn for it, a horn that sounded like a cow's anxious "MOOOOO!" I considered that fairly stylish and amusing; but as always seemed to happen, word of the horn made its way back to my father, and I received the following letter from him:

> I heard in my roundabout way that you are using that bell [*sic*] of yours on that car. I don't want to be complaining about things you do but I want to point out to you that when you exercise any privilege that the ordinary fellow does not avail himself of, you immediately become the target for display and newspaper criticism.
>
> It's all right to struggle to get ahead of the masses by good works, by good reputation and by hard work, but it certainly isn't by doing things that [could lead people to say], "Who the hell does he think he is?"

I got rid of the cow horn.

Pulling a Harvard jersey over my head and shoulder pads to play freshman football was one of the thrills of my young life. At six foot two and 210 pounds, I had the right size for a college player in those days. Making cleat marks and crashing into other solid bodies on the same field where my brothers had played—it didn't seem that life could hold anything better than that. Dad made all my home games, where he helped out the coach by pacing the sidelines wearing a beret and shouting instructions.

One dear figure's passing tempered my joy that fall. John Fitzgerald, my grandfather, succumbed to a long illness on October 2. He had been delighted in Jack's congressional victory four years earlier. Grampa's death not only marked the passing of an era; it also served as a bright line marker for the end of my childhood.

In due course, I would awaken to Harvard's intellectual bounties and find in them the building blocks for my lifelong education, in particular my grasp of national and international political thought. My fall semester, in fact, was respectable if not stellar in my coursework. But in the spring of 1951, my mind turned, or returned, to thoughts of football, and to staying in condition so that I could go for the varsity squad in the fall. There were other reasons for my gridiron passion. Most of the friendships I'd made at Harvard were through football—John Culver, Claude Hooton, Dick Clasby—and I loved being part of a team. I didn't want to lose that. In most other ways that first year, I don't remember Harvard as being a particularly hospitable place. Not for me, at any rate.

So I threw myself into the spring football drills, to the extent that my grades suffered, my Spanish grade especially. I worried that if I flunked or made a D on the final exam, I wouldn't be eligible to play football in the fall.

I expressed my concerns to a friend in the dorm, Warren O'Donnell. He jokingly suggested that I let another buddy, Bill Frate, take the exam for me. I laughed off the idea. But then Warren brought it up again, in

Bill's presence. Bill laughed and said he might get a worse grade than me. But then, trying to be a friend in need, he checked the exam schedule and saw that he was free at the time of the Spanish test. I'd already dropped the idea, but when I ran into him at dinner that night, Bill told me that if I wanted him to do it, he was willing. To my lasting regret, I said, "Great." I didn't think it through. I made an immature, spontaneous, extremely poor and wrong decision.

Bill took the exam—under the eye of a proctor who happened to be his adviser, and who knew he'd already passed a Spanish test, which had exempted him from having to take the course. Harvard sentenced each of us to a year's suspension. We were told we could come back if we'd done something useful with that time.

I felt terrible. I knew I'd screwed up. I felt even worse about having to face my father. I called up Jack and told him what had happened. Jack agreed to give Dad a heads-up while I drove to the Cape to see him. It was the longest and worst drive I ever had to make. I recall thinking as I drove that there were so many "ifs" involved: *If* I'd not confided my worries about Spanish to Warren. *If* he hadn't suggested to Bill Frate that he might take my place. *If* Bill had not been free. *If* there had been another proctor.

But in the final analysis, the "ifs" didn't matter. I knew I was to blame because I had embraced the idea.

My father met me in the sunroom. He alternated between disappointment and anger for quite a while. *Why didn't you get ahead of this?* he asked me. *Why didn't you act responsibly? See what happens when you do these things?* The more we talked, the quieter his voice would get. But then the phone would ring; one of my brothers expressing concern, offering advice. And when I came back into the room, he'd tee off on me again. "There are people who can mess up in life and not get caught," he advised me at one point, "but you're not one of them, Teddy." Boy, was he ever right.

By the next day, he'd settled down and begun to think about what my options were. We thought about other schools, but I wanted to prove myself and return to Harvard. Serving in the military made the most sense.

I signed up for the army, at the old building that still stands along the docks in Boston. My father thought the military would do me good. He was tough and he was deeply disappointed in me. But he never gave up on me. He wanted me to learn from this experience.

Another thing I recall about Dad during this crisis was that he was concerned on behalf of Bill Frate. He recognized that Bill had been trying to help me, and wanted to be supportive of him. Bill, to his great credit, took responsibility for his own actions and said he wanted to stand on his own. He went to another school for a year, then came back and graduated from Harvard.

Vicki and I still see Bill Frate and his wife, Anne. Once a year, we find a weekend to get together with some of my old football buddies and their wives for a Harvard game. Often it's the Harvard-Yale Game and the company includes Bill and Anne, John Culver, destined to be a lifelong friend of mine and an outstanding Democrat—he represented Iowa both as a senator and a congressman—along with his wife, Mary Jane, as well as Dick Clasby, who was one of the greatest ever to play at Harvard. He was a three-sport man, football team captain, and in 1952 broke loose for a ninety-six-yard touchdown run from scrimmage in the game against Washington University of St. Louis. Dick married Joe Gargan's sister and my very dear friend and cousin Mary Jo. We're joined by my dear friend Paul Kirk, who played for the Crimson a few years later, and his wife, Gail, and Bill Cleary, the All-American hockey player for Harvard and Olympic gold medalist, and his wife, Jo. Until his death, my classmate Jeff Coolidge was also part of our annual gathering. And Claude Hooton has joined us. We have a big dinner at an Italian family-style restaurant. Then the next day we go to the stadium and have a great tailgate party. Then we see the game.

But of course all this was years into the future. At the time, I wondered whether I'd ever get back to Harvard in any capacity.

I did my basic training at Fort Dix, New Jersey. I was in the 39th Infantry of the 9th Infantry Division. I worked hard through sixteen weeks of summertime heat and didn't sleep much. KP duty saw to that. I received thorough training in washing dishes and emptying garbage cans.

I also found myself in combat. Hard fighting. Against my will, and with my fists. And not with the enemy.

Up until then I'd had very little contact with African Americans. I was now at close quarters with several in our platoon, including another enlisted man named Wharton. One day Wharton and I, along with a fellow named Fessia, got gigged for having dirty rifles. Our penalty was to take some brooms, go over, and clean out the Officer's Quarters.

I wanted to get it done early because Harvard was playing football and it was being televised, and I wanted to see it. When I realized that Wharton was missing from our three-man detail, I suggested to Fessia that he go and find him. Fessia went to Wharton's barracks and returned with the news that "Wharton says he may come, or he may not."

I snapped, "That's ridiculous!" Fessia suggested, a little too casually in retrospect, that perhaps *I* should go over and reason with him.

I did. On the second floor of the barracks, I found probably eight men rolling dice against a footlocker. I said, "Is Wharton around here?" This fellow stood up—he was African American, about six foot four and 185 pounds of muscle—and said, "I'm Wharton."

I said, "Wharton, you got gigged."

"Yeah, I got gigged."

I said, "You've got to come over and clean out the BOQ like the rest of us." He said, "Well, maybe I'm comin' and maybe I'm not." I said, "You're coming." He said, "You telling me something?" Then the "reasoning" began. We launched into a really bad fight.

It was the wrestling I'd learned from Louie Andrews at Milton, and my football conditioning, that saved me. As it was, I had my hands full with Wharton. Had the fight been outdoors, on an open field, the techniques I'd learned in wrestling would have made it nearly impossible for him to stay with me. If you can take an opponent down, roll him, get a leg lock on him, you've pretty well got him. But in a barracks, you're rolling, and you roll into a footlocker, and suddenly he's on top of you. And Wharton got on top of me, pounding away and grabbing at my face. I thought he was going to put my eyes out. I put up a hand, and he bit right through it. He bit harder than the zebra.

I think I got the better of him in the end. Wrestling is defensive, and I finally managed to immobilize him. Which was good enough for me. There was blood all over the barracks, some of it Wharton's, much of it mine.

A sergeant named Maguire came storming into the room, blew his whistle, and ordered us both to get back over to the BOQ and finish cleaning it. "And you fellows can continue your fight at six o'clock on the parade ground."

Continue the fight at six o'clock on the parade ground?! I couldn't believe it. That's the last thing in the world I wanted to do. But if I had to, I had to. So at six o'clock I was pacing around the flagpole on the parade ground. And at 6:05 I was outta there. Wharton hadn't showed up. Lucky for me. I heard that in his next fight, he knocked out every tooth in the other guy's head.

With about two weeks still to go in basic training, I started formulating another idea. I would volunteer to go to Korea. I believed that it was my duty; a necessary phase of my atonement. I knew the risks. The war had stalemated, peace talks had begun, but American and Chinese troops were still slaughtering one another on the misty slopes of Bloody Ridge and Heartbreak Ridge.

On a three-day pass, I met Bobby and Jack in New York. Over lunch, I told them about my idea. Both were appalled, and strenuously argued against my volunteering. "Mother and Dad have suffered enough," one of them said to me. "We can't afford to have you go over and risk getting killed. You just can't do this kind of thing. Go where the army assigns you, and do your part."

I thought about this. I realized that I was being selfish and was risking unspeakable grief for my parents. *God, I don't want to do that*, I told myself. *I've been enough of a screwup already.*

I accepted an assignment to the Counter-Intelligence Corps Center at Fort Holabird, Maryland. CIC agents had guarded the Manhattan Project against spies during the war, and as anticommunist fervor took hold in the 1950s, the potential for spy-versus-spy intrigue promised to increase. Unfortunately, my career as a spy was fleeting. After two months, I found myself transferred to Camp Gordon, Georgia, for training with the military police.

I couldn't figure out why. Jack later learned that someone reported me in the company of one or two people at Harvard who might have had "leftist leanings." Now, that was a joke. I was a lot less interested in the left end of politics than the right end of the football line. I later came to suspect that I'd been blackballed by Roy Cohn, the anticommunist zealot and future counsel for Joe McCarthy. Cohn was just then enjoying national fame for his role in the convictions of accused spies Julius and Ethel Rosenberg. He was jealous of my brother Bobby's rise as a prosecutor, and may have been trying to intimidate or harass him through smearing me.

Whatever the case, my main achievement at Camp Gordon was to set a camp record for chin-ups, with more than forty repetitions. Then, in June 1952, I was finally assigned overseas, to the 520th Military Police Service Company at Camp des Loges, near Rocquencourt, in the Paris suburb of Versailles.

Before shipping out, I traveled to Hyannis Port to say goodbye to my parents. My mother, well-meaning to the last, asked, "Well, where are you going to be?" I told her I would be in France and Germany. She came alive with ideas for teachable moments—ideas I rather fancied: "Oh, that's marvelous, Teddy! Now, in France, they have wonderful wine, because that's where they make it. And in Germany, they have wonderful beer, because that's where they make beer. And Joe," she said, turning brightly toward my father, "I think Teddy ought to be able to drink the wine and the beer, even though he isn't twenty-one yet."

Dad's answer revealed that he was in a somewhat less teachable mood. "Rose," he said, spinning around to examine her, "are you out of your *mind*?"

That effectively took the wind out of the sails for my permission to drink wine and beer in Europe that year. I did anyway.

What my parents didn't know was that I'd begun drinking beer and wine at Harvard. Dad had made a deal with each of his sons: if we refrained from drinking and smoking until we were twenty-one, we'd receive a reward of $1,000. Later, when my twenty-first birthday came around, I confessed to Dad that I had taken liquor, but had not smoked. Dad was true to his end of the bargain: I got $500.

With the Korean War raging and the armed services on full alert, my company had orders to guard the newly built Supreme Allied Headquarters (SHAPE) near Rocquencourt, mostly by walking the perimeter of the compound. One night on leave, I decided to taste the delights of Paris. Since the city lay only about twenty kilometers from the base, I walked there. I don't remember much about the delights, but I do recall making my way back toward the barracks at about 3:30 in the morning. Upon reaching Rocquencourt, I realized I could not identify the road to the base in the darkness. I stopped in at one of the few coffee shops still open and asked directions. The proprietor was helpful, but three men sitting at a table eyed me coldly. Somehow, I realized they were communists. French communists disliked the American military even more than ordinary French people did.

I eased out of the coffee house and started down the unlit street. As I walked I began to hear a steady *choom, choom, choom, choom, choom* behind me. I was being followed. By men armed with something that went *choom, choom, choom, choom, choom* as they walked.

I began to run. Now the *choom, choom* changed to a *cha ting ta ting ting*, as if the *choom, choom* weapons were now in high gear. Sticks. Sticks, beating a pattern on the road as the three men increased their pace.

I was still in great shape from football, fighting Wharton, and all those chin-ups, so I ran at full speed until one of my pursuers lost his wind and dropped out. That still left two men in the darkness with sticks. And I had no idea where I was.

I heard the pursuers closing on me. I stopped, wheeled around, and faced them. The leader looked like a bully. The other fellow was smaller. I could see that their sticks were sharpened at the ends. Pig sticks, used for jabbing at pigs to encourage them toward the pen. Then I remembered that I was armed as well: wrapped around each leg of my MP pants, anchoring the fold where they bloused over my boots, was a bicycle chain. The chains were useful for making an MP's pants look snappy, and sometimes for encouraging drunken soldiers toward the base.

I reached down and unhooked the chains. I started whirling them over my head. They made a *whirr*—far more menacing than the *choom, choom* or even the *cha ting ta ting ting*.

With my help, the Frenchmen eventually came around to that same opinion. I concentrated on the smaller fellow first. He'd move, and I'd go at him. *Whack*, with a bicycle chain. *Whack*. He started running backwards, and then the larger guy would lunge at me. *Whack*. Soon the little guy ran out of gas, and it was just me against the real bully. I kept swinging the chains as hard as I could until he gave it up and the two faded into the darkness. Panting for breath, I found my way back to the base.

After the fistfight and the close call with the communists, there was only one event that could put a capstone on my military career: a visit from my mother.

Rose Kennedy loved Paris and she swirled into the city after I'd been there a few weeks, taking a suite at a favorite hotel, the Ritz. I arranged a three-day furlough and called for her in a rented limousine, glad to see her as always. I entered the suite in the midst of a crisis: Mother couldn't find her jewelry. She'd hidden it someplace, but she'd forgotten where. We spent two or three hours combing the hotel room for the precious stones. Finally she found them—pinned to the inside back of her purse, so that she wouldn't lose them.

We drove to the Hotel du Golf near Deauville and enjoyed an overnight visit, during which we ran into some good friends. I found myself in the midst of a black-tie party for the Grand Ballet du Marquis de Cuevas, featuring Maria Tallchief. (I think I borrowed a tuxedo from one of the friends.) It was a good break from military life.

Returning to the army base late on the final night, with my mother along for the ride, I asked the driver to let me off about a hundred yards from the entrance. I didn't want my buddies to see me getting out of a limo.

I almost made it. I'd walked through the gate and was headed for the barracks when I heard rapid, tiny footsteps and a familiar voice behind me calling, "Teddy, dear! Teddy, dear! Oh, *Teddy*, dear!"

Do I turn around or keep walking? There was only one choice, of course. I turned around.

"*Teddy*, dear!" Mother's bell-like voice was loud enough to wake the guards. "Teddy, dear! You forgot your *dancing shoes!*"

My *dancing* shoes?! I watched her hurrying toward me, her small hands clutching two shiny objects. She spent a minute or two catching her breath. "Here are your dancing shoes!" I looked at them. They weren't even my dancing shoes! I thanked Mother as politely as I could, bade her good night, and turned to face what seemed to be every man in the barracks, all of whom were engrossed in the conversation.

From that moment on, I was known around the base as "Teddy Dear." Every man had the same question for me: "Teddy Dear! Do you have your dancing shoes?"

While I was in the army in France, my siblings back home were making important strides in their lives—toward their futures, and toward one another.

In October 1951, Jack and Bobby, along with our sister Pat, set off on a tour of several Eastern and Middle Eastern countries, including Vietnam. Jack was planning a challenge to the senior Republican senator from Massachusetts, Henry Cabot Lodge Jr. He wanted to sharpen his awareness of Soviet colonial pressure in several nations as a centerpiece of his campaign. The seven-week expedition yielded an unexpected bonus: my two brothers, who had spent long stretches of time apart from one another virtually since childhood, reacquainted themselves with one another as men. (Jack was thirty-four then, Bobby just shy of twenty-six.)

Left behind during the tour was the beautiful young socialite, eques-trienne, and *Vogue* "enquiring photographer" Jacqueline Bouvier, whom Jack met at a Georgetown dinner party in May of that year. The separa-tion hardly interrupted Jack's courtship of Jackie. The two were married on September 12, 1953, in Newport, Rhode Island. Bobby served as best man and I was an usher.

Bobby resigned his job as an attorney in the Justice Department to manage Jack's Senate campaign, with organizational brilliance. He helped steer Jack to a narrow victory over Lodge, and afterward, instead of re-turning to Justice, he applied for a position on the senatorial staff of one of our father's Irish Catholic friends, Joseph McCarthy, who'd become chairman of the Senate Government Operations Committee.

McCarthy by then had made his name as a rabid anticommunist witch hunter; the *Washington Post* cartoonist Herblock had coined the phrase "Mc-Carthyism" two years earlier. The peak of the infamous "Era" that bore his name, though, was still a few years in the future. He had in fact visited our family at the Kennedy house in Palm Beach, and dated Eunice for a while.

Bobby went to work on the subcommittee on investigations for Mc-Carthy, who was just then absorbed in rooting out anti-American books in public libraries. My brother joined two other fresh appointees, chief counsel Roy Cohn and Cohn's chief consultant, David Schine. Bobby was not yet twenty-eight then, and the extent of McCarthy's vile exploitation of anticommunist hysteria had not yet fully registered with him or indeed the country.

Bobby developed an instant distrust of Cohn and Schine, perceiving their cynicism and willingness to twist the truth to fit their boss's agenda. He didn't like McCarthy's frequent collaborator and ideological soul mate, the FBI director J. Edgar Hoover, either; he distrusted him from the start. Bobby might have been an anticommunist, but he was sickened by the way Hoover and his allies destroyed lives without remorse.

Dad had known J. Edgar Hoover in the early days, back when crime-fighting was his focus. Dad liked him then, and had a lot of correspondence with him. My own memory is that until the cold war came to obsess him with rooting out communists in America, Hoover wasn't so bad.

In later years, as my own political career took hold, I came to believe that Hoover had to go. He was out of control, a law unto himself. He kept power by threat and terror. And he held his power for too long. I cringe every time I see his name on that building on Pennsylvania Avenue. He did some good things, but warrantless wiretaps and blackmail by the director of the FBI have no place in this country.

Bobby resigned his place on McCarthy's staff just months later, when Democratic members walked off the committee in protest of the chairman's unsavory methods. Yet his personal regard for McCarthy remained another matter. Even after the Wisconsin senator had been stripped of his credibility in 1954, and his career and reputation ruined, Bobby showed friendly feelings for him. He was castigated repeatedly for this, but he probably could not have made himself behave otherwise. Loyalty was one of my brother's greatest virtues, and he would not toss over a friend just because he had fallen out of favor with the world.

The following year, with McCarthy gone, Bobby rejoined the subcommittee as chief counsel. In 1955, with Arkansas senator John McClellan at the head of a reorganized committee, Bobby broke into national prominence as a tough investigator of corruption within the Teamsters Union. This image, in time, evolved into a slur that was perhaps the most offensive, and least accurate, of the many that Bobby absorbed from his adversaries over the years. It was a slur so contrary to his true nature that its use became an ironic family joke.

The slur was "ruthless."

I don't recall making much use of those dancing shoes that my mother handed me, but the remainder of my army time in Europe passed pleasantly enough: weekdays of drudge work, followed by weekend furloughs.

I used one of those weekends to win a one-man Swiss bobsled race. I'd never been on a bobsled before. In the fall of 1952, I rounded up absentee votes for Jack's Senate race among my fellow Massachusetts soldiers. In February 1953, Pat and Jean came over to help me celebrate my twenty-first birthday. We went skiing in Austria for a week.

In May, Eunice married Sargent Shriver. So Bobby was married. Eunice was married. Jack was headed for a September wedding with Jackie in Newport. Pat would marry Peter Lawford in April 1954, and Jean would be wed to Stephen Edward Smith in May 1956. It seemed incredible to me. I'd always had a curious, half-fanciful way of thinking about my siblings as regarded marriage—and myself as well.

I never expected any of us to get married. We would be brothers and sisters, unchanging, forever.

Later that spring, the army transferred me back to Fort Devens, Massachusetts, for my discharge as a private first class. I'd hardly shaken hands with Dad when I found myself on another tour of duty—one that I was pleased to accept. He asked me to travel to Chicago and Tulsa to inspect some of the family's business investments. When I returned from that assignment, I had some surprising news for my father and the family: I was considering a political career of my own.

I spent a few weeks volunteering as a basketball coach at the South Bay Union Settlement House in Boston, and then I enrolled in a pair of summer school government courses at Harvard. In the fall of 1953, I returned to Harvard as a full-time student, determined to work hard and put the past behind me. The class I concentrated on the most that semester was Spanish, where I proudly brought my grade up to an A-minus. From then on through graduation, I pursued a tough curriculum heavily weighted toward government, economics, history, and English. It was John Kenneth Galbraith who elevated my understanding of economics. In just a few years, he would be Jack's ambassador to India. Arthur N. Holcombe, another Harvard giant who had taught Dad and all three of my brothers, made the Constitutional Convention of 1787 come alive before my eyes. Political philosophy was Holcombe's specialty, and I opened myself to his stirring historical and moral insights.

I worked at public speaking with a wonderful speaking coach named Oscar Verlaine. Four times each fall, and four times each spring, Verlaine sent me and other students into such venues as South Bay Settlement and various local high schools to address civic matters, such as the Red Cross. Perhaps our topics weren't earth-shaking, but we learned how to develop bonds with our audiences via a sense of conviction, brevity, and humor, tailoring our remarks to their specific level of understanding. These engagements also reinforced in me the satisfactions of public service.

My residence now was Winthrop House, on the northern bank above the Charles River. Joe Jr. and Jack had lived there, and Jack's room is now reserved for guests at the university. Winthrop was a popular residence for athletes—and, incidentally, one of the first houses to open itself to Jewish and Catholic students. I was ineligible for varsity football when I returned to Harvard in 1953, but I played for Winthrop House. I have especially fond memories of a special game we played in the fall of that year. We traveled to New Haven to play the Eli's top residential club, Davenport, the day before the official Harvard-Yale Game. We beat the Davenport boys, 6–0, thanks partly to the pile-driving play of a certain stranger to my Winthrop teammates. It was Bobby. I'd invited him to come up from New York and watch the game, but Bobby preferred to play. He'd been wearing neckties and white shirts for ten years, writing for the *Boston Post* and working for Dad and the Justice Department. *Perfect*, I thought. *Let's see what he has left.* I found him a house uniform and set of pads; he changed into them en route. He played defensive end in that game, and for an old guy, he did pretty well. In fact, he was the star of the game. As he was coming off the field at the end, our elderly house master, Ronald M. Ferry, gave him a close look and said, "Bob, aren't you supposed to graduate fairly soon?"

In 1954, I finally realized my dream of trotting out onto the field for the Crimson varsity. It was not an easy path. I started off on the eighth squad at Harvard. That was the lowest, I think. But I hung in there; I knew I wasn't the best athlete on the team, not by a long shot, but I was determined to work hard and stay with it.

And sure enough, as the games went on, a lot of the better-ranked players started to drop off the team. They'd get hurt, or decide they didn't want to continue, or football conflicted with chemistry lab. I was lucky. Lucky and determined. I gradually rose up the depth chart. In the Bucknell game the coach finally sent me onto the field. I was so excited to be in the game that I didn't notice when I got a tooth knocked out.

I hardly even merited a sentence from the student paper's sportswriter, David Halberstam. I had a chance to earn my varsity "H" in that year's Yale classic—I needed just four minutes of playing time—but on the first play after I entered the game, an Eli ball carrier swept around my end of the line for a sixty-yard gain. Out I came, as Dad threw up his hands on the sideline and my brothers watched in disappointment from the stands. I didn't get back in and I didn't win my varsity letter, though we beat Yale and won the Big Three title. Everyone at Harvard was celebrating—almost everyone.

In my final season in the fall 1955 I not only started, but averaged fifty-six minutes a game. Those were the days when the entire line still played both defense and offense. The team itself struggled—we had a dismal 2–7 record for the season—but we never lost heart and we still gave our all. I caught a touchdown pass as we defeated Columbia on October 5, by a score of 21 to 7. My most exciting personal moment, though, came in the Harvard-Yale Game, when a pass went skidding off the hands of its intended receiver and I reached out and grabbed it and hung on to it as I rumbled into the end zone. I won my letter, but we lost the game, 21-7. This time almost everyone at Harvard was down in the dumps— but not everyone. Dad, who'd brought a couple dozen of his friends from New York and Boston by train, charged into the locker room with Jack and Bobby to noisily congratulate me. I knew they should tone it down, but with Dad and my brothers smiling so broadly over my TD catch and the earning of my letter, I can't say that I was sorry for their enthusiasm.

I graduated from Harvard in the spring of 1956, satisfied that I had proved myself both academically and on the playing field. My grades were more than respectable, and I even received a letter from the Green Bay Packers wanting to know whether I wanted to try out for the team. I declined Green Bay's kind offer, but, all in all, I was feeling pretty good.

That August at the Democratic convention, Jack made a surprising bid for the nomination as vice president under Adlai Stevenson. He'd electrified the delegates on opening night with his narration of a moving film about the history of the party, which garnered him a lot of positive attention. Jack jumped into the open nomination process. As much as Jack wanted it, Dad was not in favor of his move for the vice presidential nomination because he was sure that President Eisenhower would defeat Stevenson and Jack's political career would be over. In my mother's memoir, she writes of Jack being persuaded to run, despite my father's objections, by a Louisiana delegate who pleaded with him to stay in the race after their delegation had stuck their neck out for him. In an amazing twist of history and fate, that Louisiana delegate was my future father-in-law, Edmund Reggie, then a thirty-year-old judge, who had managed to swing the Louisiana delegation behind my brother when Governor Earl K. Long had gone to the horse races. At the end of the day, Jack didn't win the nomination, but his experience at the convention was a win all the way around: my father was relieved; Jack's eloquence and grace in concession won him enormous political capital, raising his prospects as a serious contender for the presidency in 1960; and though I could not have imagined the significance at the time, our family began a friendship with the Reggies of Louisiana that some thirty years in the future would transform my life.

Meanwhile, I was eager to see more of the world after graduating from Harvard. I asked Jack where he thought I should go, and he suggested North Africa. He was interested in the global anticolonial movements, and he wanted me to look at the African countries just emerging from

European rule: Morocco, Tunisia, and Algeria, which was still engaged in a long and bitter war of independence with France. I traveled with Fred Holborn, the distinguished Harvard political scientist who'd been an instructor of mine—my brothers and father always believed in bringing a knowledgeable source along when traveling in unfamiliar countries, especially those of geopolitical importance: a live-in tutor, so to speak. Jack had arranged meetings for us with key people in certain places, and I had made arrangements with the International News Service as a freelance reporter, just as Jack had done a few years earlier.

We drove by car across Spain and took a ferry into Morocco, experiencing our first taste of the exotic early on, high up in the steep and jagged Atlas Mountains. There we were to meet with Sidi Muhammad ibn Yusuf, the popular nationalist sultan whose exile to Madagascar by the French in 1953 had sparked an uprising. The French, realizing their mistake, returned this eminence to the Moroccan throne in 1955. Just weeks before our visit, Muhammad had negotiated Morocco's independence at Paris.

Our visit with Muhammad was memorable for a number of reasons. One was that another guest scheduled to arrive at the same time was El Glohi, a powerful Moroccan militant and recent rival of the king's. El Glohi's visit was of interest to my editor because he had tried to kill Muhammad on two or three previous occasions. The editors assured me that this meeting would be somewhat more amiable. In fact, it was to be a reconciliation; El Glohi was heading up the mountains to pay his tribute and swear allegiance to the king.

Holborn and I missed this reunion. It was held inside Muhammad's huge tent, with no outsiders allowed. We were, however, invited to the dazzling ceremonial dinner that followed. The festivities consumed most of an afternoon. The king's harem, seventy women strong, was present. There was dancing and the cutting of a calf. Out on a plain visible from the tent, bareback riders raced along on powerful horses, with rifles tucked under their arms. They would grasp the rifles with an opposite hand and, while at full gallop, hurl them fifty or seventy-five feet into the air. With-

My mother,
Rose Kennedy.
Bettmann/Corbis

My dad,
Joseph P. Kennedy.
Corbis

The wedding of
Rose Fitzgerald and
Joseph Kennedy,
October 7, 1914.
Bettmann/Corbis

My mother is flanked by her parents, Josephine and John "Honey Fitz" Fitzgerald,
at their 50th Anniversary party in Boston, September 18, 1939.
Richard Sears/John F. Kennedy Library

Jack wanted me
to be named after
George Washington
because I was born
on his birthday.
John F. Kennedy Library

9TH CHILD FOR
MRS. KENNEDY

Stork Again Visits Daughter of John F. Fitzgerald

Mrs. Joseph P. Kennedy, formerly Rose Fitzgerald, daughter of former Mayor John F. Fitzgerald and Mrs. Fitzgerald, yesterday gave birth to her ninth child, a nine and a half-pound boy, at St. Margaret's Hospital, Dorchester. She now has four sons and five daughters, the eldest of whom is a boy, 16. Her father is now the grandfather of 14 children.

Mrs. Kennedy's home is in Bronxville, N. Y., but recently she has been visiting

SON BORN THE
J. P. KENNEDYS

Is 14th Grandchild of the John F. Fitzgeralds

The ninth child of Mrs. Rose Fitzgerald Kennedy and Joseph P. Kennedy, motion picture producer and banker, a son, was born early yesterday at St. Margaret's Hospital, Dorchester.

The Washington's Birthday baby is the fourth son of the Kennedys, and the 14th grandchild of former Mayor and Mrs. John F. Fitzgerald.

Mrs. Kennedy, who has lived in New York and California for several years, always returns to Boston to await the advent of her children. The Kennedys have five daughters and four sons. She was attended by Dr. Frederick L. Good.

The family posed for a group portrait, July 8, 1934: me, Jean, Bobby, Pat, Eunice, Kathleen, Rosemary, Jack, Mother and Dad.

Bettmann/Corbis

With Bobby in Palm Beach, 1934.
John F. Kennedy Library

With Bobby, Pat, and Jean, Palm Beach, 1934.
John F. Kennedy Library

BACK ROW: Rosemary, Pat, Eunice, Mom; MIDDLE: Bobby, Dad (holding me), Jean.

John F. Kennedy Library

In Palm Beach, 1934.
John F. Kennedy Library

With Jean and Bobby on Halloween 1934, in Bronxville.
John F. Kennedy Library

With Dad in the pool.
John F. Kennedy Library

With Jack and Bobby in Palm Beach, April 1936.
John F. Kennedy Library

Being received by Pope Pius XII at Vatican City. Dad represented the
United States at the Pope's coronation, March 20, 1939. Later,
I received my first Holy Communion from the Pope himself.
Bettmann/Corbis

At the changing of the guard at Buckingham Palace, April 11, 1938.
AP Photo

With Bobby on our first day at Gibbs School in London, March 1, 1938.
Bettmann/Corbis

With Bobby at the reopening of the Royal Children's Zoo, June 9, 1938.
Bettmann/Corbis

With Bobby, Jack, Dad, and Joe Jr. in Antibes, France, Summer 1939.
John F. Kennedy Library

With Joe Jr. in Palm Beach.
John F. Kennedy Library

Sailing with Jack aboard *Victura,* Hyannis Port, Massachusetts, c. 1946.
John F. Kennedy Library

Clowning with Jack in Hyannis Port.
John F. Kennedy Library

With Jack and Bobby in Hyannis Port.
Corbis

Harvard football, 1955. I started at the bottom of the depth chart but stayed with it.
Paul Connell/Boston Globe/Landov

out looking, they would grab the guns as they descended and fire them into the air. Then they would bounce off and back onto the horses. It was an unbelievable show. That night, Fred and I were shown to our sleeping area: a corner of the tent about five feet from these horses.

This experience paled, however, beside our next destination—Algeria, where we traveled around with the Algerian army. We witnessed a prologue to the Battle of Algiers. The French, who were winning at this point, had trapped the city's leaders in the sewer system. We watched as an officer opened a manhole cover and lowered a birdcage with a dove inside—a guarantee of safety to anyone down below who saw it.

The French thought they were going to prevail, but you could get the sense that it wasn't going to happen. The French would never bring these outraged nationalists to heel. The insurrection was all around. The Algerians had experienced the most brutal kinds of torture from the colonial army, and this enhanced their hatred and bolstered the movement for independence. Nothing could stop it.

After Algeria, I made a rendezvous with Jack, as we'd planned. He joined me for a sail in the Mediterranean after the Chicago convention. I gave him a detailed report of what I had witnessed during my six weeks of travel. Jack was keenly interested; but our hiatus was cut short by an urgent message from America: the pregnant Jackie, who had suffered a miscarriage the previous year, had just suffered the second of her three such losses. My brother hurried home to be with his wife. Yet he did not forget our conversation. In a speech a little more than a year later, the new senator John F. Kennedy tacitly drew upon the views I'd shared with him to carefully advocate for a "tolerable peace" in the Algerian conflict, arguing that "the dangers of communism only become greater as settlement is postponed." This was essentially the same view my brother held regarding the still young Vietnam conflict at the time of his assassination in 1963.

With Jack in the Senate to inspire me, public service was all but inevitable now as my career of choice, and the law was its foundation stone.

I was interested in the law school at Stanford University in California—
my grades didn't quite qualify me for Harvard Law—but ultimately I
decided to follow Bobby's path to the University of Virginia Law School
at Charlottesville.

These were a rousing three years, filled with fun and learning and new
friendships. My roommate was John Varick Tunney, the son of the former heavyweight boxing champion Gene Tunney. When I met Gene, I
found him to be similar to Dad in his no-nonsense, rough-and-ready approach to life. John was destined to become a Democratic congressman
and then senator from California, and among the very closest of my lifelong friends. John is the godfather to Teddy Jr., and I am godfather to
John's son Teddy.

We lived in a converted stable a short distance from the campus,
where we staged a couple of memorable parties and had a lot of fun. The
open, empty country roads were a great escape for me, a place to feel the
fresh air on my face and contemplate the good things in life. Unfortunately, from time to time I lost track of the speedometer on my drives, but
there always seemed to be a state trooper around to remind me. Still, life
was great. I had good friends. And for a while at least, I stopped worrying
about "catching up" and savored the moment.

It was Tunney who taught me mountain climbing, more or less.
Exposed me to mountain climbing is probably more accurate. He and
I and another law student and good friend of ours, named John Goemans, spent four weeks at the International Law School at The Hague
studying contract law with the great Hardy Dillard. This put us
within range of the famous mountains among the Pennine Alps of
Switzerland—the Mischabel group that includes the Matterhorn and
the Rimpfischhorn.

Tunney, who'd climbed while at Yale, decided to let me cut my teeth
on an easy one, the Rimpfischhorn, which is only four thousand meters
high and comes to an absolute point at the top. We went up with two

brothers from the Swiss ski team, Auguste and Heinz Julen. It was probably the most terrifying experience of my life.

All of us were tied together, with me in between Auguste Julen and Tunney. I managed all right until we got close to the top. Maybe twenty feet. I saw Auguste put his foot on a little ledge and another foot someplace near that, and grab a handhold somewhere else, and boost himself up to a larger ledge. He looked down at me and said, "Now it's your turn."

After all the climbing we'd done to get to that point, my legs and arms felt like leaden weights. But I had no choice but to keep going. I was almost there. I put my foot where Auguste's had been, and my hand where I thought his had been, and I moved my other leg toward the other foothold—which wasn't there. I had just time enough to yell, "Tension! Tension!" which you yell if you're about to fall, and then boom! Down I went. I fell about twenty feet. The rope that encircled my waist slipped up underneath my arms, and I was swinging out there in space about three thousand feet above the valley. I resisted the temptation to raise my arms and grab the rope. If I raised them, I would slip through the loop and go spiraling through space. And if Auguste couldn't hold the rope, it would be lights out for all of us.

Auguste wrapped the rope around a boulder to keep it from slipping away and then slowly lowered me, letting out more and more slack. But I was beneath an overhang, and I could not touch the mountainside. I looked around and saw Tunney, just about at my level. He reached out and pulled me toward the mountain. He got me back to a very small ledge that could barely fit both of us, but it did. I was absolutely exhausted. The wind was fierce. I called out, "I don't think I can go up any farther. I really don't think I can make it. I'm too tired!"

"Boys, you've got to climb," Auguste called back. "You've got to get up to the top of the mountain." *Or perish*, was the unspoken implication.

I owe my life to Tunney. He looked around and spotted another route—a couloir, a corridor formed by large rocks. John managed to wedge himself in between the rocks and move his shoulders upward, while keeping his knees braced against the sides. In this way he managed the fifteen or twenty feet to where Auguste waited. I studied his movements carefully and then emulated them, which is why I am not hanging out there to this day.

On the far side of the peak was a funicular. We took it back down, and I found myself wondering why we hadn't taken it up as well. I made my mind up that was one sport I would never, ever get into.

The next day we climbed the Matterhorn.

Back at the University of Virginia, in the classroom, I threw myself into the study of law as never before. In this pursuit, as in our travel and good times, John and I sparked one another. We teamed up for the classic law school exercise known as moot court. The competition in this extracurricular drill consisted of seventy-five teams, with debates structured as tennis tournament eliminations. The process spanned nearly the whole of my three years at UVA.

"Free Speech" was the issue at hand, and John and I took the more liberal position. We had to write briefs that were the product of enormous research. To prepare for our oral arguments, we practiced against a team that we would not meet in the pairings, but which held the opposing view. By the time we reached the semifinals, the quality of competition had skyrocketed. The finals were in May 1959, and Bobby—who'd been through early rounds of the competition when he was in law school—and my sister Pat came down from New York to watch.

We had worked hard to get to this point in the competition and every nerve was on end. The pressure was only heightened by the caliber of our judges: retired Supreme Court justice and former solicitor general of the United States Stanley Reed; the former solicitor general and attorney general who had famously cross-examined Hermann Göring at the Nuremberg trials, the lord chancellor of the United Kingdom David Maxwell Fyfe, the Earl of Kilmuir; and U.S. Court of Appeals judge for the Fourth Circuit Clement Haynsworth (ten years into the future, as a senator, I would vote against Judge Haynsworth's nomination by Richard Nixon to the Supreme Court). Our opposing team was led by Wayne Lustig, a silver-tongued southerner who made what even John and I considered an A-plus argument. Yes, the pressure was definitely on.

In the most exciting and rewarding moment of my life to that time, and among those of all time, John and I were declared the winners of the moot court competition. We were overjoyed.

Another great tradition at Virginia Law School was the Student Legal Forum, and I was in charge of getting distinguished legal and political figures to come and speak to the students. I was successful at getting some real stars to visit the forum, because I had an ally in Jack. He helped us get Hubert Humphrey, who came down and was captivating. A thousand students showed up to hear him, which pleased Jack enormously when he heard it. We brought in Edward Bennett Williams, who was just then defending Jimmy Hoffa in court. We tried to sandbag Williams on whether Hoffa even had a tenable defense, but he blew us out of the water in about thirty seconds. We had the great union leader Walter Reuther, who was dynamic and spellbinding. We had Victor Riesel, the hard-nosed antiracketeering labor columnist, who just a few months earlier had been blinded by sulfuric acid thrown into his eyes by an assailant on a Manhattan sidewalk. Supreme Court justice William Brennan was another one of our incredible speakers.

I still wince a little when I recall the time we invited Prescott Bush, George Bush's father and George W.'s grandfather, a distinguished senator from Connecticut and an enormously gracious, dignified person. But not exactly a big marquee name at the University of Virginia Law School. As the date of his appearance drew near, we saw the reverse of what usually happened with ticket requests: instead of increasing, the demand grew less and less. We'd drawn a thousand spectators for Humphrey and eight hundred for Williams. But with Prescott Bush, as the reality of the numbers started to sink in, we realized we'd need only about four or five hundred seats. Then we thought we'd better get down to two hundred.

We ended up listening to Prescott Bush in a small room with seventy-five chairs. But he was incredibly pleasant. We had dinner afterward—and, like most speakers, he was much more interesting at the dinner.

Several weeks later, as I was driving Jack to some appointment or other in Boston, my brother reached over and honked the horn. He pointed to another car. "I know who that is," Jack exclaimed. "That's Pres Bush!" In the passenger seat was his son, George Herbert Walker Bush. Both cars stopped, and we all got out and yakked it up. The Bushes were headed up to Maine. George Bush mentioned to me that his father had told him about his visit to Virginia Law School and "the nice young Kennedy boy." I had privately disagreed with some of Prescott Bush's views, but I had a cordial personal relationship with him—just as I would have with the next two generations of Bushes.

After the family's traditional Thanksgiving dinner in Hyannis Port in November 1956, Jack and Joe Sr. left the table and repaired to the study near the living room for a private talk. When they emerged, grinning, arms around each other's shoulders, the rest of us learned that Jack had decided to run for president in 1960.

Their talk apparently had been a kind of moot court in reverse: Jack citing all the reasons why he should not run (he was Catholic, only thirty-nine, none of the party's leaders had indicated any support for such a move), and our father countering each one. Jack would not announce his decision until early in the election year. But a charge of energy ran through our family at once. Getting Jack reelected to the Senate, and then helping him become president—this had become our mission.

In October 1957, I got "aced out," courtesy of Jack, of a chance to see a professional football game, and as a result ended up meeting my future wife. The occasion was a Sunday afternoon talk that Jack "suggested" I give at the dedication ceremony for the Kennedy Physical Education Building at Manhattanville College of the Sacred Heart. Our family had donated the building in memory of Kathleen. My mother, Eunice, and Jean had all attended Manhattanville College, as had the former Ethel Skakel.

I had spent Saturday night in Dad's New York apartment with Jack. Giving a talk at a women's college was the last thing on my mind. The Washington Redskins were in town to play the 3–1 Giants, and Dad and I had planned to go see the game on Sunday. It was Jack, not me, who'd originally agreed to give the talk. But when my brother showed up at the apartment and saw me there he said, "Oh! Dad, since Teddy's here, why don't we let him do it? I want to go to the football game."

I didn't think that was a terribly good idea. I'd looked forward to seeing that game. Jack held his ground: it was going to be a great game, and *he* wanted to see it. Our father said, "Fine. Why don't you two work it out?" We worked it out, and Jack went to the football game.

I went to the college with my sister Jean. I gave the speech. It was successful enough, I suppose. After my remarks that Sunday afternoon, Margo Murray, a friend of Jean's, took me by the hand and introduced me to an exquisitely beautiful young student named Joan Bennett, who had just turned twenty-one. Jean was with Margo for the introduction, but she had not met Joan before either. I learned later that Joan had done some modeling and was a gifted piano player, which earned her a lot of points with Mother.

I definitely wanted to see more of Joan. I thought fast, and talked Margo and Joan into driving me to the airport for my flight back to Virginia. Joan and I hit it off in the car. I took her out every time I came up to New York, and almost before we knew it we were on a fast track toward marriage. The family was thrilled. She was beautiful, she was fun, and she played piano duets with Mother. It was time for me to think about settling down and getting married, and Joan seemed like a perfect match.

As for that football game—Jack had the great pleasure of watching the Giants get buried by the Redskins, 31-14.

PART TWO

Brotherhood

CHAPTER SIX

Kennedy for President
1958–1960

Jack's reelection to the Senate in 1958 was never in serious question. He was skyrocketing now as a public figure. The camera emphasized his youth, his elegance, his good looks, his quick wit. But while his reelection to the Senate was not in doubt, the *margin* of victory was very important. Jack's presidential ambitions in 1960 were now a given, at least within the family and closest advisers. That required that every public step along the way be marked with as much evidence of achievement as possible.

A great deal of Jack's charm, of course, was substantive, a factor of his unconcealed principles. His political candor was as fresh and bold as his style, and like his style, it won over audiences who might have resented it in any other candidate. He'd drawn a standing ovation in Jackson, Mississippi, after a talk in which he endorsed school desegregation; he won the support of the governor of Kansas even though he had earlier voted against high farm price supports. He accepted speaking dates before southern Protestant ministers and the American Jewish Congress in New York.

Bobby had managed Jack's first Senate campaign, but now he was absorbed as chief counsel for the Senate Labor Rackets Committee under Chairman John L. McClellan. His lacerating exchanges with the powerful Teamsters boss Jimmy Hoffa were earning him national attention. So Jack asked me to run his campaign. I relished the opportunity. I was still a year from law school graduation and was courting Joan, but the chance to help my brother, while at the same time getting a baptism in electoral politics, was irresistible.

So after my final examinations in June, I hurried home to Massachusetts and joined the senator's reelection team. Jack named me campaign manager, though I was glad to have such able hands as Larry O'Brien, Kenny O'Donnell, and Jean's husband, Steve Smith, to show me the ropes. Here were three immensely talented and loyal political professionals at the core of a group whose names would forever be associated with that of President John F. Kennedy. "A mixture of amateurs, professionals, eggheads and hardheads," the *New York Times* admiringly called them.

Larry O'Brien was an army veteran, a former union president at age twenty-two, and a Democratic operative when he came aboard my brother's 1950 Senate campaign. Like Bobby, Larry was passionate about organization. The slightly younger Kenny O'Donnell was also an army vet who was Bobby's roommate at Harvard after the war. A principled and politically sensitive man, he, along with Larry, remained at Jack's side through the presidential years as a special assistant and member.

Steve Smith was more than a brother-in-law; he was like a brother in our family. A soft-spoken and elegant man, Steve had been an air force lieutenant before joining his father's vast New York tugboat and barge empire, Cleary Brothers, Inc. An eventual heir to the fortune, he developed a genius for financial management—eventually overseeing the Kennedy family's investment operations—as well as for personnel supervision. Steve would go on to manage Bobby's Senate campaign, and my own.

A fourth member of the team was Ted Sorensen, who was virtually inseparable from Jack. (The two of them toured fifty states together between 1956 and 1959.) Ted had signed on to be the new Senator Kennedy's legislative aide in 1953, as an earnest, horn-rimmed twenty-five-year-old just a couple of years out of Nebraska. And there was Pierre Salinger. Jack had recently hired the dapper thirty-three-year-old journalist and veteran press officer on Bobby's recommendation. Pierre had impressed Bobby as an investigator for the Senate Labor Rackets Committee. He would serve as press secretary to Jack.

I took Joan to the house at Hyannis Port for a week in June to get her acquainted with my mother and father. And then we all set to work getting Jack reelected.

We held our first strategy meeting at the Copley Plaza Hotel in Boston. All the volunteers assembled in a meeting room upstairs, and Jack looked at me and said, "All right, Teddy—now you go on up and give them a speech. Talk about the organization and what you're going to do in the campaign, and then I'll say a few words." I'd never given a campaign strategy talk before. I said, "What exactly do you think I ought to say?" Jack ticked off several details about how he thought the organization should go, and then sent me up. I guess I did okay. Then Jack spoke, and, as usual, charmed and inspired everyone.

Our biggest challenge was overcoming the apathy of people who thought Jack was a shoo-in for reelection. (He probably was, but as I say, the *margin* was what counted.) And so we focused on generating turnout. We set up telephone banks and sent volunteers out for door-to-door efforts. I shuttled weekly between Massachusetts and my law classes at the University of Virginia.

We stumbled upon some unexpected controversies. One of them reflected the ancient tensions between the Irish and the Italians in Massachusetts, still intense in the late 1950s.

We'd come up with a campaign slogan for Jack, simple yet geared to our goal of a large turnout. It was: "Make your vote count. Vote Kennedy." We discovered that it wasn't so simple—certainly not in the Italian community. A group of Italian-American leaders from around the state converged on Boston and demanded a meeting with me at my brother's headquarters at the Bellevue. They sat down at a conference table opposite me and said, "This is an insult to Italians!"

I told them I didn't understand. "What we're trying to do is say, 'Make your vote count. Your vote counts for Senator Kennedy in 1958 and it's also a vote, really, for 1960. Your vote is important. Make your vote count.'"

They said, "No, no. The way we interpret it is that the vote counts if it's for an Irishman, but it doesn't count if it's for an Italian. [The Italian they had in mind was Vincent J. Celeste.] So therefore it's directed at us, and we resent it."

Pretty soon, the head of every Italian-American organization in the state was denouncing the slogan. We had to tear up all the literature and change it. I mentioned the crisis to Jack, who was as baffled as I. "I don't know. We'll work it out."

We worked it out by calling Dad up from the Cape.

We all sat down with one of his friends, an advertising man named John Dowd. Dowd worked at it all day long, trying out slogan after slogan. He was wearing a pinstriped suit, as I recall, with white checks on it, and he had suspenders and a mustache that moved when he talked, and dark, very groomed hair. He had five different pencils and pads of paper. He'd write out a slogan and hand it to Dad, and Dad would look at it and say, "No, that doesn't work, Dowd. That's not good. You can do better than that. That's not good." And then Dad went across the street to Bailey's restaurant and had his lunch, a chocolate soda. That's all he'd eat. He loved ice cream, but he didn't want to gain weight, so he had just this one chocolate soda.

He came back in half an hour. "How are you doing now, Dowd?" Dowd wasn't doing so well. By this time he was perspiring, and the dye in his hair was starting to run. After several more hours of frantic scrawling, he handed Dad yet another slip of paper with yet another slogan: "He has served Massachusetts with distinction." I thought that one, frankly, to be a little like a Schenley's whiskey ad, but my father liked it. So that became the slogan. "Kennedy. He has served Massachusetts with distinction."

One person not ready to agree that Jack had served Massachusetts with distinction was Vincent Celeste. Celeste may have understood that he had little hope of winning, but he and his people were not about to go down without a fight. I recall the night that he took the fight, almost literally, to Jack's window.

Jack had rented an apartment at 122 Bowdoin Street in Boston. This was the subject of much amusement in the family because so many Kennedys were registered to vote with that as their address. It was a small apartment, but Jack and Jackie, Bobby and Ethel, and I were all registered out of this small apartment.

Jack loved to take his bath at 122 Bowdoin to soak his back and refresh himself before evening campaign events. This was the time he valued the most in his day, in certain ways. He was then at his most relaxed and funniest, and he came away with a sense of purpose and seriousness. I always sat in the bathroom with him as he called out instructions and asked questions.

Just outside the apartment was a fairly large parking lot. One evening, while Jack was in the tub, I heard noises down there, went to the living room, and looked out the window. I saw eight or ten people lighting a bonfire in the parking lot—a sizable bonfire. Then someone began to speak at the top of his voice. It was Vincent Celeste.

Jack called to me to ask what in the world was going on. I said, "Vincent Celeste is having a rally." "What's he saying?" "He says you're a phony, your supporters are phonies, and he's going to whip you."

That caught Jack's interest. As Celeste ranted on, he kept asking from the tub, "What's he saying now?" And I'd repeat what Celeste was saying. I could see it was getting under my brother's skin, even though there were only about forty people in the crowd. But then some of the press started to show up, and so of course it became a big deal, especially to my brother. It was funny and ridiculous, and Jack laughed—but it really did get under his skin.

In the election, we got the margin we'd hoped for, and then some. Jack defeated Celeste by 874,000 votes, garnering nearly 75 percent of the votes cast, the most lopsided victory in the state's history.

On November 29, 1958, in St. Joseph's Roman Catholic Church in Bronxville, New York, Virginia Joan Bennett and I were married. Cardinal Spellman performed the ceremony. Jack was my best man; Joan was escorted by her father, Harry Wiggin Bennett, and her sister Candace was her maid of honor. My sisters were among the attendants. Among the ushers were Bobby, Joe Gargan, Lem Billings, my law school classmates John Tunney and John Goemans, and my Harvard classmates Claude Hooton and Dick Clasby. My father and mother and Mrs. Bennett were looking on.

Joan wore a white satin wedding gown and carried a bouquet of white roses. My wedding gift to her was a clover-shaped pin that had belonged to my mother.

We weren't able to take an extended honeymoon because of my law school schedule. We made up for that later. For the short time we had available, we accepted the invitation of Lord Beaverbrook to spend our honeymoon at his beautiful estate in the Bahamas. Since his time in London, my father had remained friendly with Beaverbrook, the imperious and eccentric publisher of the *Daily Express* and other British newspapers. The truth is that Joan and I hadn't expected to be quite so friendly with him on our honeymoon. When we arrived at his estate, he didn't seem to know quite what to do with us. He certainly didn't make himself scarce. We ate every meal together. For him—and therefore for us—that meant a baked potato, and only a baked potato, for lunch. Dinner was not much better. We were served exactly one daiquiri apiece before dinner and then something that was definitely not standout cuisine. Our host recommended several times that we visit a nearby little island that was completely deserted. That sounded tantalizing, but somehow his lordship never got around to providing transportation there. And so we spent all our time on his estate. We got to know it . . . well.

I graduated from law school the following June, and Joan and I finally took that deferred honeymoon vacation, a five-week trip through Chile and Argentina. We were in some of the most challenging skiing country in the world. Joan was in the early stages of her pregnancy with Kara, and was not a big skier, but she did not hesitate when I offered to help her to learn in the Chilean Andes. She grew adept in an amazingly short time. We trekked on southeastward to Argentina, traveling by riverboat and in the backs of trucks over bumpy roads, and staying at inns that had no heat. Finally we succumbed to a little luxury at a beautiful resort in Bariloche, Patagonia. We visited Buenos Aires, and then returned home, where we were massing to launch Jack's presidential campaign.

That campaign started in earnest after a meeting at Hyannis Port after Labor Day weekend 1959. It was decided that Bobby would return to his role as the overall coordinator of Jack's campaign. Steve Smith would set up the administrative and financial operations. Larry O'Brien would supervise the state primaries. Only sixteen of those existed at that time, and thus a great deal of influence over delegates was still wielded by the political establishment in each state.

Every state was critical, because Jack's nomination was a long shot. Even had he not been young, Catholic, and relatively unknown, he'd still have had to contend with Democratic party lions such as Lyndon Johnson, Hubert Humphrey, Adlai Stevenson, Stuart Symington of Missouri, and Mayor Robert Wagner of New York. Only Jack and Humphrey actually entered most of the Democratic primaries, and they yielded only 584 out of a total of 1,521 votes that would be cast at the convention. Thus several other hopefuls were focused on courting party leaders around the country for delegates. (Bobby predicted early on that LBJ, not Humphrey, would emerge as Jack's main rival, and he was right.) Nor would the perils decrease should he survive the primaries and emerge as the party's nominee: public opinion polls showed that even though Democrats were in good favor, Jack would face very stiff competition in the general election against the likes of Nelson Rockefeller or Richard Nixon.

I was assigned to campaign in the eleven western states. I'd volunteered for those states—and in the back of my mind I always kept alive the possibility of moving out there after finishing school. Joan and I had seriously discussed living in California after my sister Pat urged us to come, but we vetoed it in the end because Dad didn't think too much of the idea.

And so I never became a westerner. Not officially. But the months I spent barnstorming the Rocky Mountain states for Jack turned out to be a series of action-packed escapades that featured bucking broncos, cold-eyed strangers with six-shooters drawn, hair-raising close calls in small airplanes, and even the prospect of a guided missile attack.

The western states posed several especially thorny challenges. Support for Jack on the Great Plains and in California was anemic at the time; no one had invested much work in establishing his credentials out there. Their populations tended to be scattered, so the business of introducing his record and his agenda would entail covering a lot of terrain. I left Massachusetts the Thursday after Labor Day for Montana and the state nominating convention that would produce twenty delegates. Montana was the home of Senator Mike Mansfield, who was destined to become an American statesman: the longest-serving majority leader in Senate history, ambassador to Japan, and recipient of the Presidential Medal of Freedom. Mansfield was supporting Lyndon Johnson, and at least eight of the delegates were sympathetic to Humphrey. I had work to do.

I hitched a ride into the site of the convention, the small town of Miles City, in a twin-engine airplane owned by a friend of mine named Joe Reber. I was a licensed pilot myself by this time, having learned to fly while at the University of Virginia, but that day I relied on someone else to handle the controls. Joe and I made our way over to the convention hall where I was to speak at noon. I was wearing a suit and shined shoes, and I carried a briefcase filled with campaign materials, such as circulars. The hall was nearly empty. I asked a man, "Where is everybody?"

He said, "Ever'body's down to the rodeo."

So Joe and I went down to the rodeo. We saw pickup trucks, bleachers filled with folks who were yelling and waving cowboy hats, a loud-speaker, a lot of wranglers, and a lot of dust. Something told me there were a lot of Democratic delegates among those hat-waving fans.

The rodeo people were just getting ready for the last event of the day—the bucking bronco competition. I found someone who looked like he might be in charge, introduced myself as John F. Kennedy's western campaign manager, and asked if I could be introduced. He said nope. The only way to be introduced is if you're riding one of the broncos. I said okay, I'd ride one of the broncos.

Joe shot me an incredulous look. I knew it was risky, but something told me that unless I gave it a shot, nothing I'd say to those delegates would matter much.

The wrangler shrugged and jerked his thumb at a trailer truck. "You can go back there and get some ridin' gear and get changed," he said. "We got two ways of mountin' you up. A saddle horse. Or a horse with a surcingle."

"I don't want a saddle," I told him. "I'll try a surcingle."

I didn't know exactly what a surcingle was, but I soon found out. It is a leather strap that you fasten around a horse's middle when you ride bareback. It comes with handholds attached. That sounded reassuring.

I also came up with a cowboy hat, a black Stetson.

In the trailer, a bowlegged cowpoke introduced himself as Shorty, and asked me, "You ever done this before?"

I said I hadn't. "What can you tell me?"

Shorty said, "Well, I'm number one. They're going to let you go, I guess, after me."

I looked more closely at Shorty. His cowboy hat was beaten and tattered. His riding gloves were soaked with sweat, practically a part of his skin. For some reason they had little bells sewn on the sides. His shirt was dirty and torn in places. He looked like he'd just come from the losing end of a bar fight.

And Shorty was the bronco-riding *expert*.

"I'll show you how to do this thing," he said. "Watch me." I watched as Shorty climbed atop a slatted frame and balanced himself on the wood above a horse that was about a foot and a half below him. The horse seemed to be trying to kick the pen to splinters. When his turn came, Shorty dropped onto the mount and wrapped his fingers around the surcingle, his forearm rippling with muscles. The gate opened and the horse came crashing out, kicking his hind legs side to side. Shorty stayed on top, tipping his hat. He stayed on for about ten seconds—pretty good—and then tried to switch from the bucking steed to the tamed horse that had cantered up alongside. He missed the remount and fell to the dust. The horse he'd been riding did something that I later learned few horses do: he began to "corkscrew"—jump and twist and pivot, directly above Shorty. Shorty rolled, his shirt buttons popped, and he finally got to his feet and came limping, caked with dust and blood, back to the corral.

I blurted out, "Shorty! Are you okay?"

Shorty said, "You're next."

I'm next? I'm *next*?! "Is there anything else I ought to know?" I shouted to Shorty's retreating back. He didn't hear me. He was disappearing into the trailer, looking for ice.

My horse was named Skyrocket. I think he got his name by sending everyone who tried to ride him straight up into the air. He was already crashing against the pen. *Boom! Boom! Boom!*

I grabbed the surcingle. The gate opened, and out I lurched, the world looking like a piece of film running through a broken sprocket. I could hear the crowd—either cheering or laughing, I couldn't tell which.

Somehow, I lasted seven seconds before Skyrocket launched me where he'd launched all the others. When my head cleared I realized I was stretched out on my back, breathing dust. No bones were broken. I pushed myself upright, swatted my pants, and walked back to the corral. But it all paid off. When I walked out onstage to address those cowboy convention-eers that afternoon, they were still cheering. I didn't need my campaign literature. I didn't even have to give a talk. I just said, "You know, there's a horse called Skyrocket"—here they all cheered again—"and he wants you to vote for *John Kennedy*!"

We picked up about half the delegates.

My reputation must have preceded me to Rock Springs, just under forty miles to the north. There, they wanted to shoot a cigarette out of my mouth. I was a good sport on that one until I heard the sound of the pistol being cocked, and then decided I'd take a pass on that adventure.

After Montana, I went on to Idaho, where, through the efforts of some energetic supporters, we managed to gain a split of that delegation as well. And from there to Utah, where I had my first run-in with a real-life gunslinger. He got the drop on me when he caught me trying to rustle his car.

I'd been flying over desert land toward a political luncheon in Price, a small town at the foot of a steep mountain. My escort was a young Kennedy supporter named Oscar McConkie, the son of a prominent judge in the area. As we descended, our pilot noticed that the desert was covered by a ground fog as far as the eye could see, except for some highlands on our side of the town. We were faced with the choice of either trying to land somewhere on those highlands or fly to Salt Lake City and miss the luncheon.

Flying low, the pilot spotted a rugged dirt road and said he thought he could land there. Oscar and I jumped out of the plane after it came to a rest, and when we looked around, the pilot was taking off again.

We had no transportation. Price was fifteen miles away. We started walking. Oscar's shoes hadn't been made for walking on rocky land. Nor had mine, but since this was my show, I told my friend to wait while I walked on ahead and looked for a car to flag down. The car I found didn't need flagging; it sat by the side of the road unoccupied, a green 1956 Ford station wagon. I looked around for the owner, but the terrain was empty.

I thought, "Well, if I don't get to Price in the next twenty minutes, I'll miss the luncheon, so I might as well take the car. I'll get one of our supporters to drive it back here as soon as Oscar and I arrive."

I reached through a side window and unlocked a door. I started rummaging in the glove compartment and under the seat for a key, but came up empty. I figured I would start the car by crossing the wires. I'd never done that before in my life, but I'd seen it in the movies.

Then I heard a sound and looked out the car's window into a pistol pointed right at my belt buckle, held by about as tough-looking a customer as I'd ever seen. He'd been out in the desert trapping, I later found out. Now he'd found some quarry.

I thought fast. Before the stranger could say anything, I began jabbering about how glad I was to see him and how I'd sure appreciate some help because I'd really be in trouble if I didn't get to Price in a hurry. The pistol stayed aimed at my midsection, but the cowboy's steely gaze softened just a bit.

At this point the cavalry, in the form of McConkie, arrived. He recognized the trapper as a fellow his father the judge had once given a break to in a court case. The trapper drove us into town, where I finally talked the county Democratic convention into giving Jack's campaign what I'd come there seeking: half a delegate.

Oscar McConkie did all right for himself over the years, by the way. In 2007 the Utah State Bar named him Lawyer of the Year.

Arizona was next. As in Montana and Idaho, the old-line Democrats were supporting Lyndon Johnson; the key was to get various district committee people elected who were sympathetic to Jack, and the districts were widely separated by rugged terrain.

Flying myself in a Tri-Pacer, a single-engine plane that I'd chartered, I hopscotched from Tucson to Phoenix and several smaller towns from south to north: Globe, Show Low, Flagstaff, Prescott, and Yuma among them. I'd stocked the plane with an armload of maps, checked the weather, and then launched myself into the sky. Two things were quickly impressed on my mind as an amateur pilot flying over Arizona. One was that the terrain lacked the visual navigation aids that are common in the East: air stations, towers, lakes, rivers, railroads, and highways. The second was that airports were even scarcer than landmarks. Luckily, one could glide for many miles in any direction to find a refueling stop.

I spotted Globe easily enough from the air, after an hour's flight, and touched down for a luncheon with county Democrats and a radio interview. Afterward, Barry DeRose, the county chairman, hitched a ride with me over to Show Low, a town high up on the Mogollon Rim of east-central Arizona. (It is called Show Low, according to legend, because a couple of cowpokes who couldn't stand each other played a card game to decide who'd have to move out. The low-card holder got to stay. One of the men drew the deuce of clubs, for which the main street is named.) We tried to talk a third fellow, whose name I recall as Sadovich, into coming with us, but Sadovich doubted my piloting skills and changed his mind at least six times on the way to the plane. DeRose finally talked him on board. I got the engines going and had started to taxi when I noticed that Sadovich was twitching like a rabbit. I decided to calm him by giving him something to do. "Take this chart," I told him, "and hold on to it. And keep your eye on the main highway, because if we lose sight of it we're lost." Unaccountably, this did not ease Sadovich's mind. "Screw you fellows," he blurted, fumbling at his seat belt. "I'm not about to go with you two."

Actually, he *was* about to go with us, because we were nearly airborne. But Sadovich opened the door and jumped for it. DeRose and I could hardly stop our laughter, but I managed to get the plane in the air.

Sadovich missed a great experience. The hop from Globe to Show Low was beautiful. The rugged plateaus and pine forests were covered with a light country snow that sparkled in the sun. DeRose and I were enjoying the view so much, in fact, that damned if we didn't lose track of the highway. I shifted the bearing more and more to the north in hopes that it would reappear, but to no avail. A smog-covered town emerged beneath us, with an airport tower that peeked just above the mist. DeRose asked me the name of the tower. I checked the chart and could find nothing in the vicinity that corresponded to it. "It must be a new one," I told him, "that hasn't been put on the map yet." Something in my voice must have tipped him off that I did not entirely believe this, because he was not convinced. "Let's go back and take another look," he told me. I thought that was a pretty good idea myself.

As we circled lower, DeRose peered hard and then gasped, "My God! That's Fort Apache! I know it because I'm a counsel for the Apache Indians. I've been here before!"

This discovery meant that we were off course by some fifty miles to the east, blown by winds we hadn't been aware of. I frantically scanned the chart again and noticed that the highway leaving Fort Apache to the north continued directly to Show Low. So we followed it on to the town.

That was when we discovered that our troubles were only beginning. Neither of us could locate the Show Low airport. Everything was covered with white—the result of a four-foot snowfall. We couldn't turn back because we didn't have enough gas to get us anywhere else. I started my descent. DeRose, sounding just a little like Sadovich, asked me whether I knew how to land in snow. I assured him that I'd never had any trouble in the past—which was not a complete lie, given that I had never tried to land in snow in the past.

The landing proved to be perhaps the best I ever made, as the snow acted to slow my plane down. Two men inside the hangar, looking at us dubiously, came out to gas up the plane. DeRose and I met at a nearby roadhouse with a committee of county chairmen—all three of them. I felt as though I were winning the West, one Democrat at a time.

I took off from Show Low after eight taxis down the runway to pack the snow down, and headed for Flagstaff.

The next day started out uneventfully; in fact my flight to Prescott took only thirty minutes instead of forty-five, thanks to eighty-mile-an-hour tailwinds. I enjoyed a good breakfast meeting with another handful of party leaders, and then reboarded the Tri-Pacer to fly to Yuma. And that is when I discovered that I might be a missile target.

As I took off in the early-morning glow of the sun, I heard something through the radio static about air-to-air missiles, ground-to-air missiles, and that sort of thing. This failed to activate any warning lights in my mind—after all, I was flying over Arizona, not the Soviet Union—so I spun the radio dial until I picked up Frank Sinatra. I hummed along for a while, and then glanced down at my chart. I noticed that I'd crossed into what appeared to be a restricted zone. I flipped the chart over and read that the missile zone was open to civilian aircraft—except at times when they were conducting missile testing operations, which was in the early morning.

By this time I was in the middle of the zone, with no possibility of rezoning myself, as it were. For the next twenty minutes, I flew onward hunched over the wheel with visions of every newsreel I'd seen of those hound-dog missiles going after a drone plane and *never missing.* I made it through, and arrived in Yuma. I landed at the wrong airport. On the other hand, I landed.

I was surprised—perhaps I should not have been—that the question of Jack's religion troubled some Democrats' minds in the West. Some people were concerned when I raised the issue; others when I did not. Either way, it served to let me know that my brother would have to deal with the matter of his faith in every corner of the country.

At the University of Wyoming in Laramie in the late fall, I addressed a Young Democrats meeting with my usual talking points. I talked about the upcoming election and the national and international issues facing the candidates, Jack's strengths and relative weaknesses, and so on. I came to the topic of religion and dwelt on it for a few minutes, dismissing it as not a major issue in the election. Then I opened things up to questions from the audience.

As I stood talking to students afterward, an elderly man approached me and said, "Mr. Kennedy, I am a professor of psychology at the university here, and I would like to make just one comment about your discussion. I cannot for the life of me understand why you discuss religion as either a plus or a minus for your brother. It seems to me that from your very raising of this question, you are showing that the Kennedy people are hypersensitive about this issue, and from your discussion here tonight, I fear you are going to make a good many people conscious of that factor who otherwise might not be."

I appreciated this line of thought, and thanked the professor for his candor. I said that since I was just a beginner in giving political speeches, I found his comments especially helpful. I left the campus believing that I'd been given valuable advice on the religion issue, and that I should avoid it from then on unless it surfaced as a direct question.

The following evening I spoke again at an open meeting about the coming election. Again, I covered Jack's prospects, his strengths and liabilities, and steered clear of religion entirely. In the question-and-answer session that followed, another professor of psychology stood up, this one from the University of Colorado. "You've made a great mistake," he admonished me, "in not talking about the role that religion could play in Jack's race. It's a question that everyone is concerned about. By not bringing it up, Mr. Kennedy, you appear hypersensitive about the whole question. It's quite evident from your discussion tonight that you are going to make many people conscious of a factor, which otherwise might not be the case."

I thanked the professor for his candor. And continued on my sojourn through the West.

Looking over my faded notes from that priceless adventure of nearly fifty years ago, rereading the brief, earnest stump speech I delivered at breakfast meetings and auditoriums and college dining halls, I find a capsule glimpse of the vast changes in American politics since Jack's era. I find some constants as well, but it is the changes that interest me, because so many of them sprang from Jack's initiatives.

Twin-engine airplanes of course have long since been replaced by jets, closed-circuit TV, and the Internet. Retail politics still flourishes—putting shoe leather on the ground, pressing flesh, traveling to localities around the country.

My stump speech as written ran a little less than six double-spaced pages. While I didn't actually read it—I spoke off the cuff—I probably stayed fairly close to the general outline, usually speaking for about ten minutes in addition to the opening thanks to my hosts. I always covered three main topics: federal aid to education, medical care for the aged, and foreign policy.

Federal aid to education, in 1959, was mostly about how to pay for school construction, teachers' salaries, and school buses. *Brown v. Board of Education* was just five years old; its enforcement was a matter for the states, and not yet a part of the national dialogue. How the government should address the needs of poor and minority students, students with learning disabilities, the question of evolution versus creationism, school prayer—these were unimaginable topics in a presidential campaign, as were literacy levels, charter schools, the contents of text and library books, and guns in the classroom. Just five years later, the War on Poverty created Head Start, federal aid to low-income students, and other transformative measures. Lyndon Johnson is justly credited with steering this program to reality, but the groundwork was laid by Jack, who had been appalled at the living conditions of the rural poor when he campaigned in West Virginia, and then was galvanized in 1962 by Michael Harrington's landmark study of poverty, *The Other America*.

Medical care for the aged was an issue of some concern back then, but the problem and its solutions were only generally defined. Both candidates acknowledged a need for reform. Richard Nixon was campaigning, rather liberally, on a proposal to pay for it with a direct tax levied on every taxpayer—but disbursed only to those who would sign "a pauper's oath," as my speech argued. Jack envisioned a program to be set up under the Social Security program, covering those working men and women who paid a small fraction of their earnings into it.

This was the root idea of Medicare, which Jack was laying out in his own campaign speeches, and which came to fruition in that same breakout year of 1965, as part of Johnson's Great Society. Then there was the burning issue of World War II and Korea, which were still fresh in the American memory. The fear of communism was all-consuming. Yet the issues I addressed in that stump speech—the Hungarian revolution, the nationalist uprising in Algeria, and those monumentally strategic islands of Quemoy and Matsu—seem almost benign when contrasted to the dangers at large in the world today.

I still treasure those faded notes and the brittle pages of that earnest stump speech of half a century ago.

By early February, the West was behind me. Primary voting was set to begin in March, with New Hampshire, the traditional "first" state, leading off on March 8. Now my services were required back east, which was just fine with me for several reasons. The most important was that Joan was about to have our first baby.

She was with me out west during the earlier days of campaigning, but that became more difficult as her pregnancy advanced. She had been incredibly supportive during my long absences. She was only twenty-three then, not long out of college, and about to become a mother in a family that was busy trying to get one of its own elected president. She went to live with her parents in their Bronxville house, where she was given love and support during the late stages of her pregnancy. She and I were in constant contact by telephone during my western swing, and I'd told her that when the baby was due I would be at her side.

It was during the last of my four visits to New Hampshire that the call came. I left the campaign and arrived at the hospital in time to do the traditional pacing in the waiting room, along with Joan's family and other expectant fathers. Joan gave birth to Kara Ann Kennedy on February 27, 1960. I had never seen a more beautiful baby, nor been happier in my life. Kara's name means "little dear one," and she was then and always has been my precious little dear one. Soon afterward I reluctantly left Joan and Kara and hurried to Wisconsin, where I spent the balance of that state's primary campaign.

Jack took New Hampshire with 85 percent of the vote.

Jack understood that Wisconsin was more important to his chances than its thirty-one-delegate count indicated. Since it lay adjacent to Humphrey's home state of Minnesota, the outcome there had the potential to embarrass Humphrey, "Wisconsin's third senator," and end his bid for the nomination if he lost.

Humphrey knew this, and campaigned accordingly, with an angry, accusatory edge at odds with his usual sunny persona. He tore into Jack's voting record on farm issues in an attempt to shred my brother's "liberal" credentials, and asserted that John Kennedy had "voted with [then senator] Nixon" in the past. Humphrey surrogates painted Jack as "soft on McCarthyism." Hubert even resorted to incendiary language—incendiary for the genial Hubert, at any rate—demanding that Jack drop "the razzle dazzle, fizzle fazzle." These charges and rhetoric drew rebukes from officially neutral Wisconsin Democrats such as Governor Gaylord Nelson and Senator William Proxmire, who worried about the risk of shattering party unity.

Jack's response was brilliant. At his introductory press conference in Madison on February 16, my brother made the following pledge:

> This will be a positive, constructive campaign. Let me make it completely clear right now that I do not intend to attack my Democratic opponent, to review his record, or to engage in any arguments or debates with him. I do intend, when his name is mentioned, to speak well of him. I request, moreover, that everyone working on my behalf in this state abide by the same principles.
>
> For this is not a campaign against anyone. This is a campaign for the presidency.

But he didn't hesitate to play some other formidable cards: Kennedys, and lots of them. Mother came to Wisconsin, where she charmed the farm wives and small-town women at teas and talks. Several of my sisters joined her in crisscrossing the state, winning over audiences with their charm.

(Humphrey was heard to grumble that when the sisters or I donned rac-
coon coats and stocking caps, people thought they were listening to Jack.)

Bobby threw himself back and forth over the state's long country
roads, gaunt and fatigued by his double role as campaign manager and
speechmaker, but crackling with competitive fire. The most eye-catching
Kennedy of all, of course, was Jackie. She gamely did her share of stump-
ing for her husband and endeared herself to reporters and crowds alike.
Even James Reston of the *New York Times* allowed himself a sidelong
glance at her "carelessly beautiful scarlet coat." Jackie's soft empathy and
references to Caroline, her two-year-old daughter back home, won her
many fans. She filled in for several of Jack's speaking engagements when
he had to fly back to Washington for a vote on the civil rights debate, and
acquitted herself well, with self-effacing kindness.

As for me, I helped with organizing volunteers and telephone canvass-
ers. And I reprised my role as the campaign's designated stuntman.

It began with a dawn flight, courtesy of my friend Don Lowe, from
Green Bay to Madison so that I could witness the famous Blackhawk Ski
Club's ski-jump competition. I'd assumed that I was being invited as a spec-
tator, but figured that if by some chance there was a downhill event, I might
ski the course, perhaps carrying a KENNEDY FOR PRESIDENT banner. But
since there were only jumping events, this left me out—or so I thought.

Ivan Nestingen, the mayor of Madison and a strong supporter, picked
me up at the airport. On the way in, he suggested casually that as long as
I was going, I might as well put on some ski clothes so that I'd look like
part of the crowd. I did so, at Ivan's house. When we arrived at the site, a
friend of Ivan's asked me—just as casually—whether I wanted to borrow
his boots and skis and at least take a run down the slope. That sounded
like fun, though I noted that his skis were jumping skis. I climbed up the
hill and took the run, and enjoyed it.

When I'd climbed the hill again, Ivan said, "Why don't you go over
to the practice jump and take a look at it? But don't bother going off unless you want to."

I told myself there was no chance in hell that I would "go off" on a ski-jump run, having never attempted anything other than quite small ski jumps before, but sure, I'd go up to the top and take a look around. I climbed up with four other fellows, two of whom I learned were scheduled to compete in the "big jump" later on. When we reached the top, I heard the sounds of a brass band below. It was the Marine Band, playing "The Star-Spangled Banner." For the first time, it occurred to me that I was going to have quite a time climbing back down from the ramp without disgracing myself.

The next thing I knew, the announcer introduced the first of the four skiers. The fellow went hurtling down the ramp and off the jump, disappearing over the lip of the hill. Then the second skier went, and the third, and the fourth, and suddenly I was the only one left up there. The announcer bellowed, "Now at the top of the jump—Edward Kennedy, the brother of Senator John F. Kennedy! Edward has never jumped before, but maybe if we give him a big hand, he will try it!" Then I heard the sound of nine thousand people cheering and shouting.

Then I heard the announcer again: "Here he comes, ladies and gentlemen! What a true sport he is! I am sure the senator would be proud of him!"

The die had been cast. I bent down and clamped the skis to my boots as the Marine Band gave me a drum roll, and then I launched myself, doing my darnedest to "snowplow" slowly down the ramp. But snowplow or not, the ramp eventually came to an end. I reached it and shot into the air, 190 feet above the ground.

The next thing I recall is struggling to my feet in the snow at the bottom of the run and being escorted to the broadcast booth, where they let me say a few words. I asked the crowd whether anyone had seen Hubert Humphrey at the top of that jump, and then asked them all to support my brother John. The crowd yelled and cheered. It was the best reception I'd enjoyed since Skyrocket.

I still have a photo of that jump on my wall.

Jack's reward for weeks of long car rides and countless appearances was 55 percent of the Wisconsin vote, despite an overwhelming lead in the early polls. He'd won, but was not especially cheered by the results. He needed a larger margin to score the knockout punch against Humphrey that he had hoped for. Wisconsin voters should have been Jack's natural constituency; the labor-minded Catholic voters in cities such as Madison and Milwaukee were the ones who gave him his margin of victory. But the farmers in the great network of small towns had stuck with Humphrey. Jack had failed to break away from his rival, who was embarrassed by his defeat "next door" but still in the race. Which meant we'd have to start all over again in West Virginia.

I rushed down to be at Jack's side there after the Wisconsin victory, and found my brother gaunt and hoarse as he struggled with an unexpected crisis. He'd built up another comfortable lead over Humphrey in the early polls, and now was facing more sudden bad news. The Catholicism issue had surfaced again, but with far more intensity than I'd encountered in the West. Criticism of Jack's faith was spreading throughout the state's hills and hollows. As it did so, his poll numbers dropped, until, just four weeks before balloting, he was suddenly twenty points behind Humphrey.

West Virginia, to my young eyes, was a desolate and depressing place, an impression hardly improved by the rain that never let up while I was there, turning the many hillside dirt roads into muddy quagmires. Yet I quickly gained respect for its people: stern, resolute, gritty folk who bore their hardships with dignity. Of course West Virginia in time became a cherished state for us. In those late winter weeks of 1960, Jack forged a rapport with hardworking miners and farmers and teachers and truck drivers. But it took an all-out effort, a mobilization of resources directed by a candidate who virtually willed himself not to lose on the issue of his religion.

Dozens of friends, political allies, and volunteers flooded into the state. Franklin D. Roosevelt Jr., the bearer of a hallowed name, arrived and hit the hustings. The usual banks of telephones were set up, the household receptions arranged.

I spent about four days in West Virginia, mostly in the northwest corner. Shortly after I arrived, I made a visit—a scheduled visit, I thought— to the famous Coal House in Williamson, a building made entirely of coal that housed the local chamber of commerce. When I entered, the chamber president stood up in amazement. He thought I was to be there the following month. He grabbed his telephone and spent the next hour making calls to round up the Democrats.

During a break, the chamber man suggested that he and I pay a visit to the nearby five-and-dime store. As we crossed the street, I could hear music blaring from several loudspeakers in front of the store. Inside, along one wall, were a record turntable and a radio microphone, manned by a fellow who apparently did live interviews with customers between the tunes he played. My host introduced me to him and asked whether he would like to interview me. The radio man seemed very reluctant, and I was about to suggest that we all forget about it when he finally agreed.

For the next twenty-five minutes, the questions were these: Is it not true that Catholics are dictated to by their priests? Is it not true that the Catholic Church is a sovereignty within a sovereignty? Is it not true that people left Europe for America so that they could escape domination by the Roman church?

Before long, a crowd of about three hundred people had gathered outside the store, where the loudspeakers were carrying our interview throughout the town. My interviewer's questions were getting to be almost like speeches in themselves. By this time, all propriety had vanished. My interviewer felt no compunctions against interrupting me whenever he felt the urge, which was often, and I found myself trying to grab the microphone from the man before he could finish his questions. At the end of the interview, the local personality invited me to have the last word. As I started to rattle off something about bigotry, he slapped an Elvis Presley record on the turntable, thanked me, and sent me on my way. I had no idea how I'd be treated by the crowd as I stepped outside, but a number of the people called out supportive comments to me, which went a long way toward calming me. Later I learned from the chamber of commerce president that the radioman was a Baptist minister, and that he had treated me to one of his past sermons.

The rest of my appearances were not nearly so unpleasant. I showed up at dance halls, and probably sang "Sweet Adeline" a time or two. At community parties, I bought beers for strangers, solemn-eyed Appalachians bound to a culture of hard work and deep patriotism.

I got to know West Virginia at ground level—and below. I descended beneath the earth to grab the sooty hands of coal miners, strengthening my awareness and respect for these men and the millions of hardscrabble workers like them around the country.

I'll never forget a scene I witnessed outside a mineshaft somewhere in that state. It was nothing out of the ordinary—and that is what made it so powerful to me. The workers were emerging from the mine as their shift ended. Faces blackened, clothes heavy with sweat and soot, they trooped out one by one, slowly. I followed them into a little woodframe shack where they changed their clothes. The miners would trudge into the room, not looking at anything or anyone, and drop down onto a bench. There was no shower. The men would sit for five or six minutes, not so much as moving. Complete silence reigned. One of them would finally stand up, take off his jacket, and drop down again. Another would stand up, strip off his shirt, and sit down again. Only after a long time were these men able to complete their change of clothes, and they were still covered with dirt. Then, one by one, they would shuffle out of the room and get into their cars and drive away. The whole process took about forty-five minutes. During that time I went around the room talking to them, asking each to support my brother. I felt humble in their presence.

Jack's obvious concern for these West Virginians' plight overshadowed the resistance to his religion that he'd expected to find. So did his stamina.

He gave speeches, sometimes as many as twenty a day. He literally talked himself hoarse. As I stood at that remote mineshaft, watching those exhausted men drive away, a sheriff's car pulled up beside me, and the sheriff leaned out the window and asked, "Are you Kennedy?" I said I was. "Your brother wants you."

We drove out to a little airstrip, where I boarded a single-engine plane and we took off for Ravenswood, a town of four thousand on the state's western border, the Ohio River. George Washington surveyed and purchased the land on which it lies. Sure enough, there was Jack, waiting to whisper, "I can't speak anymore." I traveled for two and a half days with him, giving talks from notes that he'd write out. On one occasion I got a little carried away by the sound of my own fine ringing voice. "Do you want a man who will give the country leadership?" I heard myself orating. "Do you want a man who has vigor and vision?" Jack grabbed the microphone and rasped, "I would just like to tell my brother that you cannot be elected president until you are thirty-five years of age." It wasn't long afterward that he decided to send me back to the coal mines.

Some of the most colorful, old-fashioned raconteurs in the nation hailed from West Virginia. One of them was a wonderful character named A. James Manchin. He seemed to do a little bit of everything for a living: high school civics teacher, football coach, youngest state legislator ever to hold office, and Baptist minister. He went on to become West Virginia's secretary of state. His nephew Joe Manchin III was elected governor in 2004.

I'll never forget his introduction of me one night. I know I can't do it justice. He was spellbinding. But I'll give it a try.

He took out a copy of the book *PT 109* and asked the assembled crowd, "Do you know what this is? This is the book about a war hero, about a man who risked his life for his country and his crew. It's a story about the man who is going to be the next president of these United States. It's about John F. Kennedy."

Then he took out a Bible and placed it on top of the book and said, "You know what this is. It's the Good Book. It's the word of the Lord. It's the word that guides the good people of West Virginia and that guides John F. Kennedy too. And I'm gonna place it here on top of the story about this great war hero. Yes I am. The Good Book on top of the story about the great war hero, John F. Kennedy.

"And here's Old Glory, the red, white, and blue. The blue is as blue as a West Virginia sky, the white as pure as a West Virginia heart, and the red as red as the blood of all the West Virginia patriots who gave their lives in defense of this great country."

And then Manchin took out a single candle, a long taper, and he held it up and, right on cue, all the lights went out in the room. It was pitch black. The crowd gasped. Then we heard the crackle of a match as he lit the candle. "And this is the light that every coal miner in West Virginia knows. This is the light that leads you out of the darkness of the mines. This is the light to safety. This is the light that leads you home. Well, I'm here to tell you that John Kennedy is that light. John Kennedy, that war hero, who led his men to safety. John Kennedy who follows the word of God. John Kennedy who risked his life in defense of his country."

The lights went back up in the room and Manchin said, "And now we're going to hear from his brother Ted, who's going to tell you more about him."

Lucky me.

The landslide victory in West Virginia was the breakthrough for Jack's nomination. Hubert Humphrey dropped out of the presidential race after losing and heartily praised his rival—although it took years for his private bitterness to heal.

The 1960 Democratic convention opened on July 11 inside the recently finished Los Angeles Memorial Sports Arena, adjacent to the Coliseum on Figueroa Street south of the USC campus. A sense of transition was in the air, symbolized by the curving, modernistic entrance to the arena. Loudspeakers crackled, not with the old-time "Happy Days Are Here Again," but with the recorded voice of Frank Sinatra. Sinatra had met and befriended Jack through Peter Lawford, the husband of our sister Pat. His contribution to the campaign was to update his big hit of the previous year, "High Hopes," with Sammy Cahn rewriting his own original lyrics as a campaign song: "K-E, double-N, E-D-Y / Jack's the nation's favorite guy." With Lyndon Johnson and Adlai Stevenson having come in from the cold to announce their candidacies, we were thankful for every edge we could muster.

We found one further indication of transition in Los Angeles: protesters, five thousand of them, marching in the streets toward the arena. These first-ever demonstrators at a national convention were civil rights advocates. They'd been organized by the young socialist Michael Harrington and the thirty-one-year-old Reverend Dr. Martin Luther King Jr.

The delegates, aware of the protesters' visibility before the photographers and TV cameras, did in fact write a mild civil rights plank into their platform. Jack endorsed the strongest version of the plank, and affirmed his commitment to fight discrimination in a speech to the NAACP and later to King himself in a private conversation.

Jack's nomination was far from certain. Johnson declared his candidacy on July 5 and came out strong. He pounded at Jack's physical condition, demanding a public report on my brother's health. In private, LBJ denounced Jack's supposed dependency on his rich father, whose prewar diplomacy he also slurred, and pleaded with President Eisenhower to speak out against Jack. (Eisenhower refused.) Johnson infuriated Bobby, who had faced Johnson's scorn himself in the past, and intensified the mutual dislike between my brother and the Texan.

Johnson's assault on Jack, coupled with the doubts that party elders still harbored about his Catholicism and his brevity of political experience, raised the stakes for a first-ballot victory. This was to be the last national convention at which a roll-call vote actually could determine defeat or success, and all of us, Bobby especially, understood the psychological importance of putting Jack over the first time around. (Since the 1936 convention, only the 1952 balloting had gone beyond the first round.)

Balloting would occur on the third day. Bobby set up a command post at the Biltmore Hotel. He canvassed the state party leaders with even more than his usual obsessive energy. He knew the count to the precise half-ballot. His numbers told him that as things stood on the first day, John Kennedy was assured of 710 delegates of the 761 needed for the nomination. He believed that with an extra push we could put Jack over on the first ballot. The last thing we wanted was for the balloting to go to a second round, because by then new coalitions could be developing and victory would be less certain. We wanted to wrap things up on the first ballot, and all of us launched into making that push.

Our team would meet at 7:30 every morning and Bobby would walk us through all the states and their tallies. Then we'd fan out, contacting every delegation chairman on the floor to see whether we could coax any movement in Jack's direction.

By the third night, Bobby was fatigued, but as clear as ever in his calculations of probable votes. He'd worked it out that Wyoming, the last state on the roll call, could conceivably put Jack over. Before the roll call began, Jack had ten and a half of the state's fifteen votes. We knew we'd need more than that. We'd need every one. Bobby told me to get the hell over to the Wyoming delegation and nail down those votes.

This was where my hard work in the West paid off: my months of crisscrossing those states, riding the broncos, meeting the chairmen, getting to know them, remembering their names, forging personal ties. I had made seven trips to Wyoming alone, and I had developed friendly relationships. I hurried over to Tracy McCracken, a crusty newspaper editor, lawyer, Democratic National Committee member, and the person who held the most influence over the remaining votes in the delegation. I knew that McCracken personally favored Lyndon Johnson. I had to get him to commit to Jack, and in a way that would make it impossible for him to renege at the last moment. I thought I had an idea how to do that.

I walked over to McCracken within earshot of Teno Roncalio, Jack's great supporter who had become my friend in Wyoming and was the leader of the state's delegates supporting my brother. Teno and I made sure we were standing close enough to all of the Wyoming delegates that they could hear our conversation above the general echoing uproar. Speaking as much for their benefit as for his, I shouted to McCracken, "We know you have ten and a half Kennedy votes! My question is this: if we're within five votes when Wyoming is called, if Wyoming will make the difference in giving John Kennedy the nomination, will you give us the whole fifteen?"

It seemed to me that McCracken thought he was agreeing to something that he never believed was going to happen, so he said, "Sure." He got to look expansive in front of me and his delegation, by agreeing to an extremely unlikely scenario. But he didn't have Bobby's knack for counting votes.

When the roll call started, McCracken wasn't paying attention at all. But as it progressed, and the votes for John Kennedy began to pile up, he began to have a look of concern on his face. Could Wyoming *really* be the state that put him over for the nomination? I was standing there with Teno and the rest of the Wyoming delegation as the roll call continued.

I wanted to make sure McCracken held up against his Johnson people. As the roll call got closer and closer, I could see Tracy's jaw begin to clench, and the sweat starting to form. Vermont voted. And then Virginia. Washington. West Virginia. Wisconsin. Now we were within twelve votes of a first-ballot victory.

The Lyndon Johnson delegates were screaming at McCracken,

"You can't do this! Lyndon can deliver for us! We're not going for that!" McCracken was between a rock and a hard place, and he had to decide in only a few seconds. He realized that he had given his word, in the presence of the entire delegation.

The chairman's voice boomed through the loudspeakers: "*Wyoming!*"

Back came McCracken: "*Mr. Chairman, the Wyoming vote will make a majority for Senator Kennedy . . .*"

It wasn't exactly soaring oratory, but it was the sweetest speech I'd ever heard. The arena's instant eruption into bedlam supplied all the drama the announcement itself lacked. It took several minutes before things quieted enough that McCracken could officially state that all fifteen delegate votes would go to my brother. Then we all yelled and cheered again, and I waved the Wyoming standard alongside people who'd been strangers just weeks earlier, but were now dear friends. All but four and a half of them, anyway.

Jack broke tradition and arrived in the convention hall immediately after he had been nominated, to thank the delegates—and to offer a surprised Lyndon Johnson the vice presidential spot, which LBJ immediately accepted. He entered the arena to thunderous cheers and exploding flashbulbs that lit up his famous smile, with Jackie, pregnant with John Jr., and our mother Rose at his side. Dad had already slipped out of the convention hall with no fanfare. He was proud of Jack beyond all measure, but he didn't want to be a distraction. He was on the phone and constantly in touch, but he knew this was Jack's show.

On the following night, to great cheers, Jack strode beneath the blazing Coliseum lights to the podium and formally accepted the nomination. He declared that he would offer the American people challenges, not comforting promises; and he introduced a thrilling new phrase as the descriptive term for his program. "Today our concern must be with the future," he called out. "For the world is changing. The old era is ending. The old ways will not do."

And then:

The problems [of the past] are not all solved and the battles are not all won. And we stand today on the edge of a New Frontier. The frontier of the 1960s. A frontier of unknown opportunities and perils, a frontier of unfulfilled hopes and threats.

CHAPTER SEVEN

Becoming a Politician
1960–1961

That night of Jack's acceptance speech and the days afterward had the feel of emergence from a six-month trek through the winter wilderness into the Fourth of July. The endless cramped car and bus and small-airplane trips through the primary states were forgotten. The bucking broncos, the daunting ski ramps, the bad food, the fatigue, Jack's laryngitis—it had all been worth it.

We celebrated at Pat and Peter Lawford's house in Hollywood the night after the convention. Sammy Davis Jr. was there, and Frank Sinatra, and Nat King Cole. Jack goaded my college pal Claude Hooton and me to challenge Sammy and Frank to a songfest. Claude and I belted out "Heart of My Heart," and "Wedding Bells Are Breaking Up That Old Gang of Mine," and "Bill Bailey, Won't You Please Come Home." We trotted out "Sweet Adeline" in honor of Honey Fitz. Jack joined in. Frank and Sammy came back with the best they had. Frank must have sung his whole repertoire. I can't recall who won.

Politics intruded when Jack returned to the Senate. During a special session of Congress scheduled by Majority Leader Johnson, Jack bid for a leadership role in trying to push through bills for housing, new minimum wage legislation, aid to education, and medical care. The first two were voted down; the second two passed in watered-down form. These measures probably would have met the same fate no matter who was leading the fight for them—Jack or Johnson himself—but their failure allowed *Time* magazine to comment that the Democratic nominee had encountered "a nightmare series of grim surprises and jolting defeats."

Things smoothed out after that. My family, along with Jack's aides and close friends, managed a couple of sunlit days at the Cape, sailing, swimming, and bantering. It was like old times—except for the throngs of sunglassed, camera-waving tourists who suddenly filled Hyannis Port and strained against lines of policemen and barricades to peer into the grounds for a glimpse of Jack.

As campaign manager, Bobby could not wait to get going. As laughter and footballs floated across the lawn, Bobby worked the telephones, called strategy sessions, and exhorted all hands to gird for battle. He scarcely let up until election night.

Jack launched himself into action. He shored up relations with party leaders who had been skeptics: former president Harry Truman, Adlai Stevenson, Eleanor Roosevelt, whose early disdain he melted in a visit to Hyde Park. Trailing Nixon and his running mate Henry Cabot Lodge by six points in the Gallup polls at the end of July, Kennedy-Johnson drew even a month later, despite increasing Republican attacks on Jack's character and his Catholicism. Jack blunted the momentum of the latter on September 12. He addressed, on live television, a convention of southern Protestant ministers at the Rice Hotel in Houston, a move that his aides, supporters, and even the normally fearless Bobby had advised against.

Facing these conservative clerics who had regarded him as a likely agent of the Vatican whose loyalties were to the pope rather than the American people, my brother stood at ease behind the podium and delivered one of the pivotal speeches of his career. He was not the Catholic candidate for president, he told the stony faces before him; he was the Democratic Party's candidate for president who happened to be a Catholic. Speaking without a trace of defensiveness, projecting respect for the values of the clergymen in the ballroom but without apology for his own creed, Jack gradually disarmed the ministers. "If the time should ever come," he assured them, "when my office would require me to either violate my conscience, or violate the national interest, I would resign the office." He subtly peeled back the layer of righteousness regarding "the Catholic question" and exposed the bigotry that lay beneath:

> If this election is decided on the basis that forty million Americans lost their chance of being president on the day they were baptized, then it is the whole nation that will be the loser in the eyes of Catholics and non-Catholics around the world, in the eyes of history, and in the eyes of our people.

The ministers sent him offstage with a standing ovation.

Then came the event that might very well have made the difference in the outcome of the campaign: the autumn series of televised debates, or "joint appearances," between him and Richard Nixon.

Robert Sarnoff, the chairman of NBC, initiated the debate discussions on the night that Richard Nixon secured the Republican nomination in Chicago on July 27. He offered both candidates a total of eight hours of free airtime for a series of debates. Jack accepted immediately. Nixon thought it over for four days (with Eisenhower, behind the scenes, urging him not to do it) before he said yes. As negotiations evolved, all three networks agreed to telecast the proceedings. Congress suspended its "equal time" provision, which would have mandated participation even by fringe and special-interest candidates, for the occasion.

Jack's quick decision surprised none of us. He had thought a great deal about the merging of the new medium and the political process. He intuitively comprehended that his own attributes played well on the small screen. And he understood, as few did then, that one ignored the promises and perils of the televised image at one's peril. He had written a prescient article on the subject for *TV Guide* in November 1959. The "revolutionary impact" of television, Jack declared, had "altered drastically the nature of our political campaigns, conventions, constituents, candidates and costs."

The debates commenced on September 26 at the CBS studio in Chicago, with the legendary producer Don Hewitt running the show. Jack prepared, as he would for each debate, by sitting on his bed in his hotel suite, listening to Peggy Lee records, and inviting his staff to pepper him with trial questions related to the night's topic: domestic policy, in the first debate. He had a stack of file cards filled with facts and figures about every issue imaginable. When he felt he'd mastered the material on each card, he'd flip it into the air and watch it flutter to the floor.

As he donned his dark suit and knotted his tie in the hotel that first evening, he told Dave Powers that he felt "like a prizefighter about to enter the ring at Madison Square Garden." Dave shot back, "No, it's more like being the opening-game pitcher in the World Series, because you have to win four of these."

On the car ride to the studio, Jack was lost in thought. The people with him could sense his tension. At CBS, a technician took a look at his starched white shirt and told him it would flare up under the television lights. He sent Powers back to the hotel to retrieve a blue shirt, and changed into it in the greenroom.

Nixon arrived looking a good deal more nervous than Jack. He was wearing a light-colored suit, which seemed to accentuate his persistent five-o'clock shadow. Don Hewitt urged each candidate to submit to a makeup artist. Both stiffened. Jack, who'd needled Hubert Humphrey for wearing TV makeup in Wisconsin, said he would not go into the makeup room unless Nixon went first. Nixon said he would not go in unless Kennedy were seen going in as well.

And so Nixon stayed out of the makeup room, trusting in the tube of sticky film sold over the counter as "Lazy Shave." Jack stayed out, too—more or less. He ducked into his own dressing room instead, and sat still while an aide named Bill Wilson dabbed a little drugstore makeup on his cheeks and forehead to absorb perspiration.

Ted Sorensen and Bobby hung around the dressing room for a little while, then left a few minutes before airtime. Bobby recommended one final bit of advice to Jack: "Kick him in the balls."

Jack refrained; but he was inside Nixon's head long before Howard K. Smith greeted the national audience. He outfeinted Nixon, obliging the vice president to stalk onto the set first and then sit for several minutes perspiring under the hot lights. With little more than sixty seconds before airtime, people began to seriously wonder where my brother was. He was in the men's room. He strolled to his podium with only about fifteen seconds to go, calmly sat down in his chair, and glanced about placidly while Nixon stared helplessly at him. Bill Wilson later said he realized then that JFK had "psyched out" Nixon before the debate even began.

The content of those debates may have passed into insignificance, but scholars continue to study their effect as a transitional moment in broadcasting. My brother treated the camera (and by extension, each of the seventy million viewers) as an intimate friend; he gazed steadily into the lens as he spoke. During Nixon's remarks, he calmly jotted notes. His opponent darted his dark eyes from the camera to Smith to Jack to his own notes, accentuating his aura of tension. When Jack spoke, Nixon frowned at him and sneaked glances at the camera.

Richard J. Daley didn't need anyone to tell him who'd won that opening debate. As the studio lights went down, the Chicago mayor burst from the room where he'd been watching and bounded into the greenroom to congratulate my brother. It was our first sign that we'd won. Ted Sorensen recalled that on the flight back east aboard the *Caroline*, a Convair 240 propeller plane that Jack leased from our father, Jack was exhausted but happy.

My brother relaxed with a bowl of soup and reviewed his replies to questions with almost total recall. "You can always improve afterward," he told Sorensen, "but I would settle for the way it went. I thought it was all right."

Of the remaining three debates, polling showed that audiences thought my brother won the first one, 39 to 23 percent (with the rest undecided), as well as the second, originating in New York, by 44 to 28. For the third round the opponents were on opposite sides of the country: Jack in New York, Nixon in California. This was the only debate that Nixon won in the polling, by 42 to 39. Jack won decisively in the last one, 52 to 27. Roughly 120 million people saw at least one of the debates, according to NBC, forming the largest audience ever to watch and focus on one topic in history.

Now all we had to do was win the election.

The issue of race hung at the edges of the 1960 campaign, seldom acknowledged but on the minds of everyone. On October 19, Martin Luther King Jr. was arrested in Atlanta when he joined a protest at a segregated restaurant. The students involved were soon released, but King, the true target, was sent to a state penitentiary. His wife, Coretta, was understandably terrified for his safety. Many people thought it was politically unwise for Jack to get involved in the incident. The risks of advancing too far ahead of public opinion could drive white voters to the other candidate. Nixon ignored the incident. Jack didn't. He telephoned Mrs. King to express his concern. Then Bobby reached the governor of Georgia by telephone and persuaded him to order King's release.

Through the fall, all of us traveled for Jack. I spent ten days blanketing Washington, Oregon, and California. I mostly visited colleges, four or five a day. I saw lots of enthusiasm. Jack was getting young people involved.

At the outset, Nixon was heavily favored to win the election. The debates closed the gap considerably, but they didn't give Jack a lead. There was little sudden movement in the opinion polls in those days.

On the clear, crisp election day of November 8, 1960, the extended family began to converge on the Cape house. People filtered in throughout the afternoon and evening: the candidate and his wife, Bobby and Ethel, Sarge and Eunice, Pat and Peter, Jean and Steve, Joan and myself. The Gargans were there. Dad had invited some of his eclectic friends:

the former president of Notre Dame, Father John Cavanaugh; the New York theatrical producer Arthur Houghton; and Carroll Rosenbloom, owner of the Baltimore Colts. We dined on Maryland crabs and then found comfortable places for viewing the returns, most of us at Bobby's house next door.

The tallies from the eastern states came in the first hour after the polls closed. Jack won Connecticut easily. In the first couple of hours, in fact, it was looking like a blowout. Late in the night, the returns began to shift. The numbers were moving Nixon's way. Jack clung to a narrow lead, but obviously it was going to be close. Not until early morning did the trend shift back his way again. Illinois firmed up, and then Nevada, New Mexico, Hawaii. Illinois was the key state, and it went narrowly for Jack.

Even though the election was close—a cliffhanger in every sense of the word—I had always believed that Jack was going to win, even when the odds were something like nine to five against him. I suppose I believed that Jack could do anything he wanted.

And believe me, I knew the odds. I was so certain of Jack's victory that I placed a Las Vegas bet on it. My winnings would have given me enough money to buy a new car, a really fancy new car. The speedy Aston Martin DB4 had just come out of England a couple years earlier, and I really wanted one. Well, I won that bet, but I never bought the car. I made the mistake of telling Dad about it, and he hit the roof. "This is just—this just makes no sense!" he fulminated. "Foolish! I'm appalled that you'd get into this kind of thing! You're not going to collect that money." He really went after me tooth and nail. I never did collect on my bet, and I've always wondered what happened to the money. Dad was right, of course—as usual.

Bobby and I, exhausted, excused ourselves from most of the gaiety that followed Jack's victory. Along with our wives and Dave Hackett and his family, we headed for a few days of relaxation in Acapulco. (Dave, a childhood friend of Bobby's, was soon to distinguish himself as head of

President Kennedy's Committee on Juvenile Delinquency and Youth Crime.)

It was under the bright Mexican sunlight that Bobby confided in me a surprising piece of information: he did not plan to seek Jack's vacated Senate seat in 1962. Bobby was never as politically driven as the myth would have you believe. He improvised his life to an astonishing degree.

The seat was being held by a good man named Benjamin Smith, who'd been appointed by Governor Foster Furcolo to fill out Jack's term when Jack resigned shortly after Christmas 1960. I thought the world of Ben Smith. He had been my brother's roommate at Harvard, and I can remember hearing Ben say that if he had to shovel every ton of coal out of West Virginia to make Jack president, he'd do it.

The story has been told that Smith's appointment was arranged specifically to clear the way for me in 1962: he'd agreed to "hold" the seat until I was old enough to run at age thirty; then he would step aside. The truth is more complex. First, a slightly complicated bit of election background. My brother had four years remaining on his six-year Senate term when he was elected president. By law, the governor was only allowed to appoint someone to fill the vacancy for two years, until the next federal election, which was in 1962 (coincidentally, the year I turned thirty). The election in 1962 was in turn to fill the last two remaining years of my brother's six-year Senate term. Then, whoever won the election in 1962 would have to face the voters again in 1964 if they wanted to be elected to a full six-year term.

Governor Furcolo had appointed Ben to fill the first two of the remaining years of my brother's term "in the interest of promoting party unity." Jack and Furcolo had a tense relationship, and it seems that the governor had been resistant to appointing Jack's chosen person to the post. Some people felt that Furcolo himself wanted the appointment since he had run and lost for the Senate a few years before and felt that Jack had not gone all-out to support him at that time. I don't know whether Furcolo really wanted the post for himself. But I do know that there was some tension there.

The attorney general of the state, Edward McCormack Jr., was planning to launch an all-out campaign for the Democratic nomination for the 1962 election to fill out the two years remaining on the term. Eddie was the nephew of House Speaker John McCormack, and the son of Edward "Knocko" McCormack Sr., the Speaker's brother and a tough South Boston bar owner.

"Knocko" was just one of the colorful characters with colorful nicknames who have flavored Boston politics from the days before Honey Fitz down through the present time. They are part of the city's folklore. There was Peter "Leather Lungs" Clougherty, a supporter of McCormack's whom Jack never forgot because "Leather Lungs" took him for three thousand dollars once by cashing his checks. There was J. Ralph "Juicy" Granara, so nicknamed by Tip O'Neill because of his habit of chewing tobacco, though Juicy himself preferred to be called "the Colonel." Juicy was a former vaudeville dancer, an aide to several officeholders, a sometime mayoral candidate, and the Official Greeter of Boston. He made headlines in 1950 by retracing the midnight ride of Paul Revere "behind the wheel of a motor-car with the windshield wiper swinging," as the *Boston Globe* reported it, "humming under his breath, 'For I Must Go Where the Wild Goose Goes.'"

There was "Muggsy" O'Leary, Jack's longtime driver. It was completely typical of Jackie's self-humor that she used to enjoy telling of the time when Muggsy, impatient to transport her to an appointment, scowled at his wristwatch and then bellowed, "C'mon, Jackie, fer chrissake! Move yer ass."

No list of legendary Boston nicknames would be complete without "Tip"—the moniker sported by my great friend, the late Thomas Philip O'Neill Jr. The Democratic congressman for thirty-four years and Speaker of the House for ten could trade one-liners with the best of them. When a narrow vote was approaching once, Tip sought out Jimmy Burke, his fellow congressman from Massachusetts, and told him, "I need your help on this one. It's important to me." When Burke replied, dubiously, "I don't know. This is a tough one," Tip growled back, "I don't need your vote when it's *not* tough!" But as much as I relished Tip O'Neill's turn of a phrase—he once labeled Ronald Reagan "Herbert Hoover with a smile"—I revered him for his statesmanship. He took a tough, effective stand toward ending the Vietnam War, was a powerful partner with me in forging peace in Northern Ireland, and remained a staunch champion of working people. As a footnote to that salty tongue of his, Tip never made it personal. He and Reagan remained on friendly terms "after 6 p.m.," as Reagan himself put it.

Both of the elder McCormacks harbored political ambitions for Eddie. And to put it mildly, they didn't harbor a lot of love for the Kennedys. In 1947, Jack's first year as a congressman, he and John McCormack had locked horns on whether to press for Mayor James Michael Curley's release from jail. (He'd been sent up for a second time, after a conviction for mail fraud.) McCormack led the fight to get him pardoned; Jack refused to go along. In 1956, Jack and the congressman tangled again, over who would lead the Massachusetts delegation to the Democratic convention. So there was a history of tensions between the two political families.

I remember riding along with Jack Crimmins, my longtime driver, through a South Boston neighborhood one day when we passed Knocko's house. Knocko was up on a stepladder with a hammer and nails. Jack pulled the car over, leaned out the window, and called, "Hi, Knocko! What are you doing up there?" Knocko yelled down, "I'm shingling the house. And every time I pound a nail in, I think I'm pounding it into that young Ted Kennedy's tail." I didn't quite catch this, and asked what Knocko had said. Crimmins, who was holding back laughter, said, "I'll tell you about it later on. I have to park first."

I understood my sudden opportunity as soon as Bobby confided his lack of interest in the Senate seat. But did I want to make that run in '62? There were many reasons to tell myself no. Inexperience was among the biggest. What had I mastered? In what areas had I proven my bona fides? Then there was the question of public opinion. If I won, would I be seen, and dismissed, as a mere beneficiary of the Kennedy family's political power? As someone for whom it was simply "my turn"?

Of course I wanted to make that run. My reasons were hardly frivolous. All my life, as I've said, I had wanted to catch up. I'd worshipped my father as a young boy. I had been swept up by the dash and nobility of Joe Jr., and admired his wartime self-sacrifice even as I wept over it. Jack and Bobby had been godlike figures to me and my sisters. Now Jack was about to be installed as a world leader, and Bobby had already earned national recognition as Jack's right-hand man and as a warrior against crime and injustice.

I remembered again my father's words to me as a boy: *"You can have a serious life or a nonserious life, Teddy. I'll still love you whichever choice you make. But if you decide to have a nonserious life, I won't have much time for you. You make up your own mind. There are too many children here who are doing things that are interesting for me to do much with you."*

I was ready to step into the public arena alongside these men who were my father and brothers. To be of use. And to catch up.

But first I needed some seasoning. As soon as we returned to the States, I paid a visit to Jack in his Washington office. "Look," I said. "I'd like to be a part of the administration." I told him that I was interested in arms control. In fact, I cared about it passionately. This was the height of the cold war. The Berlin crisis was intensifying, fueled by the flow of refugees from the Soviet-controlled eastern sectors of that divided city to the autonomous and economically thriving West Berlin (part of the postwar Federal Republic of Germany). The exodus would lead a frustrated Khrushchev to start building the Berlin Wall the following August. The American U-2 spy plane and its pilot Francis Gary Powers had been shot down over the Soviet Union in May, infuriating the Russians. This occurred only a month after the United States had deployed ballistic missiles to Italy, adding more nuclear warheads capable of striking Moscow to the ones in place in the United Kingdom.

I knew that arms control would be a priority with Jack. An appointment somewhere in the State Department, say, would give me, at twenty-eight, the chance to learn a complex and substantive issue, to be involved with competent people, and to travel and gain experience that would help me when I was ready to declare for the Senate.

Jack considered this. Then he brushed it aside. "Just go back to Massachusetts," he told me. "Every day you're up there, you're doing yourself some good. If you get involved in arms control, the world is never going to know about you or what you're doing. Go up there, Teddy, and get to work."

And then Jack was seized by another thought. "Go up to Massachusetts," he repeated, then added, "But before you do that, go back to Africa." (He was referring to my 1956 visit to Algeria as a reporter for the International News Service.)

"Back to Africa?" I said.

"Yes. Go back and see what's going on over there. That's a continent that's going to be enormously important. There are all kinds of things happening down in the Congo. This Tshombe's on the loose. And there's this East-West struggle going on in these countries. The Belgian Congo has just obtained its independence from Belgium."

As I stammered that I had little time to put such a trip together, Jack grabbed the telephone and rang up a Senate Foreign Relations staff member named Carl Marcy. Marcy told him that a group of senators had left on a fact-finding tour of West Africa just two days earlier. "If your brother leaves tonight," Marcy said, "he can catch up with them in Salisbury, Rhodesia. He can take an overnight flight to London. We'll set up briefings for him the next day. Then he'll go overnight again to Cairo, and get on an eleven o'clock plane and fly six hours down to Salisbury. He'll arrive around six o'clock and he can join them for dinner. They'll leave again the next day."

I said, "I don't have my passport. I'm not sure Joan is going to like this. I mean, come *on*."

Jack said, "It's a great opportunity."

I left that night, December 1, for four weeks in West Africa with Senators Frank Church, Frank Moss, and Gale McGee. I joined the entourage as an observer, paying my own expenses. The senators were initially sort of glad to see me, but after the first headlines when we landed in the Congo—"Ted Kennedy Arrives with His Senate Delegation"—they cooled down just a little. Still, it was an incredible trip.

We were looking at the numerous independence movements in these countries, with an eye to whether the United States, with its various development programs, or Soviet communism would fill the vacuum of the old colonial powers.

We saw a Rhodesia still trying to yank itself free from the grip of the United Kingdom, and on the brink of violent upheaval. Years of bloody civil war between black nationalists and local European interests lay ahead. In Liberia, the small coastal republic settled by American slaves before the Civil War, we saw the economic fruits of U.S. investment and shared technology, and we also sensed the resentment of marginalized native Liberians that would erupt in bloody revolution twenty years later.

At the time of our visit, the overwhelming mood was optimism: a thrilling sense of expectations for President Kennedy. The United States was still the great symbol of hope to many anticolonialist revolutionaries, including Sékou Touré, who helped liberate Guinea from France, and who admired my brother; and Kwame Nkrumah, the brilliant prime minister of Ghana, author of the "Motion of Destiny" manifesto, leader of the Pan-African movement, soon to form bonds with Martin Luther King and President Kennedy.

I briefed the president-elect upon my return. I must say that my notes didn't provide the impact of our previous conversation about Algeria. But Jack was already ahead of the curve, on Africa and India as well. He believed that these areas would be the great testing grounds for whether democracy or communism would supplant the colonial powers.

In January 1961, Joan, Kara, and I moved to Boston, as Jack had suggested. Joan had found a small apartment on the top floor of a building in Louisburg Square on Beacon Hill. It was a wonderful little neighborhood. William Dean Howells had lived there while editor of the *Atlantic* in the 1870s. Louisa May Alcott had called it home.

Joan and I traveled to Washington to be there for Jack's inauguration. My parents had rented a house for the festivities, and we stayed with them. A day before the actual swearing in, an enormous snowstorm had hit Washington and the city was blanketed with snow. Unlike Boston, which is accustomed to clearing the streets and handling large snowfalls, Washington has less equipment to deal with snow removal and its drivers often are not proficient in maneuvering in wintry conditions. As a result, on the morning of my brother's inauguration, we almost didn't make it to the Capitol for the ceremony.

As we left my parents' rented house and piled into the cars that were to take us to the Hill, we were filled with joy and anticipation. The temperature was still quite low and everything was icy, but it was no longer snowing. As our driver tried to pull out of his parking place, we heard nothing but the sound of the engine and the whirring of the tires as they spun around and around. He tried again and again, but simply was unable to get traction on the ice and snow. None of us was happy, but my father was furious. "Hurry up. We're going to be late," he shouted. But we were stuck. Finally, my father decided to take things into his own hands. I can still see him getting out of the car in his full dress clothes, shouting and gesturing at the driver and directing him on how to turn the wheel, how to back up, move forward, while Dad finally just pushed the car, providing the necessary muscle to power the vehicle out of the parking spot. It was classic Joe Kennedy: take charge and do it right, even if it means having to do it yourself. We made it to the inauguration.

As we sat on the east side of the Capitol—until Ronald Reagan, all of the inaugurations took place on that side—we were all overwhelmed with emotion. Here we were, at the beginning of this new decade, with nothing but hope and promise ahead of us. I remember saying a silent prayer for my brother and for our country. The older brother and godfather that I had revered for my whole life, the war hero who had sneaked my twelve-year-old self aboard a navy vessel, the older, wiser brother who persuaded a young adolescent not to run away from home, the second father who had interceded when his boneheaded kid brother had screwed up at Harvard, the man I loved so deeply and had worked so hard to elect was going to be the president of the United States. At noon on the sunny, frigid Friday of January 20, 1961, my brother John F. Kennedy was inaugurated as our thirty-fifth president.

Later that same day, Jack announced his cabinet. His choice of Bobby for attorney general ignited controversy and charges of nepotism from press and party leaders alike. Jack had first offered the position to Senator Abraham Ribicoff, but he declined. Ultimately, against the counsel of his political advisers, Jack decided he wanted his brother by his side. Bobby was reluctant, but Jack and Dad (an advocate of the idea from the start) persuaded him.

The renewed bond of comradeship and trust that Bobby and Jack had forged on that seven-week tour of the East had taken deep roots. Bobby enjoyed his unqualified access to President Kennedy in moments of national and international crisis, and his counsel led to light in the darkness when even the judgments of generals and career diplomats proved inadequate to the task.

Jack learned to value Bobby's advice above all others the hard way. The first crisis of his administration that flowed from an act of aggression advocated by military minds was only weeks away.

Now it was time for me to get back to my own future in Massachusetts. Elective office had been on my mind as early as my days at Milton, where

I first learned debating. I even debated national health insurance there. I was interested in public issues by then, and I was interested in people, and everything around me—my family's civic concerns, my brothers' careers— reinforced those interests. But I had a lot of groundwork to do first. Jack counseled me to get around the state. He said he'd take some soundings to see how I was doing before he weighed in on whether or not I should think of running for the Senate in 1962. His advisers were to a person opposed to my running, but Jack wanted me to get out there to see if I had the stuff.

First, it was time to go to work. Shortly after the inauguration, I was sworn in as a dollar-a-year assistant district attorney in the office of legendary Suffolk County district attorney Garrett Byrne—the man who, among his many accomplishments, had won convictions in the million-dollar Brinks robbery several years earlier.

I vividly remember the first case I tried in Byrne's office. Now, to be totally candid, I've loved telling this story so much over the years that I've taken to "improving" it with a few flourishes and embellishments. But the essential facts are absolutely true.

I had been in the DA's office for just three days when I was handed my first file—prosecuting a fellow named Hennessy for driving under the influence. After attending a Red Sox–Yankees double-header at Fenway Park, the defendant had consumed twenty-six drinks at the Little Brown Jug and crashed his car into Kenmore Square. My assignment was to prosecute Hennessy for driving under the influence and to free the people of Suffolk County from this danger on the public roadways.

As I prepared for trial, I devoured all of Clarence Darrow's closing arguments. Even though he was a defense attorney and not a prosecutor, I was inspired by his eloquence and thought process.

On the day of the trial, I was ready. I had a bar bill showing that Hennessy had bought the twenty-six drinks. I had the waitress who was going to testify that she had served him those drinks, as well as the arresting officer, who was prepared to describe how Hennessy had fallen out of his car, glassy-eyed, and was unsteady on his feet.

Oh, yes, I was ready.

As I walked into the courtroom, I saw the clerk hand the case file to a defense attorney, who apparently was seeing it for the first time. I thought to myself, *Ha! This poor fellow doesn't have a chance.*

I put on my case and felt good about it. When it came time for the defense, they rested without putting on a single witness. They didn't offer anything until the closing argument, when the defense attorney stood up and said, "Hennessy over there has been working since he was twelve years old." Then the lawyer looked me up and down, and then the jury all looked at me. I thought, *What does that have to do with anything?* Then the lawyer said, "His principal crime is that he cheered for the Boston Red Sox." I saw the jury smile, every one of them. "And when the Red Sox beat the Yankees—in a double-header—who wouldn't want to celebrate!"

I thought, *Oh my God, what does this have to do with anything?*

The defender went on, "Hennessy is a carpenter, and if he's convicted today, he will lose his automobile license and won't be able to go from job to job. He's going to be on welfare, and he has seven children. It's going to cost the taxpayers of Suffolk County fifteen hundred dollars a month to support him if he's convicted." I thought I saw the jury looking at old Hennessy with sympathetic eyes. Then the lawyer said, "The defendant's name is *HENNESSY*." When he emphasized "Hennessy," half of the jury nodded their heads. Then he said, "My name is Bobby STANZIANI." And the other half of the jury nodded *their* heads. I knew it was all over.

Twenty-six minutes of deliberation. Not guilty!

I was a little more successful prosecuting armed robbery cases.

The people in the district attorney's office were great—and helpful. There was Jack Crimmins, who had been Paul Dever's driver when Dever was governor. He knew every road in Massachusetts. He was a great fellow. If he'd ever had an education, he'd have been president of a bank. We became good friends, and Jack would drive me around those roads as I got to know all of Massachusetts.

The cases in the DA's office lasted from ten till noon, and from two to four. Francis X. "Frank" Morrissey, a friend of my father's who had also been a great supporter of Jack's, would arrange for me to go to a different place each day after work, a social club or a lodge, and give a talk. There are hundreds of such clubs in Boston. Frank would drive. I'd talk about whatever came to mind—my trip to Africa, for instance; I could do forty-five minutes on that one, with slides. I thought I was getting to be quite the orator.

Then the president of the United States called me up and said, "I hear you're talking for a very long time. How long do you talk?" I said, "Forty minutes." Jack said, "If I can do the State of the Union in twenty-three minutes, you can do Africa in twenty-five."

I said I'd try.

Frank Morrissey introduced me to a dozen or so state representatives in Boston who became the backbone of the organization I was slowly forming. They widened the range of meetings I'd attend: Communion breakfasts on Sundays at any and every church I could get to. School dinners. I set up my office at the same old apartment at 122 Bowdoin Street that Jack had used in his campaign—and that was the registered voting address for so many of our family members. It was a small compressed place with a living room, kitchen, two bedrooms, and a bathroom, that we rented for $115 a month. When the landlord threatened to raise the rent to $125, I contemplated leaving. But I didn't. My brother stayed there one night when he was president-elect, before giving a talk to the Massachusetts legislature—he said he preferred it to a hotel.

I hired my first staff assistant, Barbara Souliotis, during that time, and she has been with me ever since. After all these years, I think Barbara can probably read my mind. Barbs has a knack for spotting and hiring talented staff members and she is beloved by our constituents. She's been called a role model for running a senator's district office. I did amazingly well in my first hire.

Perhaps the most satisfying part of this new phase of my life was that I received the full measure of my father's focus and advice. My mother writes of me in her memoir that "quite considerably more than the other three boys, he had the wonderful advantage of having sustained attention and influence from his father. . . . Joe spent a great deal more time with Ted than with the other boys, and that counted." This is true, and those times were golden to me, as when we rode horseback side by side. And yet I was a child then. I was legally an adult when I entered Harvard, but as my Spanish exam transgression showed, I had not yet put away my childish things. Now, less than a year from my thirtieth birthday, I approached my father as a man, and it was as a man that he accepted me.

In the springtime, weeks before I told him that I was privately planning to run for the Senate, I could not know for sure whether he would approve, or even think me a good fit for public office. But I had a helpful advocate in Frank Morrissey, who issued updates to Dad on my community efforts. With his gift of gab and way of "gilding the lily" on my Boston-area talks so that Dad would hear only positive things, Frank raised my approval rating with the only "constituency" who then counted. My father thought I was just on fire up there. I will never forget a pivotal conversation Dad and I had on the subject in the early summer of 1961. We were out on the boat off Hyannis Port, a couple of fellows enjoying the sunshine and the lazy roll of the boat against the blue waves. Dad was talking about Jack and Bobby, when abruptly he shifted the subject. He said, "Well, Teddy, now these boys are well set in terms of their political lives, and now it's your turn. I'll make sure they understand it."

This was a great uplift and a great thrill. I was privy to an extended seminar in Dad's extraordinary judgment. In his own way, he was as much a living encyclopedia as Honey Fitz had been. He still knew the names of people who had worked on the waterfront from years past. He knew the fishing industries. He knew the old families. He could say to Frank Morrissey, "Now, look, are the Fulhams still in the fishing business?" Frank would say, "Yes, John Fulham has taken that over." "Has he? Well, I knew his father. Have Fulham get some of those people in the industry together and have them meet Ted."

My father had a great sense of the city. He'd lived in East Boston and knew the people there. He had a good feel for the newspapers, especially the *Globe* and the *Traveler*. The *Globe* was the voice of White Anglo-Saxon Protestant Boston, and we could not assume any sympathy from its pages. The *Traveler*, the evening publication of the *Herald*, was ideologically conservative (as the *Herald* remains to this day, under Rupert Murdoch). But a man who was destined to become my lifelong friend and had been one of the paper's ace reporters became my press secretary. Edward T. Martin—Eddy—was Irish Catholic and a smart and fit product of East Boston, a marine veteran with a twinkle in his warm brown eyes. He'd covered Jack's early political career and his inauguration. His sharp wit coexisted with a political perception as sharp as that of anyone I've known, and a desire to do good in this world. Eddy died in 2006, and I still miss him.

One of the most interesting and inspiring things I worked on that year was the Cancer Crusade, where I joined with Dr. Sidney Farber, a pioneer in children's cancer research, and a Republican named Lloyd Waring. I learned so much from Dr. Farber. Our goal was to raise awareness about the disease and money for cancer research. We traveled around the state and I gave fund-raising talks to two or three audiences a night for two or three months. This experience was a cornerstone of my interest in health matters throughout my Senate career. And it was certainly an inspiration for my work years later to bolster federal funding for cancer research at the national level.

I was enjoying it all immensely. Politics and public service were in my blood. The euphoria of campaigning was almost an end in itself. I loved every corner of the state it took me to, and the people I met. I loved meeting with the students of Ware High School at nine o'clock on a cold January morning, with five more high schools still to visit before the day ended. I loved the tours of woolen factories and the people of the League of the Sacred Heart. I loved showing up at the plant gates, even when some of the workers brushed past me, ignoring my outstretched hand. I loved the summertime picnics all along Route 128, and the communion breakfasts.

I remember how moved I was at some of the plants and factories. I learned that West Virginia had no monopoly on squalor or hard labor. In some of the tanneries on the North Shore, I was advised to put covers on my shoes so the acid on the floor wouldn't take the soles off. In the shoe manufacturing plants, women and men would spend the day grabbing a length of leather and then bringing a heavy slammer down on it to shape it, or to punch eyeholes and buttonholes into it. I would walk down a line and find that many workers had lost two or three fingers. I met people who were too embarrassed to smile because their teeth were so damaged, because of what was in the water they drank.

But campaigning, of course, is hardly the whole of politics; it is merely prelude.

CHAPTER EIGHT

The New Frontier
1961–1962

Jack enjoyed being president. This was clear from talking to him, or just watching him. At the time of his election and the opening days of his presidency, he was the happiest that I'd ever seen him. For years he had been out campaigning constantly. Now he finally had the chance to do what he enjoyed best: to read and study and try to implement the ideas and programs that he'd always cared so deeply about.

I felt happy along with him, felt happy *being* with him, felt once again that old boyhood awe at being around him. It was like those days on the beach in Hyannis Port when Jack would bat a ball to me on a line like a thrown football and I'd race to catch it. Or that day I'd sailed for a few hours with him and his patrol torpedo crew. Or the times he'd enlist me as a prop in those congressional campaign luncheons. Or the time he persuaded me to come back home by telephone after I'd decided to run away—his concern for me wiping away whatever grievance I'd felt. Now we were men together, and Jack was president of the United States. Some of the happiest memories of my life are from those early, impossibly sunlit days I shared with him, when there seemed no limit to the splendid quests and triumphs that lay ahead.

Jack drew happiness as well from working with the people close to him: Powers and O'Donnell and Sorensen and Schlesinger and the rest—

certainly Bobby. These men identified themselves with the kind of nation he wanted America to be, and with the agenda he was creating to make that America a reality. He had full confidence in these close aides, and he felt that with their help he could make a really significant contribution as president.

The nation picked up on his mood. People were going about their lives with renewed vigor, taking (or trying) fifty-mile hikes and joining the Peace Corps. Jack gave me good counsel during his crowded daily routine. Even en route to the inauguration, he wanted to know how my plans were taking shape and what progress I was making. It was such an optimistic time for all of us, and for the country.

Since the end of World War II, the focus of American anxieties and the source of the cold war had been the prospect of globally ambitious communism, emanating chiefly from the Soviet Union. Thus it was that a Caribbean island of only forty-two thousand square miles proved the crucible in the early 1960s of America's reckoning with the communist threat, and with the prospect of nuclear war. As a Soviet proxy, Cuba came to enmesh itself in my brother's administration, and his destiny.

In February 1960, one year after Fidel Castro had overthrown the government of the corrupt dictator Fulgencio Batista, Cuba began shipping millions of tons of its most lucrative crop, sugar, to the Soviet Union in return for oil and grain. On May 8, its government established diplomatic relations with the Soviet Union.

Each of these moves accelerated the collision course of Castro's regime with American security interests. The president of the United States held the mandate to defend these interests, in ways accountable to the American public. But it was the State Department and the Central Intelligence Agency that shared the mandate to counter the threat to these interests. Their strategies—their de facto policies, which Jack would inherit from the Eisenhower administration—were not limited by accountability.

Within months of the coup, the CIA was monitoring Castro. The

State Department and the CIA gained Eisenhower's approval for a covert plan to support anti-Castro elements in Cuba. Eisenhower approved a CIA-drafted paper, "A Program of Covert Action Against the Castro Regime." Only a handful of State Department and CIA officials knew of it: Allen Dulles, director of the CIA; Richard M. Bissell Jr., Dulles's director for plans; and a few others.

On July 23, 1960, Allen Dulles briefed my brother, by then the Democratic nominee, at Hyannis Port, emphasizing the recruitment and training of Cuban exiles for operations against Castro. In November, Dulles handed the president-elect a copy of the covert action plan.

Cuba was not the only dot on the world map that was brewing trouble. At roughly the same time, another sliver of land in Southeast Asia was moving toward violent upheaval.

In 1949 France, which had held the southern third of Vietnam as a colony, permitted its unification with the central and northern regions. But old antagonisms persisted: Ho Chi Minh and the Viet Minh had declared a Democratic Republic of Vietnam before the French reestablished control. Ho's forces dealt a devastating military defeat to the French at Dien Bien Phu in 1954, and a debilitated France agreed that the communist Viet Minh would rule the South until elections could be held in 1956.

But the premier of the South, Ngo Dinh Diem, gambled that the United States, with its foreign-aid bounties and its phobia of communism, would provide deterrence to the North. He canceled the 1956 elections, kicked out the French military, and, with the help of his younger brother Ngo Dinh Nhu, rigged public opinion polls and elections. His armed followers decimated rival factions. He denounced communism loudly and repeatedly. And the American aid poured in.

In October 1955, Diem declared himself president of Vietnam. Resistance fighters assembled in the jungle and launched a murderous campaign of subversion that by 1959 had killed some twelve hundred government workers in the South. In December 1960, as Jack focused on absorbing the details of the plan to overthrow Castro, Ho Chi Minh took a giant step toward civil war against Diem: he sanctioned a resistance movement of several guerrilla groups that he dubbed the National Liberation Front. Jack, feeling his way through the opening weeks of his presidency, grew skeptical of the ever more ambitious and complex Cuba invasion plan. Bissell and others assured the president that the invading force (of some fifteen hundred Cuban expatriates) would overrun Castro's defenses (which eventually totaled twenty thousand); defections from Castro's army would follow; the population would rise up to embrace the invaders; and the hated regime would be ousted with minimal casualties. As history shows, the invasion was a failure, a serious one.

On Friday, April 21, President Kennedy stepped before the microphones at a press conference and accepted sole responsibility for the Bay of Pigs disaster: "There's an old saying that victory has a hundred fathers and defeat is an orphan." He added, "I am the responsible officer of the government." He never recanted that responsibility in public. But he privately, and bitterly, remarked to Ted Sorensen that he had placed too much faith in the CIA, State Department, and Pentagon men who sold the invasion to him. "You always assume," he said, "that the military and intelligence people have some secret skill not available to ordinary mortals."

Jack was very low, and Bobby knew just how to perk him up. "Let's call Dad. He always finds something positive in situations like this. Let's see what he has to say." Dad did not disappoint. "Jack, well done. Well done. You took responsibility. People like that in their leaders. Take my word for it. People like leaders who take responsibility." And then, with almost prophetic wisdom, our father told the president that "this is going to turn out to be one of the best things that ever happened to you."

Indeed, when our nation was faced with the Cuban Missile Crisis and the prospect of nuclear annihilation just eighteen months later, my brother's experience with the Bay of Pigs disaster *did* end up being one of the best things that ever happened to him—and to the country: it gave him a healthy skepticism about the military advice he was receiving, with the result being a peaceful solution to the nuclear showdown.

I found time in mid-July 1961 to launch an intense, self-financed month-long tour of several Latin American countries: Colombia, Chile, Costa Rica, Brazil, Panama, Argentina, Peru, Bolivia, and Mexico. Again, I was traveling both to bolster my own knowledge of political and economic trends in this area of the world, and to report back to the president, who was extremely interested in the region. In March, Jack had proposed a ten-year plan for economic aid, literacy education, social planning, and structures for democratic governments—his Alliance for Progress, an idea that had begun in the Eisenhower administration. It was soon to be ratified at a conference in Uruguay.

Discontent over wages, food, and living standards had begun to breed talk of revolution in some of these countries; guerrilla activity had commenced in Guatemala, and was brewing in Nicaragua. As had been the case in Africa, the specter of communism was distracting many American leaders from a clear analysis of human needs. It was these troubling movements and countermovements that President Kennedy wanted to neutralize with his Alliance vision.

The Castro fear was not entirely unjustified. I witnessed a powerful example of Cuba's influence as I visited small villages in Colombia and Venezuela. People in the region had devised an amazing bit of primitive technology: a can filled with kerosene, with a wick on top. When lit, the fuel burned at a rate just fast enough to power a small fan. The fans, in turn, generated enough electricity to power radios the size of a human fist. The radios pulled in one station: Havana. In the poorest of villages, listening to news from Cuba was a communal event. This moved me tremendously. To my mind, it was not an indication of communist passions. It was a cry for community. I was able to convey this sense of things to my brother. I believe it reinforced his determination to see the Alliance for Progress through.

I returned home in time to be present in Boston at the birth, on September 26, 1961, of our first son, Edward Moore Kennedy Jr. The joy and miracle of the birth of this child moved me beyond words. The love I felt for him that day has continued to multiply with each passing day since.

A little less than three months afterward, my world changed forever. On December 19, while Dad was playing golf in Florida, he suddenly grew weak. Cousin Ann Gargan, who was with him, drove him back to our home in Palm Beach, and from there he was taken by ambulance to a hospital. The diagnosis was severe: an intracranial thrombosis—a stroke—that paralyzed the right side of his seventy-three-year-old body.

All the family converged at his bedside. My mother went to the hospital immediately. Jack and Bobby flew down from Washington on Air Force One. Pat, Eunice, and Jean arrived.

I located a vascular specialist in Boston and persuaded him to fly to Florida with me, where I found my father conscious but near death. Pneumonia had set in, and last rites had been administered. All of us gathered for a vigil in Dad's room. I stayed there by his bedside for three days.

We learned that Dad would survive, but that he would probably never walk again. Worse, the brain hemorrhage had damaged the part of his brain that controlled his speech. He would be able to make sounds; but the familiar sharp, confident, Boston-inflected cadences that informed, inspired, cajoled, and instructed me—the voice that had read me the Sunday funnies in my early childhood and spoken for Roosevelt on the radio in 1940—was to be heard no more.

My father's illness hit me very hard. He had been so strong, so vital, so important in all our lives. And finally, for the first time in my life, the two of us had been together as men, sharing a common purpose. Now that aspect of our relationship was lost to me. It was almost more than I could bear.

There were some people around me who thought my political plans would end with Dad's illness. But that would have been at odds with everything Joe Kennedy believed in or that I had worked for. I would continue with my plans, but I had to be sure that even without Dad able to strategize with me, I would do it the right way. My close friend and brother-in-law Steve Smith made regular visits to Boston to help out. He made an enormous difference. And he gave reports to Jack and Bobby, who were following my progress very closely.

On Sunday, March 11, 1962, as rumors of my running escalated, I was scheduled to go on NBC's *Meet the Press*. I'd flown into Washington the previous Friday for a meeting with Jack in the White House. When I arrived, the president instructed his secretary Evelyn Lincoln, "Don't bother me for a while." Then he sat me down behind his desk and pretended to be Lawrence Spivak, the host of *Meet the Press*. He was very tough as he asked me questions about foreign and domestic policy, and he was not satisfied with my answers. "Well, we're going to have to sharpen these up a bit," he said as he called in Ted Sorensen and another aide, Meyer "Mike" Feldman. They peppered me for an hour and a half with the toughest questions I could possibly imagine. I was stunned. But they wouldn't let up. We went over and over possible questions and answers until we all started to feel pretty good. I learned something that day, and have followed that method of preparation for Sunday morning interview shows for all of my public life. It has generally served me fairly well.

On the morning of my *Meet the Press* appearance, Jack was down in Florida and watched the program from the Palm Beach house. Dave Powers tells the story of how my brother was so nervous that he kept walking in and out of the room, and at the end had to ask Dave how I did. Dave said I did fine. This wasn't enough for Jack. He phoned up Lawrence Spivak. I can only imagine what Spivak must have thought when he received a call from the president asking him how his kid brother did on the show. Spivak said, "He did just fine. I just never could get an answer out of him on this aid-to-education issue. I couldn't pin him down on whether he was for aid to Catholic schools or against it." Jack laughed and replied, "That's just fine, Larry. That's just where he ought to be."

I resigned my position as assistant district attorney and announced for the Senate three days after the broadcast. One of my most cherished possessions is a framed note from my sister-in-law Jackie that hangs on my wall at home:

> For Teddy
> Jack wrote this about you, and you know how proud and happy he was when you won.
> With love, Jackie

And along with that note is a press release drafted by the White House press office at the time of my announcement, with the president's handwritten changes to the draft.

Jack's press office thought he should release the following statement:

> The President has been advised of his brother's statement. The President's brother has made an independent decision to seek the Senate seat in Massachusetts. He has not sought the President's endorsement of his candidacy and he is not looking for the President's help in the campaign.

In other words, this guy is on his own! Here's how Jack edited it to read:

> The President of course knows of his brother's statement. His brother prefers that this matter be decided by the people of Massachusetts and that the President should not become involved. In response to this request, the White House will have no comment.

I walked in the St. Patrick's Day parade in Boston three days after my announcement. The crowds were jubilant and friendly, and I was starting to think that running for office was pretty grand sport, until I ran into my first opponent: myself.

I received a telephone call from Jack. "Teddy, I think it's good if we get that Harvard story out." For a moment I couldn't even think what he was talking about. I said, "What do you mean by that?!" Jack answered, "Get it out, the whole story, from beginning to end. Get it out in the early part of this campaign."

I thought, *How nice of* him *to think about this.* But Jack was right once again. Through an intermediary, our family furnished the details of the incident to Bob Healy at the *Globe.* Jack himself urged Healy to slip the cheating episode into the body of a longer profile on me. Healy refused to negotiate, and on Thursday, March 30, the *Globe* played the story on its front page.

I had a speaking engagement in Milford that night. The hall down there held about four hundred people. As I pulled into the parking lot I said to myself, *They've all read the* Globe. *I've got to go in there and face that crowd. This is going to be bad.*

I steeled myself as I walked into the hall, and once again was reminded of the basic decency of people. The crowd rose to its feet and began to cheer me. I cannot describe the feeling of uplift that I felt as I walked up to the podium. It seemed that the people in that room, at least, were willing to look beyond the stupid mistakes of a teenager. Under my breath, before I began my speech, I murmured, almost as if it were a prayer, *Maybe I can get through this after all.*

My main opponent in the primary was Eddie McCormack. (The Republican primary was dominated by familiar political names as well: H. Stuart Hughes, the grandson of presidential candidate Charles Evans Hughes, and George Cabot Lodge, son of Henry Cabot Lodge Jr.) I didn't know Eddie well, but I thought him intelligent and a good politician. He knew how to connect with people. For instance, if we made a joint appearance at a synagogue, Eddie would speak some Hebrew. He had run statewide before—he was the Commonwealth's attorney general—and he had a strong record on civil rights.

Neither the press nor academia—which still had a voice in public matters in those days—had yet accepted me. The *New York Times* columnist James "Scotty" Reston hammered at my presumption and inexperience, and the editorial page was scarcely more friendly. Vaguely scolding terms such as "dynasty" and "Kennedyism" were cropping up in press coverage, along with such questions as, "One too many?" My alma mater seemed almost to regret having given me a diploma. One law professor denounced me around the state as a "bumptious newcomer" and a "coattail candidate."

More than my own political future was riding on this campaign. Jack's advisers made no secret to me that if I lost, it would be a loss for all the Kennedys. We had more or less taken the nation by storm as a family, and the rejection of one of us in his home state would harm Jack's career.

Jack helped me, not publicly of course, but from behind the scenes. He organized a strategy session at the White House on April 27, with politicians and aides from all over Massachusetts flying in to brief him on how the candidates were viewed in the state. After that, full control shifted to Steve Smith, who proved nearly as masterful as Bobby at running a campaign. As Steve's staffers—many of them attorneys working without pay—fanned out across Massachusetts to organize support, I plunged back into the marathon round of travel and speechmaking that I'd experienced two years earlier. Only this time, I was speaking not for my brother, but for myself.

And I was having fun doing it. Back in my home state now, I could campaign the old-fashioned way, the Honey Fitz way, with marching bands, flags, drum majorettes, buttonholing people on the street. Once, as I strode the aisles of a textile machinery plant in Worcester, I spied a grimy, sweaty fellow and closed in on him with my hand outstretched. He pulled back, signaling to me that his own hand was too greasy. "Gimme that, buddy!" I yelled. I wore his worker's grime on my hand as a badge of honor the rest of the day.

Joan also visited countless women's club meetings and teas around the Commonwealth, charming audiences with her enthusiasm, her persuasiveness on my behalf, and with the home movies of our family that she liked to show.

As strange as it seems, this was really the first time in nearly four years of marriage that Joan and I were actually working together toward a goal that would affect *our* lives. Even so, our campaigning was frequently separate.

As I look back on this period of my life and at my marriage, I realize that Joan and I were young and naive about what it took to have a successful relationship. We certainly had not spent a lot of time together during our courtship, and we didn't spend the necessary time together in the early years. Almost immediately after the wedding celebrations were over, I plunged back into law school and the moot court competition, my travels, and campaign work for Jack. And so we never benefited from that critical but fleeting interval in which a young husband and wife get to know themselves and each other as a married couple.

Joan was bright and beautiful and talented. We shared the same religious faith. She was a graduate of the same Catholic college that my sisters and Mother had attended. We both had high expectations for a successful marriage. Sadly, that was not to be. Joan was private, contemplative, and artistic, while I was public, political, and on the go. We probably would have realized that we had fundamentally different temperaments if we had taken more time to get to know each other before we married, but we didn't want to wait. We thought we were in love. And I will grant that at the time I met her, I was keen to join my brothers as a married man, a family man. I certainly *wished* to be a family man. How could I not, given that "family" virtually defined my entire consciousness? Perhaps I'd assured myself that the core requirement in a marriage, compatibility, would develop naturally once the vows were exchanged.

My parents and siblings were well disposed toward Joan. Yet as time went on, the awareness deepened among all of us that something fundamental was not working right.

Our relationship atrophied. We remained together for many years longer than we were happy, but I don't think either of us seriously considered a divorce for most of those years. So many other things were going on in our lives, so many difficulties, so many tragedies, that breaking up our marriage just wasn't on the agenda. The reasons were many: our children, our faith, my career, and perhaps fear of change.

To compound our mutual unhappiness, as Joan herself has discussed publicly many times, she suffered with alcoholism. I myself drank too much at times and feel exceedingly lucky to have been spared addiction.

I do not blame Joan for the demise of our marriage. Nor do I agree with some of the accounts that she has given as to the reasons for its demise. I regret my failings and accept responsibility for them and will leave it at that.

In 1961, the worst of these troubles were still in the future. Joan, not yet twenty-five, did her best to be a mother and wife to an aspiring senator.

When I was able to get off the hustings, I'd immerse myself in long rounds of political "homework" assignments and quizzing. These were run by some of Jack's senior aides, and held mostly at the Cape house. The old house was buzzing.

By June, the time of the Democratic state convention, Steve Smith's groundwork had paid off. The party's endorsement was at stake, and our side had projected 1,196 of the 1,719 delegates. The roll call had given us 691 votes to McCormack's 360 when Eddie conceded the endorsement but demanded a primary contest in the fall, which he had a right to do. The primary contest led naturally to debates. Eddie and I had two of them, but the first was probably decisive. It was held on August 27 at South Boston High School, and carried on radio and television.

I'd flattered myself that I was a pretty good debater based on my training at Harvard and in moot court at the University of Virginia. But I was hardly ready for the ferocity of McCormack's attack. "You never worked for a living," McCormack began railing at me as he pointed a finger in my direction. "You never held elective office. You are not running on qualifications. You are running on a slogan, 'He can do more for Massachusetts.'

That is the most insulting slogan I have ever seen. It says, 'Vote for this man because he has influence, connections, relatives.'"

And this, mind you, was only in Eddie's opening statement.

As the debate went along, he dropped such insinuations as, "We need a senator with experience, not arrogance," and, "The office of United States senator should be merited and not inherited." He mocked my trips to Europe. He mentioned that I had once been arrested in Pamplona for throwing a cushion into the bullring, and was held for six or seven hours. (This happened to be true. In my defense, I will say that it was a terrible bullfight and everyone was throwing cushions.) It struck me later that the likely way Eddie could have obtained this information was through the CIA or Henry Cabot Lodge.

The papers later said my voice shook as I spoke. But I refrained from firing back at Eddie on the same level of hostility and personal attack. Instead, I emphasized the sincerity of my claim that I could help the people of Massachusetts, and the similarity of my political philosophies to those of Jack.

At the end, Eddie McCormack could not stop himself from one last ad hominem jab. "If his name was [simply] Edward Moore," he said, pointing at me again, "his candidacy would be a joke. Nobody is laughing. Your name"—turning to me—"is Edward Moore Kennedy."

I was seething, not least because of the insult to a good and decent man, Eddie Moore. Joan and I returned home—by this time we were living at 3 Charles River Square—shaken, and not knowing whether my candidacy was finished. I called his widow, Mary Moore, to apologize that Eddie's name was dragged through the mud because of me. The living room was quiet for about forty-five minutes. And then, close to midnight, the telephone began to ring, and it kept on ringing, call after call. People were telling us that although the TV newscasts had Eddie "blasting" me, the late-night talk shows struck a different sentiment from the callers. People felt that Eddie had overdone it, and they admired my restraint.

One of the calls was from the president. Jack had been so nervous he could not sit still and watch the debate. He'd asked others about it, and they'd said I held my own.

And I suppose I had. Viewers and listeners seemed to see my restraint as a virtue, a sign of dignity. And they felt Eddie had gone too far. The next morning, I was out meeting and greeting voters when a laborer came up to me and said, "Hey, Kennedy. They say you haven't worked a day in your life." Then he stuck out his right hand and clapped me on the back with his left, saying, "Lemme tell you. You haven't missed a thing!"

Eddie and I had one other debate, and it was pretty mild. Perhaps his advisers had suggested that he try a little restraint and dignity himself. It was too late, though. On primary night, the numbers were Edward Kennedy 73 percent of the vote, and Edward McCormack 27 percent.

I will always remember that evening as being enormously exciting, but also incredibly sad. The exciting part was the victory. A malfunctioning ballot box up in Salem gave us an early tip-off about the outcome: when workers opened it so they could repair it, they could see that I was winning by 60–40, and transmitted the news down to the Cape. That put everyone in festive spirits. But later that evening, my father suffered his second stroke. I canceled all the television appearances and spent time with him in the hospital. That November, I made my father proud in the best way I knew: I defeated the Republican George Cabot Lodge, by 53 percent to 44. The next day, I was sworn in as a senator.

CHAPTER NINE

Drinks with the Senator
1962

I arrived in Washington to begin my Senate career on November 7, 1962, the day after being elected. Given that I was technically filling out the last two years of Jack's unexpired term, the appointed Benjamin Smith having stepped aside, we did not wait until the new Congress began on January 3, 1963—although I was sworn in on that date too, along with the other incoming senators, including Daniel Inouye of Hawaii, with whom I still serve. The press was enormously interested in this event. I was nearly blocked by them from coming over to the Capitol from my hotel on Massachusetts Avenue. Lyndon Johnson performed the ceremony in the Senate gallery as Joan and my sisters and parents looked on from the seats.

As proud as I was of this personal milestone, I was also proud of what the 1962 midterm elections affirmed for my party and my brothers. President Kennedy and his attorney general, Robert Kennedy, had just averted nuclear war with Russia. The Soviet atomic missiles secretly installed on Cuban soil earlier that year would not, as the world had feared little more than a week earlier, be unloosed upon American cities. The most dangerous thirteen days in history had ended: thirteen days of a superpower standoff in which millions gathered silently to watch the news in fear.

Those thirteen days ended with a peaceful agreement on October 28. Some credit could be claimed by the Soviet premier Nikita Khrushchev, but most of it was due to my brothers: to their intertwined judgment, their moral and psychological acuity, and their resistance to the panic-driven pressuring of generals and cabinet members to strike, lest we be struck. Instead, the Kennedy administration ordered a naval blockade of Cuba and secretly promised to satisfy some Soviet demands. It worked.

The resolution of the Cuban Missile Crisis brought exhilaration and a wave of renewed support for the New Frontier. On November 6, voters had turned out in record numbers. The morning headlines announced "a remarkable success" for the Democrats, as Tom Wicker in the *New York Times* put it: a gain of four seats in the Senate, minimal losses in the House, and gubernatorial victories highlighted by Edmund G. "Pat" Brown's surprise victory in California over Richard Nixon. It was all the more remarkable given that a new president's party nearly always suffers reversals at midterm.

The voters understood that devastating warfare had been averted by temperate statecraft. Dad had been right in his consoling remark to Jack after the Bay of Pigs, when he'd said that this was going to be one of the best things that ever happened to him.

I had followed the crisis from a distance. I learned of it along with millions of others on my car radio on Monday night, October 22. I'd been campaigning outside Boston, debating with Lodge at a service club, I believe; and was driving home when I heard Jack's voice informing the nation of a "secret, swift, and extraordinary buildup of communist missiles" on Fidel Castro's island and announcing a "strict quarantine" of military equipment being shipped to Cuba. The deadly game was then actually at its midpoint, but Jack's address marked its disclosure to the world.

After detailing the rest of his seven steps in response, the president shifted directions and spoke to "the captive people of Cuba" themselves. (A special radio hookup was beaming the broadcast into homes on the island.) "I speak to you as a friend, as one who knows of your deep attachment to your fatherland," Jack told them, and voiced sympathy that their revolution had been betrayed by Castro, whom he did not name. The

United States, he assured Cubans, had "no wish to cause you to suffer or to impose any system upon you."

As Jack spoke, I was driving along Stonington Street in North Andover. I veered into a parking space outside a coffee shop, ran inside, and dialed the White House from a pay telephone in hopes of getting through to my brother. I reached a National Security Council member who told me, reasonably, that President Kennedy was unable to talk just now. This person did assure me that the crisis was as grave as the president had said it was, and I continued home to Joan with my mind churning. I reached Jack the next morning. He told me the outcome was still far from certain, and that he could not discuss any details over the phone. I understood.

I'd prepared a statement of my own on Cuba, but Jack's advisers asked me not to deliver it. With less than two weeks until the election, I figuratively paced the sidelines as my brothers and Nikita Khrushchev played out the fate of the world.

I still chuckle when I recall that even my *mother* was more involved in the Cuban Missile Crisis than I—although not in a way that Jack especially appreciated.

At the height of the standoff, when nuclear warfare remained a live option on both sides, the head of the KGB in Moscow burst through the door of Khrushchev's office. He carried a letter to the Soviet premier from one Rose Fitzgerald Kennedy of Hyannis Port and Palm Beach. Mrs. Kennedy wanted the premier to autograph some of his books and send them to her.

The transatlantic cables hummed with this baffling new development. When Jack found out about it, he called up our mother and demanded, "What in the world are you *doing*?!" Rose assumed that Jack knew very well what she was doing. Each Christmas, Mother made it a practice to give her children books signed by heads of state. This year, it was Mr. Khrushchev's turn, and she had methodically forged ahead according to her schedule.

"The Russians won't assume this is innocent!" Jack sputtered. "They'll give it some interpretation! Now I have to get my CIA people speculating on what that interpretation might be! The strengths! The weaknesses! The contingencies!"

The kicker is that, after the threat of World War III had been defused, Khrushchev did send Mother the autographed books.

As I began to feel my way in the Senate, I was helped by Jack's counsel. One useful piece of advice was about committees: "Take whatever they assign you; don't depend on me for a recommendation. If I get into it and you don't get the committee, that'll reflect on me." I said that was fine.

Jack also suggested that I attend the prayer breakfasts. "That's the inner sanctum of the Senate," he said, "and you ought to go on down there." And so I did, every Wednesday morning. There were about twelve or fifteen regulars—Republicans and Democrats both, but a force unto themselves. When a measure came up for a vote, unless it was an especially partisan bill, these men would generally vote together. Jack was right: they were a power clique, one of the many that I soon discovered.

The prayer breakfasts were fascinating, and Jack always wanted me to regale him with who was there and what got said. A new member got carefully scrutinized at them. The first or second time I showed up, the scrutinizer was none less than Richard Russell Jr., the powerful senator from Georgia. His statue now stands in front of the Senate office building named after him.

Senator Russell asked me to say the blessing. All eyes turned to me. Being a Catholic, I was not exactly steeped in biblical verse. I thought fast, and gave the Catholic grace before meals. It's a pretty short grace, and when I finished it the other breakfast attendees were still looking at me expectantly. I darted my eyes at them, and then said the after-meal grace. More silence. I repeated the two graces, then resolutely sat down. They seemed satisfied. Jack roared at that story.

He roared even louder the next week when I repeated a yarn about Pharaoh's daughter as spun out by Senator Willis Robertson of Virginia—

the father of the TV evangelist Pat Robertson. It more or less went this way:

"Now, the Pharaoh's daughter, she was out one morning in Egypt, just walking along the river, and she looked down in those bulrushes. And in those bulrushes she saw this little baby in a kind of a little cradle, a little boat. So she leaned down there and pulled that baby out of those bulrushes. She walked back to the Pharaoh, and she said, 'Pharaoh, I've got this baby. I found him down in the bulrushes.'

"Of course, that's what *she* said. That's how she said she got that baby. You and I know where that baby came from that she said she found in the bulrushes."

Not long after that, I walked into a Senate debate and listened to Senator Robertson speak very ardently in favor of a certain bill—the content of it eludes me now. The time for the roll call came. Impressed with the Virginia senator's passion, I cast an "aye" vote when my turn came. When the call got to Robertson, he voted "no."

I couldn't believe my ears. I went up to him afterward and said, "Senator, I just listened to your speech on this issue, and you spoke strongly in favor of it. Then you voted 'no.' I'm confused." Robertson smiled at me. "Well, Senator," he said, "in my state, the people are evenly divided on this bill. To those who favor it, I send my speech. To those who are opposed, I send my vote."

"Thank you very much," I said to him. As I walked away, I added to myself, "I think I might be able to make it here after all."

As for the committee assignments, I knew who it was I needed to go to. Senator James O. Eastland of Mississippi was chairman of the Senate Judiciary Committee, but this does not begin to express this man's influence on Capitol Hill. He'd served continuously in the Senate for nineteen years by then (after a brief stint in 1941), and would continue until his resignation in 1978 as the body's senior member. Power flowed through him and a handful of other senators, mostly southern, such as Richard

Russell of Georgia, Strom Thurmond of South Carolina, and Eastland's fellow Mississippian John Stennis. These senators were bright men, masters of procedure, and—perhaps with the exception of Thurmond—shapers of valuable legislation, in such areas as defense, agriculture, and the refurbishing of the navy. They were also segregationists to a man, although in some cases they moderated their views with the changing times.

The remarkable thing about Eastland—one of many remarkable things—was that he held his power despite being rather detached from the full life of the Senate. If you were to visit his office during the day, more often than not you would find his desk covered with oil maps. There would be oilmen in there, from Mississippi and the Gulf areas, and they'd all be bent over these maps absorbed in oil deals that they were working out. These oil meetings would go on for the better part of the week. Everything that happened on that committee, in fact, happened after 5 p.m. That's when Eastland would invite his people in for a drink. Everett Dirksen of Illinois would come in and drink with him, and Richard Russell, and Hugh Scott of Pennsylvania. John McClellan of Arkansas would stop in, but he didn't drink.

These men had little use for other committee members—people such as Charles "Mac" Mathias of Maryland, or Phil Hart of Michigan, whom I've always thought of as the conscience of the Senate at that time. It was Eastland and his reliable Old Bulls, conservatives from both parties. They knew they had the votes, and so they worked on what interested them the most: deciding which judges would get appointments and which wouldn't. They controlled Judiciary as a sort of fiefdom.

Eastland's racial views posed a moral problem for me. Civil rights became one of the defining causes of my career. How could I seek guidance, or cooperate in any way, with a proponent of segregation?

My decision regarding Eastland—in fact, my abiding impulse to reach across lines of division during my career—took strength from the concluding phrase of Lincoln's first inaugural address, on the eve of the Civil War. I decided to put faith in "the better angels of our nature." I worked with James Eastland; in fact, the two of us became friends. Then and always, I would work with anyone whose philosophies differed from mine as long as the issue at hand promoted the welfare of the people, and I would continue to await those better angels, and to remain confident in ultimate justice.

When I called on Senator James O. Eastland in his office to seek committee assignments, he rose and greeted me cordially: a tall, moon-faced man with a penetrating squint behind his dark-rimmed glasses and a resolute set to his mouth. I told him the reason for my visit, and he said, "Well, you take the weekend and figure out which committees you want to go on." I said that would be fine, and excused myself to consult with my staff.

My "staff," by the way, consisted of one administrative assistant and one legislative assistant. That's a telling figure, one of many, as one reflects on how the U.S. Senate has changed over the past half century. These days, most senators have staffs of at least fifty, including legislative directors, staff assistants, researchers, and press secretaries. I spent the weekend talking to trusted intimates, mostly Jack, about my committee preferences. We narrowed my interests to constitutional rights, civil rights, criminal law, immigration and refugees, antitrust, and perhaps one or two others. None of these seemed especially likely. The following Tuesday, the phone in my office rang, and my education in the ways of the Senate reached another colorful plateau.

"Chairman Eastland wants to see you now," the voice on the other end said.

"Now?" I replied. There seemed to be no ambiguity. I hurried over to his office.

This time, the senator's greeting was, "Do you drink bourbon or scotch?" I had not prepared myself for that particular query, but I blurted, "Scotch." Eastland summoned an aide, who brought in a tray of ice. He then placed a bottle of scotch on the table for me, and a bottle of bourbon for himself. The aide put ice in my glass, then poured scotch over the ice, and added some water. Not enough water, I thought.

"Now, I think I know what you want," said Eastland as he leaned back and swirled his drink. "Let me see if I'm right. You've got a lot of Eye-talians up there in Boston, don't you?"

Before I could answer, he went on, "You've got a lot of Eye-talians. Now, the Kennedys are always talking about immigration and always talking about Eye-talians and this kind of thing. You drink that drink there, and you're on the immigration committee."

I managed something like, "Oh, gee, that sounds great," and raised my glass. Even before I sipped, I could tell that it had the power to curl my hair. I noticed that Eastland had gotten up from his desk and crossed the office to fiddle with something. I quickly poured half my drink into some potted plants near his desk and swallowed the remainder.

Eastland returned, eyed my glass suspiciously, dropped some more ice in it, and said, "Now you have to decide that second committee." He sat down and reflected a moment. Then he filled my glass with scotch again and said, "You Kennedys always care about the Negras. Always hear about you caring about those. You finish that off, and you're on the civil rights subcommittee."

"I am?" I said. The glass in my hand looked more like a vase. But I had to give the senator credit: without even consulting me, he was two for two on my preferences. Before I could take another belt, Eastland had crossed the room again. In retrospect, he was perhaps giving me the chance to fudge my intake a little. Once again, I poured some into the potted plants and downed what was left as Eastland returned.

"Now I s'pose we have to fix you up with a third committee," he drawled. "Not a lot of people want a third committee, but I think you're always caring about the, you know, Cons'tution. Kennedys always talk about the Cons'tution. You finish that, and I'll put you on the Cons'tution subcommittee."

This was amazing. I hadn't dared hope for this level of accommodation from the senator. I began to settle into our conversation. When I checked my wristwatch sometime later, I saw that I'd been inside Eastland's office for an hour and fifty minutes. It was just coming up on noon. Both the plants and I were well lubricated.

I thanked the senator for his help, lurched out of my chair, and made it back toward my office. I found about forty people from Massachusetts outside, waiting to greet their new senator, who was weaving a bit and reeking of alcohol. The people were looking at me strangely.

"I was just, ah, getting my committee assignments," I told them.

CHAPTER TEN

1963

I badly wanted to add my voice to the issues in the headlines, but I knew it was too soon. I first needed to establish my legitimacy as a lawmaker worthy of this office, and erase the perception that I was merely the president's little brother. Building a record of independent achievement and judgment would require time and patience. My core obligation was to Massachusetts, its people, and their interests. I would focus on this obligation while I continued to study the Senate as an institution and learn its folkways.

My interest in Massachusetts is not simply or even primarily strategic. The state and the city of my birth are extensions of myself and my family. From my Boston office on the twenty-fourth floor of the John F. Kennedy Federal Building, I can look out the window next to my desk and see the lines wending across space and time. I can see where my grandfather was born, and the house where my mother was born on Garden Court Street. But for a few buildings I could see where my father was born on Meridian Street in East Boston. And as I look out at Boston Harbor, I see where all eight of my great-grandparents arrived from Ireland and walked up the Golden Steps and into the hope and promise that is America.

When I arrived in Washington, I studied the Senate. I read its history.

I worked hard to keep abreast of concerns that would make a difference in the lives of everyday people, like those back home.

So many of the events of 1963, both grave and trivial, are burned into my memory. For the exact dates of some of them, I have needed to consult the records. Taken as a whole, they contribute to the mosaic of America in the year that everything changed.

The issue of civil rights for African Americans was continuing to press forward. Yet some, like Governor George Wallace of Alabama, were determined to fight against it for as long as possible. Upon being sworn in at the State House in Montgomery, where Jefferson Davis had been inaugurated president of the Confederacy 102 years earlier, Wallace declared, "Segregation now, segregation tomorrow, segregation forever!"

On April 3, the Reverend Dr. King began his campaign of nonviolent protests in Birmingham with peaceful "sit-ins" at segregated restaurants. Nine days later, on Good Friday, Police Chief Bull Connor arrested King, the latter knowing full well he was violating an injunction against protests. Shortly thereafter, Connor unleashed his Dobermans and electric cattle prods on the demonstrators in the streets, escalating the brutality again in early May by knocking Negro schoolchildren off their feet with spray from fire hoses. Firebombings began, as well as rioting.

On June 11, my brother had to federalize National Guard troops, which in turn had to push aside Governor Wallace from an entrance to the University of Alabama at Tuscaloosa to permit the lawful entry of two Negro students. In the evening, Jack gave a nationally televised speech in which he set out his views on the crisis. His speech was historic and went further than any president before him in laying out the moral issues at stake, and it laid the groundwork for the Civil Rights Act of 1964.

"We are confronted primarily with a moral issue. It is as old as the Scriptures and is as clear as the American Constitution . . . whether we are going to treat our fellow Americans as we want to be treated."

He asked citizens to search their consciences: "If an American, because his skin is dark, cannot eat lunch in a restaurant open to the public, if he cannot send his children to the best public school available, if he cannot vote for the public officials who will represent him . . . who among us would then be content with the counsels of patience and delay?"

He pledged that he would ask Congress to make a commitment to "the proposition that race has no place in American life or law." It was the most powerful statement my brother had yet given on civil rights.

A little over two weeks later, on June 26, 1963, after a visit to the wall that the Soviets had erected to pen in those who would flee from communist control, President Kennedy stood in the Rudolph Wilde Platz in West Berlin to address a cheering crowd of at least 150,000. A fortnight earlier, he had told the American people in a different context that "this nation, for all its hopes and all its boasts, will not be fully free until all its citizens are free." Echoing those sentiments, he told the people of Berlin, "Freedom is indivisible, and when one man is enslaved, all are not free."

He continued:

> When all are free, then we can look forward to that day when this city will be joined as one and this country and this great Continent of Europe in a peaceful and hopeful globe. When that day finally comes, as it will, the people of West Berlin can take sober satisfaction in the fact that they were in the front lines for almost two decades.
>
> All free men, wherever they may live, are citizens of Berlin, and, therefore, as a free man, I take pride in the words "Ich bin ein Berliner."

I believe it was one of the finest speeches my brother ever gave. He inspired hope in an oppressed people. He delivered a message about the need for all men to be free that was consistent at home and abroad. And although he was a realist about the time it would take and the work that had to be done to achieve his vision of freedom and equality, he understood the importance of building alliances, challenging the best in people, and sowing goodwill.

On that same trip, President Kennedy made his first and last visit to Ireland, a time he often described as the happiest of his presidency. Jean, the future ambassador to Ireland, and Eunice accompanied him, along with Dave Powers and Larry O'Brien. He said on one of his stops, "When my great-grandfather left here to become a cooper in East Boston, he carried nothing with him except two things: a strong religious faith and a strong desire for liberty. I am glad to say that all of his great-grandchildren have valued that inheritance." As in so many things, I agree with my brother completely.

When he left Ireland, so moved by the reception and filled with love of his ancestral home, he told the Irish people, "I certainly will come back in the springtime."

On August 7, not quite eight months pregnant and feeling unexpected labor pains, Jackie telephoned for medical help from the Hyannis Port house and was rushed by helicopter to the Otis Air Force Base hospital in Falmouth. There, shortly after noon, Patrick Bouvier Kennedy was born via cesarean section. Bobby telephoned me the following night to report that the infant was in critical condition and that I had better get to Otis. At around four the next morning, before I was able to leave, Dave Powers called me with the news that Patrick had died. The cause was hyaline membrane disease, better known today as respiratory distress syndrome.

Jack met me at the hospital. On our way to Jackie's room, he emphasized the importance of keeping his wife's spirits up. I stayed with the two of them for an hour. It was evident that each was trying to bolster the spirits of the other.

Jack kept stoic about his loss, but those of us closest to him could see how he suffered. When he and Jackie returned to the Cape, Jack invited me over for a swim. He had John Jr. with him, and as we swam and then walked on the beach, Jack was absorbed in everything that his small son was doing. In the few months left to him, my brother showed an even greater preoccupation with the activities of his son and daughter than I had seen before. And he was concerned for Jackie, who took this loss as a tremendous blow. Over these months of diplomatic crisis, pivotal legislation, and cross-country travel, Jack's greatest concern was for his wife's and children's welfare.

On August 9, the day of the infant Patrick's death, President Kennedy set aside his anguish long enough to confer honorary U.S. citizenship on Winston Churchill. My brother honored the British statesman, absent from the ceremony because of infirmities, with his stirring remarks: "In the dark days and darker nights, when England stood alone, and all save Englishmen despaired of England's life, he mobilized the English language and sent it into battle."

Late August brought the March on Washington, nearly three hundred thousand demonstrators, mostly but not exclusively black, from across the United States. The March on Washington for Jobs and Freedom had been organized by the most illustrious civil rights leaders of that era. A. Philip Randolph, president of the International Brotherhood of Sleeping Car Porters, who had nearly brought off a similar event in 1941, conceived the idea. The planners included Dr. King; the elder statesman of the movement Bayard Rustin; John Lewis of the Student Nonviolent Coordinating Committee; Roy Wilkins of the NAACP; James Farmer of CORE; and Whitney Young of the National Urban League.

The general purpose of the march was to promote racial equality, but that message did not mean the same thing to all people. Most of the marchers supported the president's proposed civil rights legislation, but some were angry that it didn't go far enough. Malcolm X had declared the entire thing a farce and threatened to kick out any member of the Nation of Islam who attended. And to top it all off, the Ku Klux Klan and the American Nazi Party were expected to show up.

I had talked to the president about going down for it, but Jack thought that my presence might be counterproductive. I didn't want to be the catalyst that set things off between those who supported the legislation and those who thought it didn't go far enough. Violence was a concern, and Jack advised me to wait and see how things developed.

I still wanted to attend, however, and wrestled with the decision up until August 28, the day of the march. Jack thought that I should be in my office to greet any of the people who might come there, and in the end that's what I did. Still, I managed to slip out of the Capitol at one point, unnoticed and alone, and make my way to the Reflecting Pool, which seemed to be surrounded by thousands of people. It was an awesome sight. I walked back to my office and watched the speeches on television. That is where I saw Dr. King rise to deliver his prepared remarks about Negro suffering and aspirations for freedom. (As I learned later, leaders of the march had agreed with law enforcement officials that a longer speech with passionate rhetoric could conceivably trigger a riot in the nation's capital.)

I listened to those remarks and watched as Dr. King finished and turned to sit down and then abruptly turned back to the crowd. Although I could not distinguish her, and her voice was not picked up by the microphones, the great gospel singer Mahalia Jackson had blurted out to Dr. King from behind him, "Tell them about your dream, Martin! Tell them about the dream!" And Martin Luther King did. In a decade in which cataclysmic events inspired lasting oratory, the Georgia-born minister spontaneously delivered the great aria of the civil rights movement.

I was riveted, listening to the amplified cadences that echoed into my ears and into history. And if I hadn't been before, from Grampa's lessons of discrimination, from my own awakening to the plight of African Americans in our own nation, I was, that day in Washington, D.C., fully baptized into the civil rights movement. The Reverend Dr. Martin Luther King Jr. had spoken of his dream that had become my own.

Through all the turmoil of 1963, the swelling crises in South Vietnam and the American South, and through his own and Jackie's deep sorrows over the loss of Patrick Bouvier Kennedy, Jack kept touch with his capacity for playfulness and laughter. His laughter was a gift—to him, but also to all of us around him. His laughter is among the things I miss the most about him to this day.

He enjoyed guiding me through my initial months in the Senate, and his enjoyment continued through that summer. He knew all of my colleagues very well; he understood them, and when he heard reactions and reports from them about me, he would let me know what they said. On some evenings he would call me at my Senate office, often on short notice, and say he was going down for a swim; would I like to join him? We'd wind up our swim at around 8 p.m., and then talk until perhaps nine. Afterward, we'd go up to the small dining room in his living quarters and there would be a dinner prepared in the oven, and not another soul present. The table would be set, and then maybe Dave Powers or another of his friends would drop by and we'd dine. Jack would continue the conversation until ten or ten-thirty, when he'd retire to his room and start to read through reports before going to sleep.

Other times, Jack would call me just to come over and smoke a cigar with him on the balcony. He'd sit in his rocking chair, holding a cigar that he didn't pay much attention to after it was lit, and ask me questions about my colleagues. He, of course, knew them much better than I did, and I learned a lot from his queries. But mostly I just enjoyed the camaraderie of being with my brother.

When I say that the president knew and understood my colleagues very well, I am understating the case. Jack's perception of senators and congressmen, especially the key ones, was extraordinary. One Christmas Eve, before I was in the Senate, the two of us had been together in Palm Beach. We'd just been for a swim, and as we were changing clothes we fell into a discussion about one of Jack's favorite topics, the Civil War. We were trying to recall the name of a famous battle fought in 1863, in which the Confederate forces halted a Union advance into Georgia at a terrible cost of lives on both sides. The battle's name was an Indian one, and Jack, for the life of him, couldn't recall it. Neither could I.

"Dick Russell will know the answer," Jack said. He meant of course

Senator Richard Russell of Georgia, who was then chairman of the Armed Services Committee. "You're going to call up Richard Russell on Christmas Eve and ask him about a Civil War battle?" I asked. Jack nodded.

"Where are you even going to find him?"

"In his office," Jack answered matter-of-factly. He called the Capitol operator and asked to be put through to Senator Russell's office. "It's Christmas Eve, sir. Shouldn't I try him at home first?" No, my brother assured her, he really did mean the office. Of course, he was right.

Russell came on the line. "That's Chickamauga you're talkin' about," he told Jack. And proceeded to give him a detailed account of the three-day battle. There was some friendly dispute between them over which side actually won.

"How the hell," I asked Jack when he'd hung up, "did you know that Richard Russell was going to be in his Senate office on Christmas Eve?" Jack just smiled.

In summers, we'd often transport our get-togethers to the Cape. Our father especially enjoyed these times. On weekends, we would all go over to the house that Jack and Jackie had leased on the nearby section of oceanfront known as Squaw Island. (Joan and I had purchased a house there in 1961.) The early evenings were devoted to Caroline and John, who in 1963 were five and two. No matter who his guests were, Jack reserved that time of day for his children. He would tell them stories and listen to theirs. They liked to hear about his experiences flying in airplanes and traveling on boats, and about their favorite animals.

Our father got great satisfaction out of seeing Jack play with his children. It touched something deep in him. How deep, we learned not long before he suffered his first stroke. This was on a misty day in the spring of 1961, just before Jack flew off to Vienna for his summit with Khrushchev.

We were at Jack's house next door to our parents'. McGeorge Bundy, who had helped plan the invasion of Europe in World War II and now was Jack's adviser on national security affairs, had come along with us, probably to give the president last-minute advice and preparation for the consequential summit with Khrushchev.

Tradition held that we would show up for cocktails at the big house at 7 p.m. Dad would serve us daiquiris. (After all, we were grown men, and Jack was president!) If it was a Friday night, we could have two daiquiris; on Saturdays, we got one apiece; and on Sundays, none—we had to be at work the next day.

On this evening, while Mac Bundy worked the telephones next door, and Joan and Jackie chatted with Mother and Dad, Jack challenged me to a game of checkers—a chance for us to be alone for a while. There was something wonderful, something so characteristic, about the way Jack played checkers. He was good at the game: decisive, precise. He moved very quickly. And he peppered the conversation with humor, to sort of throw you off. Jack got a lift from checkers as from so much else. He played the game with a joyous frivolity.

We played and talked until my brother looked at his watch and said, "Well, it's five to seven. Let's go on over to Dad's." We walked across the lawn in the heavy mist. Caroline—she would have been three—spotted us from her grandparents' kitchen. She came running out and grabbed her father's arms. As Jack walked his toddling daughter around to the front porch, Bundy opened the screen door and said, "Mr. President, they need you on the phone. Something's come up." Jack turned to me: "Will you walk Caroline in?" I took her small hand and we headed inside the house.

Our father had been watching all this through the window. Instead of preparing the daiquiris for us, he strode alone into the dining room, half an hour early, and stiffly sat down. Jack entered the room shortly afterward and sat down next to him. None of us had ever seen this happen before. As our father sat in grim silence, Jackie, Joan, and Mother drifted in and took their seats, along with Jack. Bundy remained in the living room.

As we sat there perplexed, Dad finally broke the silence. "Jack," he said, "I know you're worried about Khrushchev. But let me tell you something. Nothing is going to be more important in your life than how your daughter turns out. And don't ever forget it."

There was an awkward silence at first, but then Jack said, "You're absolutely right, Dad." In fact, Jack was a kind and doting father, and Dad knew it; but Joe Kennedy never expected anything less than the best.

Soon the two of them were joking. Jack confided to Dad: "I have this nice boat model. If you read in the papers that I've given the model to Khrushchev, it'll mean that the talks are going well. If they don't go well, I won't give it to him. And frankly I'd rather keep that model for myself anyway. It's pretty nice."

In the end, President Kennedy kept the boat model. And Caroline turned out pretty well, too.

On September 9, 1963, Jack sat for an interview on Squaw Island with Walter Cronkite that inaugurated the expansion of the *CBS Evening News* from fifteen minutes to half an hour.

Four days after that, I sat at a luncheon table in Belgrade next to one of the fiercest figures of the embattled Diem regime. The occasion was a conference of the Inter-Parliamentary Union, which I attended along with Joan and a small American congressional delegation. Unbeknownst to us, the leader of the American delegation, Mrs. Katharine St. George, a Republican from New York, had invited the controversial head of the Vietnam delegation, Mrs. Ngo Dinh Nhu, to join us. Madame Nhu, who served as political adviser and unofficial first lady to her unmarried brother-in-law, Ngo Dinh Diem, wound up as my luncheon partner, and my conversation with her marked my first real public—albeit accidentally public—involvement with the situation in Vietnam.

My notes describe her as a woman of about five feet five inches tall, dressed entirely in white and green—green dress, bracelets, earrings, and pin; white pants and shoes. She wore deep red lipstick, rouge, nail polish, and a lot of eye makeup. She had small, delicate hands, which she moved with grace and expression, and spoke directly in a quiet but firm voice.

Madame Nhu was not the most conventional of luncheon conversation partners. When I politely asked her how long she planned to stay in Belgrade, she replied that she was often called a dragon lady, but that actually she was just a dragonfly, and that she remained in one place as long as she enjoyed it. Then the pleasantries ended.

She launched into a ninety-minute tirade, giving her spin on the current situation in South Vietnam. Propaganda is probably a more accurate description of what was essentially her monologue. She complained that the United States supported the Buddhists, who'd been stirred up by the communists at any rate. South Vietnam was a democratic country that elected its own officials; the press was free; in fact, hers was the most tolerant of all the Asian countries. I understood that she viewed me as more than just a member of the American delegation to the Inter-Parliamentary Union meeting—I was, after all, the president's brother—so she barely paused to take a breath as she continued her diatribe. She spoke of her conversations with the pope—he supposedly called her "too, too, too, too poetic" as she told him that they needed women priests to deliver the sacraments in her country—and she declared that people are only Buddhists because they are casual about their religion, and that the government is betrayed by the press. I wondered more than once how in the world I had ended up in this lunch and with this woman sitting next to me. I found it amusing when the State Department later sent a message that I should steer clear of Madame Nhu. I needed no convincing.

One of the last ceremonial events Jack participated in was an All New England Salute Dinner in his honor on Saturday, October 19. Seven thousand people paid one hundred dollars apiece to attend the event at the Commonwealth Armory near Kenmore Square in Boston. It was the most profitable Democratic fund-raising dinner of its time. Jack had attended the Harvard-Columbia football game that afternoon with Kenneth O'Donnell, Dave Powers, and Lawrence O'Brien. He was delighted at the success of the evening and with the money that had been raised.

He had noted that the 1964 campaign "may be among the most interesting as well as pleasurable campaigns that have taken place in a long time." And he made a special point of recognizing me in his speech, with his usual wit: "Teddy has been down in Washington and he came to see me the other day, and he said he was really tired of being referred to as the younger brother of the president, and being another Kennedy, and it is crowded in Washington, and that he was going to break loose and change his name. He was going out on his own. Instead of being Teddy Kennedy now, he is changing his name to Teddy Roosevelt."

The next day, Jack went to Hyannis Port for a quick visit with our parents. On Monday, October 21, 1963, the president headed back to Washington. Before liftoff, he kissed our father goodbye, then walked to the chopper that awaited him in front of my parents' house. As he was about to board, he paused, turned to look at Dad watching him, and re-traced his steps to kiss Dad again, gently, on the forehead. It was the last time the two of them saw one another.

On November 1, the South Vietnamese generals staged a coup, assas-sinating Diem and his brother-adviser Ngo Dinh Nhu, the husband of my Belgrade luncheon companion.

Jack had been traveling about the country: a five-day tour of eleven western states in September to talk about conservation and assess his po-litical standing; speeches in Tampa and Miami Beach on November 18. He made a quick trip back to Washington to take care of certain executive duties; and then, commencing on Thursday, fund-raising appearances in San Antonio, Fort Worth, and, on Friday, Dallas.

My memory of the last time I saw Jack is elusive after all the years. It filters through to me in wisps and echoes.

I think I saw him in Florida. It seems as though I was planning to fly out to Michigan to give a speech on his behalf, and I planned to needle Barry Goldwater a little. Jack was interested in what my theme would be. I showed him my prop, a little bottle with some water in it, colored gold. I planned to build a funny little story around it. "I don't think that's all that good," I dimly recall him saying. "You better get another story. Let me hear when you've come up with another story." I remember that I was somewhat taken aback by this, because I thought it was really a pretty good story.

Friday, November 22, was a dull day in the Senate. I was presiding, a duty that was passed around among freshman senators. A routine debate had begun on the topic of federal aid to public libraries; I was signing correspondence.

At about twenty minutes to two in the afternoon, I heard a shout from the lobby. I glanced over to see the Senate's press liaison officer, Richard Riedel, striding through the door to investigate. Then I saw Riedel reemerge, a strange expression on his face. He was hurrying directly toward me. The shout had come from someone who'd paused to read an Associated Press teletype machine.

"You'd better come over," Riedel told me. He meant to the AP printer.

I followed him out of the chamber. I knew something had happened, something bad, but I had no idea what it was. We reached the machine and I watched the bulletin clatter onto the tape. The president had been shot and grievously wounded. My first overwhelming sense was disbelief. How could it be true? And then horror, as I stood there listening to the *tick, tick, tick* of the teletype machine. I couldn't hear anything or anyone else. Gradually, I became aware of the voices around me. I heard someone say the president was dead.

The Senate chamber turned to bedlam. I rushed from the floor, ran down the Capitol steps, and made for my office in the Senate Building. I needed to call Bobby, who was at Hickory Hill, the house that he and Ethel had purchased in 1957.

But the line was dead. The lines all over Washington were dead. The onslaught of calls coming in and going out had disrupted telephone service. The lines were dead.

My next thought was of Joan. She adored Jack. She would be devastated by the news. I asked Milt Gwirtzman, my Harvard classmate and an adviser to Jack, to drive me to our Georgetown house. My old Texan friend Claude Hooton, in town to join weekend festivities, rode with us as we sped through traffic lights. Claude, in shock like the rest of us, brooded aloud that the president had been shot, and in his home state.

Bobby received the news by phone from J. Edgar Hoover while lunching at Hickory Hill with Ethel and the U.S. attorney for the Southern District of New York, Robert M. Morgenthau. The two had been holding meetings on the subject of organized crime. As the small party sat outside eating sandwiches, one of the men working on the house, who'd been listening to a transistor radio, began to run toward them. At the same moment, an outside telephone rang.

We located Joan at her hairdresser getting ready for a weekend with our friends. I finally reached Bobby at Hickory Hill. He confirmed what I had dared not believe: Jack was dead.

In that moment, the world lurched apart from me. I felt unmoored. But I knew that I had to keep moving. I had to put one foot in front of the other. People were depending on me. And I needed to reach out to my parents. I needed to comfort them.

I asked Gwirtzman to drive me to the White House. There, I made myself instruct an aide to telephone Hyannis Port, and waited the terrible few seconds before the ordeal of speaking the unspeakable.

My mother came on the line. She had heard. My father, in bed on the second floor, had not. Someone had to tell him face-to-face. I told Mother that I would do it.

I contacted Eunice, and together we rushed home by helicopter and jet. By the time we arrived, the anticipation of what lay ahead had burned through any numbness and replaced it with dread. I fought it by launching myself out of the plane, through the front doorway, and up the stairs to Dad's bedroom. His eyes were closed. I would let him have this last peaceful sleep. The television set near his bed caught my eye. I lunged at the connecting wires and ripped them from the wall.

The house filled with relatives through the evening. I passed a hellish night, and the following morning, I told Dad. To this day, the memory of that conversation brings me to tears.

Eunice and I brought our mother to Washington on Sunday, November 24, and prayed beside Jack's body in the Rotunda as a crowd three miles long made its way past. Jack's funeral mass was held the next day at St. Matthew's Cathedral. In recent years, Vicki and I often attend mass at St. Matthew's and walk to the spot at the foot of the altar to read the marker in the marble floor: "Here rested the remains of President Kennedy at the Requiem Mass, November 25, 1963, before their removal to Arlington where they lie in expectation of a heavenly resurrection."

I think often of Bobby's grief over the loss of Jack. It veered close to being a tragedy within the tragedy. Ethel and my mother feared for his own survival; his psychic survival at least. His friend and chronicler Arthur Schlesinger has recorded how Bobby spent the night before Jack's funeral alone in the Lincoln Bedroom, and how his longtime friend Charles Spaulding, upon leaving Bobby there and closing the door, heard him dissolve into sobs and cry out, "*Why, God?!*" He seemed to age physically. He would spend hours without speaking a word.

He delayed returning to his duties as attorney general; he found it difficult to concentrate on anything or do substantive work. Hope seemed to have died within him, and there followed months of unrelenting melancholia. He went through the motions of everyday life, but he carried the burden of his grief with him always.

I was so worried about Bobby that I tried to suppress my own grief. I felt that I had to be strong for my parents and the family. Maybe it's more accurate to say that I was afraid to allow grief to swallow me up. So I just pushed it down further and further inside.

In mid-January 1964, while Bobby was still attorney general and before he made up his mind to resign and run for the Senate from New York, President Johnson asked him to visit the Far East to negotiate a cease-fire between Indonesia and Malaysia. He was to meet in Japan with

Sukarno, the enlightened but volatile Indonesian president who had helped his country win its independence from the Netherlands. Now Sukarno, suspicious at Malaysia's recent federation agreement with Great Britain, had launched a guerrilla war against the neighboring state. Bobby's official mission was to act as peacemaker; but Johnson also hoped that the assignment would lift his spirits.

Johnson, so often perceived by Bobby as an adversary, had on this occasion performed a valuable act of compassion. Bobby invited Ethel along, and her companionship, along with the trip itself, broke my brother's cycle of depression. In Japan, Bobby and Ethel witnessed a tumultuous outpouring of friendship from the people, who wanted to show their respect and love for John Kennedy through Bobby's presence. I believe that that reception restored his faith that life was worth living after all, and that President Kennedy had achieved something lasting and worthwhile.

Late in 1964, Bobby asked me to review the Warren Commission's newly released report on the assassination because emotionally he couldn't do it. The commission had been established by President Johnson seven days after Jack was killed in Dallas, and was charged with determining who had shot Jack, and why. Johnson appointed Earl Warren, the former California governor and chief justice, to chair the commission. Its conclusion, made public in an 888-page document released in September, was that Lee Harvey Oswald had acted alone in killing Jack and wounding the Texas governor John Connally, who was riding in the open limousine with my brother and the wives of both men.

When I reached him by telephone, Warren told me he would be glad to give me a briefing and go over the parts of the report that were particularly contentious and likely to generate the most questions from the press and public. I remember the commission's office as large but spare, about half the size of the attorney general's office. I believe that Warren had one aide, perhaps a law clerk, present at the meeting. I almost certainly brought an aide along with me.

Warren gave me a full briefing, as I'd requested. I asked many questions. The whole process took about four hours. Afterward, I reported to Bobby that I accepted the commission's report and thought he should too.

Bobby agreed readily. He did not want to continue to investigate Jack's death. Earl Warren, moreover, was a strong advocate for the accuracy of the report. He told me quite persuasively that he'd felt a responsibility to the nation to get it right. He personally made the case to me, showing me its weaknesses and walking me through the thinking of the commission members.

I am well aware that many scholars and others have questioned the findings ever since they were released. There have been hundreds of so-called conspiracy theories. I was satisfied that the Warren Commission got it right: satisfied then, and satisfied now. I'm always reluctant to speak for my brother, but I know how strongly Bobby felt that it was imperative that this inquiry be thorough and accurate. In all my subsequent conversations with him, when all was said and done, I believe that Bobby accepted the Warren Commission findings too.

I must speak of what I believe to be another tragic outcome of the bullets fired in Dallas that November. Toward midsummer 1963, I was aware that my brother had qualms about Vietnam. He felt that we needed a new and different direction. He had a growing understanding that the conflict could not be resolved militarily, and I feel very strongly that he certainly would not have escalated it. I witnessed elements of this process unfolding, and Jack affirmed it to me himself in private conversations. The situation troubled him. He said that Vietnam must belong to the Vietnamese. He had spoken with McNamara about a plan for withdrawal within two or three years.

Jack's antenna was set up to find a way out. And I am convinced that he was on his way to finding that way out. He just never got the chance.

In the days and weeks following Jack's death, I sought to keep the grief from disabling me. After the funeral, I returned to the Cape to look after my parents. In fact, this time with my father proved a tremendous source of comfort to me. Even though he was disabled, Dad could find ways to communicate his thoughts, and I was there to hear them. My father had reserves of strength that I could draw upon.

I felt that I was needed by my parents now more than ever. And so I would say to myself in moments of despair, *There might be a time when you can give way to your own feelings, but not now, not in front of Dad.* And so, hour by hour, I learned to contain my grief, to not give way to it.

I drew from my parents both strength and inspiration. I would say to myself, *Mother is holding up. The last thing she needs is for me to break down or give way to a flood of tears.*

I took long walks on the beach. I was still filled with such disbelief that Jack was gone. And then the truth of it would burn through this illusion. It was in those moments, when I was out of sight of anyone else, just the sea on one side of me and the sand on the other, that I would let go of my self-control.

It never occurred to me to seek professional help or grief counseling of any kind. The times were different then. But I prayed and I thought and I prayed some more.

CHAPTER ELEVEN

Falling to Earth
1964–1965

In the end, the best way to honor Jack's memory was to take up his unfinished work.

His great dreams had included sending an American to the moon, nuclear disarmament, and the passage of a landmark civil rights bill. A lunar quest was years from feasibility. The checkered progress of disarmament was to be measured across decades.

The civil rights bill, by contrast, virtually cried for enactment. President Johnson supported it. A majority of Congress, including several Republicans, seemed to recognize that its time had come. Its main provisions would strike down restraints imposed in an agrarian age when most living Americans had witnessed slavery as a sanctioned practice. The affection that most Americans still harbored for the late President Kennedy and his dreams lent a timely backdrop for the effort to topple segregation in schools, employment, and public places.

Yet passage in the Senate remained far from a sure thing. No important civil rights legislation since Reconstruction had ever made it past the stone wall of southern resistance. Generations of senators from the old Confederacy, although a minority, had even managed to torpedo an antilynching bill. No signal existed that 1964 would be any different.

The southerners' weapon of choice on civil rights bills was the filibuster, that time-honored tradition of preventing a vote on legislation by holding the Senate floor and orating on any subject until silenced by a "cloture" vote—or, more commonly, until a compromise is forged or the opposition gives up. In the early 1960s, cloture required assent by at least sixty-seven of the Senate's one hundred members. Sixty-seven Senators were Democrats in 1964; but of these, twenty-one were from the "solid South." Among the current Republicans, only twelve of the thirty-three were moderates; the rest were conservative. A filibuster against the bill was inevitable, and we knew that the math was against us: we were nine votes short of cloture, which by all previous indicators was a hopeless gap.

The math did not in any way impede the determination and tactical shrewdness of President Lyndon Johnson, abetted by Senators Hubert Humphrey and Mike Mansfield.

Johnson sought to bolster public acceptance of the civil rights bill with speeches, appeals to the clergy, and by jawboning newspaper editors and publishers to call for its passage. He worked through Mansfield, the majority leader, to name Humphrey as manager of the bill. Humphrey homed in on the bill's most powerful adversary outside the South, Senator Everett Dirksen of Illinois, the Republican minority leader. Playing to Dirksen's aspirations to be recalled as a great man of the Senate, Hubert flattered the senator publicly, claiming in broadcast interviews that *as* a great man, he would naturally do the right thing on civil rights. Dirksen voted for the bill.

The House of Representatives passed a strong version of the bill in February 1964. Mansfield fielded it and adroitly steered it around its natural Senate starting place, the Judiciary Committee, where Richard B. Russell of Georgia awaited with the intention of shoving it into limbo. Mansfield found a creative pretext for rushing the bill directly to the Senate floor for debate. When it arrived there on March 10, Russell and his fellow Dixie Democrats launched their filibuster.

Russell was anything but subtle about his aims. He and his allies clung to the spirit of a speech he made in 1946 while filibustering a bill that would have permanently created the Fair Employment Practices Commission: he would resist "to the bitter end" any measure that would bring about "social equality and intermingling and amalgamation of the races" in the southern states.

The end this time would indeed be bitter for them. Over fifty-seven days of argument, arm-twisting, pressure, and persuasion in April, May, and June of that year—"the longest debate," as it came to be called—we virtually willed the bill to passage.

When I first entered the Senate, new members usually did not make floor speeches for at least two years. Today, they all speak almost immediately. But not in 1964. And when they finally did take the podium, members usually spoke on issues of local concern. So it was something of a break with tradition when I decided to make my maiden speech on April 9, 1964, and use it to advocate for the passage of the Civil Rights Act. But it seemed to me that civil rights was *the* issue and this was *the* time. I was increasingly involved in both the substance of the discussion and the debate and felt it was very important to speak out.

I began with a note of homage to the time-honored protocols of the Senate: "It is with some hesitation that I rise to speak. . . . A freshman senator should be seen, not heard; should learn and not teach. This is especially true when the Senate is engaged in a truly momentous debate."

I voiced my respect for the quality of debate thus far and noted that I'd planned to focus my initial Senate speech on issues affecting my home state. But "I could not . . . [watch] this issue envelop the emotions and the conscience of the nation without changing my mind. To limit myself to local issues in the face of this great national question would be to demean the seat in which I sit, which has been occupied by some of the most distinguished champions in the cause of freedom. I feel I can better represent the people of Massachusetts at this time by bringing the experience of their history to bear on this problem."

I recalled the prejudice directed against my own Irish forebears. I cited the support for the bill among hundreds of religious leaders, most particularly Richard Cardinal Cushing of Boston—who, I avowed, had made unparalleled contributions to my own racial and religious understanding.

Noting that wide areas of the South remained without integration years after the principle had been established, I warned that if Congress did not move quickly to expedite the integration decree, "it will be acquiescing in what has amounted in many places to a virtual reversal of the Supreme Court's decisions."

As for discrimination in federal programs—health, education, job training, for instance—I made what I believed to be a ringingly obvious point: "We cannot justify using Negro taxpayers' money to perpetuate discrimination against them."

After voicing a series of buttressing arguments to support these major points, I wound up my maiden speech as follows: "I remember the words of President Johnson last November 27: 'No memorial oration or eulogy could more eloquently honor President Kennedy's memory than the earliest possible passage of the Civil Rights Bill for which he fought so long.'

"My brother was the first president of the United States to state publicly that segregation was morally wrong. His heart and his soul are in this bill. If his life and death had a meaning, it was that we should not hate but love one another, and that we should use our powers not to create conditions of oppression that lead to violence, but conditions of freedom that lead to peace. It is in that spirit that I hope the Senate will pass this bill."

On June 19, 1964, a year to the day after my brother sent his civil rights bill to Congress, it passed into law on a vote of seventy-three to twenty-seven.

We knew that the Democratic Party would pay a price for this achievement. Lyndon Johnson himself put it most succinctly when he remarked, "We may win this legislation, but we're going to lose the South for a generation." And he was right; this marked the onset of the transformation of that region from Democratic to Republican.

Other Democratic leaders foresaw this as well, yet they acted to pass the bill nonetheless. I'm convinced that they acted, as had my brother in his speech, beyond political calculus: this was simply the right thing to do. Lyndon Johnson underscored his own progressive aims on May 22 when, at a commencement address at the University of Michigan, he described his vision of a "Great Society." His ideas, transformed into action by a Democratic Congress, produced a constellation of programs, laws, and agencies for social reform, some conceived by Jack and Bobby, but all championed and fought for by LBJ. They included the War on Poverty and the Economic Opportunity Act, the Job Corps, Project Head Start, Medicare, Medicaid, the National Endowments for the Arts and for the Humanities, VISTA, and others.

All were landmarks in American history.

On Friday, June 19, 1964, the same evening that we passed the Civil Rights Act, the Massachusetts Democratic Party was opening its annual convention in Springfield. I had planned to fly there after the vote and accept the party's nomination to my first full term in the United States Senate. My friend Senator Birch Bayh of Indiana had agreed to deliver the keynote. The usual flurry of floor speeches in the Senate had pushed the Civil Rights vote further and further into the evening hours, delaying our departure for the state convention, and at one point I telephoned the delegates in Springfield, my voice amplified in their hall by a public address system, to assure them I would arrive later in the evening.

The Senate roll call began at 7:40 p.m. After proudly voting "aye," I hurried and headed to Washington National Airport. There, I boarded a chartered plane along with Senator Bayh, his wife, Marvella, and my longtime aide and friend Edward Moss. The pilot, Edwin J. Zimny, was a last-minute substitute for Daniel Hogan, the plane's owner, who had decided to attend a reunion of Yale alumni. The plane was an Aero Commander, a small twin-engine painted white with blue trim. Our destination was Barnes Municipal Airport in Westfield, Massachusetts, near Springfield.

The night was heavy and humid in Washington. We headed northeast on the 360-mile trip, with the pilot navigating on instruments. An Aero

Commander is configured with seats for the pilot and copilot, plus room for five passengers. Directly behind the pilot and copilot are two rear-facing cabin seats that in turn face a bench accommodating three people. The Bayhs sat together on the bench, and Ed Moss and I both initially sat in the rear-facing seats. As we were coming in over Springfield, Ed Moss got up and said, "You people need more space, because you're working on your speeches." With that, he unbuckled himself and moved up into the empty copilot's seat. Birch worked on his speech and I went over mine, and as we were coming into Barnes airfield I turned in my seat to watch our approach for landing. I looked out in front of the plane and saw that the ground was blanketed in fog. As I knew from my own experience as a pilot, we should have been able to see the airport runway lights at about this time, giving the pilot a target for landing. But instead of runway lights as we came out of the mist, I saw a hill, scattered with large rocks, and we were about to crash into it.

The pilot glimpsed this terrifying sight at the same moment I did and pulled back on the stick to lift the plane up. Every muscle in my body tensed as I mentally went through the motions with the pilot. *Up. Up. Up, dammit!* I could see tall pine trees just beyond the rocky part of the hill. *If only the pilot can clear them . . .* He couldn't. We were flying at an altitude of only 177 feet. The whole plane was jolted as we struck the first treetop, and then we rode along the tops of those trees in what felt like a slow-motion nightmare. As we sped along and clipped those treetops, the plane teetered from side to side, until the left wing of the plane struck one of the trees with such force that the plane was thrown to the left. We crashed to the ground in an apple orchard and skidded into the earth between two rows of trees, plowing a trench two feet deep. That trench helped to slow the plane down, but we still slammed into a tree. The low branches acted as a knife, slicing open the front of the plane. The impact hurled my corkscrewed body forward into the cockpit, directly between the pilot and my friend Ed Moss.

Silence.

Silence.

On my left, I could make out the pilot slumped over the wheel. He looked in bad shape. I swiveled my gaze painfully to the right. Ed Moss looked in bad shape too. Behind me in the cabin, I could hear Birch Bayh saying, "Is there anybody alive up there? Is anybody alive?" I couldn't answer. The sleeves of my coat had come off from the impact, the shoelaces had broken on my shoes, and I couldn't move from my waist down.

Birch and Marvella managed to drag themselves out of the airplane. They were some distance away, but I could still hear them. And I still could not speak. I could hear Marvella crying in the darkness, "We've got to get help! We've got to get help! We've got to get help! We've got to get help!"

Then Birch's voice: "I smell gas. That plane might catch fire! I'm going back to see if there's somebody alive in there." It sounds very easy, as I describe it, to say that a plane's going to catch fire, we'd better hurry and get help, and for Birch to turn around, come back, and look in that plane again. But of course there was nothing easy about it. The plane could have exploded into a fireball at any moment, and Birch was risking his own life to try to save those of us still in the plane. He showed courage and compassion that I'll never forget.

When he came back to the plane, I opened my mouth and managed to say, "I'm alive, Birch!" He replied, "I can't bend over because of my back." But the prospect of the plane catching fire gave me some extra juice to try and get out of there. And so I summoned everything I had to turn around, even though I was paralyzed from the waist down. I crawled to the window and put my arm around Birch, and he dragged me out of that plane, far enough away to be safe if there were an explosion. Then I just let go and collapsed onto the ground. Birch left me to go back to the plane to try to rescue the others. But when they didn't move or answer his calls, he feared that Zimny and Moss were dead. The situation was very grim. I was having difficulty breathing as I lay on the ground in that apple orchard. I couldn't move and was fighting to remain conscious. We had crashed near a back road, and Birch and Marvella walked to the road to try to flag down a passing car for help. For a long time it seemed as though we would spend the night there. Nine cars passed them before one finally stopped. A man named Robert Schauer picked up the Bayhs and drove them to his home, where they called for help. Schauer lent them blankets and pillows and returned them to the crash site. Police and an ambulance finally arrived about an hour and a half after Birch had pulled me from the plane. I said, "You'd better go over to the others. See if they're still alive." They went to the plane and took Moss out, who was still alive. Zimny was dead.

About a half hour later they came back, loaded me in the ambulance, and transported me to a hospital. I was in so much pain that I asked for sodium pentothal. I'd dislocated my shoulder once, and I recalled that pentothal knocked you out. The doctors said, "No, no, we can't give you that." It seems that an anesthetic could have been dangerous if I had internal injuries. But as they cut my clothes away—boom! I passed out. Merciful relief from the pain. I'd suffered a broken back and a collapsed lung that had been punctured by the tip of a rib, one of several that had been cracked apart. I'd been given transfusions, and doctors had suctioned water and air from my chest cavity to keep me from suffocating. My life hung in the balance for a while. Doctors told me that I'd been lucky: had any of my broken vertebrae been cervical or thoracic, I'd have been permanently paralyzed. I was thirty-two years old, six feet two inches tall, and 230 pounds, not that far from my college football weight, and my relative youth and fitness worked in my favor as well.

I remember the first thing I saw when I woke up was Najeeb Halaby from the Federal Aviation Administration, who said, "What happened on the plane?" And I thought, *What the hell am I doing talking to this guy? What in the world am I doing talking to Jeeb Halaby about the plane?*

Then Joan arrived. She had been waiting for me at the convention, about fifteen miles from the crash site. When she heard the news, she hurried to the hospital, escorted by the governor of Massachusetts, Endicott "Chub" Peabody. "Hi, Joansie," I managed when she rushed into the room.

"Don't worry." Then my sister Pat came. Later I got the news that Ed Moss had not pulled through. I was devastated.

A White House aide, under orders from President Johnson, telephoned the home of Dr. Paul Russell, chief surgeon at Massachusetts General Hospital. Roused from sleep, Dr. Russell sped the hundred miles from Boston to my bedside, joining two Cooley Dickinson doctors. Several hours later I saw the tousled hair and concerned blue eyes of my brother beside the bed. Bobby had driven all night from Hyannis Port. My brush with death just seven months after Jack's assassination was almost too much for him to bear. I tried to ease his mind with a joke. "Is it true," I asked him, "that you are ruthless?" Bobby stayed at the hospital for two days.

I remained at Cooley Dickinson until July 9, encased in a tubing-and-strap device called a Stryker frame that kept me suspended above my bed, occasionally rotating like a hunk of barbecue meat. My father arrived on July 2 from Hyannis Port, an arduous visit for him. He rolled into my room in his wheelchair in the midst of a debate by doctors over how to treat me. There were two options: (1) to perform surgery on my back now, with a long period of convalescence and rehabilitation, to repair the break and fuse my spine, hopefully preserving my ability to walk; or (2) to spend the next six months immobilized, giving my back the chance to heal and fuse on its own. If I could not walk at the end of that six-month period, then we could consider surgery, with an additional lengthy period of convalescence and rehabilitation. Dad made his opinion as clear as if he still had the full power of speech. Whipping his head from side to side, he shouted out, "Naaaa, naaaa, naaa!" I understood that Dad was recalling the back operation on Jack that had left him in permanent pain (and no doubt thinking of Rosemary as well). I made a decision that not only honored his wishes, but mine also: I would take the more conservative option of allowing the broken bones and vertebrae to heal naturally. The chances for complications from the surgery itself were significant, and in 1964 the techniques and equipment were not what they are today. I could very well have been paralyzed because of the surgery. No, I would take my chances with nature.

I made the right choice. I would spend the remainder of my life not being able to stand fully erect and always feeling pain from my injuries. On the bright side, which is how I prefer to look at things, I would spend the remainder of my life able to walk.

When the doctors had ascertained that I'd not suffered injuries to my spinal cord, I was transferred to New England Baptist Hospital in Boston. There I began to savor the simple joys of life as soon as a little strength began to return.

Joan and the children swam back into close orbit with me. Jack's death had devastated her. My accident further distressed her, but it also lent her a new sense of purpose. I was up for election to my first full term that fall. My reelection was not in serious doubt, but we still had a campaign. My opponent was a former state representative named Howard Whitmore Jr. So, as she had in my first Senate campaign, Joan became a surrogate for me. Over the course of the next five months, she barnstormed cities and towns all over Massachusetts, charming crowds and winning votes.

President Johnson visited me at the hospital at 12:40 p.m. on September 29. We'd spoken on the phone September 6—according to my notes, he said he'd had a "hankering" to call—and he'd asked if he could visit in person during a campaign swing through New England. He said he'd been following the reports on my recovery. "I still do not understand how you can shave on your stomach, but I guess you can get used to most anything." Then he asked, "Ted, is there anything I can do to make your life more livable?"

Upon his arrival, he walked into my room and gave me a kiss on the forehead. Then he kissed Joan and told her how well she'd done at the Democratic convention. Our conversation was mostly about his reelection campaign. He mentioned that he thought TV coverage had become more important than the daily newspapers. He talked about how poorly he was polling in Alabama and predicted he would lose Louisiana and Mississippi as well. We talked about prospects for Bobby's Senate campaign, which he said he would do everything to support.

And then President Johnson confided something to me regarding Jack's assassination and the findings of the Warren Commission. He felt the real responsibility had been with the FBI. As Johnson saw it, they were aware that Oswald was dangerous and that he had visited Moscow and Mexico. FBI agents had even interviewed Oswald, but they had neglected to warn the Secret Service of their suspicions, and that's why Johnson thought the agency was culpable.

It was only a thirty-five-minute conversation, but we also had time to discuss a Detroit autoworkers' strike (he was against it); South Vietnam, which he described as a very critical situation; and Rhode Island politics, which he believed had been heavily controlled by corporate interests until Theodore F. Green had been elected governor and then senator. As always, our exchanges were easy and cordial, and when he departed, at 1:15 p.m., I was in good spirits.

During my recuperation, I began to paint again—a hobby I had not pursued since those youthful days of competition with Jack. I'd forgotten the pleasure painting had given me. I have continued to paint since then, with the sea, and sailing boats, and the Cape Cod shoreline as my favorite subjects.

My thoughts turned often to my dad. What had I left unsaid to this great man? So many things.

An inspiration hit me: I would compile a book for him, a book of essays; mine and those of others in the family, which would express to Dad all the loving memories, the respect, the moments of laughter that lived unspoken in all of us. I sent the word out through the family, and the eloquent writings came in.

I chose the title—*The Fruitful Bough*—from Genesis, chapter 49, verses 22–24:

Joseph is a fruitful bough, even a fruitful bough by a well; whose branches run over the wall: The archers have sorely grieved him, and shot at him, and hated him: But his bow abode in strength, and the arms of his hands were made strong by the hands of the mighty God of Jacob.

As I reread *The Fruitful Bough* today, I see that most of its entries—mine, Mother's, Pat's, Eunice's, Joe Gargan's, and the rest—are gilded with a love that allows no hint of human frailty in their subject. I smile as I pause over the inevitable exception. "I don't believe he is without faults," Bobby's essay begins; and, a bit later: "His judgment has not always been perfect." This is Bobby being Bobby. My brother loved and admired our father as fervently as the rest of us, as his essay shows; yet sentimentality (as opposed to true sentiment) was never part of his nature.

The hospital room became my postgraduate seminar. More receptive to ideas even than in my latter years at Harvard, and motivated now by the intellectual demands of my office, I invited a series of professors to come and offer me tutorials in a variety of subjects, complete with reading lists. John Kenneth Galbraith folded his lanky frame into a chair and educated me in economics. Samuel Beer held forth on political science. And my understanding of civil rights issues was bolstered by a number of visitors, some of them famous leaders, who briefed me on the social and constitutional history of the movement. Furthermore, my hospital stay gave me more direct insight into health care and its costs.

I entered a world, at Cooley Dickinson and later at New England Baptist in Boston, of sufferers for whom the cost of being healed was often as great a hardship as the disease itself. I met people whose stories haunted me: good working people who scrimped and sacrificed to pay for a family member with tuberculosis; families, already struggling to pay their bills, beset by catastrophic illness.

I realized that access to health care was a moral issue.

I left New England Baptist Hospital on December 16, after six months of rehabilitation. At 4 a.m. on the day of my discharge, I quietly and temporarily exited the grounds with the help of Eddy Martin, who drove me through the cold darkness to Andover, and the cemetery where Ed Moss lay buried. It was Ed's forty-first birthday. His grave was on a hill, and the two of us had to struggle upward, Eddy Martin protecting me as best he could from slipping and falling on the icy slope. We returned to the car and drove to the Moss home, where I spent time talking to Moss's widow, Katie. Then we drove back to the hospital, where I completed my formal checkout and flew to Palm Beach to spend the holidays with my family.

By then, the Vietnam War was in full swing, and Bobby was a senator-elect from New York. The war had escalated in early August following the attacks, or alleged attacks, by North Vietnamese patrol boats against a U.S. Navy destroyer—the long-disputed "Gulf of Tonkin incident." On August 7, the House and Senate, under executive pressure and lacking an accountable version of the facts, enacted Lyndon Johnson's Gulf of Tonkin Resolution, granting him authority to wage unlimited war against North Vietnam without securing congressional approval. From my hospital bed, I announced my support of Johnson's resolution.

Bobby declared his Senate candidacy on August 22, and resigned as attorney general on September 3; Johnson named Nicholas Katzenbach to succeed him. Bobby and Ethel kept Hickory Hill in Virginia and took an apartment at the United Nations Plaza. Naturally, Kenneth Keating, the incumbent Republican senator from New York, seized the opportunity to tar my brother as a "carpetbagger." Bobby handled it with his usual wit. He could have chosen to retire, he told an audience at Columbia University. After all, "My father has done very well and I could have lived off him." Nor did he need the title "senator" because "I could be called general, I understand, for the rest of my life. And I don't need the money and I don't need the office space." As the laughter and applause swelled, Bobby concluded, "Frank as it is—and maybe it's difficult to believe in the state of New York—I'd like to just be a good United States senator. I'd like to serve."

Nonetheless, his campaign was rocky at the outset, as Keating went all-out to portray my brother as hostile to the interests of blacks. These attacks roused Bobby; he wound up his campaign at a fever pitch and with the support of NAACP officials. When President Johnson, en route to his own rout of Barry Goldwater for the presidency, campaigned alongside him in late October, Keating's lead, and chances, evaporated. Bobby won the election by more than seven hundred thousand votes.

His victory made our parents unique in the annals of political families: they were the first Americans in history to have raised three senators.

Any euphoria my brother may have felt was tempered by his lingering grief over Jack. In a meeting with reporters in his office shortly after he was sworn in, one of them asked him how he felt now as a member of the Senate. Bobby replied quietly, "I regret the circumstances that led to my being here."

It is fair to say that Bobby and Lyndon Johnson had a complicated relationship. Bobby was not initially in favor of having LBJ as Jack's running mate—he worried about whether anyone who had been running so hard for the seat himself could suppress his own presidential ambitions so quickly. And I don't think either of them ever felt warmth or trust toward each other. Truth was, Bobby's close relationship with Jack prevented Johnson from ever really getting as close to Jack as he would have been had Bobby not been in the picture. It was, in my opinion, a classic "three's a crowd" scenario. But even though there was no love lost between Bobby and LBJ, I wouldn't go so far as to call them bitter and implacable enemies, as some have suggested. Johnson was capable of kindness toward my brother, and courtesy, and political support. Toward me, President Johnson was consistently solicitous and friendly. I liked him and always got along with him very well.

Still, I know that there were times that Johnson tried to play Bobby off against me, which was totally bizarre, since there was no way that a Kennedy would side with an outsider against another Kennedy. With all of his political acuity, I would have thought he'd understand that. Nevertheless, Johnson never learned it and never gave up trying. "I love Teddy and Sarge is great," he used to say. "Now what is it with this strange fellow Bobby? Why is he so difficult?" Bobby cut right to the heart of the matter. "Why does Lyndon fear me so much, for chrissakes?" he said once. "He's the president of the United States and I'm the junior senator from New York!"

Actually, Bobby's relations with Johnson in 1964 and 1965 were not all that bad, certainly not as tense as they are often portrayed in the press. Some historians have written that Bobby longed for Johnson to name him as his running mate in the '64 election, but that Johnson kept him at bay. The truth is that the vice presidency under Johnson did not loom large as an option in my brother's mind. He might have been briefly tempted, but he was never possessed by the idea. There is no denying that Bobby had been awakened by the ovation he'd received after his remarks at the Democratic convention in Atlantic City. It was so overwhelming and so extraordinary that he thought briefly of letting his name go before the convention as a candidate for vice president. But a few hours' reflection convinced him that this was not worth the try. Johnson had made his mind up about Hubert Humphrey. Still, the enormous affection and respect he enjoyed at the convention gave Bobby heart as he launched his campaign for the Senate from New York.

Bobby typically addressed his career decisions in that manner. He lived and made decisions in the moment and not in the cold, calculating way that some critics have tried to attribute to him. Bobby never really thought about what he was going to do next. He was absolutely absorbed in whatever he was doing at any given time. He started his career on the labor committee investigating racketeering, and for him, that was enough. Our father said to him, "Well, why don't you think about moving to Maryland, and then after this thing is over, you could run for the Senate?"

Bobby had by then settled into Hickory Hill. He replied to our father, "No, I'm not thinking about anything else. I just want to do this. I don't really care where I live."

As he began campaigning in New York, Bobby discovered, as he told me, that the city had a particular kind of energy that he had not thought much about until then. The writers and journalists there, he said, had a set of social concerns unlike their counterparts in Washington, who prided themselves as "insiders." As such, they tended to focus on the politics of a given situation. Many of the writers in New York were less sophisticated in practical politics, Bobby observed, but they were far more concerned about the moral and social substance of the issues.

Bobby was most stirred by Michael Harrington, whose landmark study of "invisible" poverty, *The Other America*, had been published two years earlier. JFK and LBJ were also struck by the book; it energized Jack's attention to the poor, and served as an impetus for Johnson's War on Poverty.

Bobby and I took the oath of office together on January 4, 1965—me, for my first full term. I was still navigating with the aid of a cane. Having my brother as a colleague in the Senate was wonderful. He brought energy into any room, any hearing; and his presence delighted and uplifted me as it did everyone who came into his orbit. Our new proximity brought with it the spirit of the old times; the laughter and teasing and optimism of our boyhoods; the easy intimacy of our autumn garage weekends at the Cape house.

We'd struck up our old needling even before I left the hospital. Bobby had come to visit, and as the newsmen's cameras flashed, one photographer leaned toward my brother and said, "Step back a little, you're casting a shadow on Ted." I quickly responded, "It's going to be the same in Washington."

As he recovered his old intensity and drive, my brother found the Senate's pace infuriatingly slow in relation to the changes he wanted to make. Jack had been in the Senate for five months before he made a speech. I'd been in office for sixteen months. Bobby managed to wait all of three weeks before taking the floor. He was advocating a bill that would have included thirteen upstate New York counties that bordered Pennsylvania in an Appalachian Economic Development Plan.

Bobby never wanted to give the impression that he planned to coast through the Senate on his name. He understood power well. He knew that there was an inside Senate and an outside Senate, and that his fast-blossoming idealism made him basically an outsider. Some historians have wondered if Bobby's transformation was provoked by Jack's death. I believe it was.

Bobby decided that he would take on issues that championed America's dispossessed, such as antipoverty bills and further civil rights reform. He searched out injustices and moral causes. His involvement in them lent them a sense of urgency they might not otherwise have inspired. As he grew and learned, he became more and more interested in *people*, as opposed to abstract issues.

For all our fraternal closeness, Bobby and I did not work in tandem as senators. Even when we *tried*, we couldn't manage it. Once, not long after his election, Bobby arrived late for a vote on some long-forgotten bill and looked over at me from his seat to see how I was voting. I looked back at him, not understanding what he wanted. He kept looking at me, and finally shook his head as if to ask, "Is the vote no?" I got it. I nodded back at him, meaning, "Yes, the vote is no." But Bobby thought I meant, "The vote is yes." So Bobby voted yes. I then voted no, which set the Senate buzzing—were the Kennedy brothers at odds with each other?! I looked at Bobby again and shook my head no. Bobby then shook his head no—in agreement, he thought, with the no vote. But I thought he meant, "No, I'm not voting no." So I vigorously nodded my head yes, as if to say, "Yes, you are supposed to vote no." Bobby shook his head, changed his vote to no, then bent over his desk and quickly scribbled me a note: "Now I get it. When you nod, you want me to vote no, and when you shake your head, you want me to vote no. So I guess I'm always supposed to vote no!"

We served on one committee together—Labor and Public Welfare—but otherwise chose separate legislative paths, and reinforced one another to the extent we were able. Bobby gravitated toward Vietnam-related issues, such as reforming the draft. I focused on immigration and civil rights. I was, after all, a member of the Judiciary Committee, and in 1965 especially, civil rights virtually defined the committee's agenda. Martin Luther King had received the Nobel Peace Prize in October 1964, a reminder to Americans that the world's enlightened societies supported his quest. In the spring of 1965, a voting rights bill was making its way through both houses. Its cosponsors were Mike Mansfield and Everett Dirksen. It aimed to expand upon the Civil Rights Act's social impact by outlawing literacy tests and other impediments long enshrined in southern state laws to discourage Negro voting.

Some Judiciary members, myself included, believed that the bill did not go far enough, and that liberal lawmakers had not been adequately consulted. We felt that it ignored one of the most onerous tools of disenfranchisement against impoverished black voters, the poll tax. In 1964, a constitutional amendment devoted exclusively to outlawing the poll tax had been ratified—the Twenty-fourth. But this amendment covered only voting in federal elections. In Texas, Alabama, Virginia, and Mississippi, along with stubbornly independent (and virtually all-white) Vermont, the tax was still imposed on state and local balloting.

In April 1965, I led the fight for an amendment to the voting rights bill that would ban poll taxing at all electoral levels. I drew upon an inspirational ally in this effort, the visionary NAACP lobbyist Clarence Mitchell. This was the first time I floor-managed a piece of legislation in the Senate.

I faced some unlikely opponents. Attorney General Katzenbach opposed it on the belief that federal intervention in local elections could be ruled unconstitutional regardless of the Twenty-fourth Amendment.

Hubert Humphrey, a champion of civil rights well before the movement, lobbied against it on the Senate floor. Cosponsor Mike Mansfield, a progressive on many issues, lined up against it—as did two other famous liberals, Eugene McCarthy and Vance Hartke of Indiana. At the time, I was not able to figure out why. Much to my surprise, it was later publicly revealed in Congress that Martin Luther King himself wrote to many lawmakers asking them not to vote for the poll tax removal, since he saw it as jeopardizing the passage of the Voting Rights Act as a whole.

I drew upon every scrap of procedural savvy that I had observed in my brief career as a senator. I drilled with professors from Howard University, Harvard, and several other sources, including Thurgood Marshall, until I'd mastered the constitutional underpinnings of the issue. (An extension of my hospital "tutorials," this practice would remain with me.) I kept in close touch with civil rights leaders, including Dr. King, to make sure I understood the direction and depth of their feeling. I believe that I met and spoke personally with every senator. On the Senate floor, I declared that the poll tax not only was conceived in discrimination and not only did it operate in discrimination—it was obviously *ineffectively* discriminatory, given that it would inhibit voting by the poor of any race.

I lost that battle by four votes: forty-nine to forty-five. Its defeat may have turned partly on a letter from Katzenbach, which was read by Mike Mansfield on the floor. Nonetheless, I took pride in having championed the amendment. I felt even better when my constitutional judgment was vindicated: the Voting Rights Act, signed into law on August 6, did not abolish the poll tax, but it did direct Attorney General Katzenbach to file suits against the states that used it. In the ensuing four years, Katzenbach won every one. Millions of southern blacks registered as new voters.

Soon after that, thanks to the courtesy of James Eastland, I was given my first chance at another cause that would become a career passion of mine: immigration.

President Johnson's Great Society program was redressing one social imbalance after another in the mid-sixties. One of these was to dismantle the quota system that since 1924 had allowed masses of northern Europeans to enter the United States, while keeping stringent limits on Asians, Africans, and people of color generally. Jack had cared about immigration reform, but it was what happened to newcomers once they had been allowed in that stirred his conscience: the indignities heaped on the boatloads of poor Irish disembarking at Boston, for instance.

The immigration bill before the Judiciary Committee had been proposed by Emmanuel Celler, the great Democratic congressman from Brooklyn, and was cosponsored by Senator Philip Hart of Michigan. I was happy to accept its management when Eastland offered it to me. Eastland was hardly a champion of immigration reform, but he was a realist. The momentum was running against him, and perhaps he would need a favor from me someday.

My Boston Irish constituency was not thrilled to see me at work reducing Ireland's proportionate access to U.S. citizenship, and some loud voices were raised. But I kept in touch with opposition groups in Massachusetts and managed to calm everyone's fears that the measure would lead to a deluge that would overwhelm American society. The bill passed by seventy-six votes to eighteen on September 22, 1965. President Johnson signed it into law in the shadow of the Statue of Liberty.

In October 1965, I had an experience that did not produce such satisfying results.

The issue was a federal judgeship for Francis X. Morrissey, the Boston municipal judge who'd been a friend of our family for years. He was the same Frank Morrissey who'd steered me through the city's political and jurisprudence cultures after I left law school and began to form a career, and who'd reported to Dad on my successes at giving talks and winning acceptance in Boston. Before that, starting in 1946, he had mentored Jack in a similar way, then helped manage Congressman Kennedy's Boston office.

Our father was fond of Frank. He'd seen something noble in Morrissey's classic Irish-American working-class story. Frank was a dockworker's son from Charlestown, a part of Boston across the Charles River, just north of the city proper. He was one of twelve children who'd grown up in a household without electricity. He'd studied law at Suffolk Law School in Boston, taking night courses while working as a bank teller in the daytime.

Dad believed in Frank Morrissey, and in 1961 asked Jack to appoint him as a federal judge. Jack understood the odds, and held the nomination in abeyance.

But now Jack was gone. It was four years later and Dad was frail and in decline from his stroke. I didn't want unfinished business, and I asked him whether he still cared about the Morrissey appointment. He made clear to me that he cared very much. This was the only request my father had ever made of me. Interestingly, Jack had told friends the same thing back in 1961. Jack and I both believed in our father's judgment; and his request for a favor—literally a once-in-a-lifetime event—was just about impossible for either of us to ignore. It was a matter of loyalty.

I backed Frank Morrissey for the federal judgeship. I went to the White House to personally ask President Johnson to nominate him, and the president agreed. With me sitting next to him, the president then placed a call to my father to tell him the news. According to Johnson's own White House tape recordings, he said, "Mr. Ambassador, we are sitting here with Teddy and we're getting ready to recommend your friend Judge Morrissey for the federal bench, and we wanted to tell you about it first."

Then the president handed me the phone. "Dad, well, it looks like you're the man with all of the influence," I said. "The president said he is doing it for all of you and Jack and Bob and myself, so it's really fine. But I think he is giving a little extra push because of your interest in it." My father was overcome with emotion.

As much as I wanted to make my father happy, I understood full well that there would be opposition to Morrissey. And I also wanted to do the right thing. I searched my conscience. I polled senators whose moral clarity I respected, including the deeply principled Phil Hart, whose early support of gun control and school busing inspired recall petitions against him. Senator Hart told me that Morrissey was indeed qualified to assume the federal bench: "He isn't the brightest of all the people we have, but he's certainly very competent and able to handle it." Bobby sent a letter supporting the nominee. Attorney General Katzenbach sent a report to James Eastland saying there was no basis to question the nominee's credibility. The Judiciary Committee recommended Morrissey's confirmation by a vote of six to three.

It wasn't enough. There were surprise revelations about three months of study at a Georgia law school before taking the bar exam there. That angle was featured heavily. The *Boston Globe* ran a series of articles in opposition to the nomination, and won a Pulitzer Prize for its efforts. The *Globe* claimed that the candidate had lied about his residency in order to take the Georgia Bar back in 1934. Senators who had been disposed to vote for Morrissey began to back away, including the senior senator from my state, Leverett Saltonstall.

It particularly wounded me that the leader of that insurrection was Senator Joe Tydings of Maryland. Joe and I had come to the Senate at about the same time; he and our wives had been social friends, and he'd blossomed quickly as a courageous champion of such politically perilous causes as gun registration. (The National Rifle Association got its revenge by helping turn him out of office in 1970.) He'd been a friend of Jack's and a political beneficiary of Bobby's esteem. During the hearings, though, Tydings turned on me. He spoke stridently on the Senate floor of judicial standards, implying that Morrissey did not meet them and insisting that he should not be appointed.

When I saw that I was going to be some five votes short on confirmation, I privately told President Johnson that I would abandon my fight for Morrissey. That was on the night of October 20, 1965. The following day, before a packed Senate gallery that included Joan, Ethel, and Eunice, I spoke passionately on Frank's behalf. I traced his impoverished childhood and chided his opponents for holding him to elitist standards.

Then I steeled myself and told the Senate that I recommended the nomination be recommitted to the Judiciary Committee—in effect, withdrawing it. Francis Morrissey's name was never resubmitted. He continued on as a municipal judge, served as a trustee and chair of several Boston institutions, retired in 1980, and died on December 27, 2007, at the age of ninety-seven.

That same afternoon I boarded a flight to Vietnam with a fact-finding congressional delegation that included two good friends: my old Harvard teammate and roommate John Culver, then a congressman from Iowa, and my former moot court partner John Tunney, then a California congressman. My seatmate en route to Saigon, and my roommate for the four days and four nights we were there, was Senator Joseph Tydings. It was about as long and hard an exercise in tongue-biting as I have ever had.

Was my loyalty to Frank Morrissey excessive? To this day, my heart tells me that I was right in championing this man, who was at least the professional equal of many other sitting federal judges. My reason tells me that good and thoughtful lawyers and senators looked at his record and concluded otherwise. Some historians have written that Lyndon Johnson himself played me false in his supposed support for Morrissey, intending to hoodwink me and Bobby: hoping we'd be embarrassed by a negative Senate vote. I never really bought that theory. I thought Johnson played it straight.

CHAPTER TWELVE

Thunder
1965–1967

In the scheme of things, the Frank Morrissey episode was but one small distraction in a globally tumultuous year. Vietnam was ablaze: back in March, amid his hopeful domestic social initiatives, President Johnson had authorized a "limited" aerial bombardment of North Vietnam. But like the larger war it was designed to end, Operation Rolling Thunder slipped its restraints and took on a monstrous life of its own.

Rolling Thunder had been conceived as an eight-week demonstration of America's military might—the "shock and awe" of its time. It would strike fear into the enemy as it smashed his industrial and transportation systems and decimated his troops heading south. In short, the operation would be a technological fix for a technological failure: the jungle-and-tunnel ground war that had neutralized our mass-battlefield weaponry and frontline tactics.

By the end of 1965, the bombers had been flying for nine months, and they would continue to do so until November 1968. Only after more than three hundred thousand U.S. attack sorties had resulted in nearly a million tons of bombs dropped, 745 American crewmen shot down (of whom 145 were rescued), seventy-two thousand Vietnamese civilian casualties out of the ninety thousand total, and little discernible achievement of its goals was Rolling Thunder suspended.

The bombing of North Vietnam was to become one of two cornerstones in my evolving campaign against the war. The other was refugees.

I supported the war when I arrived in Vietnam on that October 1965 visit. I still supported it upon my return. I supported it, by lessening degrees, until the spring of 1966. Supporter of the war though I was, I began to perceive almost as soon as we arrived in Vietnam that its dynamics were more complex than Americans were being led to believe. What I saw was reinforced by the findings of my refugee subcommittee, which held thirteen hearings during the summer of 1965 on the effect of our war efforts on the Vietnamese people, particularly in rural areas. A gulf had opened between what was happening in the military sphere (or what was claimed to be happening) and what was happening to the people: the civilian population. Nearly a sixteenth of them were on the run. They were essentially refugees in their own country.

Generally, we think of refugees as being people who are forced to flee for reasons of safety, but sometimes they are forced to move from place to place within their own land. Displacement is the common denominator. As I write today, for instance, there are more than two million people in Iraq who have been uprooted. They are refugees as surely as anyone who's been forced to cross a national border. The same was true of Vietnamese farmers and workers in 1965: they remained inside their country, but were constantly being forced out of home and hearth, with their lives in the balance.

The displacement most anguishing to me was that of people scrambling away from "free fire zones," areas into which U.S. forces could fire weapons without clearance from superior officers, under the assumption that friendly personnel had been evacuated and that anyone left was probably an enemy combatant.

In the four days our delegation was in South Vietnam, we received many briefings, though we were prohibited from viewing combat operations. We were briefed by General William Westmoreland, the commander of military operations there. Westmoreland told us things were going well.

With Bobby and Jack
on the beach in
Palm Beach.
Douglas Jones,
LOOK Magazine/
John F. Kennedy Library

With Bobby and Jack.
Edward M. Kennedy Collection

With Joan
at our wedding,
November 29, 1958.
Bettmann/Corbis

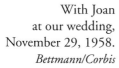

With Jack at a campaign stop in West Virginia during my brother's 1960 presidential campaign. When Jack got laryngitis on the trail, I gave a few of his speeches.
Corbis

Coming out of
Chute 4 on Skyrocket,
Miles City, Montana,
August 27, 1960.
*Edward M. Kennedy
Collection*

The night after Jack won the presidential election.
*Photo by
Paul Schutzer/
Time & Life Pictures/
Getty Images*

A campaign poster
from 1962.
Boston Globe /Landov

At a campaign rally in
Massachusetts, 1962.
Fay Foto Service

Campaigning in Medfield, Massachusetts, October 11, 1962.
Frank C. Curtin/AP Photo

With President Kennedy at a Democratic Party fundraiser, "New England's Salute to the President," at the Boston Armory, October 1963.
Cecil Stoughton/John F. Kennedy Library

With Mrs. Ngo Dinh Nhu, First Lady of South Vietnam, at a luncheon during the Inter-Parliamentary conference in Belgrade, 1963.
Bettmann/Corbis

With Kara and Teddy Jr.
John Loengard/Time Life Pictures/Getty Images

Teddy Jr. and Kara.
Bettmann/Corbis

The remains of the plane that crashed in the fog near Southampton, Massachusetts,
December 1964.
Bettmann/Corbis

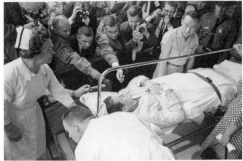

After the plane crash, being wheeled into an ambulance for my transfer to New England Baptist Hospital in Boston. *AZB/AP Photo*

Receiving physical therapy. *Leonard McCombe/Time Life Pictures/Getty Images*

With Joan, Kara, and Teddy Jr. at New England Baptist Hospital. *Bettmann/Corbis*

With Bobby in the hospital. *Bettmann/Corbis*

With Dad, December 1964.
Bettmann/Corbis

Presenting a Purple Heart
to a wounded American serviceman
during an inspection tour of Vietnam,
October 1965.
Edward M. Kennedy Collection

With Coretta and
Dr. Martin Luther King Jr.,
at a meeting of the
Southern Christian
Leadership Conference,
August 8, 1966.
Edward M. Kennedy Collection

St. Patrick's Day Parade
in South Boston.
*Burton Berinsky/John F. Kennedy
Library/Landov*

A hearing on the issue of poverty,
March 1967.
Wally McNamee/Corbis

Discussing campaign strategy
with Bobby at Hickory Hill
in McLean, Virginia, 1968.
Burt Glinn/Magnum Photos

We were briefed by the general's subordinate military leaders, who told us things were going well. We were briefed by diplomats who were involved in humanitarian undertakings. The diplomats told us things were going well.

They told us that things were getting better in the South, and that although there was systemic corruption in the South Vietnamese government and military, our special forces were training Vietnamese troops, and that they were improving and getting better organized. The South Vietnamese officials that I spoke with had a similar message.

I was impressed and accepted at that time what Westmoreland and the others had told me: that things were moving in a positive direction and the biggest concern was the danger of success by the Vietcong and the expansion of communism in the region.

I published my impressions of that visit—reinforced by an extraordinary conversation after I returned home—in an article for the February 8, 1966, issue of *Look*.

I began by acknowledging the debate "on an almost unprecedented scale" over our presence in Vietnam, and the nearly universal public awareness of this debate. An even more important related issue, though, was receiving hardly any attention, despite an address on the subject by President Johnson the previous April:

> The second conflict in Vietnam—the struggle for the hearts and minds of the Vietnamese people themselves—has not been waged with the same ferocity. There has been no one firm humanitarian policy. . . . The struggle . . . has not been one that has produced a concern for the most important element in the Vietnam situation—the welfare of the Vietnamese people themselves.

As evidence, I noted the following, among several other examples:

- That Vietnam had only eight hundred doctors, five hundred of whom were in the military, leaving three hundred for a civilian population of sixteen million. (Of these, nearly one million had become refugees by December 1965.)

- That 80 percent of Vietnamese children suffered from worms.
- That the country's social institutions were being decimated by war: not one of the sixteen thousand villages or their officials had escaped assassination or terror.
- That the government in Saigon was indifferent to these and related problems: "Government officials assured me that the refugee situation was well in hand—yet I inspected one camp of over six hundred people without a toilet. Construction was started on seven refugee camps in anticipation of my visit. Work stopped when my plans were temporarily altered. It began again when it was finally possible for me to go."

I witnessed and understood quite clearly these effects of the war. They troubled me. Yet the ultimate transformation of my position on the war was spurred by the critical conversation awaiting me back in the United States.

The figure I spoke with was Bernard Fall, the extraordinary French journalist and historian who'd been writing about Vietnam since his country withdrew as a colonial power. Fall had invited Tunney, Culver, and Tydings to his Washington apartment shortly after they returned home to compare their impressions with his. When I next saw them, they urged me to seek this man out myself.

I found myself edified by a fit, lean-jawed, bespectacled man of thirty-nine, who looked as though he would be more at home in a camouflage jacket than a scholar's study. Fall was a man of penetrating ideas *and* fearless action. His parents had been part of the French resistance in World War II and paid for it—his father killed by the Gestapo, his mother dying in a concentration camp. Bernard had taken up their activist ideals. He'd observed combat as a journalist traveling with French forces in Vietnam in 1953, and had predicted France's downfall. He had accepted a professorship at Howard University, but returned to Southeast Asia, where he applied brilliantly unorthodox measurements to his study of the war. On his last visit there, two years after our talk, Fall was killed by an exploding land mine while on one of his many forays into the field—this time with a platoon of U.S. Marines pursuing the Vietcong down the fabled Route 1, which he had trod with the retreating French more than a decade earlier.

The structure of our conversation was the itinerary of my own visit to Vietnam. I would name a location and Fall would ask, "Now, who did you get briefed by?" I would reply, "Well, it was the State Department and the land reclamation people and the economic development people, and they told us that there was more rice being produced than ever."

Fall would shake his head and reach for a folder. In it would be statistics for rice production in that region before the war—say, three hundred thousand tons. I would be perplexed: "Oh? That doesn't really square with what I was told on this. It was a much lower figure." Fall would then ask, "And what was the price of rice? And what did that price tell you about security?" I would consult my notes and quote some rice prices, wondering what they had to do with security. Fall would produce a pamphlet from the Department of Agriculture, quoting rice prices at various hamlets within a region. "Why is there a 200 percent increase from this village to this one? Don't you suppose it is because this second village is not secure?"

Thus Bernard Fall, sitting in his study and drawing only upon American documents, would contrast what our official sources had told us with what could be inferred from our government's own statistics. And thus he raised the most serious questions I had yet encountered about honesty, truthfulness, and candor in war.

Back in the Senate, I resumed work on issues tangential to the war. I began on a reform that would take years to be enacted into law: an overhauling of the Selective Service System to create a fairer process for the military draft.

The draft method then in use had changed little, in structure at least, from the late 1940s. It required all men aged eighteen to twenty-six to register for conscription into the army, with the option of volunteering for the navy, marines, or air force. The length of commitment, including active duty and reserve time, was six years. Local draft boards would select names from these lists, in theory starting with the oldest registrants first.

The problem with this method was that as the years went on and the threat of war receded, the SSS built in an ever-expanding array of deferments, or available excuses for avoiding military service. The reason for this was bureaucratic survival: the officers in charge of running the draft did not want Congress to abolish their administrative authority in favor of an all-volunteer army. Lieutenant General Lewis Hershey, the system's director, actually argued that the prospect of being drafted had the power to terrify young men into enlisting, in the hope of getting the best possible deal for themselves. These layers of deferments led inevitably to a de facto system of class privilege for those who claimed "other priorities": potential college students, who were mostly white, could avoid or delay the draft, while young black men, with no college prospects, could not.

I began to face the fact that while draft reform was well worth pursuing, it was subsidiary to the overarching question of the war itself. In the spring of 1966 I began addressing this question. I was not yet ready to call for an American pullout from Vietnam. But I was ready to challenge Lyndon Johnson on a cornerstone strategy in his prosecution of the war.

An occasion presented itself: a meeting the president called at the White House on the evening of June 29. He'd invited some thirty-five members of the House and five senators: George McGovern, Fritz Mondale, Joe Tydings, John Cooper, and me, all of whom had traveled to South Vietnam. He wanted our input—or so he declared.

My notes on that meeting provide a window into the president's leadership style and "consultation" with Congress. President Johnson came in at about 6:15 p.m. and asked Secretary of Defense Robert

McNamara to give us a report on that morning's bombing of petroleum tank farms near Hanoi and Haiphong Harbor.

The president mentioned that the congressional response he had heard to date had been principally critical of the bombing. He was distinctly uneasy as he went around the table asking for our comments. His concern quickly evaporated, however, as the first members to speak indicated that they wanted the president to go even further. *They* were concerned that he was holding back and hadn't taken the wraps off the air force and the military completely. Johnson visibly relaxed.

When the president called on me, I broke the mood. "I regret that I have to sound the first note of discord this evening," I began. I felt we should be moving in a different direction because aerial bombing had never been successful in bringing people to a peace conference table. I quoted the mayor of Hamburg, Germany, as saying in May of 1945 that although the city had suffered forty-five thousand civilian casualties under Allied bombing, the will of the people had never been stronger in defense of their city and country. I said that we should halt the bombing in the North and do what was necessary in the South to maintain the security of our forces, while continuing the search-and-destroy efforts. If it was necessary to send additional troops to achieve this goal, then that step should be taken. In the silence that followed, I added that what disturbed me the most about the current phase was that we appeared to have given up our diplomatic efforts.

What does the future hold? I asked. Will we continue the bombing of Hanoi and Haiphong? Are we prepared to respond at this time if Chinese ships enter this port or Chinese planes attack our bombers? Are we going to stop them or destroy them? Are we going to bomb the port facilities?

The president dismissed my concerns. According to my notes, he said, "What would anyone do in this situation? Everyone wants an easy answer. When a fella is about to hit you, what do you do? If fifty trucks come down the road, do you just crawl under the rug? Or do you hit 'em back? I've given this a lot of thought. I think we should hit 'em back."

McNamara expressed his own concern about ending the bombing: "How do you tell American [infantry] to face fifty trucks of ammunition when you have planes and bombs to take them out?" Johnson then said that he hadn't received a letter from one soldier in Vietnam who wanted the U.S. military to withdraw from the country. And until the North Vietnamese get more discouraged than they are today, he said, we would not be able to reach any agreement with them. By bombing Hanoi and Haiphong, we would raise the cost of the war to them to such a level that they would no longer be interested in it. It was obvious that the administration had made up its mind. George McGovern and Joe Tydings asked about the nature of our objectives in Vietnam. But George Ball summarily dismissed their questions just before the president broke in and said, "We have already stated the problem twice—what our objectives are in Vietnam." Tydings said he'd seen a recent speech by Secretary of State Dean Rusk that he felt left open the interpretation about our fundamental objectives. He thought they should be clarified.

Before that could happen, Congressman Howard "Bo" Callaway interrupted to declare that he was a West Point graduate, that he had some one hundred friends in Vietnam, that he'd spent two weeks there. He pronounced the president's bombing strategy long overdue. Morale among the boys on the aircraft carriers, after their strikes on Hanoi and Haiphong, had never been higher.

When the congressman was finished, the president said that that was the finest statement that he'd heard on Vietnam all evening. By this time in the evening, President Johnson had relaxed completely. His spirits rose as he became sure of the support of the House members.

I left the meeting with Senators McGovern, Mondale, and Tydings. McGovern shared my frustration, saying it was impossible for him to communicate effectively with the president about Vietnam: "Something happens to you when you get into the Cabinet Room with all those charts, maps, and aerial reconnaissance photos around the room."

And so Rolling Thunder continued.

A different thunder rolled through American cities in the hot summers from 1965 through 1969 and, sporadically, beyond: the thunder of gunfire and explosions and police tear gas canisters as Americans fought one another in urban streets; the thunder unleashed by the violent collision, as the Kerner Commission would later phrase it, of "two societies, one black, one white—separate and unequal."

The inaugural of the 1960s race riot era—the six-day spree of fires, deaths, and terror in the Watts neighborhood of south-central Los Angeles—was almost a year old when, on August 8, 1966, I traveled to Jackson, Mississippi, to address the annual convention of the Southern Christian Leadership Conference. I shared the platform with Martin Luther King Jr., the organization's first president (though unfortunately I never got to know him well).

I began with praise for the group's commitment to nonviolence. "You have been jailed and bombed, beaten, and stoned," I told them, "but your work has persevered."

I ticked off the recent milestones in black America's fight for equality: the passage of three civil rights bills since 1959 with a fourth soon to come, the registration of more than two million Negro voters in the South, the advent of the War on Poverty.

I acknowledged the realities that remained. "After all of the programs that Congress has passed," I asked, "how much has the life of the average Negro really changed? Not very much. What good is a desegregated motel if you can't afford to stay there? What use is the right to vote if you must risk your job and even your life in order to vote?"

None of us, perhaps not even the rioters themselves, could then fully imagine the breadth of combustible despair and anger that curled about the nation's most alienated streets, black and white, awaiting the spark of ignition. Parts of San Francisco, Omaha, Waukegan, Lansing, and Chicago went up that summer. The next year would see the conflagration of Newark—five days, twenty-six deaths, more than $10 million in property damage. No city, it began to seem, was safe: Tampa, Buffalo, Memphis,

Milwaukee, Washington, Baltimore, Youngstown, Hartford, Fort Lauderdale—the list went on. As did the sniper fire, the clubbings, the flames, the deaths of police and civilians, the ruined small businesses and churches and schools, the incalculable economic devastation: $45 million in insured damages in one hundred cities by early 1968, to cite but one of many figures.

"How is it possible?" President Johnson asked. "After all we've accomplished? How could it be?"

It was a question that many in Congress must have asked themselves. It implied a crushing sense of betrayal. Here we were, by our own sights, a collection of affluent, well-educated, politically successful white men who had devoted years to a constellation of causes that might well have led to electoral defeat for any or all of us. School desegregation. Desegregation in universities. Desegregation in transportation and public gathering places. The Civil Rights Act. The Voting Rights Act. The poll tax repeal. We acted, as I have said, because we believed that the principle of equality and justice among the races was a cause larger than our own ambitions. We believed that our victories in these causes would change history. And at the very moment in American time when we were anticipating a mood of joyfulness and uplift, our cities were exploding in violence. How could it *be*?

There were no easy answers. There never are.

In early 1967, the tide of events began to pull the Kennedys again toward the responsibilities and perils of the highest office in the land. A January poll showed Bobby beating Lyndon Johnson, who was entangled in the coils of the Vietnam War. While it was Bobby alone who took on the burden of contemplating that ultimate choice, all the family reached out to share the weight with him. What he decided would transform all our lives.

The background of Bobby's presidential campaign of 1968 probably had its roots two years earlier, when he and I were campaigning in the Midwest for Democratic senatorial candidates. One of them was Paul

Douglas of Illinois. Douglas was a brilliant but aging figure, a decorated hero of World War II and a close friend of Jack's. He had good ideas about economic policy and urban redevelopment, but he remained a hawk on the war. In the late summer of 1966, embroiled in a close race with the Republican Charles Percy, Douglas asked my brother and me to come out and help him.

We arrived at a pivotal moment in a decade festering with pivotal moments. The antiwar movement, galvanized the year before by Johnson's bombing campaign over North Vietnam, had spread across the United States, with university campuses forming its central nervous system. Senator Douglas had been shocked by the vehemence from students that greeted his speeches. Because Bobby and I agreed with him on nearly all the other issues, we went to bat for him on the campaign trail.

We were both accustomed by now to the raw passions of the civil rights movement, but the fury of the antiwar demonstrators was new to us. The placards, the chants, the shaking fists, the interruptions as we tried to speak to crowds—all of this told us that something profound had taken root in American society.

Bobby returned East after a few days, but I moved on to the University of Wisconsin at Madison to speak on behalf of Gaylord Nelson, who, like Douglas, was up for reelection to the Senate. Nelson was considered a liberal—he founded Earth Day in 1970—and in this year was edging toward an antiwar position, but had not yet declared it. This was not good enough for the three thousand students who awaited us in the lecture hall.

Our first sign of trouble was a display at the back of the hall, whose broad contours were soon to become familiar: an array of white sheets with skeletons drawn on them in charcoal—graphic, and almost ghoulish. Other sheets depicted the explosions of bombs and artillery shells.

I was the first to speak—or try to speak. The crowd erupted in a roar as I walked to the microphone. I looked out at a sea of thrashing arms, writhing bodies. I asked, shouting into the mike, whether they were going to let me speak. "NO! NO!" they thundered. An antiwar chant welled up.

Finally I shouted, "I'll let one of you come up! I'll listen to you speak, and then you listen to me!" A young man approached the stage from the crowd. To this day, I can remember his last name: Schultz. He was from New York. He took the podium and gave an impromptu antiwar talk—I must say, a *stirring* impromptu antiwar talk—that lasted about seven minutes. At the end, waves of roaring approval resounded in the hall.

I decided to honor the mood of the crowd. "You can keep going," I shouted to Schultz. "Keep going!" He cited a couple further facts, and then stopped again. I renewed my gesture: "Keep going! This is a major issue! Keep going!" But Schultz had run out of gas. "I don't have anything more to say," he told me. "You don't have anything more to say?" I repeated. "That's all you had to say?" I had made a tactical mistake: the crowd thought I was browbeating him, and directed boos at me.

At length, things quieted down enough that I was able to speak for the same amount of time as Schultz. My own doubts about the fundamental validity of the war—the seeds planted by Bernard Fall and my own concerns for refugees and the humanitarian aspects of the war—were forming themselves, but I had not yet declared a sweeping opposition. So I spoke critically about one of the two or three issues that orbited this central point: our military's lack of a coherent exit strategy.

Yet the time for declaring oneself was drawing near. By 1967, as U.S. troop levels in Vietnam topped four hundred thousand, the antiwar movement, ignited by the bombing of North Vietnam, swelled toward its peak. Returning veterans disillusioned by the war began to publicly burn their draft cards. In January Martin Luther King declared himself on the dissidents' side, arguing that the war was starving vital domestic legislation.

It was in this atmosphere that my brother, in the early spring of 1967, delivered the Senate speech that set him irretrievably on a course apart from that of President Johnson. Its message was simple: Stop the bombing. Negotiate with North Vietnam for peace.

Bobby had spoken with Johnson before his speech. He'd traveled through Europe weeks earlier, meeting with President Charles de Gaulle, the Socialist leader François Mitterrand, and the Far Eastern specialist Etienne Manac'h in France; Chancellor Kurt Kiesinger and then foreign minister Willy Brandt in Germany; and, in Italy, the Italian foreign minister Amintore Fanfani and President Giuseppe Saragat. All had expressed variations of the same conviction: that America's course in Vietnam was wrong, and that it was harming U.S. relations with Europe. The well-connected Manac'h had added the provocative view that Hanoi, though it had lost trust in President Johnson's peace overtures, was prepared to negotiate without preconditions except one: that America halt its bombing of the North.

On his return, Bobby had met privately with Johnson and told him frankly what he thought the president should do—told him, in essence, the thrust of the speech he was contemplating.

And then Bobby made a serious offer to Johnson. He proposed that the president give him the authority to personally negotiate for peace. He would shuttle back and forth between Washington and Saigon, and would even travel to Hanoi and China if necessary—and Moscow—if Johnson would trust him to be the U.S. government's agent in these secret negotiations.

If the president had accepted his offer, Bobby certainly would have been too immersed in the peace process to become involved in the 1968 presidential primary. But Johnson just couldn't accept his offer at face value. He worried about Bobby's sincerity and whether he had ulterior motives. Bobby didn't. He just wanted to end a war.

And so on March 2, 1967, after a night of drafting and redrafting his speech, with the knowledge that American opinion tilted against him and that the political repercussions would be harsh, Senator Robert Kennedy stood up in the Senate and spoke for the record about his break with America's conduct of the Vietnam War.

He absolved Johnson of personal responsibility for the conflict, and accepted some responsibility, along with the late President Kennedy, for failures of policy. Yet this ever-widening war must end, he declared, and

it was Congress's and the president's responsibility to end it. Given that
Hanoi was reported to be ready to negotiate, the United States should test
that readiness by a cessation of the bombing. An international group
should monitor the borders for signs of further escalation by the North,
and United Nations forces should gradually replace U.S. troops as negotiations moved forward.

Johnson increased the bombing missions.

I respected the courage and moral clarity that Bobby displayed with
this declaration. And I was moving closer to my own public break with the
administration's war policy. I had privately urged the administration to
pursue diplomacy instead of bombings, but those efforts had obviously
been futile. I then publicly declared that the Great Society itself had become a casualty of the Vietnam War. We had been forced to spend so much
militarily that there were no longer resources for domestic programs.

In May, I disputed the official estimates of war casualties among South
Vietnamese civilians. I reported to Neil Sheehan of the *New York Times*
that my subcommittee staff and I had determined that the dead and
wounded amounted to more than one hundred thousand a year—double
the figure announced by the administration.

I also kept up my criticism of the deplorable state of medical care
available to Vietnamese civilians, and in July the president responded—
or appeared to respond—by sending a team of physicians over to study
the situation. The doctors' findings proved nearly as worthless as the
facilities they examined. To their credit, they called for increased spending, especially on surgical resources. But they dismissed my casualty estimates as far too high. They rejected my call for building three new
hospitals in the country. I convened public hearings on the issue. The
doctors again pointed to underfunding by the Johnson administration.
We were getting nowhere.

In August McNamara admitted to a Senate committee that the bombing of the North was not working. In November he announced his resig-

nation, and his intention to join the World Bank as its fifth president. Johnson replaced him with Clark Clifford.

Lyndon Johnson had reasons to resent the Kennedys, and Bobby in particular. Public opinion polls showed a tide of popular support for my brother's candidacy for president as 1967 went on, and a corresponding drop in LBJ's popularity. Bobby had said nothing about running for president then, although privately he had burned to challenge Johnson at least since the summer of 1967—not from personal animosity, but because he wanted to stop the war, among other priorities. I talked him out of it at that time. I did not see how we could pull things together to win the nomination against a sitting president, and even if we did, I didn't see how we could win in November.

Now my brother was beginning to attract people who agreed that Johnson must be challenged from within his own party: people such as activist Allard Lowenstein, who soon would head the Americans for Democratic Action, and California's Jesse Unruh. Bobby continued to hold back from any inclination to run, even as he kept up his criticism of the war, and Senator Eugene McCarthy seemed poised to declare as the candidate of the antiwar left. Yet the opinion polls, the urgings of friends, the rigidity of LBJ as his popularity sank—all this, coupled with Bobby's own anguish over the continued waste of humanity and resources in Vietnam— made it impossible for him not to contemplate the prospect.

On October 8, 1967, a group of us met at the Regency Hotel in New York to discuss Bobby's plans over the next year. Bobby did not attend the meeting, but he had called and specifically asked me to be there. In addition to me, the group consisted of Chuck Daley, Joe Dolan, Fred Dutton, Dick Goodwin, Ivan Nestingen, Kenny O'Donnell, Pierre Salinger, Steve Smith, Ted Sorensen, and Bill vanden Heuvel. We had a good give-and-take and decided at the end of the day not to confront Johnson at that time, but not to endorse him either. In the meantime, the team would start to make contacts with the Democratic organization in different parts of the country (we saw this as essential no matter what steps we ended up taking in '68) and would take soundings in New Hampshire right away. We agreed to get together again in a month or so.

On Tuesday, November 28, Eugene McCarthy came to my Senate office to let me know that he was going to announce his candidacy for president. He told me that he would enter four primaries, but that for the time being Massachusetts was not one of them. He expected to keep the Massachusetts decision—and New Hampshire—under review for three or four weeks and would let me know before he made any announcements. I told him that I would have to keep open the possibility of running as a favorite son and he said fine, that he understood anything along those lines that I would do. At that time, McCarthy understood that my running as a favorite son would be intended as a placeholder for LBJ, but the whole situation was one I was eager to avoid. I indicated to McCarthy that there was a Massachusetts Democratic State Committee meeting on December 2 and that a resolution was going to be voted on at the time, but he seemed only vaguely interested in that. Our meeting lasted about fifteen minutes.

McCarthy publicly declared his candidacy on November 30. And on December 2, with a bit of behind-the-scenes work from our people, the Massachusetts State Committee voted to support LBJ and his policies by a vote of forty-five to four. Within hours of that vote—and without notice to me—McCarthy publicly announced that he was entering the Massachusetts primary. He came by to see me briefly on December 6 to "explain" the reason for violating his commitment to talk to me before he made any announcements about my state. He felt that the State Committee vote had left him no choice. They had "thrown down the gauntlet." He hoped I would understand. Then he said that when you enter these campaigns, sometimes you go past the point of no return.

On Sunday, December 10, a small group met at Bill vanden Heuvel's apartment in New York to discuss Bobby's plans. This time, the forty-two-year-old potential presidential candidate was there as well. In addition to Bobby, Bill, and me, the participants in that meeting were Fred Dutton, Dick Goodwin, Pierre Salinger, and Arthur Schlesinger.

Schlesinger opened with a fiery argument for Bobby making the run. Goodwin offered some strategic thoughts about how Bobby might enter the primaries on the assumption that McCarthy would soon withdraw, leaving Bobby to face Johnson at the convention. Bobby himself spoke up from a moral perspective. He wondered whether the world could endure another Johnson term, and whether that question alone should propel him into the race.

I believed, and Ted Sorensen agreed with me, that the 1968 elections would not be a good time for a run by Bobby. We both believed that Johnson would win reelection and that my brother should wait until 1972, when he would be the logical successor. The meeting ended with an agreement to take a look at the situation again after the first of the year.

The year 1967 had held its moments of relief for me from the weights of Vietnam and urban racial violence. In the spring, I worked with Howard Baker, then a freshman Republican senator from Tennessee, on "one man, one vote" legislation, basically reforming congressional districts in the United States into roughly the same size in terms of population. Bobby knew and admired Baker and had suggested that we join forces.

The Supreme Court had ruled five years earlier that population imbalance in legislative districts could be challenged in court as unconstitutional. Proportional population was a tough issue to sell in practice, though, because both Democrats and Republicans valued having congressmen in small rural districts. The House had just passed a bill that would permit a 30 percent differential between the most and the least populous districts; the Senate Judiciary Committee, over my objections, increased the margin to 35 percent.

With Baker working the press, and me working the phones and the meeting halls to galvanize the support, we began to progress. The process took several months, and we faced many strategic delays. But in November, the momentum swung in our favor and we won on a Senate vote of fifty-five to twenty-two. I was exhilarated.

Even more satisfying was the birth on July 14 of Joan's and my second son, Patrick Joseph Kennedy. Patrick was a gift of pure joy. This new baby embodied so much of my hopes and dreams for the future. I couldn't even imagine then the pride I would someday feel serving alongside him in Congress. With our expanding family, Joan and I needed a bigger house. So we found property along the Potomac River, not far from Bobby and Ethel in McLean, Virginia, where we proceeded to build a new home.

CHAPTER THIRTEEN

Bobby
1968

My second visit to Vietnam grew out of my conviction that an even greater gap existed between rhetoric and reality there than during my first trip, in 1965.

I had dispatched a team of advance men to explore the terrain held by U.S. forces—villages, refugee camps, hospitals—and to scout for sources who could take me beyond "official" versions of what was happening. My traveling companion on the flight over was Dr. John M. Levinson, a physician who had spent time in Vietnam studying medical care and health issues.

We arrived in Saigon on January 1—two days before Senator Eugene McCarthy stunned the Democratic Party by announcing he would enter the New Hampshire primary against Lyndon Johnson as a test of the Vietnam issue. Over the twelve dangerous and heartbreaking days we spent on the ground, I refused to settle for canned pronouncements and packaged tours. When a colonel greeted us with a schedule for a given day, I would demand double or triple the agenda. I made sure we kept on the move, and in one instance, at least, it was that constant motion that kept us alive. We'd been scheduled to have dinner one night in Can Tho at the residence of the heroic young pacifist David Gitelson of the International Volunteer Service, a sort of private version of the Peace Corps. Gitelson, who'd been an honor student at the University of California at Davis, was living like a peasant in Vietnam, teaching modern farming methods to people as he roamed the Delta region. He was just then involved in building a library at Ba The. As the hour approached, I suddenly decided we needed to be somewhere else, and canceled the dinner in favor of breakfast the next morning. A bomb, planted in a car outside the house, exploded at the dinner hour, blowing out the front of the building.

Gitelson survived. But a month later, he was shot to death by the Vietcong.

Memories from the trip: We raced at midnight across wild jungle roads in a car driven by John Paul Vann, the civilian adviser, in clandestine search of a notorious mental hospital where the inmates were forced to feed on garbage. We didn't find it.

A young air controller sobbed as he described his job to me, flying around in a small plane looking for figures in black pajamas so that he could report their positions to fighter pilots. He had no way of knowing whether the figures were Vietcong or peasants.

I found photographs of Jack on walls of tarpaper shacks in Saigon, and heard shouts of "Ken-uh-*dee*, Ken-uh-*dee*" in a refugee cemetery behind a church in the city.

I met with President Nguyen Van Thieu, as well as U.S. military commander General William C. Westmoreland and Ambassador Ellsworth Bunker on the day before departure back home. Their stonewalling of questions and their boilerplate optimism made me wonder whether they were speaking about the same torn nightmare of a country as the one I'd just seen. In response to my queries about refugees, whose festering camps I'd seen myself, they declared that the refugees were being well cared for. To my report that I'd heard of American artillery fire being directed into an area that might have held civilians, Westmoreland assured me that no civilians could possibly be injured or die from indiscriminate U.S. fire. Why not? Because there was no indiscriminate fire. The handbooks forbade it.

I left Vietnam with one further thought in my mind: I could no longer support this atrocity of a war. I drank a great deal of liquor on the flight home.

My mood was not improved by a briefing with President Johnson at the White House on January 24, not long after I returned. As the president's white-haired dog Yuki romped on the lap of my aide Dave Burke, covering him with dog hair, I began to outline my observations: that corruption was rampant in the government of the Republic of Vietnam to the extent that it was inhibiting our goals, and that President Thieu of South Vietnam showed no inclination to combat this corruption. The result was that morale among civilian-program workers was suffering. The president broke in to remark that he was aware of the corruption, and yes, it certainly had to be corrected. He asked me for an evaluation of U.S. civilian personnel in Vietnam, and I told him that although some in the mission were long-serving, dedicated, and able, too many others saw their work as a form of adventure and escapism, a chance to break away from their wives and earn some easy money.

The president mulled this over and suggested that before I continued, Dave and I might like some tea, coffee, or a Fresca. We politely declined. The president persisted and asked Dave, "Aren't you going to have a Fresca with your president?" David said, of course, he would have a Fresca.

LBJ seemed preoccupied with our soft drink needs as that meeting went on, Burke's especially. Every time Dave found an opening to voice his opinions on Vietnam, Johnson would interrupt to ask whether he would like another Fresca. It finally became clear that the president was trying to keep Dave off balance—and off the topic of Vietnam.

The president gave me a little more leeway than Burke in speaking my opinions—but not much. After much fencing, I finally was able to turn the topic to how I would suggest reducing the war to more moderate levels, as was my stated wish. I urged him to change our strategy from "search and destroy" (essentially, going out gunning for the enemy) to one of "clear and hold" (securing territory). LBJ told an assistant to write out a memo along those lines. We all want to do the right thing, he observed.

Finally, Johnson asked me whether I'd seen any progress in the war since my trip in 1965. I formulated as tactful a reply as I was able: perhaps I had seen some, I told him, but I was not sure the measures of progress we were using were in fact related to the real war, the war we should be fighting for the Vietnamese people. Lyndon Johnson thought that over for a moment, and then became philosophical. It is difficult to evaluate the war, he said. You have some progress when you have half a million men and all that equipment, but where and how do you start evaluating true progress? Two times zero is zero, he noted, but two times one-half is one. And that is some progress.

Then the president leaned toward me. "I believe we are all trying to do the right thing," he said again, and added, "If we flop on this one, then Nixon will be in there, and we don't want that, do we, Ted?"

On that note, the meeting ended.

Two days later, in an address before the World Affairs Council in Boston, I abandoned all restraint. The *Lowell Sunday Sun*, among other papers, printed the text of my remarks, and added the comment, "This speech could mark the beginning of the end of U.S. involvement in the Vietnam war."

I acknowledged the limited optimism I had felt after my 1965 visit, but told my audience, "I am forced to report to you, and to the people of the Commonwealth, that continued optimism cannot be justified . . . that the objectives we set forth to justify our initial involvement in that conflict, while still defensible, are now less clear and less attainable than they seemed in the past." I praised the bravery and professionalism of the young Americans who were fighting for us. Yet, "I found that the kind of war we are fighting in Vietnam will not gain our long-range objectives; that the pattern of destruction we are creating can only make a workable political future more difficult; and that the government we are supporting has given us no indication, and promises little, that it can win the lasting confidence of its own people."

This war was unlike the traditional wars the United States had fought, I said. "Our country was not attacked. Our cities were not threatened. We do not seek to overthrow an enemy government, capture ground, or achieve unconditional surrender. We seek only to allow the people a free choice. For these reasons the war is more nebulous, more vague in its ends, than the conflicts of our past . . . we must be careful in applying the traditional canons of patriotism, or the clichés of the past, in judging this war."

I pointed out, in reference to America's concern with the spread of communism, that political ideology meant little to the suffering peasants of Vietnam. Their concerns and hopes were not identical to ours. I brought up the question of refugees: "twenty-five percent of that nation's population, all of whom are disaffected, all of whom hold a strong resentment for whatever side tore them away from . . . their lives. . . . I found a great deal of resentment to the United States among these people."

I spoke of the corruption among Vietnamese officials, and gave examples: the siphoning off of money to aid the refugees, for one.

"I believe," I told my audience toward the end, "that if we cannot achieve negotiations in the very near future, we should begin immediately to moderate . . . our activities in South Vietnam to levels . . . more commensurate with our limited aims." Those aims, I suggested, should be defensive—protecting and holding heavily populated areas—and conditional on demanding and receiving more of a commitment from South Vietnam to defend and govern itself.

With this speech, I was now on record, along with Bobby, that time and events had outpaced our original mission in Vietnam, and that the war was a perversion of our original ideals.

On the issue of Vietnam, I was shoulder-to-shoulder with my brother. And yet as I watched his trajectory veer toward a bid for the 1968 presidential nomination, I continued to find myself unable to embrace it wholeheartedly.

Don't mistake me: I thought that Bobby *should* be president. And I thought that Bobby *could* be president. But I believed that 1972 would be a better year to run. If LBJ prevailed in the primaries but lost the election, Bobby would be blamed. But whether LBJ won or lost, I thought that Bobby would be the likely nominee in 1972. He would be the one to bring the party together.

Bobby was torn by his personal desire to stay out of the race and his growing opposition to the war. Ethel and my sister Jean urged him to commit. Bobby edged toward running, but remained wary. "What bothers me is that I'll be at the mercy of events," he remarked.

On January 31, less than two weeks after I returned from Vietnam, the Tet Offensive erupted. As Bobby breakfasted with members of the National Press Club in New York and told them he would not oppose Johnson "under any conceivable circumstances," more than eighty thousand North Vietnamese and Vietcong troops broke an announced religious-holiday cease-fire and rose up along a front throughout the South, attacking villages, towns, and cities. The communists eventually paid a terrible price in casualties for this surprise offensive, which had been conceived as an effort to stalemate the war. U.S. forces won the battle, but its initial severity outraged the American public. Coupled with an unrelated attack by North Korea on the U.S. intelligence ship *Pueblo* a week earlier, Tet spurred the Joint Chiefs of Staff to request more than two hundred thousand new troops.

Not "under any conceivable circumstances," Bobby had declared at the Press Club. I was glad that the alert Frank Mankiewicz, his press secretary, prevailed on him to change "conceivable" to "foreseeable" for release to the press. In 1968, scarcely anything was foreseeable.

Nor was Bobby as hardened against running as his declaration made him sound. On my return flight from Vietnam in mid-January, I had stopped over in Hawaii, intending to try and clear my mind in the sun there for two or three days. I was in my hotel room, getting undressed and ready to drop into bed and sleep off my fatigue, when the telephone rang.

It was Bobby. "Come on back now," he told me. "We're going to meet out at McLean, either tomorrow or the next day." I climbed into my clothes again, checked out of the hotel, found a plane, and flew back. I felt that I knew exactly what I was going to find out upon my arrival: Robert F. Kennedy would join the race for the Democratic presidential nomination. I'd heard it in his voice on the phone.

But Bobby was still not ready to commit himself. Not publicly. The meeting at Hickory Hill in McLean turned out to be a discussion of options, strategies, weighing political pluses and minuses. I continued to oppose his entry, but save for Ted Sorensen, I had no allies.

On February 1, we knew who Bobby's Republican opponent would most likely be. Richard Nixon announced for the nomination. His only criticism of the Vietnam War was that it was not being waged efficiently enough.

On February 8, Bobby abandoned what was left of his own restraints and ambiguities regarding Vietnam. At a book and author luncheon at the Ambassador East Hotel in Chicago, where he'd been invited to speak about his forthcoming book, *To Seek a Newer World*, Bobby unleashed a denunciation of the war, and ensured wide coverage of his remarks by instructing his aides to distribute copies of his talk to the national press corps in Washington. He excoriated all the war's facets, from muddled U.S. policies and prosecution to the corruption of the South Vietnamese regime—a regime that was an American ally "in name only." Declaring to the writers and editors that "it is time for the truth," my brother rebuked any official assurances of progress as "illusory." To the contrary, an American military victory was not in sight and probably would never come. I believe the Tet Offensive caused the last of his reservations to fall away.

The fissioning dynamics of 1968 now accelerated. On the same day as Bobby's speech, George Wallace of Alabama announced he would run for president as an independent, and a peaceful demonstration by black students at South Carolina State University—they wanted a bowling hall in the town of Orangeburg to be integrated—triggered gunfire by state troopers. Three students were killed and twenty-seven were wounded.

Bobby remained interested in my opinion on his candidacy. My brother and I had several direct soul-searching talks on the topic, starting with his phone call to Hawaii, summoning me to Hickory Hill. On or about February 13, Bobby asked me what I thought Jack would counsel him to do. I told him I wasn't sure about that, but I knew what our father would have said: Don't do it. As for Jack, he might have cautioned against it as well; but he probably would have made the run himself in similar circumstances.

National attention whipsawed from campus unrest back to the war again on February 27, when Walter Cronkite, at the end of his CBS newscast, famously editorialized that the war was likely to end in a stalemate.

The following day, the moderate Republican governor of Michigan, George Romney—who'd converted to a critic of the war after saying he'd been "brainwashed" into supporting it a year earlier—dropped out of the race.

Lyndon Johnson's incumbency, and the power and prestige that flowed from it, had stood paramount among the strategic reasons for Bobby's hesitation to declare. (During an early strategy meeting, I'd wondered aloud what would happen if Johnson should pull out of the race. No one took the question seriously—myself included.) But on March 12, America woke up to more stunning news about McCarthy: he had come within seven percentage points of upsetting the president in New Hampshire.

Overnight, Johnson had become beatable. He'd won the balloting, and won it entirely on write-in votes; he'd not even entered the primary. Still, McCarthy's showing, propelled by his antiwar stance and the idealistic college students who canvassed for him, made it clear that the president's worst fears might be realized.

That afternoon, Bobby taped an interview with Cronkite for airing on the *CBS Evening News* a few hours later. A group of us were waiting for Bobby at Jean and Steve Smith's house to explore the implications of

McCarthy's near-upset on Bobby's prospects. At 7 p.m. we tuned in the news and watched the interview. At the end of it—though my brother still had stopped short of declaring his candidacy—I knew, along with everyone else in the room, and everyone who'd watched the broadcast, where his intentions lay. When Bobby himself arrived at the Smith house and walked into the room, sleeves rolled up and grinning his best sheepish grin, we all stood and gave him a great rousing cheer. None of my misgivings mattered anymore. My brother was running for the presidency, and I intended to do everything in my power for him.

Historians like to analyze Bobby's decision to run for president almost exclusively in the context of the Vietnam War and his opposition to it. But Bobby's concerns about America extended far beyond the war. He was bothered by the deterioration in our cities: the poverty and decay, and the growth of gun violence. He did not see Eugene McCarthy paying any particular attention to these problems. I am convinced that had McCarthy begun to talk about the cities and put forth plans to restore them, Bobby would not have run. But McCarthy had demonstrated no interest whatever in these issues. And when one examines the record, one finds that his interest in the war came pretty late as well.

Nor can one fully understand Bobby's candidacy without recalling his engagement with rural hunger and poverty: his emotional interlude with the near-comatose, starving child that he held in his lap inside a shack in the Mississippi Delta, and his vow as he arose that "I'm going back to Washington to do something about this." (The occasion was a visit to the state by a Senate subcommittee on poverty in March 1967; my brother asked Charles Evers to take him on a tour of the Delta.) There was his visit to California for a meeting with Cesar Chavez, the great farmworker activist, who was then on a hunger strike. There was his chairmanship of the Indian Education Committee, in which he held hearings about boarding school abuses being visited on children on western reservations.

Even his war concerns went beyond the fighting, and engaged the issues of what the war was doing to American society. The inequities of the draft, for example. My work on the random-selection revisions in the draft was spurred by his criticisms of the status quo. I remember walking into his house in 1966 and him launching into an attack on the way Selective Service worked: how it was disproportionately the poor and the black who were fighting and dying, while the sons of the white middle class took advantage of the education deferment, the marriage deferment, the skill deferments.

It was not just the war that made Bobby decide to run. It was the war, and how the war was propelling the direction of America, especially the young people, the underprivileged, the underserved, those struggling for their civil rights. It was the inflaming of the cities and the failure to deal with the root causes of the flames. It was the cutting back on appropriations, the underfunding of the Office of Economic Opportunity, for example, because funding for the war took priority. Bobby felt that we were witnessing the deterioration of President Kennedy's legacy. And when people came to Bobby as they did, saying, "You can change this. You can do it. It's possible. It's feasible. We're prepared to help you do it," he felt an obligation to do something.

Our organizational meetings shifted in tone from "further discussion" to "campaign mode." We assigned key people to campaign tasks—organizing volunteers, arranging an itinerary.

By the middle of March, Bobby was perhaps 90 percent resolved that he would run, but he held back, pending one final consultation with Eugene McCarthy, whose viability could not be dismissed. I flew to Green Bay, Wisconsin, to meet with the senator and deliver two messages from my brother. The first was that if McCarthy would pledge to speak out as forcefully about the crises in our cities and about urban policies in general as he was speaking out against the war, Bobby would stay out of the race. The second was that if McCarthy refused to make such a pledge, Bobby would listen to any ideas about a joint effort to defeat Johnson. If the Minnesota senator spurned both options, Bobby would get in.

In the interest of discretion, I flew with a small group of aides to

Green Bay at night and, instead of risking detection by taking an elevator, trudged up the back stairs of the Northland Hotel, where Gene and Abigail McCarthy were staying. I should have saved myself the climb. At the eighth floor, stationed in the stairwell with his cameraman, hovered the CBS correspondent David Schoumacher, who'd been assigned to travel with McCarthy. He asked me, "What are you doing here?"

Abigail answered my knock. I waited an hour and half for McCarthy to appear. It was a difficult meeting. As soon as he entered the room, it was clear to me that he was completely uninterested in what I had to say. I assume that he had watched my brother's interview with Walter Cronkite, and had a pretty good sense that Bobby was going to get into the race. He certainly got it from me that Bobby was going to get in unless the two of them talked. Gene was still riding the high of New Hampshire and felt he was pretty much in the catbird seat. The meeting was respectful, but I really hadn't expected much from it.

McCarthy had always had a little edge of anger, or perhaps contempt, for the Kennedys. I believe he'd felt himself more Catholic, more liberal, and more intellectual than John Kennedy. I'd maintained a decent relationship with him in the Senate, but there was never any warmth between us.

I said goodbye to McCarthy in the wee hours of Saturday, March 16. At which point McCarthy gave the whole story of our meeting to the waiting David Schoumacher, spinning the thrust of it in his own favor.

On Saturday morning, March 16, 1968, Bobby entered the Caucus Room of the Old Senate Office Building and announced his candidacy for president. He stood in the same spot where our brother Jack had made his own announcement in 1960. "I do not run . . . to oppose any man, but to propose new policies," Bobby avowed. The divisions in the party and in the country made clear by Senator McCarthy's showing in New Hampshire took the race beyond a mere clash of personalities and made it a test of policies and the nation's moral character. He expressed personal respect for President Johnson and gratitude for LBJ's kindness toward the Kennedy family. But, "I must enter the race," he declared. "The fight is just beginning, and I believe that I can win."

Fifteen days after my brother entered the race, a weary and war-haunted Lyndon Johnson sat down in the White House television studio and delivered a stunning announcement. He began by renewing his calls for peace talks with North Vietnam. He promised a significant unilateral reduction in the bombing. And then he concluded with the words, "I shall not seek, and will not accept, the nomination of my party for another term as your president."

By that time, Bobby was campaigning with all the energy and clear purpose that the president lacked. Photographs of him amid the crowds are part of the national memory. I still smile when I recall his lightning appearance in Boston the day after his announcement. It was St. Patrick's Day, the occasion of Boston's grandest parade. I was walking, as I did every year, and this time Bobby decided to join me. He arrived while the parade was in progress and walked by himself for a couple of blocks. I spotted him and hurried ahead to join him, but by then he'd noticed that he was getting a great reception. I have a terrific photograph that shows him sort of pushing me away with his right hand. He was saying, "I'm doing fine, Teddy. You don't have to join me. I'll see you later."

At the far end of the parade, in a manner of speaking, lay Indiana. The state now dominated our thinking. Its primary was scheduled for May 7; the filing deadline for candidates was March 28. Should Bobby enter? The risks were high. Indiana was a conservative and pro-war state, despite having elected two antiwar Democratic senators. It was the home to the Ku Klux Klan, a stronghold of the Teamsters, whose membership still resented my brother's investigation of Jimmy Hoffa, and a large conservative agricultural community. Its tough Democratic governor, Roger Branigan, had entered the primary as a stand-in for Johnson. Its two leading newspapers, the Indianapolis *Star* and *News*, reflected the anti-Kennedy opinions of their owner, Eugene Pulliam, a wealthy and right-wing Republican from Arizona.

Despite the odds, we decided that we had no alternative but to enter that primary. No one on the campaign seemed to have focused on the fact that Indiana would be the first test after Bobby announced, and that he stood a very good chance of getting licked there. The early polls did not look good. And if Bobby lost right away, before he got into the other states, it would amount to a devastating setback—especially given the small number of presidential primaries back then relative to today.

In April, as my brother opened his Indiana campaign, I helped set up the state, along with several of our friends and Bobby's aides. We were starting with almost nothing. And so we scrambled. We barnstormed the cities and towns as in the old days for Jack in Wisconsin and West Virginia, collecting signatures for Bobby's entry, building an organization from the ground up. We tried to find out the people's impressions of our candidate. We found that Indianans didn't necessarily like Bobby's "super-hot" style. And they didn't like the similar style of some of his advance people who rolled into the state. Bobby softened his approach and smoothed over some of the local feathers that had been ruffled by overeager staffers, but he didn't slow down his pace.

Every evening in Indiana, after his day's round of speaking and appearances, Bobby would sit down at the hotel bar and have a drink with members of the press. They would talk until two in the morning, and only then would he go to bed. After a three-day run with this schedule, he'd be exhausted. Yet he kept it going. Bobby went beyond political "straight talk." He would talk about Albert Camus, and poetry, and literature that inspired him.

These sessions exacted an incredible physical toll on Bobby. Yet the rewards were great. By the end of the campaign, those press people—suspicious at the outset toward this "ruthless," "arrogant" figure—had formed a completely different view of Bobby. Richard Harwood of the *Washington Post*. Jules Witcover of the *Washington Star*. Jack Newfield of the *Village Voice*. Sandy Vanocur of NBC, who interviewed my brother in the early evening of June 4 in Los Angeles, and then reported live throughout that horrible night from the Ambassador Hotel. All of these fine reporters came to see Bobby as he really was.

After my brother's loss, these members of Bobby's press entourage organized themselves into a group that, each year, gives a press award for a high school essay or editorial on the subject of poverty or civil rights (they present awards to professional journalists as well). They hold an annual presentation in Washington, raising the money themselves.

I have another very personal memory of Bobby in Indiana. I was following him up a stairway to his hotel room, after a long day of campaigning. Bobby told me that he was worried about his then twelve-year-old son David, who had been caught throwing rocks at cars. My brother stopped and looked straight at me.

"Teddy," he said, "I want you to know that if I don't make it this time, I am not interested in running again. This all takes too much. I have to be there for David and the other children."

In the early spring of 1968, America found itself in shock from a loss that in and of itself would have marked the year as catastrophic. On April 4, Martin Luther King Jr. was shot and killed as he stood on a motel balcony in Memphis.

On that same day, Bobby had arrived in Indiana to begin his campaign. He'd kicked it off with an address in Muncie. Then he boarded a flight to Indianapolis for a speech in one of the most troubled African-American neighborhoods in the city, at a children's playground at Seventeenth Street and Broadway. Before his plane left the ground, Pierre Salinger reached my brother by telephone with the news that Dr. King had been shot. Upon his arrival in the city, Bobby learned that King was dead.

Most white political figures would have made any excuse to avoid standing before a black crowd in a ghetto under any circumstances in the summer of 1968. My brother did not hesitate, even when cautioned against it by the Indianapolis mayor. Carrying with him the news of King's assassination, Bobby moved ahead toward a moment that I believe encapsulates his life entire: a moment of conviction, compassion, courage, and eloquence.

Standing hatless on the floor of a flatbed truck under harsh lights on a rainy, windy night, in an enclave of desolation and anger, above a crowd whose reaction could not be predicted, Robert Kennedy broke the news with the directness of a family member: "I have some very sad news for all of you, and I think sad news for all of our fellow citizens, and people who love peace all over the world, and that is that Martin Luther King was shot and was killed tonight in Memphis, Tennessee."

Bobby invited the grieving people before him to make a choice: "You can be filled with bitterness, with hatred, with a desire for revenge." Or, he said, "we can make an effort, as Martin Luther King did, to understand and to comprehend, and replace that violence, that stain of bloodshed that has spread across our land, with an effort to understand with compassion and love."

He quoted Aeschylus: "'In our sleep, pain which cannot forget falls drop by drop upon the heart until, in our own despair, against our will, comes wisdom through the awful grace of God.'"

And Bobby closed with another invitation, this one offering no options at all, other than hope: "Let us dedicate ourselves to what the Greeks wrote so many years ago: to tame the savageness of man and to make gentle the life of this world. Let us dedicate ourselves to that, and say a prayer for our country and for our people."

Upon the news of King's murder, more than a hundred cities across America erupted in rioting and burning. Indianapolis remained calm.

I've always thought in very personal terms of the power of my brother's words that evening. I believe the people of Indianapolis responded to the sincerity of a man whose own life had been touched by such profound loss and grief, by a man who understood.

Sixty-one days later, it was my brother himself who was cut down by an assassin's bullet. Even as I write these words, they still seem almost unreal.

Those sixty-one days were mostly days of sunlight for Bobby; days when tens of thousands of Americans lined the streets of his campaign trail or watched him on television, and came to know him at last in the fullness of his personality, the fullness I'd known and loved since boyhood. He seemed to thrive on his exposure to crowds, although the crammed schedule, the constant travel, and the sheer intensity of it all deepened his exhaustion. As with the reporters in the hotel bar, his contact with the crowds paid dividends. Through his hesitations, his quick banter and self-parodying jokes, his humanity shone through.

He won Indiana on May 7, beating McCarthy by 42 percent of the vote to 27. On the same day he defeated Hubert Humphrey, who'd finally entered the race, in the District of Columbia, 62.5 percent to 37.5. Then on May 14 he won Nebraska. He lost Oregon to McCarthy, who had grown increasingly bitter. He campaigned in South Dakota, which would vote on June 4, and in California, which had its primary on the same day.

California was crucial. I campaigned for Bobby among labor leaders there. McCarthy had stung us in Oregon, but it was Humphrey who led in national delegates. Humphrey was not running in California, where the winner would capture all 172 delegates. Thus, coupled with New York, whose primary was two weeks later, a victory here could give Bobby enormous momentum. We were scraping for every vote we could get.

The signs looked good. My brother's natural constituency—Hispanics, urban blacks, farmworkers—formed a great mass of California voters, and they turned out in throngs for Bobby, cheering his speeches as his train moved up the fertile farmlands of the Central Valley toward Sacramento. He encountered rough spots: a fractious meeting with black militants in Oakland, a spitting incident amid hostile students at San Francisco State College. But on June 1, my brother answered McCarthy's challenge for a televised debate. Nearly half the state's voters watched, and of these, nearly 60 percent thought Bobby had won.

California voters went to the polls on June 4. At a party for campaign workers in San Francisco that evening, I watched the TV networks track Bobby's rising numbers as he came from behind McCarthy en route to a

45 to 42 percent victory. I watched as my brother, with Ethel smiling at his side, received the cheers from his supporters near midnight in the Ambassador Hotel ballroom in Los Angeles. I watched him proclaim America to be "a great country, an unselfish country, and a compassionate country."

And then I left the party and went to my room at the Fairmont Hotel. There, I turned on the television news again.

My mind went black.

Dave Burke was with me. He took care of the details.

A police escort to the airport, a hastily arranged military plane for the flight to Los Angeles, a helicopter ride to Good Samaritan Hospital. John Tunney and John Seigenthaler were there.

We arrived around 3 a.m., just before doctors began their surgery to remove what they could of the three bullets fired by Sirhan Sirhan. Bobby died at 1:44 a.m. the next day, June 6, 1968.

At the funeral mass for Bobby at St. Patrick's Cathedral in Manhattan on June 8, after a night of sleeplessness, I managed to deliver these thoughts:

"Love is not an easy feeling to put into words. Nor is loyalty, or trust or joy. But he was all of these. He loved life completely and lived it intensely.

"A few years back, Robert Kennedy wrote some words about his own father and they expressed the way we in his family feel about him. He said of what his father meant to him, 'What it really all adds up to is love—not love as it is described with such facility in popular magazines, but the kind of love that is affection and respect, order, encouragement, and support. Our awareness of this was an incalculable source of strength, and because real love is something unselfish and involves sacrifice and giving, we could not help but profit from it.'

"Beneath it all, he has tried to engender a social conscience. There were wrongs which needed attention. There were people who were poor and who needed help. And we have a responsibility to them and to this country. Through no virtues and accomplishments of our own, we have been fortunate enough to be born in the United States under the most comfortable conditions. We, therefore, have a responsibility to others who are less well off."

I read a brief speech that Bobby had made to the young people of South Africa on their Day of Affirmation in 1966, in which he acknowledged the world's evils—slavery, slaughter, starvation, repression—but then affirmed "that those who live with us are our brothers; that they share with us the same short moment of life; that they seek—as we do—nothing but the chance to live out their lives in purpose and happiness. . . . Surely this bond of common faith, this bond of common goal, can begin to teach us something."

And I concluded my own remarks:

"This is the way he lived. My brother need not be idealized, or enlarged in death beyond what he was in life, to be remembered simply as a good and decent man, who saw wrong and tried to right it, saw suffering and tried to heal it, saw war and tried to stop it.

"Those of us who loved him and who take him to his rest today pray that what he was to us and what he wished for others will someday come to pass for all the world.

"As he said many times, in many parts of this nation, to those he touched and who sought to touch him:

"'Some men see things as they are and say why.

"'I dream things that never were and say why not.'"

Life, and politics, went on. But not in the same way. Not for me. I was shaken to my core. I was implored to rejoin the political whirlwind less than an hour after Bobby expired. The activist Allard Lowenstein found me on an elevator at the hospital and blurted that I was all the party had left. In subsequent days and weeks, Mayor Daley of Chicago led the voices of those who sought to enlist me as a standard-bearer against Richard Nixon. I told them all no.

I understood very well the stakes of the forthcoming election. I simply could not summon the will.

Hubert Humphrey now dominated Eugene McCarthy in the delegate count, and seemed certain to be the Democratic nominee. The convention was scheduled to begin in Chicago on August 26. Four days before that, Hubert paid an early-morning visit to my house in McLean, and I spent about forty-five minutes with him. We had a warm conversation about my accepting the vice presidential place on the ticket. He understood my personal difficulties, but he wanted me to run with him. If I did, he said, the ticket would win. If I did not, he faced a very difficult uphill fight.

Hubert and I had always had a good relationship, even though he had opposed both Jack and Bobby in presidential primaries. The two of us worked easily together in the Senate. And yet as much as I liked him, I was not prepared to sign on. It was too much, too soon. I was not about to put my family through all this. And anyway, Humphrey had not distanced himself from the war, and I reminded him that a large part of the reason Bobby had decided to run for president was the Vietnam issue. I still felt myself to be a part of this cause that Bobby had created and championed and that had inspired millions of people. It was not necessarily Hubert's cause. If I joined him on the ticket, I would be betraying the whole effort and movement that my brother had stood for—had died for, really. And so in the end it was not even a close decision. I would not stand for vice president.

Hubert told me that once he got the nomination, he could state more accurately his true position on the war. Given that Bobby had staked everything on an explicit antiwar candidacy, I did not find this inspiring. The conversation about the vice presidency ended cordially, and I invited him to breakfast.

The months following Bobby's death are a blur in my memory. One day I decided that going back to work would help relieve the emptiness. I got into my car and drove toward Capitol Hill. When the Senate Office Building came into view, I began breathing heavily. I turned the car around and went back home.

When I finally was able to enter the building, I found that I could not concentrate on my Senate work. I would go and visit my father on the Cape for a couple of days, and then I would go sailing. Sometimes I sailed alone. Sometimes I sailed with a friend. Sometimes I sailed for long distances. Sometimes I sailed to Maine.

I surrendered myself to the sea and the wind and the sun and the stars on these voyages. I let my mind drift, when it would, from my sorrows to a semblance of the momentous joy I have always felt at the way a sailboat moves through the water. I love sailing in the day, but there's something special about sailing at night. And on these nights in particular, my grieving was subsumed into a sense of oneness with the sky and the sea. The darkness helped me to feel the movement of the boat, and the movement of the sea, and it helped displace the emptiness inside me with the awareness of *direction*. An awareness that there is a beginning to the voyage and an end to the voyage, and that this beginning and ending is part of the natural order of things.

A sail from Cape Cod to Maine, with a southwest breeze, is a glorious adventure, and it's a trip that Bobby and I had enjoyed together in years past. About twenty miles from Hyannis, you see a sweep of sand dunes. And as the sun descends, only a few lights appear onshore, and so you head off into the darkness. Yet in the darkness you can see well into the distance, once you have learned where and how to look. The Cape gradually disappears, and the shore lights with it. After a while, new distant lights, small and bright, appear along the shoreline. And then the full darkness descends. Seldom is there another boat in sight.

And that is the truly magical time of sailing, because the North Star appears: the North Star, which has been the guiding star for all seamen through time. The North Star guides you through the evening. Its light is the most definite thing you can see on the surface of the dark water. And so you have the North Star, and the sound and swell of the shifting water. And sometimes the fog will come in and you must go by the compass for a period. But you are always waiting to see the North Star again, because it is the guide to home port; it is the guide to home. And so the voyage becomes all-inclusive; you are enveloped in the totality of it: you are a part of the beginning, you are a part of the end. You are a part of the ship and a part of the sea.

I gazed at the night sky often on those voyages, and thought of Bobby.

PART THREE

On My Own

CHAPTER FOURTEEN

The Shock of Silence
1969

I returned to shore—to the Senate, to what was left of my world—consumed with the need to spur myself forward into activity. Devastation about Bobby's death—and with it, all my pent-up grief about Jack—threatened to overtake me. My only defense against giving in to it was to keep active, keep moving, keep churning forward. I feared that despair and darkness might overtake and smother me if I slackened my drive.

On New Year's Eve 1968, three weeks before the inauguration of Richard Nixon as the thirty-seventh president, I announced to Mike Mansfield that I would challenge Russell Long for his position as Senate assistant majority leader. It was a bold move, in terms of Senate tradition, and it surprised a lot of my fellow senators. Not many of them thought I had a chance to unseat the Louisiana icon, and some thought I had no right. I certainly could show no claim to seniority: I was just thirty-six and had been a senator only six years. I held no committee chairmanships.

The Louisiana incumbent whip cut a picturesque figure in the Senate, though hardly as picturesque as that of his towering father, Huey Long, back in the 1930s. As governor of Louisiana and later its junior senator, "the Kingfish" had blazed his way into folklore as a gifted rustic populist with oratorical tactics and presidential ambitions. I liked Russell: as a specialist in tax law with a conservative's antitax positions, he differed in his politics from me; but his racial views were far more moderate than those of his southern colleagues. More often than not, Russell and I would sit next to each other during Democratic Caucus meetings and he'd tell stories. He was witty, a great teller of jokes—one of the most entertaining senators I've known. There was never any hostility between us.

He also knew how to get things done. He had perfected a trick of persuasion that reminded me of Lyndon Johnson: he would lean into you during a discussion, bringing his face in close to yours and draping a heavy arm around your shoulders, pulling you to him against your will. He'd get inside your space, your comfort zone. Senators would find themselves agreeing to whatever he wanted, just to get away. And when he was at the top of his game, he was a master. He'd take four weeks to push one bill through, not letting it be finished until he was finished lining up his votes. He was unique in that way.

But Long, who'd first been elected to the Senate in 1948, was running out of gas. He was beginning to be more interested in pursuing his oil interests than in attending to the duties of the whip. I sensed that he was vulnerable. I made up my mind before Christmas that I would make the challenge, and on January 3, I ousted Long as whip by a vote of thirty-one to twenty-six.

I continued to drive myself as hard as I could. But sometimes things happened that made me realize that my deepest fears were closer to the surface than I wanted to believe.

As I walked in a St. Patrick's Day parade in Lawrence in March 1969, a burst of popping firecrackers caused me to freeze in my tracks and prepare to dive to the pavement. I stayed upright by an act of will. Years later, on another occasion, I was enjoying a walk in the sunshine near the Capitol with Tom Rollins—then my committee staff director—when a car backfired down the street. Tom recalls that I was suddenly nowhere to be seen. Turning around, he saw me flattened on the pavement. "You never know," Tom recalls me saying. His memory is probably true.

Even now, I'm startled by sudden noises. I flinch at twenty-one-gun salutes at Arlington to honor the fallen in Iraq. My reaction is subconscious—I know I'm not in danger—but it still cuts through me.

In the months and years after Bobby's death, I tried to stay ahead of the darkness. I drove my car at high speeds; I drove myself in the Senate; I drove my staff; I sometimes drove my capacity for liquor to the limit. I might well have driven Joan deeper into her anguish, but the sad truth is that she needed no help from me. Bobby's assassination had devastated her.

We suffered together. And we suffered apart.

I generally managed to keep my public duties and my private anguish separated. Whatever excesses I invented to anesthetize myself, I could almost always put them aside in my role as senator. Almost, but not always.

Among my subcommittee chairmanships was Indian Education. The previous chairman had been Bobby; I'd taken it over after his death. On April 8, 1969, I led a delegation to Anchorage for visits to schools in Eskimo and Indian villages. The other members included Senator Walter Mondale, four other Republican senators, and one GOP representative. The trip was marred at the outset by political tension: after a long day of touring remote villages with newsmen and photographers in tow, three of the Republicans decided that I was exploiting the event for publicity and with great fanfare pulled out of the visit and returned to Washington. Mondale, Senator Ted Stevens, and Congressman Howard Pollock—the latter two of Alaska—and I continued our investigation, and in fact we were later able to pass legislation that improved conditions for the schoolchildren.

The aurora borealis, the northern lights, burned brightly while we were in Alaska. The lights burned especially bright one night during a side visit by Ted Stevens and myself, via a small airplane, to a locale so ancient and so remote as to almost seem suspended in time: Arctic Village, a tribal settlement of fewer than two hundred people and more than forty-five hundred years old. It lay, and still lies, in the lonely far north tundra of the Yukon.

The only landing strip lay several hundred yards from the hamlet, and so Senator Stevens and I, accompanied by some reporters and guides, traveled to it by dogsleds from the plane. We inspected the pitiful facilities, talked to people, made notes on what had to be done, and began our trek back to the airplane. Not far outside the village, I spotted something illuminated dimly by those green and red flashes of light from the heavens. What I saw made me halt my dogsled, disembark, and walk down a path that cut through a nearby woods. I had spotted a child, shivering in the cold, with no shoes and no bottom to his clothing. I unzipped my parka, lifted this little fellow, and tucked him inside against my chest. I could feel his icy skin begin to grow warm as I set out, with Ted Stevens, in search of his mother. We found her, in an igloo in that hamlet. She hadn't realized that her toddler had wandered off.

On the homeward flight to Seattle, I drank too much in an effort to numb myself. The accounts that eventually surfaced, of my resulting rowdiness and leading everyone in childish chants of "Eskimo power!" were on target. Someone later quoted me as saying, in the course of one of those legs, that if I were to run for president, "They're going to shoot my ass off the way they shot off Bobby's."

My family, especially my children, provided hope and balance in those hard months. I focused on the responsibility that now had fallen to me, at age thirty-seven. My father would remain our paterfamilias for as long as he drew breath, but the family now looked to me for guidance and leadership in a new way.

I accepted my new role, insisted on it, and discharged its duties as though Dad's blue eyes were still watching me from the window of the Cape house. I became closer to the children of my brothers and sisters: those of Jack and Jackie, Bobby and Ethel, Peter and Pat Lawford, Sarge and Eunice Shriver, Steve and Jean Smith, Joan and myself; and, later, Caroline and Curran, Vicki's daughter and son. Thirty-two total, just from that group alone. I wanted to do for them what my family had done for me when I was young; what all the Kennedys always did for one another: cherish them, look out for them, show them hope and joy and the delights and miracles of this world.

Memories of how I'd received these gifts came flooding back to me. I recalled the way my parents made the household and the dinner table places of inclusion and learning; the dolls and soldiers that Dad brought home from his travels; the endless larking competitions on the lawn and by the shore and out in the open waters of Nantucket Sound; the way we'd joke as children that none of us would marry because we were having such a good time with one another. I recalled those walking tours with Mother around Boston to see Milk Street and the Common and Paul Revere's home, and the trips with her to Plymouth, to Walden Pond— excursions that Honey Fitz had led for his eldest daughter Rose at the twentieth century's turn; excursions he later led for me.

I recalled how Jack and Bobby, who were altar boys, trained me to be an altar boy—and how that training tightened the fraternal bonds among us.

I recalled watching Jack as he used to take the hand of his small son John and lead the boy to the shore in front of the Cape house; watching the two of them bend over an elegant miniature sailboat, a gift of the Italian government, I think. How Jack would actually trim the little boat's sails and rig its steering.

Then memories came rolling in: all of Bobby's children filling the sunlit waters offshore with swimming and sailing, their cries of excitement floating along in the wind, their father splashing among them.

And I knew that my role now was to ensure a continuum in this beautiful process, this precious tradition of the Kennedy family, regathering itself, replenishing its young with knowledge and love.

And so I became the family uncle. I was counselor, skipper, and mentor to the sailors among them. I organized an annual hiking and camping trip in western Massachusetts, and we kept it going, with a revolving cast, for probably fifteen years. I got a Winnebago and we toured the Massachusetts countryside, the Berkshires, always with a stop in Stockbridge, where we visited Norman Rockwell's studio and the summer studio of Daniel Chester French, the sculptor of Lincoln's figure at the memorial in Washington. Then on to Pittsfield, where we visited Melville's Arrowhead house. Then on again to the Riverside amusement park and its spine-tingling Cyclone roller coaster. As the nephews and nieces grew older, I rented a bus and expanded my itinerary to include the great Civil War battlefields, the ones where Jack had taken me. Over the past fifteen years, the circuit has variously included Manassas, Gettysburg, Antietam, Fredericksburg, Baltimore, Richmond, and Harpers Ferry, among many others.

I traveled constantly, almost compulsively, in the early months of 1969. In mid-May I flew to Los Angeles for a ceremony honoring the great organizer of migrant farmworkers, Cesar Chavez. Cesar had formed a powerful friendship with Bobby. This was my first return to the city since June 1968, and every boulevard, every palm tree took me back to that awful night.

My first impulse had been to decline the invitation. Both Chavez and I would be out in the open, among large crowds, and would be easy targets. But at the last minute I decided the hell with it, boarded a flight, and went.

In my hotel room at Los Angeles, I wrote a letter in longhand to the Los Angeles district attorney, requesting that the life of Bobby's assassin, Sirhan Sirhan, be spared. Sirhan was then awaiting sentencing for his act, and the gas chamber appeared to be his fate. I told the presiding judge that Bobby would not approve the taking of a life in retribution for the taking of his own. The sentence, I argued, should be decided with respect for compassion, mercy, and God's gift of life. The next day I had copies of the letter made and sent them to Ethel Kennedy, to our mother, and to Eunice, Pat, and Jean. All of them agreed with me. I mailed the original letter to the judge, Herbert V. Walker, a week or so after returning from Los Angeles.

Walker disregarded the letter and sentenced Sirhan to the chamber. His life was spared by the California Supreme Court. As he sat on death row in 1972, the court ruled the death penalty unconstitutional. Sirhan's sentence was changed to life in prison.

Meanwhile, the Vietnam War had just reached its peak of escalation, with 543,400 troops in country at the end of April. The mad futility of that escalation was just then on display once again: a ten-day battle of breathtaking, needless carnage. I took the Senate floor on May 20, the concluding day of the slaughter that came to be known as Hamburger Hill, and gave my outrage full cry. It was "both senseless and irresponsible," I declared, that U.S. Army generals "continue to send our young men to their deaths to capture hills and positions that have no relation to this conflict."

The day of my speech marked the twelfth and final infantry assault upon the lethally fortified Ap Bia Mountain in the jungles near Laos. Our troops inflicted and absorbed heavy casualties. After the American survivors had taken the hill, the generals—as I'd predicted; as they so often had—abandoned the mountain as being "of no strategic value."

In subsequent days, and folding the abandonment of Ap Bia into my argument, I repeated my denunciation of the battle to the New Democratic Coalition in New York and to other groups.

On June 2, Everett Dirksen unleashed a strong and lengthy rebuke to me in the Senate. I was absent from the chamber on that day, delivering a commencement speech in Arizona. Senate protocol requires that a senator notify a colleague if he intends to refer to that colleague by name on the floor, but Dirksen was clearly not in the mood for niceties. He declared that my criticism of the generals "jolted" his estimation of my wisdom and judgment and that I had no doubt undercut troop morale and discipline. Radio Hanoi was already broadcasting my dissent to the North Vietnamese populace. Moreover, battlefield tactical decisions are never the province of "homefront critics"—they must always be left to the generals.

Given that Dirksen spoke only after a well-publicized meeting with congressional Republicans attended by Nixon himself, it was hard not to conclude that this was part of a consensus strategy to avoid responding to war criticism on its own terms.

The strategy failed. The sacrifices of American boys on Hamburger Hill and in similar battles that week, condemned by me and many others, outraged many citizens. The public outcry led General Creighton Abrams to fundamentally revise the U.S. prosecution of the war from one of massive force against North Vietnamese troops to one of "protective reaction" against attacking troops. The policy of "Vietnamization" soon took hold—in public, at least.

There was an increasing perception in the country that Vietnam was no longer "Johnson's war," it was now "Nixon's war"—a scalding rebuke to a president who'd campaigned on the promise that he had "a secret plan" to end the war. I always doubted Nixon ever had such a plan. But as American casualties mounted in the spring of 1969, he began to improvise secret tactics. One of them was the bombing of presumed enemy supply lines in neighboring Cambodia. This operation did not remain "secret" for very long, as leaks to the press began around the same time as Hamburger Hill. Nixon's outrage over leaks and supposed leaks escalated his impulse toward surveillance: telephone taps, procurement of personal records, and, ultimately, the bugging of the Democratic offices at the new Watergate apartment and office complex in Washington.

Speaking of Watergate, not long after Nixon's inauguration in 1969, I took over the chairmanship of an obscure Senate subcommittee, Administrative Practices and Procedures. I could not have anticipated, at the time, how pivotal this subcommittee was destined to become.

On June 8, I gave a talk in Kentucky, and allowed the Associated Press reporter Joseph E. Mohbat, with whom I'd been friendly, to accompany me and some aides back to Hyannis in a small plane. June 8 fell two days after the first anniversary of Bobby's assassination, and the heaviness of it had caught up with me in spite of my constant attempts to stay busy.

Mohbat sensed my reflective mood, and took the opportunity to draw me out on my thoughts regarding my political life and my future.

When asked about a possible presidential run in 1972, I shared my misgivings: "I mean, is the country going to be receptive? Will it be the time? And if it is, is it really the best thing for me to do? And what kind of contribution could I make, even if . . . ?"

Mohbat noted in the piece that I spoke hesitantly, in half-sentences, and he offered some examples: "I'm really very unresolved right now . . . Maybe over the summer . . . some sailing . . . the family . . . I think perhaps by fall I'll be settled, have some idea . . ."

In response to my flying companion's pleasantry about a "good crowd tonight," I could summon little enthusiasm: "You know, these kinds of things kind of turn me off now. When I first came on into this in 1962, it was really good, easy. But the kicks aren't . . . I mean, meeting Molly Somebody and hearing all about her being Miss Something."

I added, coming close now to the heart of it, "What's it all for? I used to love it. But the fun began to go out of it after 1963, and then after the thing with Bobby, well . . ."

The reporter then ventured one of those formulaic questions that almost seem to invite an equally superficial reply: whether I thought the Kennedy name would still be "magic" in 1972 or 1976. My response was probably unreflective and offhand, yet it hinted at deeper feelings.

"I just don't know," was what I told him. "I really think all these things are predestined."

June gave way to July. My calendar remained cluttered with dates for speeches and appearances around the country, and I continued my frenzied travel pace to fulfill all of them. Toward the calendar's lower right corner, the square marking July 18 read, "Edgartown regatta."

The Kennedys had a long history in the regatta. Joe Jr. and Jack had raced in it before World War II. Joe Gargan and I had always competed as kids. This was the regatta where Jack had swooped in from the skies from Washington one year to skipper for Joe and me on *Victura*, then swooped up and away again.

This summer would mark my first return to the regatta since Bobby's death.

There was an event that would be held on the same day and in the vicinity—on Chappaquiddick Island, separated from Edgartown and the rest of Martha's Vineyard by a narrow split of the Sound—a reunion of the six young women who'd served on Bobby's campaign staff, doing the hard necessary work of answering phones, getting out press releases, overseeing schedules and accommodations, and dealing with the press.

Such gatherings, I knew from experience, tended only to increase my difficulties in dealing with the grief. But Nance Lyons, one of the six who was then on my staff, let me know that it would mean a lot to the others if I attended. And so I decided to stop by the gathering.

I flew from Washington to Boston that morning, then made a small-craft connection from Logan airport to the Vineyard. Tip O'Neill was my seatmate out of Washington, and I recall telling him, "I've never been so tired in my life."

That night on Chappaquiddick Island ended in a horrible tragedy that haunts me every day of my life. I had suffered sudden and violent loss far too many times, but this night was different. This night I was responsible. It was an accident, but I was responsible. One week after the accident, I purchased airtime to discuss the details of that night as best I could recall them. I gave the best account of it in my power at the inquest at Edgartown in January 1970. I've touched on it in interviews. And that, aside from many apologies, to the Kopechne family, to my constituents, to my fellow citizens, and in prayers for forgiveness, has pretty much been the extent of my public comment.

I have been told that upwards of twenty books have been published that deal in whole or in part with what has been known for forty years as "Chappaquiddick." Newspaper and magazine articles on the subject over the years are probably uncountable. I am aware that there are many who are skeptical of my explanation. And I am aware that there are others who are contemptuous, with the unchecked chatter in the blogosphere even going so far as to spin totally false, bizarre, and evil theories that do not deserve to be repeated here.

People have asked why I have not attempted to knock down each of these theories, as though my silence somehow gives credibility to every horrible allegation that people choose to make. Throughout my life, not just with this accident, I have refused to respond to false gossip and innuendo. I have never, not once, responded to a story in the tabloids, even when the story got repeated in the mainstream press. I knew that once I started, I would be forced to engage in a back-and-forth on every allegation, no matter how ludicrous or impossible. And I knew that no matter what I said, it would not satisfy those who had already made up their minds.

But whatever attacks and misrepresentations I have suffered as a result of Chappaquiddick, I know that they have been nothing compared to the grief endured with dignity by Mary Jo's father, Joe, who died on Christmas Eve 2003, and her mother, Gwen, who died in 2007. I know that my public discussion of that terrible night would only have caused them more pain.

I also have a personal distaste for self-justification. I grew up in a family of people who didn't want to hear you complain, and, quite frankly, I don't have a lot of respect for people who whine or go around feeling sorry for themselves. I do not intend to re-create all the details of a night that happened forty years ago, as I write this book. I couldn't. From my forty-year vantage point, what I am left with now are mostly memories of memories, and even those older memories lacked clarity, as records of the time show. My thoughts through the hours that followed the accident were disrupted by shock, terror, and the concussion that I received on impact. In any event, I gave testimony about those events at the time, and that testimony is the best evidence of the chronology of that evening. But I do want to share the general story and my more personal feelings.

I landed at Martha's Vineyard airport in the early afternoon that Friday and was met by my driver Jack Crimmins, who had previously brought my Oldsmobile sedan to the island. Jack drove me across the Vineyard to Chappaquiddick Island. We crossed the narrow spit by ferryboat and went on to the small cottage that Joe Gargan had rented for the weekend festivities. I took a swim and then went back to Edgartown. Joe had reserved rooms at an inn near Edgartown for the women and at another inn for the men, including me.

Besides Joe, Jack Crimmins, and myself, the men included my friends Paul Markham, the former U.S. attorney for Massachusetts; Ray LaRosa, a former fireman and stalwart campaign worker; and another campaign aide, Charles Tretter, a lawyer and head of the New England Regional Commission. The young women, besides Mary Jo and Nance Lyons, included Nance's sister Mary Ellen, Susan Tannenbaum, Rosemary Keough, and Esther Newberg.

Later that afternoon I skippered my Wianno Seniors sloop, *Victura*, in the regatta, with Joe Gargan as part of my crew as usual. My recollection is that we finished in the top half of the fleet. After celebrating a while with the crew of the boat that won the race, I returned to my hotel to freshen up for the evening. Crimmins drove me to the cottage for the cookout. The guests, transported from the ferry site by Joe, had all gathered by about 8:30. We all talked, told fond stories about Bobby, listened to music, danced a bit, and had cocktails until dinner was served a little before ten.

During the evening, I began speaking with Mary Jo Kopechne. I did not know her socially before that evening. Perhaps I had met her before, but I did not recall it. We reminisced about Bobby, and we both became emotional. I needed to get out of that party. I needed to get outside, to breathe some fresh air. When Mary Jo said that she wanted to go home, I was grateful for the excuse to leave. I asked Jack Crimmins for the car keys and left with Mary Jo. My intention was to take her to the ferry and back to Edgartown and to her hotel.

With Mary Jo in the car, I drove the short distance from the cottage to a T-intersection. It was very dark. I had not been to this part of the island before that day, when I had been a passenger in the car and not the driver. I turned onto what I now know was Dike Road. The road was unlit, and a narrow car bridge for crossing the pond came up suddenly and unexpectedly in my headlights. It had no guard rails and headed in a leftward angle from the road. My car slipped off the side of the narrow bridge and into the water and flipped upside down.

To this day, I cannot tell you how I escaped that car. Most probably, I squeezed through the window on the driver's side, a reprise of escaping through the window of the crashed airplane, with Birch Bayh's help, five years earlier.

I dived back into the water several times, trying to get to Mary Jo. I could not see her in the car. I hoped she'd been able to escape, too. That's what I wanted to believe, even though I knew it was unlikely. I ran back to the party to get help. I returned with friends who also dove, but could not see her.

What I said and did in the ensuing hours has been copiously recorded, examined, disputed, and debated for decades: my devising and rejecting scenarios with Joe and the others that flashed compulsively through my feverish thoughts; swimming across the channel to Edgartown; delaying in reporting the accident. I am not proud of these hours. My actions were inexcusable. Perhaps I have not made my acknowledgment of this clear enough over the years. And perhaps I have not fully acknowledged the following points as well:

I was afraid. I was overwhelmed. I made terrible decisions. Even though I was dazed from my concussion, exhaustion, shock, and panic, I was rational enough to understand that the accident would be devastating to my family. They had suffered so much, and now they would be forced to suffer again because of me. And I knew it would be damaging to my political career as well.

I also worried that people would leap to false assumptions about Mary

Jo Kopechne and me. We had no romantic relationship whatsoever. Yet I understood that my reputation was such that many people would seize on the circumstances to attack Mary Jo's character. And mine. The sad fact is that my flawed and wrongheaded actions had the opposite effect of having people link Mary Jo to me in a romantic way. I am deeply sorry about that. Mary Jo Kopechne was an innocent young woman who had done nothing more than been loyal to my brother and his cause. And she lost her life in an accident when I was at the wheel. I've had to live with that guilt for forty years. But my burden is nothing compared to her loss and the suffering her family had to endure. She also didn't deserve to be falsely linked to me in a romantic way. She deserved better than that. And God knows her parents did.

When I finally did stumble off into the darkness after my futile efforts to rescue Mary Jo, my mind was a jumble of mutually conflicting thoughts. I believed that the young woman was dead, and the thought buckled me with grief and horror. At the same time, I'd managed to convince myself that she surely must have escaped, given that I had not seen her in the car. Perhaps I had misperceived while I was in the dark water. Perhaps I could wish it all away.

But I could not wish it all away. I had suffered many losses during my life. I had lost all of my brothers and my sister Kathleen. My father had been lost to me in many respects because of his debilitating stroke. And now this horrible accident. But again, the difference this time was that I myself was responsible. I was driving. Yes, it was an accident. But that doesn't erase the fact that I had caused an innocent woman's death.

Atonement is a process that never ends. I believe that. Maybe it's a New England thing, or an Irish thing, or a Catholic thing. Maybe all of those things. But it's as it should be.

On Saturday, November 15, my frail father suffered the latest in a series of strokes that had ravaged his eighty-one-year-old body and slipped into unconsciousness at the Cape house in Hyannis Port. He never awakened.

Three days later Joseph P. Kennedy quietly passed from this world, lying in bed in the same second-story room, with its view of Nantucket Sound, from where his blue eyes had tracked us children as we'd scampered home at twilight so many summers, and lifetimes, ago. The core of his surviving extended family kept watch at his bedside in the final hours: my mother, Ann Gargan, Pat, Eunice and Sargent Shriver, Jean and Steve Smith, Jackie, Ethel, Joan, and myself.

Condolences came in from all over the world. President Nixon graciously noted Dad's passing and the role he played in shaping American history.

Dad's old friend Richard Cardinal Cushing presided over the simple services two days later at the small nearby church where Kennedys have worshipped over the decades, St. Francis Xavier on South Street. It was November 20, Bobby's forty-fourth birthday. My remarks at the service were brief. There was too much to say, and too many tears to hold back. I observed quietly that this was not so much a final prayer for Dad as a reminder to the rest of us of the deep love he held for us, and our obligation to lead the kind of lives he would want us to lead.

We walked on the beach, singly and in small groups, heads down, hands in our pockets, shoulders hunched against the November wind. Mother walked with Jean and Pat; I walked with Ann Gargan and my son Patrick, who was eight.

Later, I walked alone, letting the tears come, and struggling with thoughts more wrenching than those following any of my previous bereavements. I wondered whether I had shortened my father's life from the shock I had visited on him with my news of the tragic accident on Chappaquiddick Island. The pain of that burden was almost unbearable.

CHAPTER FIFTEEN

The Hospital

1970

On July 25, a week after the accident, in a television address carried nationally, I asked the people of Massachusetts to give me their advice and opinion as to whether I should resign as their senator. The polls were in favor of my continuing on. I took this as a validation of my legislative efforts but also as an affirmation of their faith and goodwill.

My constituents underscored their previous summer's vote of confidence in me by returning me to the Senate in November 1970. I defeated my Republican opponent, the businessman Josiah H. Spaulding, winning 61 percent of the vote.

Naturally, there were questions about whether I would run against Richard Nixon for president in 1972. I made it clear every time I was asked that I had no interest in such a run. I supported George McGovern in that election, though I turned down his invitation to run on his ticket for the vice presidency. "I just can't do it," I told him. I held fast even when Ted Sorensen gave me a memorandum asserting that it was constitutionally possible to be a vice president and also a cabinet member. It was not the prospect of being bored or isolated in that office that held me back. It was my concern about my family, and my responsibilities to them.

As I settled back into the Senate, into something like a state of equilibrium, I recognized that I had grown almost completely devoid of a state of mind I'd taken for granted since my early childhood. That state of mind was joy.

What amazing fun it had all once been. What adventures, what friendship and laughter and travels I had shared with my brothers and sisters. What a thrill I'd felt at mounting a wild bronco in Montana, or diving off a cliff in Monaco, or setting my sails into the teeth of a squall, or even facing off against old Wharton in the barracks at Fort Dix. What a lift to the spirit it had been, watching Jack and then Bobby soar into the stratosphere of world events, and to watch each of them accomplish mighty and good things; and then, incredibly, to join them on that plane, standing with them to engage history, with laughter and good cigars and the pranks we still played on one another. No more.

I had looked upon my winning the majority whip position from Russell Long in January 1969 as a high point of my Senate career. In January 1971, as I accepted the new realities of my situation, I lost it to Robert Byrd of West Virginia.

My downfall was due in part to the loss of some key allies who had supported me when I unseated Long. Warren Magnuson and Henry "Scoop" Jackson, both of Washington, peeled away because I had opposed appropriations for supersonic transport, which they supported along with Byrd. Boeing was too important to their home state for them to do otherwise.

And then there was Bill Fulbright. The Arkansas senator had voted for me against Russell Long. Our paths had parted since then over an opportunity to secure the names of American prisoners of war in Vietnam, an objective we both supported.

I'd received a communication from the North Vietnamese in 1970, offering to release the names to a representative of mine. After notifying Senator Fulbright of the offer, I sent a trusted emissary named John Nolan, who had worked with Bobby to get prisoners out of Cuba after the Bay of Pigs. John was given the names, returned to the United States, and presented them to the State Department.

I sat next to Fulbright the following Tuesday, during some piece of business on the Senate floor. I leaned to him and said, "Bill, remember I called you last week about securing those names?" Bill replied, "Yes, that's right. We're going to have a committee meeting this afternoon to decide what to do." I wasn't sure he'd heard me right. I said, "I've already sent someone over there, and we have the names." And Fulbright replied, icily, "That's a matter for the Foreign Relations Committee."

He maintained an edge toward me from that point. I suppose he believed that I was still overreaching, though I had notified him about the matter. And so he joined the opposition to me.

Byrd never did openly announce for my whip position, though he had been hard at work behind the scenes. One of his most influential allies was Richard Russell, but Russell lay dying of cancer at Walter Reed Hospital. Russell had given Byrd his proxy vote, but had he died before the balloting took place, it would be meaningless. On the day of the balloting, Byrd checked the hospital. Russell was still alive. He gave the go-ahead to his supporters—including four incoming senators who had all assured me of their support. Byrd scored a stunning upset, a vote of thirty-one to twenty-four. Russell died four hours later. Had the incoming senators voted the way they'd promised, I would have beaten Byrd by one vote, twenty-eight to twenty-seven. I figured out how they'd actually gone by a pair of telltale misspellings among the Byrd ballots: "B-I-R-D." No one who enjoyed more than a distant knowledge of the West Virginia senator would make such a mistake.

The fact is, those four did me a favor—they and the others who voted to oust me as whip. Robert Byrd went on to do an admirable job in the role, and eventually became a distinguished majority leader. As for me, the defeat served as a prompt to immerse myself more deeply in the necessary basic work of a U.S. senator.

And so I burrowed in. I gave myself over to contemplation and study. I absorbed the Senate's history, the careers of its greatest members, the principles that lent it constancy over the years, and the many social movements and powerful figures that at times altered its influence and character. I reread the Constitution in the context of the mandates it prescribed for the Senate; and, in doing so, reexperienced the awe of this document that had first been opened to me by the likes of the great Arthur N. Holcombe, my teacher at Harvard.

I grew interested in every aspect of the Senate: its arcane rules both permanent and new; its parliamentary procedure; the functions of its many committees and subcommittees, some of which were well known and others half-forgotten or unsuspected, and therefore of potentially great use. I doubt that anyone has ever managed to completely internalize the immense font of knowledge that these areas comprise, but I committed myself to learning it as thoroughly and in as much minute detail as I could.

As I had during my hospital days in 1964, I sought out mentors. I called once again on John Kenneth Galbraith of Harvard and on another distinguished economist, Carl Kaysen of MIT, who had once been an aide to Jack in national security affairs. I also asked business executives and union leaders to meet with me for luncheons at which I asked endless questions about their expectations of this body and about its impact on their lives.

Always available to me in his office, or so it seemed, a pipestem caught between his fingers and a scowl of contemplation narrowing his dark eyes, was Senator Mike Mansfield. In his late sixties now, the majority leader looked every inch the statesman he was. Mansfield conveyed his understanding of and reverence for that institution to me.

Instead of doing this research during my Senate workday, I always did it outside the Senate: it was genuine "homework." I have a policy of not reading memos or signing letters during office time. I use that time for Senate business, committee work, meetings with other senators and constituents. My homework begins as soon as I'm in the car, headed to or from Capitol Hill. A staff member drives me, so I can use that time to make phone calls or read memos. And then, after dinner, I make my way through The Bag.

The Bag is divided into several compartments. There is the "must do" compartment, which includes material that needs action ASAP. Another section holds briefing memos from the staff on various issues, correspondence to be signed, correspondence to be read. Then I might dive into the section jammed with news clips from Massachusetts and around the country, Capitol Hill news, current newspapers, and magazines that I might not have yet seen.

By definition, we senators are generalists. But we must at least know more about the issues that fall under the jurisdiction of our committees than about other issues. That's one of the main reasons for my "policy dinners" and for my regular meetings and talks with experts.

I'm certainly not alone in my determination to master policy. I had a wonderful experience a few years ago with Mike Enzi, the popular Republican senator from Wyoming. I was chairing a subcommittee meeting on safety in the workplace. The first item on my agenda was toxins in the workplace, and Mike spoke up, saying that he'd just gone to a conference on that issue and had very specific recommendations. A little later I said, well, let's move on to poisons in some other aspect of the workplace, and he had specific recommendations on that too. He had gone to a conference on *that*. I raised a third issue, and Mike knew all about that issue as well, because he'd gone to another conference on that one. In just a few minutes, Mike Enzi showed us what a superb legislator he was and what it took to be a good one: knowledge, information, hard work. There's no substitute.

As I studied and contemplated the Senate, I kept myself involved in the great issues that had always mattered to me. Refugees, to name but one example. I had led the fight for U.S. aid to the millions uprooted from their homes and communities in Vietnam. Now a fresh wave of terrified, starving victims of war welled up—this time in Africa.

Biafra, a territory of seven million people, most of them Catholic Ibos, on the southeastern coast of Nigeria, had declared its independence from the much larger and heavily Muslim federation in May 1967. (Nigeria itself had only just gained independence from Great Britain in 1960.) Riots and armed fighting between these religious and ethnic adversaries had flared up for years, but Biafra's secession triggered an immediate full-scale civil war, with catastrophic results. It took weeks of horrific fighting, marked by massacres on both sides, but a quarter million Nigerian troops finally overwhelmed the tiny breakaway state, gunning down and starving the Ibos by the tens of thousands. By the time of Biafra's capitulation in 1970, the total dead on both sides exceeded one million. Well before that, the victors' merciless crushing of the rebel state had begun to smack of genocide.

In my first Senate speech following Bobby's death, on September 23, 1968, I pointed out that while the United States and other nations did nothing to intervene, more than seven thousand Biafrans were dying of starvation each day. After that I spent weeks pressing administration officials and State Department leaders to do their humanitarian duty. By the end of that year, my lobbying had produced results. Some relief planes were flying into the devastated area, but several were shot down—by both Nigerians and Biafrans.

The war itself was nearly at an end when I called hearings before my refugee subcommittee in early January 1970. But the suffering was far from over: the victorious Nigerian armies were running unrestrained through Biafra, ransacking households, murdering and raping. After testimony on the extent of the brutality, I renewed my call for America to intervene in this open-ended massacre. The hearings generated enough press coverage that President Nixon, encouraged by Henry Kissinger, joined with Great Britain to once again ship tons of food and medicine to the helpless Ibos.

On the domestic front, I committed myself to the issue that had already caught my passion. I recognized that improving health care, and ensuring Americans' ability to pay for it, would be my main mission, and I would fight for it for however long it would take.

I knew that this mission would require many years and a great deal of energy. How many years, and how much energy, I could not then imagine. Health care, and its inadequacies, have been woven into the fabric of my life.

As a young boy I had witnessed Rosemary's struggles. I had watched Jack endure his many ailments, diseases, and near-death experiences. I had shared the family's shock over my father's stroke in 1961 that robbed him of his speech. I had tried to comfort Jack and Jackie in 1963 as they grieved the loss of the newborn Patrick Bouvier, who died from inadequate lung development. In 1964, with my broken back, I had been personally introduced to the pain and helplessness of a debilitating injury, and to the numbing routine of lengthy hospitalization. And these family crises of health were but prologue for what was to come.

My family's good fortune had insulated me from the desperation that for most Americans compounds the trauma of drastic illness or injury—the effort to meet crushing medical bills and, often, of having to make life-and-death decisions imposed by the enormity of those bills. Perhaps it has been this acute awareness of my own good fortune, as well as the suffering of so many of my loved ones, that has spurred me to always look beyond mere statistics, beyond conventional cost-benefit analyses, and to insist that "health care" be rooted in care.

I was in fact an activist in this area—a "foot soldier," as I've called myself—even before I entered the Senate. As I've mentioned, I had the extraordinary privilege of working with Dr. Sidney Farber in 1961 on the Massachusetts Cancer Crusade. Dr. Farber is recognized as being the father of both modern pediatric pathology and of chemotherapy as a treatment for neoplastic (tumor-forming) disease. He taught me about the ravages of cancer in American society, the depths of suffering caused by it, the self-defeating and unnecessary shame felt by victims and their loved ones, and the staggering costs of the disease.

I could never have dreamed back then how intimately I was destined to experience cancer's dark realities. Or how transformative those informal seminars were to prove, to me personally as well as to the cause of cancer research. It was this singular physician who ignited my long campaign as a senator to increase funding for this research.

The morass of genetic, environmental, and human-intake causes and the intricacies of its play among human cells, make cancer perhaps the greatest of all challenges to medical science. In 1971, still inspired by Farber and aware that the annual death toll from cancer was at nearly 340,000 and rising, I felt the time was right for a major offensive against the disease. I wanted to pass a National Cancer Act, and bolster it with enough funding to offer realistic hope for new discoveries and breakthroughs. I had recently become the chairman of the health subcommittee, and I was in touch with several of America's most distinguished health advocates and economic experts who felt the same way.

Besides Dr. Farber, these included some giants of their times, people whose contributions, like those of Walter Reuther, have regrettably faded in the public memory. One of them was Mary Lasker. The wife of the wealthy Albert Lasker, a pioneer of modern advertising, Mary was herself a pioneer: she fought for higher health standards and for medical research in America for most of her long life, and received a Congressional Gold Medal before her death at ninety-four. Mary brought prestige and tactical wisdom to our efforts.

Another valuable partner was Benno Schmidt. The well-connected New York investment banker shared my belief that cancer research was a critical national duty. His financial expertise told him that the country could and would support our quest for as much as one and a half billion dollars, a fourfold increase in research funding. That estimate became our figure in the bill.

Our intention, expressed in the legislation's early drafts, was to bypass the then ineffectual National Cancer Institute, an appendage of the National Institutes of Health, by creating a new independent agency structured along the lines of NASA. Mary Lasker had long advocated for such an agency. In her early seventies then, she lent her distinguished reputation to a round of speeches and published essays advocating for our bill.

We faced a powerful competitor for our goal: the Nixon administration, anxious to put its own stamp on cancer research, but at a much lower price tag than ours. In January, the president proposed a bill with an increase of $100 million in spending for this purpose, thus capturing temporary cachet as the leader in the fight. "Temporary" could easily become "permanent" unless we outflanked him: he was hardly likely to cede the momentum, and the credit, to a liberal Democrat in Congress—especially one named Kennedy.

My allies and I were now in a fight for the initiative and, along with it, a truly adequate research budget. We needed a bipartisan thrust; this effort must not get tangled up in partisan politics. And so I formed a partnership with an eager Jacob Javits, the Republican senator from New York, to get our bill written and moving through Congress.

A final obstacle remained: Nixon could not bring himself to sign a landmark bill that had the Kennedy name attached. So I immediately said to take my name off the bill, though I felt badly that Jacob Javits was also being denied the credit he deserved because of Nixon's feelings about me.

Nixon had insisted that his own bill, not the one created by our team, be the one submitted. So we replaced the language of the Nixon bill with the language of ours, and kept it labeled as the Nixon bill. The measure passed by a vote of seventy-nine to one and was signed by Nixon in 1971. The new department created by the act, the Conquest of Cancer Agency, remained within the NIH, as the Republicans wished. But administratively it would report not to NIH but directly to the president. And it carried our budget figures. The important point was that cancer research had entered a new era of federal funding and productivity.

Many others, of course, have felt the same urgency as I about health care. Progressives' calls for some sort of federal health-cost protection for Americans had fitfully arisen and subsided since the days before World War I. President Roosevelt considered a health insurance provision in the Social Security Act of 1935, but omitted it out of concern that its projected costs would scuttle the act, a cornerstone of his New Deal. He later

With Prime Minister Indira Gandhi, at a celebration marking the 24th anniversary of Indian independence, August 1971.
Bettmann/Corbis

With a refugee child in Calcutta during a fact-finding mission to India, August 1971.
Bettmann/Corbis

With members of the Vietnam Veterans Against the War during a 1972 demonstration on the Washington Mall. John Kerry is visible at bottom right.
Steven Clevenger/Corbis

Speaking with Vietnam veterans during the 1972 demonstration on the
Washington Mall.
Leonard Freed/Magnum Photos

Meeting with
Jewish Refusniks
in Moscow, 1974.
Ken Regan/Camera 5

With Howard Cosell
at the RFK
Tennis Tournament,
in Forest Hills,
New York, 1975.
Ken Regan/Camera 5

With
Walter Cronkite
at the 1976
Democratic
National Convention
in New York City.
CBS /Landov

Being received by
Pope Paul VI during
a private audience
in Vatican City,
November 12, 1976.
AP Photo

With Mother in
Hyannis Port,
1978.
Ken Regan/Camera 5

With Pat and Jean,
campaigning for the 1980
presidential nomination.
Ken Regan/Camera 5

With Leonid Brezhnev
and a Russian interpreter,
1979.
Ken Regan/Camera 5

In China, 1979.
Ken Regan/Camera 5

With Dick Drayne, Jim Flug, and Paul Kirk at the Democratic convention, watching Tip O'Neil on TV.
Ken Regan/Camera 5

Campaigning in Illinois, 1980.
Ken Regan/Camera 5

Andy Warhol helped raise $300,000 for the Kennedy for President Committee through the sale of these large red, white, and blue posters. Kerry Kennedy (l) and Jean Kennedy Smith aided the fundraising.
Bettmann/Corbis

Shaking hands with Jimmy Carter at the conclusion of the
Democratic National Convention, August 14, 1980.
Bettmann/Corbis

With President Ronald Reagan at a ceremony in the White House Rose Garden,
to honor my brother Bobby, June 5, 1981.
Bettmann/Corbis

With my sister Jean,
Cardinal Bernard F. Law,
and Pope John Paul II
at a Very Special Arts
(VSA) performance
at the Vatican,
January 23, 1985.
AP Photo

With Teddy, Kara,
and Patrick,
Parade magazine cover, 1982.
Ken Regan/Camera 5

With Jacqueline Kennedy Onassis, John Kennedy, and Caroline Kennedy, at John's
graduation from Brown University, Providence, Rhode Island, June 4, 1983.
AP Photo

Giving away the bride
at Caroline's wedding,
July 19, 1986.
Denis Reggie

With the mother of the bride
at Caroline's wedding.
Denis Reggie

Being introduced
by John at the
Democratic National
Convention in
Atlanta, Georgia,
July 1988.
Bettmann/Corbis

asked Congress to include adequate medical care as part of an "economic bill of rights," but was rebuffed. When President Truman proposed national health insurance to Congress in 1945, the American Medical Association mobilized a virulent opposition campaign, aimed at the heartland, portraying the idea as "socialized medicine." Senator Robert Taft of Ohio took up that charge, and a House subcommittee member went even further, labeling it "a communist plot." Medicare was passed in 1965 under Lyndon Johnson, with my strong support. Still, large disparities remained. With eighty million Americans uninsured and a national outlay of $60 billion in health-related costs, *Time* reported on May 11, 1970, that "there is a growing consensus that some national insurance blanket must be thrown over the ailing body of health care." True enough—and the scatter-quilt of federal programs was hardly a remedy.

In a December 1969 speech at the Boston University Medical Center, I declared that the time had come to begin phasing in such a program, despite its unarguably high costs. I expanded these views and enfolded them into a larger arraignment of the American health care system in my 1972 book *In Critical Condition*. As a member of the Labor Committee's health subcommittee, I had been in communication since the end of 1968 with Walter Reuther. Reuther is remembered as the progressive president of the United Auto Workers union, but his larger legacy, all but forgotten to history, is that of a social visionary whose humanitarian concerns included but extended well beyond the members of his union. When Reuther himself called for national health insurance in November 1968, I'd sensed an alignment of forces that could produce a new opportunity for action. In January 1969, when he invited me to join his new Committee of One Hundred for National Health Insurance, I did not hesitate. Reuther was killed in a small-airplane crash in May 1970, but the committee's work went forward, and in August 1970, drawing on its contributions, I introduced the first bill of my career for national health insurance. It was defeated: the first setback in a long, long struggle.

Still, with the help of others, I was able to gain some important early victories. In 1965, two physicians on the faculty of Tufts University, Jack Geiger and Count Gibson, came to one of the semi-regular policy dinners that I held, this time in Boston. The discussion that evening involved health care, and in the course of it the two doctors began to focus on the need to eradicate the barrier of distance that often discouraged poor and working people from visiting their doctors. From our conversation was born a plan for community health centers, modeled on experimental centers in the third world, notably Africa. The idea was not only to redress illnesses and injury, but to educate the community in prevention and healthy living. Excited by their concept, and aware of funding possibilities through the new Office of Economic Opportunity, I introduced an appropriation bill in 1966 that would expand upon their concept, providing $38 million to make it a reality. The original plan was for two neighborhood health centers, one at Columbia Point in Boston and the other in Mount Bayou, Mississippi.

In searching for allies, I approached Adam Clayton Powell Jr., the charismatic congressman and social activist from New York's 18th District, which included Harlem. As chairman of the House Education and Labor Committee, Powell had championed Jack's New Frontier programs, and helped steer many of them into law. He'd done the same for Lyndon Johnson's Great Society initiatives.

In 1966, Powell was fifty-seven, still handsome with his neatly trimmed mustache, and still very much the master of his congressional domain. When I visited his committee to make my pitch, he obliged me to wait for several hours as they went through their other business. Yet when he finally turned to me, I received the full force of his famous spark and dazzle. "Teddy Kennedy!" he began. "You want these neighborhood health centers?" I said that I did. "How many are you going to have for thirty-eight million?" he asked. I said that it would cover two and (quickly anticipating Powell's own interests in backing me) perhaps four. Powell shot back, "You write in there that one of them is going to be in my district, and you've got it!" I told him that that would be fine with me. I wrote it in; Powell steered the bill through the House; the Senate passed it; and that was the beginning of neighborhood health centers across the United States.

My battle against cancer first struck home in 1973.

Teddy was a seventh grader at the St. Albans School in Washington that fall. He'd turned twelve on September 26 and was proud to be a member of the Bulldogs' football team despite his slight build. Thinner and smaller than I had been at the same age, he was nevertheless a good athlete in the style of Bobby, whom he'd adored—a good runner especially.

He was an even better student, thanks in part to his own perseverance. He'd determined to keep up academically in this highly demanding school. He was exceptional at memorization. This was something he and I worked on when he was a small boy, and I remember almost to the moment when he dazzled us with his first big breakthrough. It was during a ski weekend with Bobby and his family at Stowe, Vermont, one spring. After a hearty dinner, I reminded my son that it was time for him to go and learn his next assignment: "Casey at the Bat." Triumphantly, Teddy announced that he'd already memorized it—then recited it at the table, to everyone's applause.

At St. Albans, he and the other students were required to memorize one poem each week. I remember listening enchanted as Teddy mastered Yeats's "The Second Coming": "Turning and turning in the widening gyre / The falcon cannot hear the falconer . . ."

On November 6, Teddy came down with a cold and remained home from school at our McLean house, where he padded about in a bathrobe. I was in the library, just winding up a briefing session with staff. As I walked out, I spotted my son and noticed that the area just below his right kneecap was discolored by an ugly reddish lump. He grudgingly admitted that it hurt a little—which meant, in Kennedy lexicon, that it hurt a lot. I assumed that it was nothing more than just a football bruise. (Teddy himself said later that he'd thought it was Osgood-Schlatter disease, a common affliction to fast-growing young knees that several of his class-mates had experienced.) I asked our governess, Teresa Fitzpatrick, to tele-phone Dr. S. Philip Caper, who had been affiliated with Harvard Medical School, but was then in Washington as a staff member for my Senate health subcommittee.

The doctor rang our doorbell scarcely half an hour later. He was en route to a formal event and was dressed for the occasion, yet he examined my son with fully professional concentration. It was probably nothing to worry about, Phil said, but we should keep an eye on it. He'd check back in a couple of days.

I flew to Boston on Thursday, November 8, to complete some work out of my office there and had planned to fly down to Florida the next day for a brief visit with my mother in Palm Beach. But when Teresa called me to say that Teddy's leg was not better, I really became concerned. I told Teresa to call Dr. Caper, and I made plans to return to Washington the next day when my Boston events were finished, instead of visiting my mother. Phil arranged for Teddy to see the chairman of orthopedic sur-gery at Georgetown University Hospital, Dr. George Hyatt. Dr. Hyatt examined my son and had X-rays taken.

As I flew back to Washington the next day, I began to have an almost overwhelming sense of dread, but I willed myself not to think of the possi-bilities. In truth, they *were* unthinkable. Phil Caper met me at the airport, and the expression on his face made me brace myself. He told me the situation was serious: that Dr. George Hyatt at Georgetown felt certain that we were looking at a bone tumor. We immediately went to George-town, where Phil and I met personally with Dr. Hyatt, and he repeated the same devastating news. He added that if we were indeed looking at bone cancer, then Teddy's leg would most likely have to be amputated. He wanted to bring Teddy into the hospital for more tests and to consult with a broader group of experts from other institutions as well. I readily agreed.

Later that day, my good-natured twelve-year-old son checked into the hospital for more X-rays and blood tests and examinations. He was so innocent and trusting. I could barely absorb the realities of the situation, and I didn't feel that it was the time to discuss it with him. Joan was traveling in Europe, and I hadn't even been able to talk to her yet.

After two days of tests, the news was no better, but the doctors let me take him home for the rest of the weekend. We wanted his life to be as normal as possible for as long as possible. When we got back to our home in the Washington suburbs, I grabbed a football, went out to the lawn, and threw passes to my son. As he ran to catch them, I was fighting not to be crushed by emotion, knowing that this was probably the last time that Teddy would be able to run on two legs. I didn't tell him what the future held. There would be time enough for that. I just played ball with my son and savored every moment and prayed that he was going to survive. There had been so much loss. But please God. Not Teddy.

I called Joan. She needed to come home from Europe. We were facing a life-and-death situation for our son.

Teddy returned to the hospital after the weekend and on Tuesday, November 13, the doctors operated on his leg to remove a small slice of the tissue believed to be malignant. The tissue was analyzed immediately by Dr. Lent Johnson of the Armed Forces Institute of Pathology, the country's leading expert in analyzing this kind of tumor.

I did not leave the hospital. Dr. Hyatt delivered news both devastating and hopeful: Teddy's right leg would have to be amputated above the knee, and quickly, in an attempt to overtake the cancer that was probably spreading. The hopeful news was that the type of cancer seemed to be chondrosarcoma, which attacked the ligaments and was a good deal less deadly than osteosarcoma, cancer of the bone, which took the lives of 80 percent of its victims within five years. Still, no one was sure.

The surgeons made plans to amputate Teddy's leg on Friday, November 16. Only Teddy's persistent cold prevented them from operating the next day, as they'd have preferred.

As of Thursday, I still had not told Teddy of what lay ahead. I'd consulted a child psychiatrist to get help on how to break the news. He said that we shouldn't tell Teddy too far in advance, to minimize his level of anxiety, and we had to tell him in the right way. On the day before Teddy was to have surgery, I went with Phil Caper and Dr. Robert Coles, the renowned child psychiatrist from Harvard, to deliver the news to my son. I'd heard and delivered more than my share of bad news in my life, but this was the worst of the worst. My twelve-year-old son started crying, and I was fighting back emotion with every ounce of my being. I held Teddy in my arms and told him that I'd be there with him, that we'd face this problem together, that surgery would take care of the problem so he could be well, that we would have many happy days still ahead. I needed to believe those words as much as he did. In the end, he accepted the news bravely, but I'm not sure that his young mind could truly absorb what it really would mean to lose his leg above the knee.

My visits to the hospital had attracted press attention, and few secrets can be kept in great urban hospitals. I decided to prevail on the essential humanity of the reporters, who were by now asking insistent questions. I told them the facts, but asked them not to print their stories until the following day, when the operation would occur. The reporters said they would comply. Just in case someone had not heard of the agreement or elected to ignore it, I removed Teddy's radio and TV set. I made the excuse that we were offering them to other children in the hospital who could not afford such luxuries.

Because of Teddy's lingering cold, the doctors postponed the surgery again, until 8:30 Saturday morning. This posed a distressing new dilemma. Saturday, November 17, 1973, was a date I'd circled on my calendar many months ago. My niece Kathleen was to be married on this day: Kathleen, the sparkling, great-hearted eldest child of Bobby and Ethel. Kathleen, named in honor of our late sister "Kick," the eldest grandchild of Joe and Rose and the first to be wed. Her thick shock of raven hair has always reminded me of Bobby, as has her devoutness, her curiosity, and her passion for public service.

At 11 a.m. on this day, Kathleen was to marry David Townsend, then a doctoral candidate at Harvard in history and literature. The church was Holy Trinity, where Jack had worshipped during his time as president. I had promised to give my niece away at the ceremony. Kathleen had offered to postpone the wedding after she'd heard about Teddy's operation schedule, but I dissuaded her. I wanted nothing to cloud her memories of this milestone in her life. But the delay in Teddy's surgery caused me anguish. I needed to know that my son was going to be all right before I left the hospital.

At around ten that morning, the doctors appeared from the operating room to announce that the surgery had been a success and Teddy, still anesthetized, was well out of danger. Only then did I rush the several blocks to Holy Trinity to walk Bobby's firstborn down the aisle on her wedding day. As soon as the nuptial mass was over, I rushed back to the hospital.

As difficult and painful as the surgery and the loss of his leg were for him, Teddy's positive and upbeat nature carried him through his recovery and rehabilitation. But even as Teddy was working hard on his exercise regimen and enjoying visits by special guests (the entire offensive line of the Washington Redskins, for example), the doctors were revisiting their conclusion that his cancer was strictly chondrosarcoma. Pathology lab results showed dreaded bone cancer cells indeed present in my son's tumor.

This fresh blow to my hopes for Teddy left me stunned at first; but a more aggressive emotion quickly took hold: defiance. *If the cancer has escalated, we'll escalate back.* However unwittingly, I began to form the template for future counterattacks against the disease in my family, including my own test thirty-five years on.

I got on the phone and called doctors from around the United States who I knew were working on experimental forms of treatment—doctors I'd gotten to know in our shared crusade for cancer funding. I convened a meeting at my home in McLean. The practitioner whose results seemed the most promising to me was based right in Boston: Dr. Edward Frei III, of

Children's Hospital. In this period before the general advent of chemotherapy, Dr. Frei had found success administering a drug called methotrexate, which destroyed cancer cells efficiently. (Sidney Farber was experimenting with this drug in the 1940s as well.)

The other doctors agreed on this treatment, and on February 1, 1974, my resolute twelve-year-old commenced a rigorous pattern that would be repeated without interruption over two years. Every three weeks, I would fly with Teddy from Washington to Boston, where he would endure six hours of lying nearly motionless in his hospital bed while a needle dripped medicine into his bloodstream, followed by another long period of citrovorum injections. The entire process covered three days.

Helping Teddy recover took precedence over every other activity in my life, including my duties in the Senate. I slept beside him in his hospital room. I would hold his head against my chest when the nausea overcame him. In time, I learned the technique of injecting him myself, so that we could cut the visit short by a day and get him into his classroom on Monday mornings.

My many hours at Boston Children's Hospital were precious in another way. While Teddy was asleep or in treatment, I wandered the halls and the waiting rooms, and sought out other parents who, like me, were keeping vigil over terribly ill sons and daughters—many of them with the dreaded osteosarcoma. These were mostly working people: salesmen, secretaries, laborers, teachers, taxi drivers. Their long hours and modest savings allowed them to raise their families comfortably and with hope—until catastrophe struck. It was in these conversations that the inhumanity of our health care system truly hit home to me. We shared common ground in our anxieties about whether our children would live or die, or survive with debilitating frailties. But for my new friends, this was only one terrible part of a larger nightmare.

Teddy's treatment, like that of the other children suffering from cancer, was free in the first six or seven months, because it was part of an NIH experimental grant: a clinical trial with uncertain results, to which we had all agreed. The results in fact proved highly promising for all the young patients, a dividend of the rise in research funding. But this happy news brought with it a heartbreaking downside: once the usefulness of the treatment and medicines had been verified, the experiment ended, and the patients' families were billed for the remaining treatment.

I will never forget sitting down and listening to those parents. Suddenly they were faced with finding a way to scrape up three thousand dollars for each treatment. The treatments were necessary every three weeks for two years. These families were terrified. They could not begin to afford it. They would tell me of being reduced to a grim, almost macabre calculus: How much of a chance, they would ask the doctors, did their children have if they purchased the resources for only a year? Or eight months? Or six months? They were not being stingy. They were bargaining based on how much they could afford. Many had already borrowed to the limit. Others had sold or remortgaged their homes. Several had run the risk of being fired from their jobs for the crime of taking time off work to be with their son or daughter. In a few cases, debt or bankruptcy was compounded by the knowledge that the child would never recover: the illness had no cure, because funding in that field remained inadequate.

I began directing my Senate health committee's work toward the realities of lives such as those: the uninsured, the underinsured. I held hearings—but not always just ordinary hearings. Whenever feasible, I would take my committee and witnesses to hospitals in rural and inner-city neighborhoods. I wanted my colleagues to be taken out of their comfort zones, as I had been taken out of mine. I wanted them to experience the ravages of preventable illness and death as I'd learned to experience them: not as abstractions on a printed page, but as blood, and bandages, and needles, and wails of pain down a hospital corridor, and tears, and mourning.

The field hearings did not produce instant, dramatic results—cries of empathy from hardheaded Senate conservatives, a raft of new legislation, fresh winds of enlightened consensus. I never assumed that they would. I had no illusions about the battle for health care. But now that battle had my complete attention. I had even won an early fight in it: my son would live.

CHAPTER SIXTEEN

Nixonian Radicals
1969–1973

There was not much reason for me to distrust Richard Nixon at the outset of his presidency. The early stages of my acquaintanceship with him were congenial. He was both interesting and entertaining. In the spring of 1953, when I came home from the army, I went down to Washington to visit my brother the new senator, and Nixon, the new vice president, spotted me in the Capitol. (As president of the Senate, the vice president has an office in the Capitol building.) He invited me in, and we spent a cordial forty-five minutes in conversation.

Jack liked him as well back then. My brother and Nixon had both been elected to Congress in 1946, and the two of them would often chat and joke with each other. Jack respected that Nixon was also a navy man, and he found him to be intelligent and pleasant. I suppose that neither of us had been paying all that much attention when Nixon ran his less-than-pleasant campaign for the Senate in 1950, which he won by attacking his Democratic opponent, Helen Gahagan Douglas, as a communist sympathizer and dubbed her "the Pink Lady—pink right down to her underwear."

In later years, Nixon did not feel quite so pleasant toward me or members of my family. He was bitter over his narrow loss of the presidency to Jack in 1960. And he had lost the governorship of California to Pat Brown just two years later. Still, he came back again to win the presidency over Hubert Humphrey in the rubble of all that had disintegrated in the year 1968. He won by less than a percentage point, as the third-party candidate George Wallace of Alabama swept five traditionally Democratic states in the Deep South and pulled away more than 13 percent of the total votes.

It was clear I'd infuriated Nixon with my May 1969 speech denouncing Hamburger Hill and, by extension, the Vietnam War policies that he now administered. Almost immediately after that, I began tangling with the administration over a series of Supreme Court nominations that I and others felt were antithetical to the court's independence from ideology. My base of operations was an obscure Judiciary subcommittee that I had agreed to chair in that same year: Administrative Practices and Procedures.

In the past, "Ad-Prac" wielded little legislative influence, and few people outside the Senate even knew it existed. But my growing understanding of the ways the Senate operated told me it had the opportunity to be otherwise. It was true that Ad-Prac had statutory jurisdiction over only a small number of areas. But as I discovered, it enjoyed a surprisingly broad mandate—essentially the entire federal bureaucracy—for administrative oversight. Over the ensuing years, our subcommittee was able to change federal policy in varied and substantial ways. For instance, with the help of a young staffer who served as special counsel to the committee in 1974, we deregulated the airline industry and abolished the Civil Aeronautics Board. That young staffer was Stephen Breyer, now associate justice of the United State Supreme Court.

My opposition to the administration's policies was not personal, but Nixon took things quite personally indeed. I quickly drew his distaste, as well as his need for control and vengeance. By 1971, although I didn't know it at the time, I was a member of his infamous "enemies list." Since the tally of those "enemies" eventually reached forty-seven thousand, I was never really able to savor a sense of prestige at being included, even after I found out about it.

In May 1971, the president directed his chief of staff, H. R. Haldeman, to wiretap my telephones, along with those of Ed Muskie, Hubert Humphrey, and several other Democrats. He also had assigned his operatives to research and put their own spin on the Chappaquiddick tragedy to maximize the damage to my reputation and perhaps end my Senate career. He ordered his aides to plant two spies within my Secret Service detail. Their assignment would be to catch me in the company of another woman. It is not clear whether that directive was ever carried out. A batch of recently released papers from the Nixon Library included one of Haldeman's notes, reminding himself, "Get him—compromising situation. . . . Get evidence—use another Dem as front."

As to Nixon's Supreme Court appointments and his other misadventures with the Constitution:

My daughter Kara not long ago gave me a lovely Christmas present: *200 Notable Days: Senate Stories, 1787 to 2002.* It was written by the splendid Historian of the United States Senate, Richard A. Baker. Its narratives contain several references to James Madison's seminal *Notes of Debates in the Federal Convention of 1787,* the event known familiarly as the Constitutional Convention. Madison shows clearly that the last major decision on the appointing of justices effectively divided the responsibility between the president and the Senate. This principle—"advise and consent" is its familiar label—is far too often overlooked during consideration of appointments to the federal bench. The president is usually able to convince the American people that he has sole authority and responsibility for these appointments, and that unless one can find an egregious circumstance, the overwhelming requirement on the Senate is to defer to the president and approve the nominee. But the Founding Fathers did not intend it that way. Quite significantly, they stipulated that justices would have *lifetime appointments*—which implies enormous responsibility for interpreting the Constitution. To help regulate that responsibility, they provided for the utmost deliberation, and assigned that deliberation to the Senate.

These different views on the standards for confirmation didn't really come into play, however, until Richard Nixon put them to the test. Prior to his administration, nominations were made based on suitable judicial temperament, experience, integrity, independence, and knowledge of the law, and there was a strong bias in favor of confirmation. Nixon skewed the process, however, by substituting political ideology for judicial independence. For many of us, that change in nomination procedures meant a change in the level of confirmation scrutiny.

The first confrontation erupted in July 1969, just six months into the administration's first term. Abe Fortas, a liberal-leaning associate justice and close friend of Lyndon Johnson, resigned from the Court after questions arose over a retainer he had accepted from a financier friend who later went to prison for securities violations. Nixon's choice as a replacement was a solid southern conservative: Clement Haynsworth of South Carolina, then chief judge of the Fourth Circuit Court of Appeals. This was the same Clement Haynsworth who had been a judge in Tunney's and my winning moot court argument at the University of Virginia back in 1959. He was the first southerner to be nominated to the high court since 1942.

The early support for him was strong, and consensus had it that he would be easily confirmed. But almost immediately, several civil rights groups declared their intention to oppose him. They charged that Haynsworth had contrived to undercut the mandates of *Brown v. Board of Education* at a time when the law required him to expedite school desegregation. They also pointed to his judicial opinion upholding the right of a hospital that practiced hiring and patient discrimination to receive federal funds. There was also strong opposition from organized labor. In my questioning, I handled the nominee gently at the outset. Anticipating that he would refuse to discuss specific cases, I tried to elicit whether Haynsworth was sensitive to the dynamic social forces of the times, and in particular with the grievances of the young, the poor, and the minorities of America. If he showed that he was not, I reasoned, one could argue that his votes on freedom of speech and defendants' rights might reflect his indifference, if not hostility, to such forces.

Haynsworth saw it coming. We fenced carefully. I tried several variations of my inquiry. How did he view the frustrations of young and poor people? What did he see as the underlying causes? But the dignified Haynsworth stuck to artfully bland responses. The committee voted to recommend confirmation by a vote of ten to seven. I coupled my dissenting vote with a request to President Nixon that he withdraw the nomination. Media and public opinion had by now turned sharply against Haynsworth, and some Republican senators joined me in this request. Nixon refused. In the sharp floor debates that followed, there were allegations of a conflict of interest, and Democratic and Republican support for the nominee further eroded. In November his confirmation was rejected, fifty-five to forty-five, with seventeen Republicans, including several members of their leadership, voting no.

The Senate's repudiation of the president's chosen candidate for the Supreme Court sent shock waves through Washington. It was a game changer. A president's nominees would no longer be rubber-stamped by a compliant Senate.

The defeat exposed Nixon's deeper propensities for control and revenge. The outraged president vowed in effect to stuff his next nomination down the Democrats' throats. He is reported to have ordered an adviser to "go out this time and find a good federal judge further south and further to the right." Nixon's reasoning was that the Haynsworth defeat had given him carte blanche: liberal Republicans would not dare buck their president in a second straight confirmation process, and many Democrats would feel equally reluctant—enough to make a second repudiation next to impossible.

Nixon's designated adviser was Harry Dent. Dent was the conceptual thinker behind Nixon's "Southern strategy" of increasing his base and converting Democrats in the South by assuring them that he would not force civil rights laws on unwilling states.

Dent went out and found G. Harrold Carswell, a U.S. Court of Appeals judge from Tallahassee, Florida. Florida newspapers promptly published a speech Carswell had made in 1948 while campaigning for the state legislature: "I believe that segregation of the races is proper. . . . I yield to no man in the firm, vigorous belief in the principles of white supremacy."

The day after the Florida press disclosures, a damning bill of particulars surfaced via the offices of Marian Wright Edelman, the visionary activist lawyer and founder of the Washington Research Project and the Children's Defense Fund, who had warned us that we were making a mistake when the Senate confirmed Carswell to the 5th Circuit without a serious fight in June of 1969. Listing Carswell's efforts to slow desegregation in Florida schools, his uncivil manner as a judge toward black lawyers, and his refusal to hold hearings on habeas corpus petitions involving black defendants, Edelman and her fellow lawyers concluded that Carswell had been "more hostile to civil rights cases than any other federal judge in Florida."

Nixon's tactical calculations were uncomfortably close to the truth, at least at the outset. At a meeting on January 23, 1970, Birch Bayh, Joe Tydings, and Phil Hart agreed with Birch's oft-voiced perception that it requires staggering resources and energy to defeat even a bad presidential nomination.

I could not attend that meeting, but was represented by a first-rate young staffer, Jim Flug, a Harvard Law School graduate. Flug had made a meticulous head count of senators likely to support Carswell, those likely to oppose him, and those on the fence who might respond to "go along with proper kinds of brotherly pressure" and oppose the nominee. It appeared that Carswell could indeed be defeated. We went to work. As the Judiciary Committee hearings began on January 27, I bore in on news reports that Carswell, then a U.S. attorney, had maneuvered to keep a Tallahassee municipal golf course segregated even after such discrimination had been ruled illegal. He denied involvement in any such thing.

Three days after that, another Flug memo, titled "How to Beat Carswell," listed sixty-one senators who might oppose the man "if we can get the full civil-rights apparatus working, which it's beginning to do."

Birch Bayh was an outstanding leader in this battle and wanted to delay the committee vote on Carswell for two weeks to allow public opposition to grow. He managed it via a clever parliamentary maneuver that outfoxed Strom Thurmond.

Nevertheless, on February 16, the Judiciary Committee voted to recommend the confirmation of Carswell by a vote of thirteen to four. Bayh, Hart, Tydings, and I were the four "no" votes. We authored a joint dissent that hammered at Carswell's "lack of achievement and eminence in the law," and at his basic competence as a judge. Meanwhile, our strategy of letting opposition grow was working. It soon reached a flood tide among dozens of law school deans and professors, poverty lawyers by the hundreds, and several of the most influential law journals. Liberal Republicans began to back away. And then on March 16 came what many feel was the coup de grâce against Carswell—delivered not by the opposition but by a blooper from his own floor leader, Senator Roman Hruska of Nebraska.

The thickset and pugnacious Hruska, flailing for any kind of toehold as the tide turned against his man, blurted to a radio interviewer that even if Carswell was mediocre, there were lots of mediocre people in the country, and they too were entitled to representation on the Supreme Court. "We can't have all Brandeises and Frankfurters and Cardozos and stuff like that there," Hruska stoutly affirmed. It proved the most enduring quotation of his career.

Still, Nixon hung on, trying to marshal a counteroffensive against the backlash. Several southern judges endorsed Carswell, as did the American Bar Association; but these had little impact. In March we achieved another valuable delay, persuading Mike Mansfield to hold up a full Senate debate. This had the happy effect of giving the Senate time to complete action on the Voting Rights extension bill, which included a provision I'd long championed, lowering the federal voting age to eighteen. The extension passed, and we turned our energies back to the Supreme Court nomination fight. The *New York Times* had predicted that Carswell would narrowly be confirmed, perhaps by a forty-nine to forty-seven vote. But the actual results showed another embarrassment for Nixon. His nominee was rejected by fifty-one to forty-five, as thirteen Republicans joined the majority. (Seventeen Democrats, mostly southern, voted to confirm.)

Nixon publicly held his rage in check; he remarked icily and artfully at a press conference that the Senate, "as presently constituted," would not confirm a southern nominee who shared the president's vision of strict constructionism. A few weeks later, reportedly at the suggestion of Chief Justice Warren Burger, he nominated Burger's fellow Minnesotan and close friend, Harry Blackmun, to the Court. Blackmun held strong conservative credentials as well; but his answers to my questions at his hearing—he affirmed that the Court should continue to be "the real bastion of freedom and liberty" in the nation—told me he would be an acceptable choice. He was confirmed unanimously, and eventually became one of the most effective and outspoken progressives on the Court until he retired in 1994, and was replaced by my former counsel, Stephen Breyer.

Racial insensitivity continued to run through Nixon's Supreme Court nominees. When Hugo Black and John Marshall Harlan announced their impending retirements in September 1971, Nixon's first choice for the nomination was Congressman Richard Poff of Virginia. In 1956 Poff had signed the Southern Manifesto protesting the Court's landmark *Brown v. Board of Education* decision outlawing school desegregation. Poff declined Nixon's offer.

Eventually, Nixon nominated former assistant attorney general of the Office of Legal Counsel William Rehnquist and Lewis Powell, a moderate conservative from Virginia. I was lulled, at first, into a sense of relief when I saw these names. At least these were men of reputation and some accomplishment. And in fact Powell, who was confirmed easily, served as a centrist and consensus-builder on the bench for fifteen years.

Rehnquist was another matter.

I knew that Rehnquist's conservatism ran deeper than Powell's. He was rumored to have held questionable positions on race matters. Still, hoping with everyone else that a third standoff with the president could be avoided, I withheld any final opinion until the hearings. In retrospect, given the historic consequences, perhaps I should have pounced right away. But it probably would not have mattered. Nixon played this round with the instincts of a chess master in the endgame. He understood the steep odds against another standoff.

Controversy erupted almost immediately. As with the earlier nominees, the civil rights community mobilized its opposition to Rehnquist. Revelations surfaced that in 1964, just seven years earlier, he had testified in opposition to desegregating public accommodations in Phoenix—at the same moment, virtually, that Congress was en route to passing the Civil Rights Act. He was shown to have favored restrictive covenants in housing and to have fought school desegregation, remarking, "We are no more dedicated to an integrated society than we are to a segregated society. We are instead dedicated to a free society."

Charges also surfaced that from 1958 through 1964, Rehnquist, as a lawyer working for the Republican Party in Arizona, repeatedly had confronted black and Hispanic citizens at polling places in Arizona and tried to prevent them from voting. The NAACP released affidavits sworn to by two African-American men that they had witnessed Rehnquist challenging black voters at a Phoenix precinct in November 1964. One of these men added that a black woman had come to him in tears: as she'd stood in line, Rehnquist approached her and demanded that she recite the Constitution as a prerequisite to voting. After a scuffle involving the two men and Rehnquist, police removed the young lawyer from the precinct. He later returned in a car. Rehnquist responded by insisting that he'd been near the voting lines only to supply legal advice to people who were in fact challenging voters.

My opening-day questioning of Rehnquist on November 4, 1971, focused on the nominee's assaults on civil liberties. I grilled him on his role in supplying legal justification for the administration's use of wiretapping, electronic surveillance, and "no-knock" entries of residences in drug cases. I also pressed him on his role in "containing" the anti-Vietnam rally on the Washington Mall earlier that year, which resulted in the arrest or detention of twelve thousand peaceful demonstrators. That particular action was later voided by the courts on First Amendment grounds.

There was opposition fatigue, in the press, in the nation, and even in the Senate. No revelation of insensitivity on issues of race or violations of civil liberties seemed to resonate or stir opposition to Rehnquist. The nominee proved adept at deflecting the queries with platitudes. And then the administration claimed executive privilege to prohibit the committee from gaining access to memos that Rehnquist had written to Attorney General John Mitchell on these issues. Rehnquist also protested that disclosure of the memos would violate the privacy of the "attorney/client" relationship. Given that the client of the attorney general is the American people, I did not understand how this relationship could be "private." Nevertheless, we saw the same arguments being used decades later by President George W. Bush to block the committee's access to documents in the confirmation hearing of Rehnquist's former law clerk, John Roberts, to succeed his old boss as chief justice of the United States.

Newsweek released a bombshell a day after the hearings began. On November 5, the magazine published the contents of a memo written by Rehnquist in 1952, when he was a twenty-seven-year-old clerk for Justice Robert H. Jackson.

The memo, "A Random Thought on Segregation Cases," could not have laid out its argument more candidly or clearly: "Plessy vs. Ferguson [the infamous 'separate but equal' doctrine handed down by the Court in 1896] was right and should be reaffirmed." Under that reasoning, *Brown v. Board of Education* should not have overruled *Plessy*, but instead should have upheld the constitutionality of segregation in our public schools.

Its conclusion read, "To the argument . . . that a majority may not deprive a minority of its constitutional right, the answer must be made that while this is sound in theory, in the long run it is the majority who will determine what the constitutional rights of the minority are."

In other words, as long as we're in the majority, we can decide what the minority is entitled to. We're the boss.

How did Rehnquist justify his majority-rule view of racial fairness? He said the memo did not reflect his views. "I believe that the memorandum was prepared by me as a statement of Justice Jackson's tentative views for his own use," Rehnquist wrote in a letter he delivered to James Eastland, the committee chairman. Why Justice Jackson, who in fact voted to strike down school desegregation in *Brown v. Board of Education*, would ask for such a memo was never explained. Jackson died in 1954, shortly after his vote on the historic *Brown* decision, and thus was unavailable to answer Rehnquist's allegation.

Rehnquist's confirmation (by a resounding vote of sixty-eight to twenty-six) owed much, I believe (and as Nixon had foreseen), to the Senate's institutional reluctance to repudiate a president a third consecutive time. The unfortunate result was, in my opinion, a justice whose record was disqualifying on its face.

What we now call "Watergate" was in fact a confluence of at least three currents that began flowing in 1971. The first was the International Telephone and Telegraph scandal, which involved essentially the same players, the same atmosphere, and the same activities that comprised the larger chain of wrongdoings. The second involved Nixon's firing of the special prosecutor he'd appointed to investigate the many allegations. The third was Watergate itself: the illegal break-ins by clandestine agents seeking to gain information about Nixon's adversaries, the illegal payoffs to those agents, and the illegal cover-ups of both activities.

The ITT affair began to surface in the summer of 1971, at about the same time the *New York Times* and *Washington Post* began publishing the Pentagon Papers and nearly a year before the storied break-ins at the Watergate office complex. This was not entirely a coincidence. Daniel Ellsberg's bold procurement of those papers—the Defense Department's top-secret history of the war that revealed a pattern of official lying about its prosecution—had driven the secrecy-obsessed Nixon to his catastrophic spree of surveillance and revenge. In September 1971, summoning the same "plumbers" unit that a year later would try to bug the Democratic offices at the Watergate complex, Nixon authorized a burglary raid on the office of Ellsberg's psychiatrist. Their mission was to scavenge for files that would call into question the former defense analyst's sanity.

In July 1971, the Republican National Committee announced that San Diego, Richard Nixon's preferred city, would be the site of its 1972 convention. A little more than a week later, the Nixon Justice Department revealed that it was dropping the appeals of three major antitrust suits involving ITT—appeals that had seemed likely to be upheld in the Supreme Court. This news was quickly followed by the abrupt resignation of Richard McLaren, the chief of the department's antitrust division, who'd built the cases and had a reputation as a relentless watchdog of conglomerate mergers. Just days after his resignation, McLaren was given a federal judgeship in Chicago, the appointment brokered by Deputy Attorney General Richard Kleindienst, who persuaded the chairman of the Judiciary Committee, Jim Eastland, not to hold confirmation hearings. I immediately smelled a rat, but could find no evidence that the judgeship was tainted, or any reason why it might have been. The syndicated columnist Jack Anderson smelled one as well, and said so in a December 9 column—an artful solicitation, as Anderson himself later admitted, for more information from anyone out there who might possess it.

Things grew more intriguing when Kleindienst—a longtime Arizona friend of William Rehnquist and a colleague of his at Justice—turned up in early 1972 as Richard Nixon's nominee for attorney general. He would replace John Mitchell, who'd resigned to spearhead Nixon's reelection campaign.

Kleindienst's original confirmation hearings elicited some opposition on the Committee, but not enough to prevent him from being reported out favorably. However, Kleindienst's troubles were just beginning. On February 29, and again on March 1, Jack Anderson published columns that called Kleindienst's integrity into question. His trial-balloon column had paid off: an informant, whom Anderson never named, appeared at the columnist's Washington offices and presented an internal ITT memo that amounted to the first "smoking gun" of the long Watergate affair. It explained why the administration had quietly dropped the antitrust investigations against ITT: the company had struck a secret deal with the administration to donate $400,000 to bankroll the San Diego convention. (The city itself had refused to finance the event.)

Why San Diego? Nixon was a Californian who loved the coastal stretches and the political climate below Los Angeles. He'd purchased his San Clemente estate, just an hour's drive up the highway from the city, in 1969. The region was a good deal more conservative than Los Angeles or San Francisco, and Nixon wanted a televised show of popular enthusiasm to contrast with that of his likely opponent, George McGovern.

The memo's author was an ITT lobbyist named Dita Beard. Beard asserted that Mitchell and Nixon not only knew about the company's donation, but had approved the terms under which it had been given. The go-between had been Kleindienst.

Kleindienst immediately demanded that the Senate reopen his hearings so that he could clear his name. In a hastily arranged private meeting with me in my Senate office on March 1, he insisted that he had never talked to Mitchell or anyone else at the White House about the ITT case, and that he certainly had never brokered any illegal agreements. He was lying.

He certainly got his wish about the hearings, and then some. Eastland agreed to reconvene the hearings. We started on March 2 and went on for twenty-two sessions. Eastland was, as always, very fair to me, and allowed me to call most of the witnesses I wanted and to use my Ad-Prac subcommittee staff to do the necessary investigatory work. Those hearings were the most intense I'd participated in since my arrival in the Senate, and I wanted them that way. (In certain respects, they formed a procedural template for the Watergate hearings themselves.) Often the sessions would last well into the evening, after which I'd convene my weary staff at the McLean house at around 10 p.m. to discuss the draft questions for the next day.

Kleindienst appeared five times, but we had plenty to talk about even in his absence. Just about every day brought new revelations: of meetings between ITT executives and Justice Department officials; of document shredding in the ITT offices; of skewed financial studies by the corporation for the White House. My fellow Democrats and I pressed the White House hard for documentation covering the antitrust settlements, and the White House, after strongly resisting us at first, complied. I asked Kleindienst for the record whether he had had any contact from the White House on the cases, and he replied, "No, sir"—a perjury, as it developed.

Dita Beard herself was a piece of work, as I discovered when five other senators and I visited her in Denver on March 26. I felt that as the author of the fateful memo, she should come and testify in the hearings, but when we learned that she was confined to an osteopathic hospital in Denver with a weak heart, Eastland authorized a bipartisan delegation to go and take her testimony there. We arrived at Rocky Mountain Osteopathic Hospital to find a crusty, fast-talking woman in her early fifties who sprayed jumbled thoughts in salty language at us as she alternately sucked on cigarettes and gulped from her oxygen mask.

It was not the most productive of testimonies I've witnessed, but it was among the most colorful. As we senators, a court reporter, Flug, and a lawyer for Eastland stood awkwardly around her bed, she smoked and coughed and denied having written the memo, which she'd earlier owned up to until the week before the hearing. She dropped administration names and called various people sons of bitches. When the Florida Republican Senator Edward Gurney asked her what she knew about Kleindienst, the arrows on her blood pressure machine went straight up, and she gasped and clutched at her throat until the doctor stopped the session and ushered us out of the room. I looked at Phil Hart, and saw that he was nearly as pale as Mrs. Beard herself. "That's it," Hart declared. He was not going to go back into that room, for fear that our witness might seize up and die.

Mrs. Beard was tougher than Hart thought, however. The week before the hearing, she had received an undercover bedside visit by one of Nixon's "plumbers," E. Howard Hunt, who showed up under a bizarre red wig and equipped with a voice-alteration device, apparently to persuade her to renounce the memo. I'm still amazed by it all: the appearance of a stealthy figure, cloaked in disguise, trying to interrogate and intimidate a hacking, chain-smoking, oxygen-gulping, bedridden emphysemic with a foul mouth.

Despite the overwhelming indications of governmental cover-up and illegal agreements presented to the committee, Kleindienst sailed once again to confirmation, over the objections of me and three others, which we laid out in a long, detailed minority report. We could not know it at the time, but damning evidence against him existed, spooled within one of the notorious White House tapes that Nixon maintained. It did not surface for another year and a half, when special prosecutor Archibald Cox listened to it and related the following passage to me:

NIXON: I want something clearly understood, and, if it is not understood, McLaren's ass is to be out within one hour. The IT-and-T thing—stay the hell out of it. Is that clear? That's an order.

KLEINDIENST: Well, you mean the order is to—

NIXON: The order is to leave the goddamned thing alone. Now, I've said this, Dick, a number of times, and you fellows apparently don't get the message over there. I do not want McLaren to run around prosecuting people, raising hell about conglomerates, stirring things up at this point. Now, you keep him the hell out of that. Is that clear?

KLEINDIENST: Well, Mr. President—

NIXON: Or either he resigns. I'd rather have him out anyway. I don't like the son of a bitch.

KLEINDIENST: That brief has to be filed tomorrow.

NIXON: That's right. Don't file the brief.

KLEINDIENST: Your order is not to file a brief?

NIXON: My order is to drop the goddamn thing. Is that clear?

KLEINDIENST: Yeah, I understand that.

This episode, I believe, was the true beginning of Watergate. Nixon now felt the heat of curiosity from congressional Democrats and the party's leaders. His instinct was to dive more deeply into the murk. Five days after Kleindienst assumed office, on June 17, 1972, came the celebrated break-in at Democratic headquarters. Larry O'Brien, one of my brother Jack's closest and most valued aides, was now the chairman of the party, and it was his conversations the intruders were seeking to tap via an electronic "bug." Their arrests on the scene were the beginning of the end for Nixon's reign of secrecy and imperialism.

Kleindienst might have clamped down on the Watergate abuses before they metastasized, but he apparently lacked the nerve. The day after the break-in, "plumber" G. Gordon Liddy himself told the new attorney general that the scheme was traceable to the White House, and that he should act to get the five men released. To Kleindienst's credit, he refused. But he failed to report what amounted to a criminal confession. He resigned his office the following April, was convicted of a perjury misdemeanor for his false testimony to our committee, and given a suspended sentence and fine.

Now events began to quicken, as the *Washington Post* and other newspapers fastened onto the possibility of a massive political scandal. In late September, the *Post's* Bob Woodward and Carl Bernstein reported that John Mitchell controlled a secret fund of as much as $700,000 that financed equally secret intelligence-gathering and sabotage operations. On October 10, FBI agents produced evidence that the break-in at O'Brien's office was part of this massive campaign.

Watergate was by now "Watergate" in press coverage. But the American public had not yet focused its attention on these developments, or perhaps could not yet summon the belief that they were real. Political party leaders, though, were paying very close attention indeed. The presidential election was only weeks away. Nixon remained popular in key sectors of the electorate. McGovern, who'd been nominated at the "New Politics" Democratic convention in Miami Beach, was seeking a mandate to end the Vietnam War; but since April he'd found himself smeared as the candidate of "amnesty, abortion, and acid." He was further damaged by the revelations that his vice presidential choice, Thomas Eagleton of Missouri, a good and decent man, had been hospitalized in the past and treated for depression, including receiving electric shock therapy. In those days, receiving psychiatric treatment alone might be considered as a disqualifier for public office—there was still a lack of understanding and terrible stigma associated with mental health issues in general. Adding hospitalization and electric shock to the mix sadly compounded the problem. In 1972, unlike vice presidential selections since then, there was no extensive vetting process that would have turned up an issue that might not play well in public. In fact, McGovern had settled on Eagleton as his running mate only after rejecting—or being rejected by—several other candidates. I found myself in this field: McGovern had invited me to run on the ticket with him when I telephoned to congratulate him on his nomination. The vice presidency had never really interested me; certainly not as an alternative to the Senate, where I could directly affect public policy. But given the party's low standing in the polls and the urgency of electing a Democrat after the wreckage of Nixon's reign, I briefly considered it. In the end, I turned it down.

McGovern then sounded out Gaylord Nelson, the Wisconsin senator who'd been the principal founder of Earth Day in 1970. After Nelson said no, McGovern talked to Senator Abe Ribicoff of Connecticut, who'd placed his name in nomination, with similar results. His list of possibilities after that showed flashes of what we now call "thinking outside the box": Leonard Woodcock of the United Auto Workers, the CBS News anchor Walter Cronkite, Father Theodore Hesburgh of Notre Dame, Mayor Kevin White of Boston, and the Texas Democrat Frances "Sissy" Farenthold.

Among McGovern's earliest choices was his eventual running mate, my brother-in-law Sargent Shriver. But Sarge, who was in Moscow at the time, initially demurred as well. And so the choice came down to Eagleton. After the Missourian left the ticket following the disclosures about his psychiatric history, McGovern first spoke to Hubert Humphrey and then to Ed Muskie about joining his ticket.

In early August 1972, I had a conversation with Hubert and told him that I would make the case to McGovern if he were interested. Humphrey said that first of all, he liked McGovern; second, he wanted to beat Nixon; but third, he'd taken quite a knocking around and felt that people would say, "There's good old Hubert. He comes out every time the bell rings." Humphrey ultimately turned it down.

I had a conversation with McGovern in the back of the Senate on Thursday afternoon, August 3. He told me that he was interested in Sarge, but that he wanted to approach Muskie first. The next evening, I went to the Cape for dinner at the Shrivers' and told Sarge that if Muskie turned it down I thought he would be offered the job.

McGovern called Sarge the next day and he came to see me before he accepted. Sarge said that he would not accept the offer if I objected. Some people were concerned that if Sarge were the successful vice presidential candidate in 1972, he would be making it more difficult for me to run for president in the future.

It is true that there was lingering unhappiness among some RFK supporters who thought that in 1968 Sarge should have resigned or taken leave from his post as ambassador to France and returned to America to help out with Bobby's presidential campaign. I personally had steered clear of this controversy. It just didn't bother me. I felt the same way about Sarge's being on the ticket in '72. I raised no objection.

I began to receive calls and visits from Democrats frantic to resurrect McGovern's campaign by a formal investigation of Watergate. They wanted me to convene hearings. I wanted to convene hearings as well. But the process was hardly as simple as it sounded.

Stewart Alsop laid out the difficulties in his *Newsweek* column of October 2, a week before the FBI report. He noted that two Senate bodies were tailor-made for such a probe: Sam Ervin's subcommittee on constitutional rights and John McClellan's Government Operations Committee. But given that both men represented southern, anti-McGovern states—North Carolina and Arkansas, respectively—this was unlikely.

Noting that "the Watergate affair is a snake that badly needs to be scotched," Alsop declared that the mandate for action lay with me: "It is a case of Kennedy or nothing." But obstacles lay in my own path as well. Alsop predicted that I would be attacked "all-out as a demagogue using his . . . chairmanship to play politics, compromising the rights of the accused in the process."

Alsop was referring to my Ad-Prac subcommittee, and he was partly correct. I had indeed hesitated to advance my subcommittee, believing that an investigation would be more credible with the public if led by a chairman more conservative than myself. I too thought that either Ervin's or McClellan's bodies would be a good choice. Ervin in particular was known as a great civil libertarian aside from his views on civil rights. But I wanted in, and I had no doubt that Ad-Prac's mandate would take the investigation deeper than even my colleagues imagined. The ideal entrée for Ad-Prac would be an invitation from one of these conservative southern Democrats to urge Ad-Prac to take the lead. I thought I knew a way of getting this to happen.

On October 3, I wrote to Ervin, exhorting him to get things going through his constitutional rights subcommittee. He replied in exactly the manner I'd hoped: "It seems to me appropriate for the Administrative Practices and Procedures subcommittee to investigate this matter and I want to assure you of my support should you decide to open an inquiry along these lines."

I moved quickly. Two days later, I notified my subcommittee members that we were going forward. On October 12, I ordered a "preliminary inquiry" into the matter, which included subpoena power. My plan, which had Ervin's support, was to bypass the Watergate burglars—who in any case were being prosecuted criminally—and train my sights on the Justice Department itself, sending out subpoenas to any official who might have known, participated in, or controlled the bugging and sabotage operations. And so it happened: we went after telephone and banking records of people under suspicion, and compelled testimony from several of the key figures. Among the first of these, whom we called to testify in November, was Donald Segretti, the young "dirty tricks" specialist from the Committee to Re-elect the President, who admitted that his source of funds for forging campaign literature was none other than Nixon's personal counsel (and bagman) Herbert Kalmbach.

Richard Nixon crushed George McGovern in the November election, winning more than 60 percent of the vote—and proving, incidentally, that none of the Watergate transgressions had even been relevant to his reelection. But as 1973 began, a steady cannonade of new revelations, convictions, resignations, and hearings erupted and dismantled his administration piece by piece. On April 30, 1973, the core of his brain trust—H. R. Haldeman, John Ehrlichman, and Kleindienst—resigned, and White House counsel John Dean was fired.

In the early spring, Mike Mansfield persuaded Sam Ervin to chair the hearings looking into Watergate. I was not a member of Ervin's special Senate committee, respecting Mansfield's view that my status as a possible candidate for the presidency in 1976 would have raised conflict-of-interest questions. On May 18, the Senate Watergate committee began its nationally televised hearings. White House tapes of February 1973 revealed Nixon and his counsel John Dean discussing the new Ervin committee and how they might spin it as merely a front for me and my own pernicious vendetta against the president. Ervin, Dean declared, was only a puppet for me; in fact, I was "behind" the entire creation of the hearings. He assured Nixon, "The partisan cast of this will become more apparent."

I supplied Ervin's committee with the vast body of testimony and findings developed by my Ad-Prac subcommittee, and they used it to great effect. It included a complex chart that interconnected the many people and many groups implicated in the overlapping scandals.

Most Americans of a certain age recall the highlights of Watergate's long denouement: the bombshell remark by witness Alexander Butterfield on July 13 that Nixon had taped all conversations and phone calls in his office since 1973; the protracted struggle for possession of the tapes highlighted by the "Saturday Night Massacre" of October 20; the bizarre "eighteen-and-a-half-minute gap" on one of the key subpoenaed tapes on December 7; the Supreme Court's unanimous ruling on July 24, 1974, that Nixon must turn over the tapes of sixty-four previously unreleased conversations; and, finally, on August 8, 1974, Nixon's resignation as president and the swearing in of Gerald Ford.

I want to return briefly to the "Saturday Night Massacre," because I had some personal experience with its heroes.

The seeds of it lay in Nixon's appointment in May 1973 of Elliot Richardson, the distinguished war veteran, Harvard Law School graduate, and, at the time, secretary of defense, as his new attorney general, succeeding Kleindienst. I admired Richardson, a liberal Republican with a long record of achievement in several cabinet posts, but I'd made it clear to him that he would not be confirmed by the Judiciary Committee unless he agreed to appoint a special prosecutor. My committee colleagues and I were convinced by this time that only a strong prosecutor independent of party loyalties or control would be credible enough with the public and the press to demand the hardest truths from this administration. After a series of private conversations with me, Richardson promised he would make such an appointment.

Richardson approached several possible candidates, but in late May settled on what I thought was a masterful choice: Archibald Cox, the legal scholar who had served my brother Jack as adviser, speechwriter, and, later, solicitor general. I admired Cox's ability, intelligence, and integrity, and I was determined that he function without the slightest hint of pressure. So I spoke again with Richardson, insisting—against his own wishes at first—that he agree to one condition, and one condition only, under which he would fire Cox or carry out a presidential order to fire him: "extraordinary impropriety."

It did not take Richardson long to understand the importance of this condition, and he agreed to it. Better still, he stood behind it when the inevitable phone call from Nixon reached him.

That call came on October 20. Since July, Cox (backed up by a district court order) had been demanding that Nixon release his newly revealed tape collection to Ervin's committee. Nixon resisted, growing more and more defiant as the weeks passed. On October 19 the desperate president concocted a scheme: he would offer a compromise. He prevailed on

Senator John Stennis, the Mississippi Democrat, to listen to the tapes and send Cox a summary of them. The ridiculousness of this plan was obvious. Stennis and Nixon enjoyed a warm friendship. And Stennis was nearly deaf.

Archibald Cox unconditionally refused this transparent ploy. Nixon exploded; he picked up the telephone on October 20, called Richardson, and demanded that the new attorney general fire Cox. An historic crossroads was at hand. Would Elliot Richardson cave in? Had he done so, oversight of the tapes would almost certainly have defaulted to Stennis, Nixon would then have escaped the threat of impeachment, and his illegitimate power would have continued to stain American governance.

Richardson held strong. Nixon responded by firing him, then firing Deputy Attorney General William Ruckelshaus for his refusal to fire Cox. Solicitor General Robert Bork became acting attorney general and he finally carried out Nixon's order. The president had won the night. But he had only succeeded in raising the level of suspicion against him—and of calls for his impeachment.

A final footnote to Watergate: virtually since the moment the existence of the Oval Office tapes became public knowledge, Americans have wondered where Richard Nixon came up with the idea of recording the conversations that ultimately brought him down.

I believe I know the answer: he got it from my brother Jack.

President Kennedy had a taping system in his office. He was not the first president to do so, nor the last until Nixon. Franklin Roosevelt recorded a few hours of press conference conversation with a large, unwieldy prototype. Both Harry Truman and Dwight Eisenhower experimented with the idea. But it was Jack's system that seems to have caught Nixon's imagination. My brother in fact recorded the fewest number of hours of any president, and nothing was confidential. But they included the intense and historically invaluable deliberations over the Bay of Pigs, the Cuban Missile Crisis, and the early debates over going into Vietnam.

Perhaps Richard Nixon envisioned compiling a comparable record of his own presidential triumphs. His fatal modification was to install a voice-activated mechanism, which removes the user's volition. Jack and other presidents, by contrast, relied on the conscious procedure of flipping a switch.

CHAPTER SEVENTEEN

Backlash in Boston
1974–1976

In handing over to Sam Ervin's committee documents that Ad-Prac had accumulated, I'd largely fulfilled my role in the Watergate matter. And so in the spring and summer of 1974, I turned my energies to other matters, ranging from nuclear arms testing to the Boston school busing crisis.

I had been invited by the Soviet Union for a six-day round of talks in Moscow related to arms control. I had some topics of my own that I intended to raise. I decided to take members of the family with me.

Along with Joan, Kara, and Teddy Jr., I arrived in the Russian capital on the evening of April 18. (Patrick was still too young for this kind of trip.) Waiting to greet us were several deputies of the Supreme Soviet and the chief editor of the government newspaper, *Izvestia*. I made a brief statement at the airport, noting that I wished to discuss the issues of free emigration and civil liberties in the scheduled meeting with the premier. Given that the Russian leadership and the Russian people in general were well aware of Watergate and the impending collapse of the Nixon presidency, I felt it appropriate to assure them that the Democrats were at least as committed to detente as the Republicans.

My host, the general secretary of the Communist Party Leonid Brezhnev, welcomed me. I understood (as I subtly tried to keep my grip as firm as his) that I was in the presence of a classic Russian strongman and shaper of history. Brezhnev's broad face beneath those famous eyebrows conveyed the toughness of his working-class roots and his rank as brigade commissar in World War II, where he served alongside Nikita Khrushchev.

Brezhnev honored me with what the press back in America described as a "four-hour luncheon," although I will admit now that two of those hours consisted of making polite conversation, through interpreters, with the other guests in the Kremlin's formal dining room as we waited for Brezhnev to appear.

Arms control, the main agenda item for my visit, was politely side-stepped in this early, ceremonial phase of my visit. No one, however, could ignore its urgency. The secretary, while professing his wish to end the arms race, for years had been investing Russia's wealth in an ongoing buildup of its armies and their weapons, to an extent that modernization of industry was neglected, the vast agricultural system had failed to keep pace with population increases, and the economy as a whole was stagnating. The USSR and the United States had signed the first Strategic Arms Limitation Treaty (SALT I) when Nixon had visited Moscow two years earlier, but Russia's continued testing of nuclear weapons was a matter of great concern to the U.S. government.

I opened up the subject the next day, when I gave a talk that stressed the dangers to peace inherent in weapons testing, and directly questioned why the Soviet Union continued to build and test missiles. The day after that, April 21, I spoke to an audience of some eight hundred people at Moscow State University. About half of this audience suggested to me either a dense infusion of party apparatchiks, or that students in Russia were considerably older than in the United States. I began by attempting to poll the audience on the issue of Soviet defense spending, but it went nowhere. An awkward silence dropped over my listeners, and a professor in the audience barked out a sharp rebuke.

I raised the issue of Jewish emigration, which resulted in more fur-rowed brows. I finally coaxed some smiles when, asked about whether I would run for president in 1976, I cupped a hand to my ear and pretended that I hadn't heard the question. When the two or three laughs had died down, I assured everyone that my only intention was to run again for my Senate seat. I responded to a question about the Warren Commission report on my brother's assassination by stating my belief that its conclusions were correct.

Though I'd been forthright in disavowing any intention to seek the highest office, I well understood why Brezhnev had been so receptive to my visit. He and other Soviet officials believed that I would be America's next elected president, and that I was an honest advocate for control of the arms race. This was confirmed when the two of us finally sat down for serious discussion on the topic. I had brought with me a draft treaty built around a call for a total ban on nuclear testing. The secretary nodded in silence from time to time as the document was translated for him.

"If you were president of the United States now," he told me when it was finished, "I would ask you to sit over here in front of this fireplace. We would light a fire, and we would have some vodka, and both of us would sign it and celebrate a great step toward halting nuclear expansion."

During my visit, Brezhnev averred expansively that our countries should not be threatening each other. I told him that I agreed. He grew emphatic: his country was *not* threatening the United States. One unfortunate tradition that fed false suspicions was that of restricted access: the Soviet Union restricted where American visitors could travel, and Americans restricted Russians' freedom of movement as well. Brezhnev believed that between the two countries, the Soviet Union was far more liberal.

"Let me show you," he said. We both arose, and I followed Brezhnev to a map of his country. "Americans cannot go here or here," he conceded, as his thick finger stabbed at various locations. "Or here, or here. Or here. But outside of that, Americans are able to go anyplace they want."

I tried to memorize the places where Brezhnev's finger had fallen. When I returned home, just for the fun of it, I showed the locales to a military expert, who told me that each was a top-secret site where the Soviets stored their missiles.

It was doubtless the prospect of my possible presidency, coupled with the innate hospitality that Brezhnev shared with his fellow Russians, that prompted the secretary to offer his private jet to my entourage for a side trip before we returned to the United States. Before we departed, I had one further item to take up with Secretary Brezhnev. Leonard Bernstein, the esteemed conductor and composer who had been a great friend of President Kennedy's, had called me before I left the States and said he knew I was interested in the release of Soviet Jews. He had a request: see what Brezhnev will do, he urged me, about the release of Mstislav Rostropovich, the sublime cellist and conductor who was effectively imprisoned within Soviet borders.

Rostropovich was perhaps the greatest cellist of the twentieth century. Both Prokofiev and Shostakovich had composed pieces for him, and in 1950, at the age of twenty-three, he was awarded the highly prestigious Stalin Prize. Rostropovich's social ideals were as bold and enlightened as his art was exquisite. An outspoken believer in free speech and democratic values, he earned the enmity and scrutiny of the Soviet leaders. In the early 1970s, official Russia held him in disgrace, canceled his concerts, and, in 1972, prohibited his travels outside Russia.

Joan's training as a classical musician made her a strong advocate of the artist's release as well. During a photo opportunity in front of the Kremlin on our arrival, she had relayed to Russian officials the petitions of Bernstein and others in the worldwide artistic community that Rostropovich be granted an exit visa. Now, toward the end of our meeting on Monday, I repeated the request to the premier. I could see that he'd picked up on the importance that we, and by extension the influential American arts community, had accorded this matter.

Brezhnev said to me, you will hear back from us very soon.

We flew from Moscow for Tbilisi, the historic capital of Georgia, and then Leningrad (since restored to its original name, St. Petersburg), where we visited the massive Piskarevskoye Cemetery with its roughly half million dead and buried in mass graves from the infamous nine-hundred-day World War II siege. Accompanying my entourage was an aide to Brezhnev, A. M. Alexandrov-Agentov, clearly present to keep an eye on my contacts and behavior.

On the return flight to Moscow, I frankly told Alexandrov about a plan I intended to carry out, a plan that involved some risk to me as well as potential outrage from my hosts. I wanted to speak personally to some of the dissident Jews being held without exit visas in Moscow. Alexandrov was predictably shocked, and we argued about it, but he shrugged helplessly when he saw that my mind was made up—though I knew he would report my intention.

I'd arranged a dead-of-night meeting with a group of the dissidents at the small apartment of one of them, a distinguished scientist and a pioneer in cybernetics named Alexander Lerner. He had applied to leave for Israel in 1971 and was refused. I was accompanied by the courageous Grace Kennan Warnecke, the daughter of the former ambassador George Kennan, who challenged our driver to take us there despite orders to the contrary from the KGB.

Like Rostropovich, these Jews were hostages within the Soviet Union, and hungered for the right to immigrate to Israel. I promised them that once back home, I would do all in my power to see that their dreams came true. In the end, the Soviets, though furious about my visit, did indeed grant exit visas to some of these people.

Nor was that all the good news. When the flight back home made its first landing outside the Soviet Union, I received a call from the Soviet ambassador saying that Rostropovich and his wife would be released.

After we returned to the United States, Joan and I had a welcoming party for Rostropovich and his wife, Galina, at our home in McLean, Virginia. They were exceedingly gracious. When the maestro met Teddy later in the evening, I could see that he was moved by my son's positive spirit in the face of his ongoing battle with cancer. In a spontaneous act of generosity, Rostropovich said that the only way he could ever thank me for helping to secure his freedom was to teach my son the cello. As it turned out, Teddy did not take advantage of this formidable opportunity; but neither my son nor I ever forgot the offer.

Rostropovich became musical director and conductor of the National Symphony in Washington, was awarded the Medal of Freedom by President Reagan, and sat on a metal chair at the Berlin Wall as it crumbled in November 1989 and played a Bach suite with tears streaming down his face. He reconciled with his homeland in the 1990s. When he died in Moscow in 2007, Soviet president Vladimir Putin called his death a terrible loss for Russian culture and praised the musician as a firm defender of human rights.

Back home and at work, I started to address the other urgencies that had crowded my calendar during the Watergate ordeal. Health care and national health insurance, for example. Ending the oil depletion allowance. Reforming campaign finance laws. Easing restrictions built into the 1966 Freedom of Information Act. Addressing tensions in Boston ignited by the issue of busing. And, in the early months of 1974 at least, considering my prospects for a presidential run in 1976. I could not help but notice that in May, a poll for *Time* reported that 55 percent of Americans called me an "acceptable candidate" as opposed to 43 percent for Vice President Ford.

I'd begun to move ahead on some of these well before the House Judiciary Committee passed its three articles of impeachment in late July 1974 and Nixon announced his resignation on August 8.

I harbored no doubts that Nixon had to go, yet I could not shake a sense of sadness that the country had been put through this ordeal. The saving truth was that our system had worked. The right outcome had occurred.

As the news was announced, the Senate cloakroom was nearly empty, but not completely. One other senator remained there, sitting in silence beside me as we watched Nixon's small, hunched figure trudge down the walkway to the waiting craft, mount those steps, then suddenly spin about and thrust both arms over his head, giving the double "V for victory" salute with his fingers as he prepared to leave the White House for the last time. The two of us watched without speaking as Nixon disappeared inside.

The senator sitting next to me was Gene McCarthy. McCarthy and I, alone together in the cramped, L-shaped cloakroom, frowning in concentration at the TV set as Nixon vanished into the sky.

We didn't have a conversation. I don't recall that we spoke, although courtesy probably prompted us to acknowledge each other. We just sat there and watched, each of us consumed with his own thoughts about what might have been.

After Eugene McCarthy died at age eighty-nine in December 2005, of complications from Parkinson's disease, in a retirement home in Georgetown, I attended his funeral. He'd been a difficult fellow in many ways, but I wanted to pay my respects.

In mid-1974, the next presidential election primaries lay only a year and a half in the future. Some candidates in both parties had in effect launched their campaigns already. I knew that I would very soon have to make my own decision. Feelers were coming in from thoughtful and substantial Democrats, urging me once again to make the run. Although I had insisted both in public and in private that I would not be a candidate, I admitted to myself that I had some serious thinking to do.

Many of the friends, aides, and followers who envisioned an Edward Kennedy presidency were basing their hopes on a romantic and ultimately irrelevant model. Whether consciously or not, they seemed enthralled by the dream that the dash and vaulting aspirations of the early 1960s would return again.

My actual vision of the presidency, to the extent that I turned it over in my mind, was a good deal more complex and less romantic.

It was and remains a given that my brothers established a soaring standard for public service, and that their standard to a great extent has defined my life and my aims. I have always measured myself against that standard. Jack and Bobby were my heroes.

But my concept of myself as president had little or nothing to do with Camelot. It had nothing to do with that old preoccupation with "catching up" that I've mentioned earlier. It wasn't about Jack, or Bobby, or my father. The eras that shaped them had passed. The present era was quite different in mood, in collective experience, and in the challenges the nation faced. Jack's and Bobby's great legacies inspired me, but cold reason told me that I could not run as their surrogate, nor could I govern according to their templates. My goals, my style would derive from my own judgments as to what I wanted to accomplish.

The most important reason I declined to make the race in 1968, aside from my debilitating grief, derived specifically from that refusal to be a surrogate. I knew that if I ran, I wouldn't be running as myself. I was in grief, and I wasn't ready. In 1972, it still felt too soon, and my son's health took precedence.

Heading into 1976, I weighed the actual opportunities it would provide me for advancing my social and political ideals against the sacrifices my family would have to make. Joan and I remained together largely for the children, and I worried about her role in the campaign. I was far from certain that my children, in particular Teddy Jr. as he continued to reshape his life as a cancer survivor and youthful amputee, would not be damaged by my necessary absences. And I was far from certain about my safety as president. I had made my personal peace with the prospect of assassination. Making peace with its effect on my mother, sisters, wife, children, and friends so close that they amounted to family—this was another matter.

Although it was not a determinant in my decision-making, I also knew that it did not help my presidential prospects that Chappaquiddick came spinning back into the nation's consciousness. On July 14, 1974, five days before the fifth anniversary of the accident, the *New York Times Magazine* published a retrospective essay by the journalist Robert Sherrill. Irrespective of its merits, the piece attracted great attention. Though the election was still two years away, my adversaries would almost certainly continue to make an issue of it.

In the late summer, just before Labor Day, I gathered my family for a conference on the Cape to make certain I understood their feelings on the matter, and that they understood mine. What transpired led me, on September 23, to call a press conference in Boston to announce that I would not be a candidate for president in 1976. I made it as unequivocal as words would allow.

My primary responsibilities were at home, I told the reporters and cameras. "It has become quite apparent to me that I would be unable to make a full commitment to a campaign for the presidency. I simply cannot do that to my wife and children and the other members of my family." My decision, I stipulated, was firm, final, and unconditional. I would accept neither the nomination nor a draft.

If I needed any further reminder how deeply my loved ones agonized over the thought of my running for president, I received it a year and a half later, by way of my mother.

Rose Kennedy was eighty-five in January 1976 when she trustingly consented to an interview in Palm Beach with a *National Enquirer* reporter named Charles Van Rensselaer, who'd developed some acquaintanceships among the Kennedys. When I learned of my mother's comments, I realized afresh the anxieties that coursed beneath her resolutely cheerful exterior.

"I feel Teddy may be pressured into running for president this year," Mother was quoted as telling the reporter. "I don't want him to, but the pressures may force him.

"He promised me, he promised me faithfully, that he would not run. I told him I did not want to see him die, too, that I could not stand another tragedy. . . . But even though he has given me his promise that he will not run, I realize there are considerations that could make him change his mind. He may feel it is something he has to do. . . . And if that is his decision, I would support him. I'll campaign for him, anywhere he wants me to. You know, I'm quite a campaigner.

"But he shouldn't run, though. Oh, no. No. We've had so many tragedies already. I have prayed so much about this and I have asked God that

Teddy will be led to the right decision. But in the end I have put it all in God's hands and I will follow His will, no matter what it is."

With the question of my candidacy resolved, I turned my attention to a matter of much greater importance. Racial tensions had escalated in my home state over the issue of school busing to achieve integration. American schools had been desegregated by law since the *Brown v. Board of Education* decision of 1954. Yet urban housing patterns in which populations remained stubbornly sealed within neighborhoods of their own ethnic and racial identities ensured that true integration would remain an unattainable ideal. Finally, the courts of the nation took it upon themselves to enforce the ideal.

Boston was one of several American cities that had stalled for years in designing a desegregation plan, but it was among the most volatile, as events proved. Francis W. Sargent, a moderate Republican, was governor then. He advocated support of the busing order, but was tarred as an elitist by opponents. Kevin White, the mayor of Boston, also tried to play a constructive role, but there was no groundswell of support. The business community simply did not get involved. In those days, they were essentially isolated from this kind of thing.

The Catholic Church, a potential bulwark for restraint, did not play a constructive role. Richard Cardinal Cushing, my father's old friend, was in the waning days of his life and physically too frail to be a force. Sadly, some local priests actually went on the anti-busing marches.

At that time, Boston didn't have someone like Lenny Zakim, the late civic leader and civil rights activist who was known for building bridges between people. The civic leaders at the time of the busing crisis gave money to support the arts, but they really were not involved in this kind of community healing effort. We were not entirely bereft of people and groups who understood the common good and worked bravely for it. I think of some of the members of the African-American community like the Snowdens, Otto and Muriel, the creators of Freedom House in 1949, who remained vital and active through this era. I think of the great educator and NAACP activist Ruth Batson, who stood up to the Boston School Committee when it counted. Or Ellen Jackson, whose constructive work on behalf of affirmative action earned her tremendous vituperation. A Boston high school now bears her name.

In that same year, Judge W. Arthur Garrity Jr. ruled in the United States District Court for the District of Massachusetts that the Boston Public Schools showed a lingering pattern of racial discrimination, and mandated busing as the remedy: transferring children out of their community schools by bus to those in distant and racially dissimilar neighborhoods to achieve the balance required by the law.

Civil chaos tore through the city within weeks.

Several anti-busing leaders had been elected to the Boston School Committee, the governing body of the Boston Public Schools. This group successfully had blocked implementation of Garrity's ruling. Towering above them all was the determined Boston lawyer Louise Day Hicks, who, with her severely parted black mane, her mouth set in a thin straight line, and her universally recognized catch line—*"You know where I stand"*—had nearly won the mayor's race in 1967. (She served a term as a Democratic congresswoman from 1971 to 1973, and in 1976 became president of the Boston City Council.) Hicks and her equally confrontational comrade-in-arms, Elvira "Pixie" Palladino, cofounded the aptly named ROAR (Restore Our Alienated Rights) in 1974. And there was John Kerrigan, the heavy-browed, caustic school committee chairman who spewed patently over-the-top claims and castigations to keep himself on the news and in the limelight.

It is significant that Hicks, Palladino, Kerrigan, and others at the forefront of the anti-busing movement were Democrats. Hicks in fact voted for the Equal Rights Amendment as a congresswoman, and Palladino rather creatively tried to frame busing as a women's issue. Activists were holding public rallies all over the city in the early 1970s.

Some of the opponents of busing were focused only on race, and I knew I couldn't have any impact on them. But others were concerned and bewildered, troubled and filled with anxiety about what was happening to their children, and I thought that maybe I could reach these parents. They had legitimate concerns. They were worried that their children would be far away from home if they fell ill at school. And they were upset because they were being denied access to the school in the neighborhood to which, in some cases, they had moved to specifically because of the school district. I understood those concerns.

In August, I made a televised appeal for calm. Others did the same, and we had some success urging support for the courts. The federal courts had been instrumental in helping to break down the walls of discrimination, and I deeply believed that the worst thing we could do was to cast doubt on the legitimacy of the courts' decisions.

But in retrospect, it may have been this very appeal, and others like it, that branded me as an enemy of the outraged dissenters. In their eyes, I had become just one more of those Boston elitists who didn't care about ordinary people and their children.

I issued another plea for restraint shortly before the opening day of public schools. But as that day dawned, September 9, the entire nation seemed focused on South Boston. I went over to see it for myself: television trucks and reporters everywhere, swarms of police, rocks flying at school buses, mobs of red-faced people yelling insults at the African-American children as they walked to their schoolhouse doors, where metal detectors awaited them.

A huge anti-busing rally was forming at City Hall. I debated whether or not to make an appearance there. I had not been invited, and so it would have been easy to stay away. The prospects for violence were enormous. But I felt a responsibility to go. Boston was my city, and busing was *the* issue of the day. Hundreds of good people of both races were putting themselves on the line, trying to find a way through this struggle. There was no choice but for me to face this issue where it counted: at ground zero, on the street. That was when I discovered the price of calling for calm.

When my car pulled up to City Hall, a massive crowd swelled the area between it and the John F. Kennedy Building. People screamed through bullhorns.

I decided to walk to this crowd. I told my aides to stay behind: I did not want it to appear that I was coming with a group to protect me. As I walked alone across the mall toward them, I could hear voices say, "There he is! There he is! There he is!" They began yelling insults. But they did fall back a little and open just enough of a path for me to get to the podium.

As I approached the microphone, a man shouted at me, "What do you want to do, speak? You're not going to speak! You've taken away our rights! We're going to take away your rights! How do you like that?!"

With that, everyone in the crowd turned their backs on me and sang "God Bless America." A busing protester took the podium and gave a five-minute fire-and-brimstone speech. When I walked toward the microphone again after he'd finished, some of his supporters covered the mike with their hands. The crowd turned its back again and sang another song. The hostility level was rising fast. I was catching insults from both the crowd and those on the podium. I started down the stairs at the side of the podium. The crowd opened just a sliver. They raged insults at me that knew no bounds: "YOUR ONE-LEGGED SON! SEND *HIM* OVER HERE!" Eggs and tomatoes were in the air now, and there was pushing and shoving.

I stopped on my way away from the plaza. Crowds such as this one are filled with cowards. If you turn and face them, they're reluctant to close the distance. I stopped a couple times more, and the crowd stopped. But it was showing signs of turning into a full-fledged mob. I was now about thirty yards from the doors of the JFK Building. The mob was still stopping, but it had edged ever closer to me. I turned resolutely and strode toward the doors. As I passed through them, the rocks started hurtling toward me in earnest. Window glass shattered, but police were inside the building, and my pursuers didn't try to enter.

The crisis, for me at least, could have ended there. It almost did. I got into an elevator and started to take it down to the basement garage to get into a car that would whisk me to the airport, from which I would fly to Washington. Then it struck me: *They'll say they ran me out of town.* There was no way I was going to let that happen. I rode the elevator back up to street level and let them see me. Then I took the elevator up to my office on the twenty-fourth floor.

More dangerous still was a situation that developed after a speech I gave in Quincy not long afterward. This time ROAR was an even more aggressive presence among the several hundred demonstrators outside the building. I realized that I would have to move through them on my way to my car. My driver, Jack Crimmins, usually stayed with the car on such occasions, but this time he left it and walked back to the meeting hall to give me and my aide Jimmy King some extra protection.

We made it back to the car with people screaming and spraying spittle in our faces. The car's tires had all been punctured. Dog feces were smeared on the door handles and all over the windshields. The demonstrators had nearly encircled us. There was no security.

Jack and Jimmy and I started to walk. I didn't know where the hell we were walking. It was a neighborhood, but one completely unknown to me. We walked on. The thing was to seem purposeful, resolute. I asked Jack, "Do we have friends around here? Is there a house?" But Jack knew of no one. We didn't even know the name of the street we were on. We kept walking. The mob followed us. It was starting to grow larger. The people in it were getting nastier. Then, out of the corner of my eye, I saw a subway station. I looked at Jimmy and said, "Jimmy, we've got to get in there." But what I was thinking was, *My God, we'll be in the subway and we'll be waiting there for who knows how long for the train to come.* We broke for the entrance. Our pursuers ran after us. There was one gated doorway leading to the tracks. We squeezed through, and Jimmy somehow braced it shut against the mob. We boarded a train and were safe.

Probably the most excruciating encounter of them all, though, was an event that wasn't physically threatening. I'd agreed to meet with some seventy South Boston parents in my office.

They all crowded in and formed a semicircle around me, behind my desk. ROAR was ably represented by my old friend Pixie Palladino. She did not disappoint. But the woman who really burned her name into my memory on that long, long day was an organizer named Rita Graul. She was the toughest cookie I'd ever seen. I remember thinking, *If I were ever to be fighting against the German lines, I'd want Rita Graul to be in that foxhole with me.*

Rita never spoke—formally, that is. She just introduced each one of the seventy people. Each of whom spoke. One. At. A. Time. The meeting lasted seven hours. Rita was the emcee, if that is the term. She knew every single person in that group; knew which neighborhood they came from; what part of Ireland their ancestors had come from. "Oh, golly," she'd say. "Now we'll hear from Mary over here. Mary O'Sullivan. You know, the O'Sullivans used to be a great community resource in the school there. But now—" She'd sigh, and go on in that quivering voice of hers, "Why are you torturing Mary's kids, Senator? She's got two nice children: Megan and Sean. Sean was on the baseball team. But he can't play baseball anymore, Senator, because he is being bused. Senator, do your kids play baseball? Why are you doing this to us, Senator? Why are you doing this to me?"

Seven hours of it.

The wounds inflicted on the people of Boston by the years of racial strife never reached a dramatic moment of healing. I wish I could say otherwise—but such is true in the nation as well. I certainly take comfort in the progress made since then: the fact that Massachusetts schools, in the fourth and eighth grades especially, are now among the very best in

the country. More success has been achieved in reducing the racial dispar-
ity in Boston schools than in almost any other state. The enlightened
business community has championed reforms that goaded government
into taking action.

Yet the scars remain: by the time the busing experiment ended in
1988, white flight to the suburbs had generated a kind of social segregation. The Boston school district, once a hundred thousand students
strong, stood at fifty-seven thousand, only 15 percent of whom were
white.

The bicentennial year 1976 witnessed the election of Jimmy Carter as
president over Gerald Ford. Carter won without any help of consequence
from me. This was not my decision, but Carter's. I had in fact told him
that I would go anywhere on the trail he needed me to go. I suggested,
though, that he accompany me in these appearances; he declined. I believe
that the prospect of standing alongside me in public activated his political
insecurities.

Jimmy Carter baffled me. He baffled many potential allies in his own
party—Hubert Humphrey, Ed Muskie, and George McGovern found
themselves as unwelcome as did I in their overtures to campaign on his
behalf—but I believed then and now that he reserved a special place in his
animus toward me.

The year 1976 also saw my reelection to the Senate, an especially
heartening outcome in light of the recent turmoils in Boston. The massed
anger of the anti-busing voters of South Boston was still fresh in my
memory, as was my sorrow that those furious crowds consisted mostly of
people whose heritage I shared and respected, Irish Catholics. I doubt
that many in those troubled neighborhoods had mellowed enough to
vote for me—my opponent, after all, was the ROAR counsel Robert Em-
met Dinsmore—but the Commonwealth returned me with 74 percent of
the vote.

Jimmy Carter's electoral victory over Gerald Ford seemed to cheer up the nation, but not everyone in the political world, even among liberal Democrats, was as charmed. The moment was certainly right for Carter. The electorate was hungry for a newcomer, a moral crusader who would play against Washington and its politics of cynicism. The smiling Georgia peanut farmer who campaigned on the studied folksiness of "My name is Jimmy Carter and I want to be your president" arrived on the scene just when American governance was ripe for transformation.

Looking back, I think he simply had convinced himself that he was going to do it his way. He was an outsider, and he was going to run things from an outsider's point of view. This was true of his dealings with the Senate, and one of the principal reasons that he never won that body's cooperation.

It seemed as though Jimmy Carter looked on me as a potential spoiler for his presidential hopes from the very outset. We first met when he was still governor of Georgia, in May 1973, when I traveled to Georgia to speak of my Soviet Union trip, and he invited me to stay at the Governor's Mansion in Atlanta. What I did not know then was that he had already decided to run for president in 1976, and regarded me as a competitor in the Democratic primaries—this even though I'd stated my intention to keep out of the race, and though these primaries were filling up with other serious contenders. I did notice that he was puzzlingly changeable in his manner toward me, a trait that would continue. In Georgia, he was cordial one moment, as when he extended the mansion invitation, and callous the next, as when he offered me and my aides the use of his official airplane for our flight to the University of Georgia at Athens—and then withdrew the offer on the morning of the talk, obliging us to speed by car along the seventy-five-mile route in order to get there on time.

At the 1976 Democratic convention that nominated him for president, Carter chose not to offer me a speaking role. Still, as his administration began in 1977, our relationship was harmonious enough. I'm not a person who holds grudges or keeps political score in that way. I've never found it to be particularly conducive to getting things done. I was with him on most votes. We had started to work then on such important issues as airline deregulation, tax reform, arms control, human rights, energy independence, and the Panama Canal Treaty that Carter advocated and signed in 1977 to transfer sovereignty of the Canal Zone from the United States to Panama. I supported his stands in all those areas.

Another important area on which we found common purpose was Northern Ireland. British rule of the Protestant North, and the marginalization of the Catholic minority there, was of course an ancient and seemingly settled fact of history. It traced back at least as far as 1690, when the invading King William III of England and Scotland wore down the Catholic Jacobites at the Battle of the Boyne. The harsh peace terms that followed ensured British control of the six-county North and bitter resentments among the conquered Catholics for centuries to come. The Partition of 1921, which followed armed conflict in the South between British forces and the Irish Republican Army, created home-rule policies for both the North and the twenty-six counties of the South, but its unintended consequence was oppression for the Catholic minority in the northern counties. This led to Catholic civil disobedience in the North, which morphed into violence, which in turn provoked savage reprisals by Protestants. A cycle of death and devastation took hold, with arson, bombings, and shootings shredding the fabric of civilized life. The Irish Republican Army—the IRA—then turned into a Catholic nationalist paramilitary force, and waged a decades-long battle to end British rule of Northern Ireland.

"The troubles," as they were known in Northern Ireland, remained off the United States' diplomatic radar until the late 1960s. America's close relationship with Great Britain, reinforced during World War II, lent a patina of self-interest to our official disinterest in this "internal affair" of the United Kingdom. But this cycle of repression and killing had to be stopped.

My understanding of the situation in Northern Ireland really began to evolve after I met John Hume, a brilliant young member of Parliament from Northern Ireland. We had met briefly in 1972, after I cosponsored a resolution with Abe Ribicoff calling for withdrawal of the British troops from Northern Ireland and establishing a united Ireland. But it was really in late 1972 that John began the great education of Edward Kennedy about Northern Ireland and established the seeds that grew into a wonderful relationship.

John Hume was a charismatic figure who believed in nonviolence. He believed in the political process rather than the bomb and the bullet, and that the different traditions should be able to work out their differences through mutual respect. Unlike those of us who said that the first step was for the British to withdraw troops, John believed that the ultimate resolution of the conflict would come through political evolution rather than by unilateral actions by any of the parties. As a native of Derry (as the Catholics always call Londonderry), John was outraged by the violence on January 20, 1972—Bloody Sunday—when a British paratroop regiment had fired on Catholics marching in Derry to protest the British policy of internment. Thirteen of the demonstrators were killed on the spot and a fourteenth lost his life a few months later. But he was adamant that retaliatory violence would only spark more violence.

Hume's views of the situation made a very powerful impression on me and influenced the work I did on Northern Ireland from then on. I thought it important to listen to someone who was on the ground and suffering and experiencing the harshness that he was experiencing and risking his life in nonviolent protest. In 1976, I worked with Congressman Bruce Morrison of Connecticut, who was very involved in Irish issues, to address the issue of Northern Ireland for the first time in the Democratic platform. Although I did not have a strong personal relationship with

Jimmy Carter, we were able to work with his staff, with his knowledge, to include the following language: "The voice of the United States should be heard in Northern Ireland against violence and terror, against the discrimination, repression and deprivation which brought about that civil strife, and for the efforts of the parties toward a peaceful resolution of the future of Northern Ireland."

Hume urged that I encourage Irish Americans to withhold their support from organizations giving money to the IRA—a counterintuitive viewpoint for many such citizens, who tended to romanticize the IRA as freedom fighters, perhaps not understanding the endless cycle of violence that was being created. I sought out some other prominent Irish Americans to back me up in delivering the message. First, I was able to secure an alliance with the new Speaker of the House, the popular and credible Thomas P. "Tip" O'Neill. Then New York's Senator Pat Moynihan and Governor Hugh Carey soon joined us as well.

We became known as the Four Horsemen. Our first joint statement, issued on St. Patrick's Day 1977, was two-pronged. We urged all organizations engaged in violence to renounce their campaigns; and we called on Americans to renounce actions that supported such violence. *Newsweek* made our subtle point explicit. The Four Horsemen, the magazine said, "forced Irish Americans to consider the bloody use of their guns and money."

Jimmy Carter committed his administration to supporting a form of government in the North that would "command widespread acceptance throughout both parts of the community," meaning Catholic and Protestant, and added the incentive of economic assistance in the event of a settlement. By this gesture, Carter ended the era of official nonintervention by America in the Irish conflict, an admirable accomplishment. Later, he built on this by stopping the sale of weapons to the Royal Ulster Constabulary, a force that many Catholics viewed as oppressive and dangerous.

And so Jimmy Carter and I did find common cause in certain areas, after a fashion. The overarching political cause for me, however, was health insurance, and that is where the comity really broke down between us. In fact, health care and health insurance were the issues that damaged our relations beyond repair.

CHAPTER EIGHTEEN

Sailing Against the Wind
1976–1980

A little more than two weeks before I first met Jimmy Carter in Georgia, he had unveiled his views on health care in a speech to African-American medical students. It was obviously tailored to the hopes of the United Auto Workers as expressed by the late Walter Reuther. Carter declared that coverage should be universal and mandatory. Later he told reporters that his plan was nearly identical to the one I had been shaping with Congressman James Corman of California. I had my doubts. He was certainly paying lip service to "universal" and "mandatory" coverage, but he never talked specifics. My father had a great rule of thumb: bet on what you think a man will do rather than what he says he'll do and you'll be right more often than not. I just wasn't sure with Carter.

My suspicion deepened, and was essentially confirmed, once Carter took office. He announced soon after the inauguration that his first priority was an energy bill; health care would have to come later. "Later" proved to be an understatement. The president assigned Joseph Califano, secretary of Health, Education, and Welfare, the responsibility to draft a plan. It seemed to me unlikely that the administration would have a bill ready for the 1977 Congress, but I did not slow my own Committee's efforts in moving forward.

My staff and I worked hard to craft a plan that would be capable of having broad-based support. Specifically, we negotiated long and hard in 1977 to persuade Lane Kirkland, the secretary of the AFL-CIO, and Doug Fraser, president of the UAW, to compromise on their strong commitment to a single-payer system, where health care providers would be paid from a single national fund like Medicare—and agree instead to support a plan built on our existing system of private insurance provided that coverage was mandatory and universal. I had personally supported single payer in the past and understood the benefits of it, but I also knew that it would be politically impossible to pass.

In November 1977, Califano finally presented a series of options on national health care to the president. We then had extensive discussions between his staff and mine, incorporating the work we had done earlier in reaching agreement with Kirkland and Fraser. But there were tensions between HEW and our position. They seemed to be putting a negative spin on our proposal, and despite our efforts, Carter made it clear that he had no intention of bringing us into the process to work with his team to hammer out a legislative proposal. Instead, he told us he needed to take a month-and-a-half here and a few weeks there to have meetings and read memos and more discussions with his Cabinet officers and staff. Then, he'd get back to us and we'd have a chance to make comments on what they'd decided. I thought that was a recipe for failure.

The moment called for bold leadership and swift action built around a single piece of legislation. We continued to work toward that end. And Carter continued to slow down the process. By the summer of 1978, I felt that the president was squandering a real opportunity to get something done. The Jimmy Carter who had declared that he wanted mandatory and universal coverage and had a plan that was nearly identical to mine had now been replaced by the President Carter who wanted to approach health insurance in incremental steps, over time, if certain cost containment benchmarks were met—and after the 1978 midterm elections. According to my notes, I spoke with Carter by phone on June 26, 1978, and was very direct in laying out how politically untenable his position was: "I don't think you can go to an elderly group and say, 'You're in . . . the second phase [of coverage], but if we pass the first [phase] and if hospitals keep their costs down and the economy doesn't go so much into a deficit, then you might be phased in.'"

When I met with Carter and his team two days later, he continued to pay lip service to the desirability of a single bill, but he clearly had no intention of going in that direction. He wanted to move slowly, through a series of small bills. After leaving the meeting, I knew he wasn't committed, and I didn't plan to wait around. The issue was too important to me. I called Califano to let him know that I was being besieged with calls about our meeting and was going to have a press conference explaining my differences with the White House. As I learned later, Carter regarded my efforts as a platform to challenge him for the presidency. If that's why he slowed things down, then he made a poor political calculation. If we had passed comprehensive national health insurance together, it would have been a huge victory for Carter. And it would have been much more difficult for me to have challenged him for the nomination, as I ultimately did.

Clearly, President Carter was a difficult man to convince—of anything. One reason for this was that he did not really listen. He loved to give the *appearance* of listening. He made a point, for example, of bringing eminent people to the White House for colloquies in the summertime. You'd arrive about 6:00 or 6:30 p.m., and the first thing you would be reminded of, in case you needed reminding, was that he and Rosalynn had removed all the liquor in the White House. No liquor was ever served during Jimmy Carter's term. He wanted no luxuries nor any sign of worldly living.

He apparently considered boating a luxury and a sign of worldly living as well: in April 1977 he sold at auction the presidential yacht *Sequoia*. I knew *Sequoia* as a magnificent 104-foot teak vessel that had been built in 1925, bought by the Commerce Department six years later, and first used by a president in 1933, when Herbert Hoover borrowed her for fishing getaways. *Sequoia* had served as a floating retreat for every president since then. Jack had held strategy meetings aboard her during the Cuban Missile Crisis and had celebrated his last birthday aboard her. After Carter got rid of her in the name of frugality, she endured many undignified years of changed ownership, lawsuits, and dereliction until she was designated a National Historic Landmark in 1987.

At any rate, if you were a guest at one of these gatherings you would get to the White House, and you would mill around, and you'd go through the buffet line and eat quickly. And then for the next three hours Jimmy Carter would conduct a seminar: on Africa, for instance. He would let you know that he knew every country in Africa and the name of every president of every country in Africa. He would have the secretaries of state and defense talk about what was happening in these regions that would affect the globe. He could count on about a third of the Senate in the room every time, and about thirty members of the House.

I will not deny that it was well worth attending these events. They were informational—you could say they were nothing if *not* informational. But they were so broad-gauged as to not be of much specific importance. They were personal tours de force, and every one of my colleagues recognized them as such, designed to impress us that the president knew so much about the minutiae. In contrast, when you read about Franklin Roosevelt, you realize that he was the master of the situation he needed to know about. He didn't know every name and every place, but he knew what was worth knowing: the key people, and what motivated them, and why they were doing what they were doing.

Through all this, I told reporters, and myself as well, that I expected President Carter to be renominated and reelected in 1980, and that I intended to support him. I informed Carter himself of this intention.

On Christmas Eve 1977, I embarked on my first and only visit to China. I brought along a large entourage that included Joan; our three children; Eunice; Caroline and Michael Kennedy (both were then sophomores at Harvard); the Harvard law professor Jerome Alan Cohen; and some aides and reporters. Joan had moved out of our McLean house that fall and into our old Beacon Street apartment in Boston, but we still traveled as a family. I had notified the government of the People's Republic that I wanted to meet with the vice premier and de facto leader of the country, Deng Xiaoping. A tough-minded survivor of political purges by Mao Zedong, and little known in the West, Deng was just then making his mark as an architect of China's recovery from the calamitous Cultural Revolution. His Four Modernizations, in agriculture, industry, science, and technology, would soon transform the vast country, earn him recognition as *Time*'s Man of the Year for 1978, and propel China's economic rise.

My main mission was to serve as an unofficial ambassador for the United States: specifically, to try to firm up diplomatic relations with China despite the United States' refusal to acknowledge the People's Republic's claim to Taiwan. At the same time, I hoped to secure a commitment that the mainland would not use arms to enforce its claims upon the island nation of sixteen million people. As in Moscow in 1974, I brought a list of detained people—twenty-two Chinese, in this case—who sought to leave the country. And Joan encouraged several members of the Beijing Symphony to request permission to study the following summer with the Boston Symphony.

The trip produced no significant breakthroughs, certainly not in the matter of Taiwan's hopes for independence. But I was happy to hear one high-ranking diplomat strongly hint to me that the island could expect "a peaceful and prosperous future."

By the summer of 1978 my associates and staff had done their consensus-building job well, and we had in place the elements to move ahead on the comprehensive health program. And so I began negotiations with Joe Califano, the president's secretary of Health, Education, and Welfare. Like his boss, Califano wanted to pass legislation that would be sequenced: when a bill was passed to cover one element of our plan, we would have to come back to Congress to initiate another one. I saw that approach as completely unworkable. It was too risky; it gave Congress too many chances to say no. I spoke to Carter himself about this in late July, but I could not convince him. The failure signaled that on health care, at least, the president and I were irrevocably on separate tracks.

Still, I remained committed to his reelection.

My commitment buckled a bit in the fall of 1978, when some friends of mine inside the administration leaked to me some portions of Carter's proposed budget requests. It was clear that in the name of harnessing inflation, the president intended to starve some important domestic programs that mattered a great deal to me. Health care legislation was clearly among those endangered programs.

I had the chance to express my outrage at this timidity shortly afterward, at a December symposium on health care in Memphis. It was part of the Democratic "mini-convention" that attracted twenty-five hundred grassroots stalwarts of the party, such as campaign workers, teachers, union people, and officeholders from the cities and states—people who passionately embraced the traditional core principles of our party.

"There could be few more divisive issues for America and for our party," I told the receptive audience, "than a Democratic policy of drastic slashes at the expense of the elderly, the poor, the black, the cities, and the unemployed." Rebuking the tactic of presidential pandering to the presumed selfishness of the middle class, I chose an abiding metaphor from my life as a sailor. "Sometimes," I declared to the crowd, "a party must sail against the wind!"

The phrase drew cheers and applause from the crowd. The symposium's chairman, the young governor-elect of Arkansas Bill Clinton, later said he had never experienced anything like the crowd's reaction.

I returned to the Soviet Union in September 1978. Again, Brezhnev welcomed me on a Saturday morning, despite the fact that I'd sent him a series of rather blunt but private messages stating my wish for further easing of restraints against dissidents. I took his willingness to meet as a positive sign, particularly since he was not feeling well and had declined to meet with President Carter's representative the day before.

When I arrived, I presented him with gifts of native foods we had acquired on our travels—bread from Tashkent, melon from Samarkand, and apples from Alma Ata. We had been able to carry the crate of fruit into Brezhnev's office and set it down on his desk without so much as a question from his security guards. He expressed delight in receiving what he described as the best food in the Soviet Union.

Brezhnev showed how little he really understood about our country in general and me in particular when he tried to separate me and President Carter for his own political advantage. "Concern about human rights has become an unclean political game," he declared, a spurious attempt to bring pressure on Russia. I felt obliged to reply that American demands for human rights were legitimate; I reminded him that I shared them, and warned that no real breakthroughs in arms control could be achieved unless this area could be resolved.

I could see that I was putting him to sleep—literally. As the aging leader's eyes grew heavy and unfocused, his aides signaled to me, in essence, that it was time to end this phase of the negotiations because the general secretary of the Communist Party of the Soviet Union was ready for a nap.

Back home, I began to deal with the reality that yet another presidential election cycle was nearing, and that speculation among Democrats once again centered on me. I had not seriously considered running against the president in 1980. For his part, late that same year, Carter invited me to lunch and asked me to make a "Shermanesque statement"—that under no circumstances would I run for president or accept a draft from my party. I declined to do that.

If give-and-take is a sign of a healthy alliance, which I believe it is, ours was not healthy. A good example of the president's refusal to offer reciprocity of any sort involved Archibald Cox, the superlative lawyer and noble figure of Watergate. When a vacancy came up on the First Circuit

Court of Appeals in March 1979, as head of the Judiciary Committee I strongly favored the former special prosecutor whose firing by President Nixon further sealed Nixon's demise. Shortly afterward, Attorney General Griffin Bell telephoned me and said, "The president isn't going to do it." I replied that I wanted to talk to Carter personally about it. "It won't do you any good," Bell warned. I said I still wanted to talk to him.

Carter invited me into the Oval Office and we had our conversation about Cox, or the appearance of a conversation about Cox. He certainly allotted a generous amount of time. Expecting a fifteen-minute talk, I found myself spending close to an hour with the president. But as it developed, he wanted to talk about several other matters: health, the economy. When we did finally get around to the topic at hand, Carter told me bluntly and preemptively why he could never, ever support Cox for the First Circuit. In later years, Carter would claim that it was Cox's age—he was nearly sixty-seven then—that made him an unacceptable choice. That is not the way the president represented it to me in his office. He could never, ever support Archibald Cox, he said, because Cox had supported Morris Udall (instead of Carter) in the 1976 Democratic primary.

I had witnessed a lot of political grudges in Washington, and I knew that though they generally led to punishment of some sort, overt revenge was far from the only means of settling them. I pressed on: "Well, that was back then, and you defeated Udall. Cox's support for him certainly does not mean he has no admiration for you." Carter shrugged and said he knew that Cox had been close to the Kennedy family and to Jack in particular, and that made some difference to him, but not enough. (Reflecting on this later, I suspected that it made the wrong kind of difference.) I then framed the nomination from a political context: Cox, I pointed out to Carter, is the most respected lawyer in the country. Putting him on the First Circuit would be a "ten" for you. It would be a "nine" for me recommending him, but it would be a "ten" for you.

Jimmy Carter gave me an icy stare. He said, "Even that isn't going to override my strong feelings against Archibald Cox for supporting Udall."

His words had a certain ring that I have always remembered. It seemed as though Carter was experiencing real pleasure in telling me that he was not going to support Archibald Cox. As for the other subjects that we covered, I always felt that he wanted credit for talking to me for an hour, rather than just fifteen or twenty minutes, so he could claim to have reached out to me. But whatever his reasons, it was clear he wasn't really interested in my views on Cox.

Any thoughts I still held about supporting Jimmy Carter in a reelection bid I put firmly to rest on July 15, 1979. On that evening the president appeared on the three major television networks to deliver the most self-destructive address of his administration.

Fatigued from the rigors of a recent economic summit in Tokyo and, just before that, a round of touchy negotiations on arms limitations with Leonid Brezhnev; distressed by American outrage over the energy crisis gas lines that had driven his approval ratings down to 25 percent; and badly shaken by an alarmist memo from his pollster Pat Caddell that warned him of a sharp decline in the nation's trust in him, Carter looked into the camera lens and fulfilled Caddell's prophecy. He lectured the people of the nation on their contribution to what he called "a fundamental threat to American democracy." This contribution, he declared, was a collapse of confidence and of faith, in government and in themselves.

"It is a crisis that strikes at the very heart and soul and spirit of our national will," Carter intoned. "We can see this crisis in the growing doubt about the meaning of our own lives and in the loss of a unity of purpose for our nation.

"The erosion of our confidence in the future is threatening to destroy the social and the political fabric of America."

This was the address that would become famous as Carter's "malaise" speech, although the president did not use that word in his remarks. (It had appeared in Caddell's memo.) It was a speech born of panic, as the details of its genesis soon made clear: the product of a ten-day "domestic summit meeting," as the press called it, at Camp David earlier in the month. Battalions of advisers and experts from various fields, plus his wife, Rosalynn, barraged the president with advice on how he might reverse declining poll numbers, a perceived erosion of national confidence, and his own image as a leader. "It became a question of saving his presidency," an aide admitted to the *New York Times* soon afterward.

I watched the televised talk with mounting incredulousness and outrage. This message was contrary to—it was in conflict with—all the ideals of the Democratic Party that I cherished. It was in conflict with what the country was about. I tried to imagine President Kennedy or Bobby Kennedy ever abandoning their optimism in the face of adversity and giving vent to sentiments remotely this melancholy. If this message was truly reflective of Carter's feelings, I couldn't see how he was really going to address the central problems we were facing, both in the economy and foreign policy.

It was in the aftershocks of this speech that I began thinking seriously about running for the presidency in 1980.

Inflation, a malady of the past several years, was at double digits now, and the president in my view had abdicated his responsibility to deal with this issue. As for health care reform, he had had nearly three years to demonstrate the commitment implied by his campaign promises, and had either misrepresented or misstated what that commitment would be.

Crowning all these was the overall leadership issue: what the Democratic Party historically stood for, what I had *seen* it stand for. This president had said that he believed that the spirit of America was in crisis. I recognized that Jimmy Carter, although he was of my own party, held an inherently different view of America from mine.

In late August Ronald Reagan edged ahead of Carter for the first time in the presidential preference polls. Those same polls showed me with a lead over Carter, among Democrats, of 62 to 24 percent. They also indicated that I would defeat Reagan handily.

First, though, there was the matter of actually defeating Jimmy Carter. I believed that I could do this. But even before my campaign officially got started, I ran into some unpromising harbingers.

For me, getting up to speed in a political campaign has always taken time. There are many good campaigners who can leave the Senate floor on a late afternoon and be red-hot on the campaign trail that night. Not me: it takes me two or three days to get warmed up and into the mood. For some reason, in 1979 and early 1980 it took even longer than usual for me to get going.

One of the most damaging indicators of my sluggish start was the now famous two-part interview I taped with Roger Mudd of CBS News in September and October 1979. The edited interview ran as an hour-long news special on Sunday night, November 4, just three days before I announced my candidacy.

Mudd himself dwells on this interview in his 2008 memoir. He observes, correctly, that he and I had known one another socially in past years. "Because of these connections," Mudd writes, "perhaps there was in 1979 the assumption by the senator and his staff that this would be a softball documentary." He correctly notes that the filming took place weeks before I declared my candidacy.

Mudd, as he recalls, wanted two sit-down interviews, one at my Cape Cod house "about family and personal matters" and one at my office or at McLean "about senatorial matters." I consented to allow a CBS crew to follow me around for several days, filming me on Capitol Hill, in my office, in Hyannis Port, and in other informal situations.

I remember the circumstances of that interview a little differently. I recall, for example, that I'd granted the interview to Mudd as a personal favor, during a critical moment in his CBS News career. I had run into Roger at the Waldorf-Astoria in New York in June of that year, when I attended a reception for the president of Mexico, José López Portillo y Pacheco. As I walked out of the hotel at about 10 p.m., Roger approached me and said—I cannot recall the words verbatim—"I'm in this contest with Dan Rather for the anchor position at CBS News, and I'd love to get an interview with your mother." (It was common knowledge that Mudd had been expected to replace Walter Cronkite when he hit the age of mandatory retirement at CBS, but Rather was giving him a serious run for his money.)

I replied, "Well, my mother doesn't do interviews. She's older, and she just isn't up to the demands. But let me think about it, and I'll get back to you." Roger said, "It would make a big, big difference if I could ever do that interview down at Cape Cod. Everybody's always wanted that interview with your mother."

I talked to my mother and my sisters about it. We decided that Mudd could do the interview with Mother as they walked along the beach, but I would have to be with them. The two of them could chat back and forth, but we just didn't want to have a sit-down or to leave Mother on her own. Roger said that was fine. I added, "Our children are going to the Cape, so that's going to be the setting." Roger said that was fine too.

A day or two before the scheduled interview, my mother fell ill and left the Cape for Boston. At about that same time, Kara received an invitation from the Hopi tribe in Arizona, the only matriarchal tribe in the country. They asked her, as one interested in Native American culture, to come there and be a part of a large ceremony they were planning. Kara wanted to go, and so she was out of the interview tableau. And finally, for a reason I can't recall, Teddy said he could not be available either. That left Patrick, who had just turned twelve, and me.

I telephoned Roger, explained the situation, and tried to put off the interview. "Oh, no," he replied. "That'll be all right. I'll come on down. We'll do you and the sea and Cape Cod, and what the sea has meant." I thought I could easily talk about that: how I used the sea as a place of rest and reflection, and what this place meant to me and the family.

Roger and his crew arrived and set up for the interview at Squaw Island, the area half a mile west of the Cape house where I owned a seaside cottage. I had asked no staff members to be present, and I had done no preparation for an interview that dealt with political or personal topics. The agreement, as I'd understood it, was that our topic was to be the sea, and the connections between the Cape and the Kennedy family. I should have had my political antennae up. In retrospect, it is almost inconceivable to me that I did not.

As we took our chairs out in front of the house, the camera rolled, and we talked for some forty minutes about the sea and the Cape. During a break, I looked at the time, and said, "That's about it, isn't it?" Mudd replied, "Yes, just about." I turned to my twelve-year-old son, who was watching, and said, "Patrick, why don't you go down and get the boat and pick me up? I'll see these people to their van."

When Patrick had disappeared, Roger excused himself and consulted with two CBS executives, who'd accompanied him and had stood nearby, watching our interview. Then Roger walked back to me and surprised me by asking, "Can we do one more segment?"

I replied, "Well, I'd really like to go. I think we've done it." "No," he said. "We'd really like to do just one more." And so I agreed to do one more. (Mudd later wrote that he and the other two newsmen had compared notes on the conversation thus far and pronounced it a "disaster.")

The cameraman put in a fresh roll of film and Roger resumed his questions. The first had to do with Chappaquiddick. Then he asked about my marriage. My discomfort and unhappiness with the line of questioning was more than apparent on my face and in my halting answers. I was further distracted by my awareness that Patrick was on the water by himself, struggling with a twenty-five-foot sailboat. I needed to go down there and help him.

At last it ended, and the CBS crew packed its equipment, Mudd and I shook hands, and they drove away.

When Patrick and I were on the water I told him my sense of the interview: a disaster.

I telephoned Mudd the next day and said, "Look, if we're going to do this thing, I want another crack at it." Mudd agreed. Our understanding called for two sessions anyway; and so on October 12 we sat down again, this time in my Senate office in Washington. The cameraman signaled that the film was rolling, and Roger Mudd asked:

"Why do you want to be president?"

I had not yet publicly declared my intention to challenge President Carter and had no intention of announcing my candidacy in this interview with Roger Mudd. I wrestled in my mind with just how far to go. After a long pause, I began:

"Well, I'm—were I to make the announcement, and to run, the reasons I would run is because I have a great belief in this country. That it is—there's more natural resources than any nation in the world; there's the greatest educated population in the world; the greatest technology of any country in the world; the greatest capacity for innovation in the world; and the greatest political system in the world. And yet I see at the current time that most of the industrial nations of the world are exceeding us in terms of productivity and are doing better than us in terms of meeting the problems of inflation . . ." and on in that vein for 336 words, by courtesy of Roger's own count—of which CBS used the first 242.

My displeasure with Roger Mudd unfortunately spilled over into my interview performance. I regret that. If I had already declared my candidacy, I suppose I would have had a more polished answer to Mudd's question, but the essence would have been the same.

On November 4, 1979, the same day as the airing of the Mudd interview, Iranian Islamist revolutionaries seized fifty-two U.S. diplomats at the American embassy in Tehran. The nation plunged into shock. At the time, none of us could have anticipated that this crisis would continue for 444 days.

On Wednesday, November 7, I went ahead with my plans to announce my candidacy for my party's nomination as president of the United States. As I stood quietly behind the lectern in Faneuil Hall, I was enveloped in the moment. My personal past, my family's past, the Boston past, the American past—it had all coalesced in this room, where patriots had once gathered before the Revolutionary War to shape the American future. Honey Fitz had pointed to this building and told me its stories as we strolled past it on those long-ago Sundays. Jack had made his final 1960 campaign appearance here. I was forty-seven years old, one year older than Jack when he died. Jackie smiled at me from the audience of some 350 friends and relatives—three generations of my family, from my mother to my children—and half again as many reporters.

And so now here I stood. I'd chosen not to make my announcement from the Senate Caucus Room in Washington, where both Jack and Bobby had delivered theirs. This setting symbolized my wish to be understood not as the third Kennedy brother in a line of succession, but as a candidate entirely of my own volition and purposes.

My announcement speech was brief, just a little over fifteen minutes. Emphasizing my strong antipathy toward Carter's view of a weakened American spirit, I stressed my belief in the hope and daring that had made the country great, and cautioned against "the myth that we cannot move." At the conclusion, to warm applause, I embraced my family, who had joined me at the lectern. And then it was down to business. I hit the campaign trail at once.

Jimmy Carter was waiting for me. In fact, he had been cleverly using the power of the presidency to pick off my potential supporters before I even announced. His operatives canvassed work programs around the country that had received operational funding. They told the people in those programs they had to vote for Carter because he could guarantee their funding. They reached out to mayors and local leaders in these towns and cities that were important electorally. They asked these people, "What do you need? What are you asking for?"

When I was in Washington just after I announced, the Illinois congressman Dan Rostenkowski came over and said, "We're going to do the same for you in Chicago that we did for John Kennedy. You can relax. You can depend on me to do it." About ten days later, at a gathering of Democratic congressional leaders at the White House, I spotted Rostenkowski. It seemed that he was avoiding me. I called him up the next day, but I couldn't get him. Four days later, he announced for Carter, who had pushed through funding for Chicago's transit system.

Some of the other supporters I was counting on were simply missing in action. At Eunice's Special Olympics in New York State, Pat Moynihan had made a big point of pulling me over and saying I had to run. He'd said he'd do anything for me. In a New York meeting, Hugh Carey had said the same thing: I had to run. He'd do anything for me. But once my campaign got started, I never heard from either of them again.

Then my campaign funding took a serious hit after my defeat in the Iowa caucuses. On January 21, 1980, in our first head-to-head contest, Jimmy Carter won the caucuses by an unexpected two-to-one margin.

Iowa was a learning experience for me as a grassroots campaigner. Unfortunately, the lessons I learned came too late.

The sluggish start that I mentioned showed up in the initial fuzziness of my message, but it hurt in other ways as well. We were slow in organizing, and the campaign had a jump-start feel in the early weeks. My campaign manager and close friend Steve Smith worked capably, but he was burdened by angst about my safety and the question of adequate security. We were not quick to realize how the hostage crisis had changed the whole electoral atmosphere and strengthened support for the president.

My nephew Joe Kennedy II, later elected as a congressman from Massachusetts, saw the debacle coming. He was the one person on my team who sensed that Iowa was going to be a bigger-than-life state, and that it was not in my pocket despite the good poll numbers. After he visited there he told us, "This is not a caucus. This is a primary state. There's so much activity and involvement."

No one really paid sufficient attention to him. We did Iowa the old-fashioned way, from the top down: we located the state's local Democratic leaders who were leaning toward us and counted on them to turn out the voters on caucus night. I made a strenuous tour of the towns, hitting many of them two, even three times. I noticed that the turnouts were not

gigantic—quite small in some cases—but attributed that to the thin population.

On the evening of January 21, we counted more Democrats in our
column than had shown up in either of the previous two presidential
races. I looked at the numbers and said, "I'm going to win this thing. I'm
going to win it."

I didn't win it. We'd misread that surge of Democrats who favored
me. They were a minority faction in one of the largest turnouts in Iowa
history, more than a hundred thousand people. And most of them declared for Carter, by a margin of roughly 60 percent to 30.

I could not believe it at first. I had campaigned with everything I had.
I'd visited Iowa's cities and towns again and again—Ottumwa, Ames,
Cedar Rapids, Davenport, Council Bluffs. What had gone wrong?

I finally got the answer from Harold Hughes, the former governor
and senator from the state. Hughes was a supporter, but other obligations
had kept him away from my campaign. "I'll tell you why you lost," Hughes
said. "The reason was, you'd arrive in one of these little towns, and there'd
be a hundred people waiting for you at the church or the meeting hall.
But you'd bring twenty Secret Service agents with you, and they would be
pushing people around, telling them to sit over there. And then there
would be thirty TV cameras.

"Now, when I campaigned in Iowa," Hughes went on, "I would drive
into, say, Ames myself, at the wheel of a car or a pickup truck. I'd get out,
and I'd go into the meeting hall by myself, and I'd shake everybody's hand
and tell them my name. Then I'd write their names down. And after my
talk I would go back to the motel, and I'd take that list of names out, and
I'd write a note to everyone on it. That's what you have to do when you
campaign in Iowa."

Hughes's folksy approach made sense to me. Unfortunately in my
case, it was an impossibility. The Secret Service agents and the mass of TV
people were following me around, on the assumption that I was a marked

man. And so the heavy Secret Service was assigned. And the television crews were along to preserve it for posterity should it happen.

Was I worried about my physical safety? I suppose so. But I never brooded about it. I could not live my life dwelling on that kind of thing. Threatening letters are regularly sent to my office. We deal with them in a professional way, but I don't read them. I choose not even to know about them unless absolutely necessary. I've decided that I would not live out my life in fear of the shadows.

I flew back home from Iowa to McLean, where I listened to the results. When it became clear that Carter had carried the caucuses, I braced myself for a very unhappy duty. I knew I had to call my mother and tell her the bad news, that I was the first Kennedy who had lost an election. Her voice came on the phone, and I broke it to her as gently as I could. And I received one of Rose Kennedy's priceless, endearing reality checks.

"Oh, that's all right, Teddy dear," she replied. "I'm sure you'll work hard and it'll get better."

And then: "Teddy, do you know that nice blue sweater I gave you at Christmastime? Do you remember that?" I said I remembered it, yes. It was a turtleneck, and it had a small pocket on the front. It had been made in France.

"Have you worn it?" I said, "Well, I'm not sure that I've worn it." She said, "Is there something special about it? Because I just got the bill for it, and it was two hundred and twenty dollars. Will you check it out, Teddy? And if you haven't worn it, will you send it back, because I've got another blue one here that I think is just as nice and is not nearly as expensive."

By the next morning, I was ready to go into battle again. I was scheduled to speak at Georgetown University in less than a week, on January 28. I decided that if people were waiting for a strong message, they were going to hear it that night. No more fumbling or fuzziness.

From my opening words that night at Georgetown, I took the fight directly to Jimmy Carter. Specifically, I assailed what I saw as the futile stridency in the "Carter Doctrine" that he'd unveiled five days earlier, in his State of the Union address. The doctrine was a response to the Soviet invasion of Afghanistan on Christmas Eve 1979, which had triggered shock and anxiety throughout the free world.

Citing Carter's remark that he was "surprised" by the Soviets' strike, I pointed to the warning signals that the president had missed: the obvious Russian buildup of forces, and the murder of the U.S. ambassador to Afghanistan while Soviet military advisers looked on.

I drew attention to the hostage crisis in Iran. The Muslim students' detaining of American diplomats there, in retaliation for the U.S. admission of the deposed shah for medical treatment, was in its eighty-sixth day. "This is a crisis that never should have happened," I told the audience, because the administration had been warned of exactly this response to allowing the hated shah inside our borders. "The president considered those warnings and rejected them in secret."

Expanding from there, I rebuked the president for his failure to resolve a number of issues affecting ordinary Americans as he groped for a coherent foreign policy: rising inflation, unemployment, and energy prices. I called for gasoline rationing and for freezes, followed by controls, on prices, wages, profits, dividends, interest rates, and rents.

"Today," I concluded, "I reaffirm my candidacy for president of the United States. I intend to stay the course. I believe we must not permit the dream of social progress to be shattered by those whose promises have failed."

Press reaction in the following days ratified my sense that the speech had infused my campaign with the snap and focus it had so far lacked. "He gave some real reasons for running, based on issues," Anthony Lewis declared in the *New York Times* of January 31. "And he sounded like a man who wanted to run."

Contrary to all doubts that might have arisen at the time or since, I did want to run. I did want to be president. The bad news, though, was that the campaign coffers were running on empty. We were nearly broke. The big money began to fade away after the Iowa caucuses.

There were some on my team who wanted it to end. My two hundred campaign aides had worked without pay since mid-January, but pay was not the issue for them. They were willing to continue, and did. Their concerns were not for themselves, but for my political future.

I can remember Steve Smith telling me on that night, "Look, no money now. We're in debt. If you get out now, no one will really blame you. You took a crack. Your career is still intact. If you go back to the Senate, it's not a real blemish on your record. But if you stay in . . . I have the poll here from Massachusetts. You're getting beaten by twenty-five points in your home state. If Carter beats you in Massachusetts, your career is gone. Finished. That's what you're looking at. You have no money, and I don't know what's going to turn this thing around."

That was a very tough conversation. I remember walking around outside for a while after Steve spoke his mind. I'd told him, "I think I'll just wait a couple of days before I make my mind up." After a couple days, I said, "I'm staying in it."

My reasons were not complicated. I genuinely cared about the issues I was running on, and I knew that my team did as well. I felt we could get traction with our message and win some of the upcoming primaries and keep faith with our supporters around the country.

There was hardly any shortage of issues to care about in that year: health care, the economy, foreign policy. One frustrating problem in propounding my stand on these issues was simply being heard. I competed for airtime (and often lost) on the evening news with the Iran hostage crisis and then the Russian invasion of Afghanistan. Some in the press continued to raise the issue of Chappaquiddick.

We won some. We lost some. We won some more.

We were in constant need of funds, but delighted with creative sources. Politically engaged artists created lithographs for us to sell on behalf of the campaign. James Rosenquist. Jamie Wyeth. Andy Warhol. Bob Rauschenberg. These artists probably raised a couple of million dollars for us. They kept us going.

As the weeks and months went on, I was able to refine my message in interviews and speeches, yet that did not neutralize the media obstacles to getting that message out on a daily basis. Several times, I challenged Carter to a public debate. In late May I even offered to drop out of the race and release my delegates if the president would debate me before the convention. Carter and his people deflected these offers, perhaps finding it impossible to believe that I would leave the race if my beliefs for the party received an adequate hearing.

We broke new ground in campaigning openly for gay rights. Toward the end of the campaign, I was the beneficiary of a fund-raiser at the Hollywood Hills home of a couple named Clyde Cairns and John Carlson. As my entourage made its way toward the party, someone informed me that it had been declared off-limits to the news media. I asked all the cars in the caravan to stop while my staff phoned up news outlets in the city and invited them to come along. We were overwhelmed by TV cameras. No major-party candidate had ever appeared at a fund-raiser organized by gay supporters.

I opened up a question-and-answer session at the event, and the complexity of some of the questions really fascinated me. One person wanted to know whether a partner from another country without legal status to remain in the United States would face deportation. Others raised fairness issues about the tax code and health care. I did a lot more listening than answering that night, and left with greater awareness of issues lawmakers were not yet confronting.

I met with Carter at the White House on June 5, to discuss the campaign and a way that we might go forward. We sat opposite each other in front of the fireplace, with a vase of flowers between us.

I tried to set a formal tone. I told him I certainly understood that, mathematically, I didn't have the delegates to win the nomination. But I felt that I was representing the concerns of millions of Americans who deserved to have their voices heard. The president had ducked debating me for the entire primary season, and as a result the people in our own party had been deprived of a give-and-take on the issues that mattered to them. I said that I was concerned about the economic issues facing our country and wanted to have a public dialogue with him about them. I also said that I was in the process of making decisions about how I was going to proceed in the next few weeks as we moved toward the convention, and that what I was most interested in was this dialogue. Finally, I told him that if we had a debate on economic issues and were able to make some progress through good-faith, constructive efforts on both our parts, then I would say that I would support the party's nominee.

It was a respectful exchange, about fifteen minutes. He listened to what I had to say, and raised only a few points of contention. After I told him that I was not interested in being divisive, he criticized the "harsh" tone of my campaign rhetoric and said he had never attacked me personally.

I responded, "Mr. President, those ads of yours aren't handling me with kid gloves."

At one point, he said, "You know, I too grew up in a family that was political, and we were very combative."

When I raised the prospect of a debate, Carter asserted that no incumbent had ever debated in the history of our country. Besides, he said, people understood our policy differences. Ultimately, his response was: You present your views to the platform committee. I'll present mine. And we'll stay in touch through our people. No debate.

As our conversation drew to a close, he asked me whether there was any part of the campaign I had enjoyed. I said it was least satisfactory when things were electronic, rather than person-to-person. He said he couldn't agree more.

The 1980 Democratic convention was set to begin on August 10 in New York. I maintained my candidacy through the convention, so that I could speak to the issues and address the delegates and the people I'd been fighting for. We had been on the trail for nine months, 100,000 miles, through forty states, and we were not victorious. But neither were we defeated.

Our cause, I declared, was the same as it had been since the days of Thomas Jefferson: the cause of the common man and the common woman. Our commitment had remained, since the days of Andrew Jackson, to all those he called "the humble members of society—the farmers, mechanics, and laborers."

I spoke out of a deep belief in the ideals of the Democratic Party, I went on, and in the potential of that party and of a president to make a difference. I offered the promise of the dignity of useful work to those who were idle in the cities and industries of America. I called for the re-industrialization of America. I asked for a resolution against the risk that prosperity be purchased by poisoning the air, the rivers, and the great natural resources of the continent. I affirmed the need to defeat inflation, reshape the unfair tax structure.

And finally, avowing that we cannot have a fair prosperity in isolation from a fair society, I reaffirmed my stand for national health insurance: "We must not surrender to the relentless medical inflation that can bankrupt almost anyone and that may soon break the budgets of government at every level."

I congratulated President Carter on his victory, and voiced my confidence that the Democratic Party would reunite on the basis of Democratic principles. "And someday, long after this convention, long after the signs come down and the crowds stop cheering, and the bands stop playing, may it be said of our campaign that we kept the faith. . . .

"For me, a few hours ago, this campaign came to an end.

"For all those whose cares have been our concern, the work goes on, the cause endures, the hope still lives, and the dream shall never die."

The delegates' response was warm and generous. NBC News said they were still cheering after forty-five minutes. I didn't know it was that long. But it was gratifying. Our message got through.

I returned for the final night of the convention to be on the stage after President Carter's speech. I reached the convention floor shortly after the speech ended, but a whole crowd of other Democrats were already there. The cheering after the speech had not gone as long as some had expected, so the platform was filling up earlier than anticipated. Tip O'Neill was right behind me, and behind him was the former party chairman Bob Strauss, and then Fritz and Joan Mondale, and party leaders of all kinds.

I shook the president's hand, and then Mrs. Carter's hand. I did not elevate his hand, and he made no effort to elevate mine. But then the press began to point out that I had not elevated Jimmy's hand, and that became a sore spot that has lasted, I suppose, to this day.

I thought that what we did on the podium was proper enough. Had he made an effort to raise our hands together I certainly would not have resisted. It just wasn't a big deal—certainly it wasn't as if we'd just gone fifteen rounds in the ring for a heavyweight championship.

President Carter continues to believe that I weakened him for the general election and caused him to lose the presidency to Ronald Reagan. In fact, he makes a point of saying so frequently, especially when he speaks in Boston. But I'm not really sure he needed any help from me.

Carter's approval rating in the summer of 1979—before his "malaise" speech—was 25 percent, lower than Richard Nixon's after Watergate. The nation was suffering through an energy crisis and double-digit inflation. The American people were looking for new leadership. And Ronald Reagan was capturing the imagination of the American people with his sunny optimism. Having said that, President Carter was still quite successful against me. His political strategy worked. And my improvement in the closing weeks was too little too late.

What would have happened had I gained the nomination?

Frankly, I don't know that I could have beaten Ronald Reagan. He was more than a candidate at that time; he was a movement.

After the election, I phoned President Carter on December 15, as his administration was nearing its end. He asked me if I was looking forward to the new administration.

I answered, "Not one day sooner than they take office."

He said he would be staying in the White House until the last possible day. (There had been reports that Mrs. Reagan had suggested the Carters should vacate the residence prior to January 20, 1980.)

I thanked him for nominating the former Senate Judiciary Committee counsel, Stephen Breyer, to the U.S. Court of Appeals. The president said he didn't know Breyer personally but had heard a lot of good things about him.

It wasn't a long conversation. He asked me about Reagan's cabinet nominees, and I said they would not be subject to much dispute, except, possibly, Alexander Haig. We also talked about the status of fair housing legislation. And skiing. (We both had trips planned for the holidays.)

Then we wished each other a Merry Christmas and said we hoped to stay in touch.

CHAPTER NINETEEN

The Reagan Years
1980–1988

One of my first encounters with President Ronald Reagan was on St. Patrick's Day in 1981 during a small luncheon at the Irish embassy. We were seated at the same table. He was warm and friendly, full of laughter and small talk.

He told us of his recent meetings with Canadian prime minister Pierre Trudeau, whom he described as a rather lonely man; and Mexican president José López Portillo, who showed Reagan his detailed doodlings of horses while expressing a desire to become a painter after his term ended.

When he was asked about British prime minister Margaret Thatcher, Reagan said, "I hope Senator Kennedy will excuse me here." Then the new president proceeded to tell us how Thatcher had advised him to enact his entire program at once; otherwise, opponents would nibble away at it. So, he told us, that was what he was going to do.

Toward the end of the meal, Reagan was asked whether he planned to travel much for the next three years, or whether he would host visitors. "You know, I just don't know the answer to that question," Reagan said. "I never get my schedule until five o'clock in the afternoon about what I'm going to do the next day. Here I am, the most powerful man in the country, and my wife has to tell me to take my coat off. But to tell you the honest to gospel truth, I really don't know what I'm doing the next day until I get my schedule at night."

Someone at our table said, "Well, you must have some idea."

Reagan responded, "Oh, I'm sure they've all got ideas about where to send me traveling or who I'm supposed to see; but, you know . . ." And then he just smiled and laughed. "To tell you the truth, they just come up and tell me about the trips."

The questioner at our table persisted. "Well, does this continue for the next three years?"

Reagan said, "Well, to tell you the truth, I don't even know the answer to that. I don't know if they do it more in the first year, or more in the third year. I'll have to find out more about that."

I realized at the outset that Reagan's ascendancy would require a fundamental adjustment of my role in the Senate. For the first time in my career I found myself in the minority party. More challenging still, many colleagues whom I'd counted as reliably liberal began to move rightward from the issues we had championed together over the years.

The action commenced almost at once. In February 1981, Reagan, laying the groundwork for his assault upon the tax code, announced his wish to consolidate eighty-eight federal programs into seven block grants targeted to states and communities. At the same time, he presented a plan to trim federal spending by 15 percent. He said he wanted to "reduce waste" and "give local governments more flexibility and control."

I thought this was nonsense, and came out on the attack. At a glance, it was clear that the powerful petroleum companies were going to be shielded from sacrifice, while the "flexibility and control" of individual families would shrivel, as states would continue their long-standing habits of spurning the poor, the helpless, and the hungry—especially hungry children.

I called on such allies as the liberal Republican Lowell Weicker on the Labor Committee to help me in opposing Reagan's block-grant proposals, and we were able to rescue a good deal of federal aid for health and education programs from dilution into block grants, though as in most other areas, we couldn't prevent slashes in spending.

Nor could we really stem the full onslaught of the Reagan revolution, though we fought on every battleground that opened up.

The administration's long-anticipated first full-scale offensive commenced in July, with the unveiling and swift enactment of the largest tax-cut program in American history. Reagan's Economic Recovery Tax Act of 1981 called for $150 billion in tax reductions over the ensuing three years, and the president made clear that he would comb the federal budget for corresponding cuts in social (if not military) programs. I voted against this bill, one of a handful of senators to do so, and immediately launched out on a series of speeches and position papers excoriating its likely social effects. It was "scorched-earth economics," and would vitiate job training, elementary school education, unemployment compensation, cancer research, and science research in general, as it would cripple the National Science Foundation. Several months later, when these programs had indeed begun to achieve these effects, I groused to a meeting of Democratic loyalists that "Ronald Reagan must love the poor; he is making so many of them." .

My objections to President Reagan's policies are far too vast to enumerate, but one of them seemed to me to be based more on science fiction than reality—and it required us to spend enormous sums of money that might otherwise have gone to addressing our domestic needs.

On March 23, 1983, the president took to the prime-time airwaves, raised the terrible specter of the Soviet Union launching a nuclear attack on America, and then asked, "What if free people could live secure in the knowledge that their security did not rest upon the threat of instant U.S. retaliation to deter a Soviet attack; that we could intercept and destroy strategic ballistic missiles before they reached our own soil or that of our allies?"

This was the world's introduction to Reagan's Strategic Defense Initiative, on which, a few weeks later, I hung the nickname by which it would be known: "Star Wars." (I admit it, I had gone to see the movie. At the time, I'd seen the evening as an escape from reality.) The idea was that "the scientific community" would "turn their great talents now to the cause of mankind and world peace" and "give us the means of rendering these nuclear weapons impotent and obsolete." Then we could change the course of human history.

I will avoid a long recitation of what the scientific community was expected to create—the extended-range interceptors and exoatmospheric reentry-vehicle interception systems and X-ray lasers and chemical lasers and neutral particle beams and the rest. Suffice it to say that although some of the technologies developed in the pursuit of this notion proved useful in other antiballistic missile applications, Star Wars never quite got off the ground. In 1993 President Clinton significantly trimmed back its scope and budget and renamed it the Ballistic Missile Defense Organization (it's now known as the Missile Defense Agency). One legacy of the budget-trimming Reagan's vision is a continuation of space-based defense research that has totaled well in excess of one hundred billion dollars. But unlike the movie its nickname evokes, Reagan's Star Wars never really had a successful sequel.

On the question of American diplomacy in Northern Ireland, Reagan and I found a reason for some agreement. Reagan traced his ancestry to the village of Ballyporeen in County Tipperary, and visited there in the summer of his reelection campaign.

There was continued violence in Northern Ireland and, in my view, an underappreciation of the need to stop the violence on *both* sides of the conflict. We drafted a series of statements and got them out to Senate and House members of both parties, to keep their awareness high. Tip O'Neill was very strong. He began a series of Speaker's lunches, and invited President Reagan to attend. At the same time, a number of us persuaded the taoiseach (the Irish head of state) and other key officials that this was the time for them to come to the United States. One incentive was that they would have an opportunity to talk with President

Reagan about policy, most likely at the Speaker's lunch. And so they began coming.

Reagan did not discuss policy at these lunches. That clearly was not his intention. The first few times he came, his aides told all of us very clearly that we were simply there to tell funny stories. Reagan would lead off by telling a couple of tales, and then Tip would call on people around the room. At first the president called only on the Americans at the table—our Irish guests must have wondered what they were doing there—but gradually as time went on, he would call on some of the Irish. They would dutifully tell their stories, but they'd also manage to sneak in some comments about the situation in the North.

Eventually those lunches evolved into occasions for serious talk about substantive issues. They became an important and significant framework for dialogue, and continue today. Just as important, the luncheons helped motivate Reagan to prevail on his close friend Margaret Thatcher to somewhat soften her stance toward the Catholic minority in Northern Ireland. Thatcher had coldly responded to the Hunger Strike of 1981, but in 1985, she signed the Anglo-Irish Agreement, which gave the Republic of Ireland a role in the affairs of Northern Ireland for the first time.

Tip O'Neill privately joked with me that he doubted Reagan was really Irish because he could never take any of his kidding. Once, Tip ran into the president at a party to celebrate the launch of *USA Today*. Tip said to him, "Why don't you give me a call sometime, Mr. President, and have me come on down? I'll straighten out all those mistakes that you've made in the past two years." Tip was just joking, but he could see Reagan's fists getting clenched.

On a personal level, I found myself among the countless people who enjoyed Reagan's company. In November 1981, I accompanied my mother and Ethel Kennedy to a White House visit with President and Nancy Reagan to express appreciation for a medal given to Ethel in memory of Bobby. In the car on the way over to the White House, I showed Mother a gift I intended to give to the Reagans, some of Jack's handwritten notes about football and politics. Mother was more concerned with knowing the where-abouts of the medal, in case she was asked any questions about it.

When we entered the Oval Office, the president said to Mother, "I'm sure you recognize the desk over there."

Mother said, "What about it?"

"That's President Kennedy's desk," Reagan said, "with the little doors where John played."

The president seemed genuinely interested in Jack's handwritten notes as I read parts to him. Then he said he had a gift for us too, but that it wasn't nearly as nice or personal.

He presented us with a jar of jelly beans, noting the improvements in the quality of the candy in recent years. They used to taste a little bit differently according to the colors, he told us, but now there were jelly beans that tasted like steak and peas and other sophisticated flavors. "You can reach into a jar and pick up a whole meal," he joked.

Mrs. Reagan added, "I wish we had bought stock in the company."

He lit up a room, and he could summon laughter, intentionally or otherwise. In fact, sometimes it was hard to tell whether his whimsical side was intentional. The best examples of this were the times we met in the Oval Office to discuss whether to protect the American shoe industry from imports, and ended up discussing . . . shoes.

The question of import quotas on consumer products was a critical issue in the 1980s. Massachusetts was among the states whose industries were struggling the hardest to compete with the flow of cheap foreign goods. Our shoe and textile industries especially were hurting.

I was involved in drawing up legislation to curb imports on these products. My bill, like the two-hundred-odd similar bills floating around Congress, was strongly opposed by the White House. Reagan in fact vetoed two quota bills during his presidency, even as shoe imports soared toward a 90 percent penetration of the market.

Several senators and I asked to speak with the president to press our cases, and he agreed to a meeting. About ten of us were on hand. John

Danforth, the Missouri Republican whose state was hemorrhaging its small shoe plants and who favored some quotas, was present, as was the Missouri governor, Kit Bond. Strom Thurmond sat glowering as a defender of free enterprise to the bitter end. The president's response to our various presentations, everyone felt, could go far in determining the future of his administration's policy. And so we were all steeped in preparation.

The president strode briskly into the Oval Office with his famous arm-swinging gait after we'd all arrived, and took a seat right next to me. His aides told us that we would have half an hour, total, to present our cases. John Danforth was chosen to go first. He got only as far as, "Good morning, Mr. President." Reagan was looking me over. He said, "Ted, you've got shoes on, haven't you?" I replied, truthfully, "Yes, I do, Mr. President." He studied them and said, "They look like Bostonians." I glanced down at the shoes on my feet. Bostonians? I wasn't sure. Why hadn't I checked the label on my shoes before I put them on that morning? But the president was moving on ahead.

"Bostonians," he repeated. "That's incredible. Do they still make the Bostonian shoes around here?"

I had no idea, but I ventured, "I believe so, Mr. President."

Reagan seemed to want hard facts. "Does anybody know where the Bostonian shoes are made?" he demanded of the gathering at large.

Kit Bond cleared his throat and said, "I know they produce shoes just like them down in Missouri."

Someone else said, "You know, you can get the best shoes, shoes that are better than those shoes, if you come on up to Maine. They've got good shoes up there."

Reagan said, "They do have good shoes up there, don't they? Do they give them a real good polish?"

"Yes, Mr. President, they give them a good polish."

Reagan said, "You know, my father owned a shoe store, and I used to sell shoes. So I know all about them. To measure the length of the foot, you go across the top, like this." He began to demonstrate how to measure people's feet for shoes. "You can also put them in the foot measurer, and you turn the knob like this until you know exactly what size shoe will fit. And then to break them in, you take the heel in one hand, and the toe in the other, and you push toward the middle. That gets the leather to soften and bend, you see."

He went on in this vein for twenty minutes. Several of us began conspicuously to glance at our watches. At some point, I tried politely to intervene: "Uh, Mr. President, we've only got, uh—I mean, while you're here, we'd like a chance to—"

"Well, Ted, it's been a wonderful meeting. And I hope we can continue this discussion at another time. I really enjoyed it. Thank you and do come again."

And it was over! No one ever got a word in about shoe or textile quota legislation. The ten of us got up and walked out of the White House like goofballs to face the thirty or so TV reporters who wanted to know what sort of progress we'd made on the issue.

A larger assemblage met in the Cabinet Room to address the same topic on June 15, 1981. This time the gathering was about equally divided between Republicans and Democrats. Vice President Bush was present, and also Secretary of State James Baker, Secretary of the Treasury Donald Regan, and several others.

This time the focus was on the Orderly Markets Agreement put into place three years earlier to limit shoe imports by Taiwan and Korea. The Trade Commission had indicated that the limits should continue on Taiwan, but not Korea, because the imports of the latter were no longer a serious competitive threat to the United States. When my turn to speak came I told the president that what we were arguing for, essentially, was a continuation of the status quo. We felt that the status quo, combined with the administration's new tax program, would motivate the American shoe industry to invest in expansion, which would provide more employment. I also stressed that we were not looking for long-term arrangements, just temporary measures to stabilize the shoe industry over the short haul.

Senator William Cohen of Maine began his presentation in a way that might connect with Reagan's sense of humor. He said he remembered the time when Nikita Khrushchev banged a shoe on the podium at the United Nations to emphasize a point. We want to make sure, Cohen went on, that Americans were going to keep on having shoes in case they ever wanted to follow a similar procedure. Turning serious for a moment, Cohen emphasized the importance of the shoe industry to Maine, and said he'd just received word of two additional shoe plants shutting down in the state.

Paul Tsongas and Robert Byrd followed with closely reasoned, emphatic arguments. A couple of others spoke. And then we sat back and awaited Ronald Reagan's response.

He said—well, the fact is that he asked about cowboy boots. He wanted to know whether cowboy boots would be protected. Then, after getting some assurance on this point, Reagan told all of us that he was particularly interested in this issue. He was interested because his father had owned a shoe store. And so he, President Reagan, had always thought when he was a young man that the sign of really having made it in the world was wearing a pair of Bostonians. He wondered whether there was still a Bostonian company going. This time I'd done my homework. I told him there was.

On those occasions when one did manage to get Reagan to focus on the issue at hand, the net results could be about the same: just a little bit maddening. In that same month of June I secured another meeting with the president, to discuss gun control. I began by assuring him that I just wanted to make a few points very quickly, because I knew his time was limited.

I told him that I'd grown up in a family that did not own guns, but I respected families that do, and I respected the gun tradition in rural America. I hoped, I said, that we could make some progress on gun control with respect to the types of weapons that really had no sporting purpose whatsoever. I wanted to work with his administration, I told Reagan, to eliminate some of the terrible gun problems in this country. Sentencing for gun crimes was one issue of interest to me; another was one that had worked well in the president's home state of California: a twenty-one-day waiting period, to allow background checks on a firearm purchaser that would help keep guns out of the hands of psychopaths. To put a waiting period into federal law might make some sense. And it would amount to a compromise, if gun opponents in return would be willing to put less emphasis on the manufacture and distribution of certain weapons.

President Reagan nodded and looked thoughtful. He said that he had thought about the gun issue for some time. Yes, it was true. In California they had a good law: mandatory sentencing. But those legislators in California had written into the law an exception for "extraordinary circumstances" that could mean everything under the sun. They'd just taken the heart out of that law. Yes, something more has to be done out in California.

I said that that was interesting. This waiting period, I went on carefully. That might help.

Well, Reagan replied, what would happen? Suppose we passed a national law that required the states to have a waiting period? I don't like mandating the states to have this waiting period. But if we did, then what would we do in the twenty-one days? Will we have to ask Washington to set up a whole new bureaucracy to review all these gun applications? If someone wants to buy a handgun in Mississippi, does that mean *Washington* is going to make the judgment whether that person can or cannot make the purchase?

I said: What about running these matters through local law enforcement, and let them make the judgment?

Well, Reagan said, then we're still mandating it at the federal level. I think that setting up a whole new kind of process and whole new regulations is not wise. It would be very good if the states did that on their own, of course, and we ought to encourage them to.

Then Reagan reflected some more and went on: But, you know, there have never really been definitive studies linking the availability of guns and deaths. And I'm just not sure that, if we banned "Saturday night specials," we'd be doing very much about the problem. There's a study being done by a foundation out on the West Coast that shows that it isn't just Saturday night specials; it's handguns in general.

Reagan cited the example of Great Britain—where, as he told it, they had a presumption that if you were carrying a gun, you were going to use it. They tried you with the presumption that you had the intent to kill somebody. So it was a very strict law over there. The burglars didn't carry guns and you didn't have as many shootings.

That, President Reagan pointed out, is a different concept than we have over here; but that's what happens in Great Britain.

I responded that I knew other countries had other laws. But what I was interested in, I repeated, was reaching some common ground on the gun issue in America.

Well, said Reagan, I think it's difficult to mandate to the states any kind of requirement.

I heard the door to the Oval Office open behind me, and felt the presence of someone who had walked in and was standing behind me. It was a signal that my time with the president was up.

This conversation took place about two months after John Hinckley stepped from a crowd outside a Washington hotel and fired a shot that ricocheted into President Reagan's lung with a German-made "Saturday night special" that was traced to a pawn shop in Dallas. Hinckley struck two others with the shots he fired. The pistol contained six foreign-made explosive cartridges, illegal in the United States. (None of the shells exploded.) Had the bullet struck the president directly, he could easily have been killed.

Reagan could be warmly gracious. He offered an eloquent tribute to Jack's memory in a 1985 fund-raiser to endow the John F. Kennedy Library, held at my home in McLean It was a wonderful evening.

When the president arrived, he took special care to talk to the children in attendance and pose for individual photos with them. There was a joke

about where to stand, and Reagan remarked how important such directions were, particularly in the movies, because if you didn't hit your mark
it could upset the whole scene. Many times, he said, scenes were ruined
because an actor would start off on the left foot instead of the right.

Caroline and Jackie were in attendance. Jackie seemed somewhat surprised when Caroline asked the president whether he had any microphones in the Oval Office. Reagan denied it, but Caroline said she thought
she had detected one on a previous visit.

I asked the president about his ranch and whether he was able to get
there often. Reagan brightened at the mention of the subject and spoke
for about fifteen minutes about how he'd had to give up his old ranch
when he was elected governor of California because the taxes on it were
half of his salary. Since then, he'd found new property in a mountainous
area that he referred to as goat country. Mrs. Reagan said it was full of
trees and pastures, terrific for riding.

I have remained a close friend of Nancy Reagan. She was a dedicated
ally in lining up support when we both fought in vain during George W.
Bush's administration to restore funding for embryonic stem cell research.
(Nancy, of course, was motivated partly by her husband's tragic affliction
with Alzheimer's disease.) She said, "Give me the names of people you
want me to call." I gave her the names, and she called every one of them.
She called back and said, "Give me some more names."

On January 21, 1981, Joan and I finally accepted the inevitable and di-
vorced. It was amicable, and we agreed to share the duties of raising the
children. Joan moved into the apartment in Boston; I maintained residence
in the McLean house.

I faced a reelection bid for the Senate in 1982, and while I did not feel
that my seat was in serious trouble, I always took elections seriously. I was
mindful that there might be political fallout from my run, and loss, for the
nomination in 1980 and that outstanding senators and good friends—
John Culver, Birch Bayh, and Frank Church—had just lost their reelec-

tions when Reagan swept in to victory. It was also the first time I would be running as an unmarried man. My team produced a number of TV ads for the 1982 election. I trusted the voters of Massachusetts to respond to messages of hope, frankness, and humanity. One ad featured Luella Hennessey Donovan, the beloved nurse and governess from my childhood, who described how I had slept in a chair beside Teddy's hospital bed while he was recuperating from his leg amputation. Another featured Frank Manning, an eighty-three-year-old advocate for senior citizens, who avowed, "He's not a plaster saint. He's not without his faults. But we wouldn't want a plaster saint. . . . We want an average human being who has feelings and likes people and who is interested in their welfare."

Even these mild excursions into persuasion caused me some personal discomfort. With them, and also with the tireless organizing of a first-time campaign manager named Kathleen Kennedy Townsend, I won my fourth reelection to the Senate that year, defeating the Republican businessman Ray Shamie with 60 percent of the vote.

In the waning months of 1983, I delivered two speeches that have remained dear to me. The circumstances and the audiences for the talks were about as divergent as it was possible to get. The first was to an audience of students and faculty at a famous evangelical college in Virginia. The second was to a far smaller gathering of family and friends at a memorial mass in Washington. And yet on a deeper level they shared a great deal. What unified the two talks was the presence in them of my late brother John F. Kennedy.

I had not eulogized Jack on any of the anniversaries since his death on November 22, 1963, though I quoted him and invoked his vision in nearly every commemorative speech I gave. For several years, the risk of being overcome with emotion dissuaded me. Then, as I began to seriously be mentioned as a presidential candidate, and in fact moved actively into that arena, I held back out of concern that any tribute I paid my brother be misconstrued as a play for voters' sympathies. But in 1983 I was not an active candidate. Moreover, the escalating demolition by the Reagan administration of my brother's accomplishments, and its tacit repudiation of Jack's historic vision, compelled me to remind Americans of the principles Jack had stood for, and how deeply imperiled those principles were.

I sifted through my mail folder on a late summer day in 1983 and found myself staring, with great amusement, at an envelope with an instantly familiar return address. I opened it and withdrew a promotional invitation designed to look like a passport. It was a membership card to the Liberty Baptist College in Lynchburg, Virginia, home base of the Reverend Jerry Falwell, who routinely used me as a whipping boy for his homilies on godless liberalism and immorality. The pitch was sweetened with an invitation for me to join up and help fight "ultraliberals such as Ted Kennedy."

The mailing had reached me via a computer error so sublimely improbable that as a practicing Christian, I could hardly help wondering whether it was divinely inspired. I passed it along to a reporter friend who wrote a whimsical item about it. The item came to the attention of Cal Thomas, then a vice president of Falwell's Moral Majority. Thomas wrote me an equally whimsical invitation to come and visit the campus sometime. I wrote him back, cordially but not at all whimsically, that I'd be delighted to come; and that I wanted to speak as well. Thomas forwarded my suggestion to Falwell.

Thus it was that on the evening of October 3, 1983, I stood behind a microphone in the auditorium of Liberty Baptist College and made ready to speak to five thousand expectant young evangelicals and their teachers. Falwell himself looked on with the tightly composed smile of a genial host. It was easy to imagine that a fractious hour lay ahead. Boos, hisses, people filing out of the hall—any of this would have played into popular stereotype. But as I looked into the young faces, I saw no hatred, no defiance—only the opaque but attentive stares of intelligent young people that are well known to any college professor at the outset of a lecture.

I began with a gentle joke: "They seem to think that it's easier for a

camel to pass through the eye of the needle than for a Kennedy to come
to the campus of Liberty Baptist College." This received a gratifying ripple
of laughter. I built on it: "In honor of our meeting, I have asked Dr. Falwell, as your chancellor, to permit all the students an extra hour next
Saturday night before curfew. And in return, I have promised to watch
The Old-Time Gospel Hour next Sunday morning." More laughter, and I
sensed some relaxation in the auditorium, certainly in myself. I moved
ahead into the heart of my message.

I'd come, I told them, to discuss my beliefs about faith and country,
tolerance and truth in America. I knew we had certain disagreements; but
I hoped that tonight and in the years ahead, we would always respect the
right of others to differ, and never lose sight of our own fallibility, that we
would view ourselves with a sense of perspective and a sense of humor.

I mentioned the bane of intolerance, citing Dr. Falwell himself as a
victim of it for advocating the ecumenical church. Then I moved quickly
to the more pressing question of whether and how religion should influence government. "A generation ago, a presidential candidate had to prove
his independence of undue religious influence in public life, and he had to
do so partly at the insistence of evangelical Protestants. John Kennedy said
at that time, 'I believe in an America where there is no religious bloc voting
of any kind.'" I contrasted Jack's stance with that of one of the students'
idols. "Only twenty years later, another candidate was appealing to an
evangelical meeting as a religious bloc. Ronald Reagan said to fifteen thousand evangelicals at the Roundtable in Dallas, 'I know that you can't endorse me. I want you to know I endorse you and what you are doing.'"

To many, I said, that pledge was a sign of a dangerous breakdown in
the separation of church and state. Our challenge was to recall the origin
of the principle, to define its purpose, and refine its application to the
politics of the present. I recounted our nation's long history of religious
intolerance: "In colonial Maryland, Catholics paid a double land tax, and
in Pennsylvania they had to list their names on a public roll—an ominous
precursor of the first Nazi laws against the Jews."

The real transgression occurs when religion wants government to tell citizens how to live uniquely personal parts of their lives. In cases such as Prohibition and abortion, the proper role of religion is to appeal to the conscience of the individual, not the coercive power of the state.

"But there are other questions which are inherently public in nature, which we must decide together as a nation, and where religion and religious values can and should speak to our common conscience. . . . The issue of nuclear war is a compelling example. To take a stand . . . when a question is both properly public and truly moral is to stand in a long and honored tradition." I cited the evangelists of the 1800s who were in the forefront of the abolitionist movement; the Reverend William Sloane Coffin, who challenged the morality of the war in Vietnam; Pope John XXIII, who renewed the Gospel's call to social justice.

"And Dr. Martin Luther King Jr., who was the greatest prophet of this century, awakened our nation and its conscience to the evil of racial segregation."

I was gratified to note that the students and faculty had begun interrupting my speech—not with jeers but with applause.

The end of my speech was approaching, and I drew once again upon the words of Jack. I cited a talk he had given in November 1963 to the Protestant Council of New York City to reaffirm what he regarded as some fundamental truths. "On that occasion, John Kennedy said, 'The family of man is not limited to a single race or religion, to a single city, or country . . . the family of man is nearly three billion strong. Most of its members are not white and most of them are not Christian.' And as President Kennedy reflected on that reality, he restated an ideal for which he had lived his life—that 'the members of this family should be at peace with one another.'

"That ideal," I concluded, "shines across all the generations of our history . . . as the Apostle Paul wrote long ago in Romans, 'If it be possible, as much as lieth in you, live peaceably with all men.' I believe it is possible. As fellow citizens, let us live peaceably with each other; as fellow human beings, let us strive to live peaceably with men and women everywhere. Let that be our purpose and our prayer, yours and mine—for ourselves, for our country, and for all the world."

In the months and years that followed, Jerry Falwell's public references to me softened. For what that said about living peaceably with each other, I've always felt grateful.

The second meaningful talk of that autumn, my twentieth anniversary eulogy of Jack, came in Washington after I had spent a quiet evening at the Cape house with my mother and Jackie. We flew together to Washington and were driven to Holy Trinity, where my brother had worshipped on the morning of his inauguration. President and Mrs. Reagan sat in the front pew at the mass.

I began with some memories of Jack from my childhood: "Walking along the beach at home, he said to me when I was very young, 'On a clear day you can see all the way to Ireland.'" I recalled the gentle, natural ways in which he would look after Rosemary—always including her in the sailing expeditions with the rest of us. "Compassion was at the center of his soul," I said, "but he never wore it on his sleeve."

I evoked his wit, which I said "marks our love for him with laughter." I recalled how after he'd talked Bobby into accepting the attorney general post, he made a simple request: "Please, Bobby, just comb your hair."

I summed up, as succinctly as I could, the list of his great achievements: championing the American landing on the moon; building the political foundations of the Civil Rights Act; standing firm in Berlin and during the Cuban Missile Crisis; creating the Alliance for Progress and the Peace Corps; bringing us, in his last months, the test ban treaty and the beginning of an end to the cold war.

Let me acknowledge here that a loyal and loving brother cannot provide a dispassionate view of John Kennedy's presidency. Much has been written about his personal life. A lot of it is bullshit. All of it is beyond the scope of my direct experience.

There were conversational boundaries in our family and we respected them. For example, I had no idea of how serious Jack's health problems were while he was alive. It would never have occurred to us to discuss such private things with each other.

Historians will come to their own judgments about President Kennedy. Here is how I choose to remember him:

> He was an heir to wealth who felt the anguish of the poor. He was an orator of excellence who spoke for the voiceless.
>
> He was a son of Harvard who reached out to the sons and daughters of Appalachia.
>
> He was a man of special grace who had a special care for the retarded and handicapped.
>
> He was a hero of war who fought hardest for peace.
>
> He said and proved in word and deed that one man can make a difference.

I did not want to see a second Reagan administration, yet I could find no Democratic figure on the horizon who convinced me that he or she was capable of unseating the force of nature who was our president. And so in 1982 I asked my aide Larry Horowitz to explore the feasibility of another run. My explorations did not last long. The decisive forces were my three children. Actually they were no longer "children" now, but young adults— Kara was twenty-two, Teddy not quite twenty-one, and Patrick fifteen. And yet of course they were still my children.

Over the late summer and early autumn of 1982, I sounded them out in several searching conversations about their feelings on another presidential campaign. I will never forget this series of talks with them. What they had to say made all the difference.

Our first occurred as we sailed to Nantucket from Hyannis Port on September 26, Teddy's twenty-first birthday. The water was quiet and peaceful, and the sun shone on their faces. Teddy spoke up first. He had reservations, he admitted. He felt that in my 1980 run I had stood for and expressed all the things I believed in, and that now my place was in the Senate. Then he got to the heart of the matter: another campaign would put the family through a great deal of turmoil. He did not say so specifically, but I sensed that the turmoil would center on my safety. Of course, he said, as Kara and Patrick nodded, if I made the decision to run, all of them would support me. But—did it really make sense?

We all kept on probing the topic, in a relaxed way, for more than an hour, as the boat cruised gently toward Nantucket. Kara was somewhat more open-minded to the prospect than Teddy, but Patrick agreed rather strongly with his brother. I thanked all of them at the end, and asked them to give it some more thought.

I learned a good deal more about the depth of Patrick's feelings when the two of us went to the Cape house by ourselves for one of those delicious late fall weekends, of the kind that Bobby and I spent together so many years ago, walking on the beach and building campfires and sleeping in the chilly garage. My son and I enjoyed a good meal and some talk about what was happening at his school, and then it was late and I decided to turn in. I said good night to Patrick and went to my father's room to sleep. I was dozing off when I became aware of a presence in the room. Patrick had come in silently, and when he knew I'd seen him, he sat on a chair, but remained quiet. It was easy to see that he was troubled.

"Are you concerned about the future?" I asked him. He nodded, and murmured that he was. He really did not want me to run, he said, and his voice grew husky. If I were elected president, he said, I would not have as much time to spend with him as he wanted—as it was, he didn't see enough of me. It would create an absence in his life that would be hard to fill. He became rather teary-eyed, very sweet about it, and then went to bed.

On the last week of my Senate reelection campaign, Patrick and I were driving over from Hyannis to Oyster Harbors. I asked him whether he had changed his mind at all. He said he had not.

The next time we broached the subject was on November 2, the night of my Senate reelection. I told my children honestly that I was giving serious consideration to the run, and that I wanted to have one more intense conversation with them about it—perhaps on Thanksgiving weekend, when we would all be together for a few days. I could tell by their faces this time that each was deeply troubled by the prospect, more troubled than I had realized.

On that weekend I asked Larry Horowitz to come to the Cape and brief the children and other family members as to where we stood politically. Over two and a half hours at Jackie's house, Larry reviewed the various polling data and how it reflected the positive view that people had of me after watching those TV spots in focus group sessions in New Hampshire. This was an encouraging and even rather significant trend, given that at the same time, Reagan's poll numbers were rising while those of his likely challenger, Walter Mondale, were slipping down.

The children inferred from this session that my aides and I were gearing up seriously to make a run, and I must say that they were right. Everyone in the room could see the likelihood of my gaining the nomination, and also that the election campaign would be hard-fought and probably be decided by the television debates. Yet the Reagan administration was showing some signs of missteps—they'd been talking lately about taxing unemployment insurance, which would outrage many of their moderate supporters. I really felt that this was the race for me. All of the other times I had taken a pass on running were because it wasn't my time. Those earlier races wouldn't have been about me; they would have been about my being a surrogate for my brothers. And in 1980, as much as I had wanted to win, I felt almost forced into the decision by what I saw as Carter's dragging down of the country and the party. But 1984 would be my race on my terms. And I thought I had a good chance.

I did not ask for reactions from the family at that meeting. My nephew Joe wished me luck, but went on to say that from what he'd heard, the family anticipated a great deal of anguish and anxiety, and that I should give that prospect very serious consideration. My sister Pat seemed to be leaning toward a run; Jean was against it. Steve Smith thought it would be an extremely difficult battle.

The Sunday after Thanksgiving, my children and I went to the Squaw Island house. I told them how much I respected their grasp of the political realities of a run, and of what a campaign would entail. Then I asked them whether they'd formed a final judgment.

Once again, Teddy was the spokesman. He told me that he and Patrick had been having many serious discussions between themselves, and that they both felt strongly that I should not run. I would continue to be a force in the Democratic Party, he pointed out, and in the Senate. People would continue to pay attention to my views. He, Patrick, and Kara were not asking me to step out of public life, he stressed. But given the existing turmoil resulting from Joan's and my divorce, and the change and uncertainty for all of them that that entailed, a run for the presidency might amount to unbearable strain.

I looked at Patrick, who was obviously uncomfortable: he did not want the brunt of my decision placed upon his shoulders. He assured me that he would support any decision that I made. Should the decision be to go, he said he was quite prepared for it—but he just thought the family would be happier if I didn't make that decision to go. There was plenty of time in the future . . .

I shifted my gaze to Kara. She agreed totally with Patrick: if I felt there was a moral imperative to run, they were prepared to sign on and be part of the team. But quite clearly their choice and recommendation were not to go forward with a campaign.

The meeting lasted about two hours, and by the end of it, as far as I was concerned, the decision had been made. If the children felt that strongly about my not running, then I would not run. They all came back to the Big House with me and we had dinner with my mother. I could clearly detect the relief in their minds and in their attitudes and their general dispositions.

A couple of days later I announced that I would not be a candidate for the presidency in 1984. After the press conference, I had a chance for quiet moments with each of the children and asked whether they thought they made the right decision. The response was so uniform, so complete, so overwhelming—it was the right decision. But it was fifteen-year-old Patrick who really brought it home for me. When Patrick and I were sitting together after the announcement, just the two of us, I looked at his face and his smile. He was so happy and obviously so enormously relieved. If I ever harbored any second thoughts about the decision, they vanished at that moment.

I braced for new battles on even more hostile terrain when Reagan, at seventy-three, won reelection in November 1984. The oldest elected president in American history rolled up the highest electoral vote in American history, 525 to 13, against Walter Mondale.

Reagan had made a laudable choice in his first high court appointment, in 1981. Honoring a campaign promise to nominate a qualified woman, he chose the Arizona Republican Sandra Day O'Connor, who replaced the retiring Potter Stewart. She did not become the predictably conservative vote that the Republican right might have hoped. She became famous for avoiding predictability, as the Court's leading "swing vote" on politically charged cases, including upholding *Roe v. Wade*. Reagan's next high court appointment was to nominate William Rehnquist to be elevated from associate justice of the Supreme Court to chief justice of the United States.

As an associate justice, Rehnquist had staked out a position on the Court's far right and held it unwaveringly. I was opposed to his elevation to chief justice for the same reasons that I had opposed his nomination to the Court in the first place. But I understood that the odds were strongly in favor of his confirmation. In the Judiciary Committee on July 29, 1986, I bore in strongly on Rehnquist's string of lone dissents as an associate justice. "The framers of the Constitution envisioned a major role for the Senate in the appointment of judges," I declared. "It is historical nonsense to suggest that all the Senate has to do is check the nominee's IQ, make sure he has a law degree and no arrests, and rubber-stamp the president's choice."

Along with Howard Metzenbaum of Ohio, I resurrected the two damaging pieces of evidence that Rehnquist had shown racial bias in his past. These were the charges that he had harassed black voters at the polls in Arizona in the 1950s and '60s, and the memo he'd written in 1971 maintaining that "separate but equal" should be reaffirmed.

None of it mattered. Rehnquist sailed past the committee by a vote of thirteen to five, and he was confirmed by a vote of sixty-five to thirty-three. Still, he received the most "no" votes ever cast against a chief justice nominee up to that time.

Lewis Powell announced his retirement that same year. Powell was a true moderate on the bench and was often a swing vote, sometimes bridging differences between his more liberal and conservative colleagues. I had a strong sense that Reagan's nominee to replace Powell would not share his qualities of moderation.

By the time Powell resigned, on June 26, 1987, I had prepared myself to seize the initiative against the likely replacement nominee: Robert Bork.

I'd had my eye on Bork since he fired Archibald Cox during Nixon's "Saturday Night Massacre." I'd watched him closely and believed his legal theories were totally out of the mainstream. And he had a written record that set forth his extreme views for all the country to see. On July 1, within forty-five minutes of Reagan's announcement that Bork was in fact his nominee, I arose on the Senate floor and spoke out against Bork and his vision of America.

I knew my speech was red-hot even before I delivered it. I wanted it that way—immediate and fiery—because I wanted to frame the debate. I knew I was making myself a target by being so heated in my rhetoric, but it was a price I was willing to pay to keep this man off the court.

In what came to be known as the "Robert Bork's America" speech, I urged Bork's rejection on several grounds: that he stood for an extremist view of the Constitution and the role of the Supreme Court; that he'd opposed the Public Accommodations Civil Rights Act as well as the Supreme Court's "one man, one vote" ruling in 1964; that he saw the First Amendment as protecting only political speech, and not literature or works of art or scientific expression.

"Robert Bork's America," I continued, "is a land in which women would be forced into back-alley abortions, blacks would sit at segregated lunch counters, rogue police could break down citizens' doors in midnight raids, schoolchildren could not be taught about evolution, writers and artists could be censored at the whim of government, and the doors of the federal courts would be shut on the fingers of millions of citizens for whom the judiciary is—and is often the only—protector of the individual rights that are at the heart of our democracy." I closed with the declaration that President Reagan "should not be able to . . . reach into the muck of Watergate, and impose his reactionary vision of the Constitution on the Supreme Court and on the next generation of Americans. No justice would be better than this injustice."

On summer weekends, I turned the house at Hyannis Port into a command center, from where I invited or telephoned dozens of legal scholars, my fellow senators, advocates for African Americans and women—anyone I could locate who had an informed opinion as to issues at stake. I listened, debated, researched, synthesized, and finally began to draft the input into an argument.

An early head count by the Democratic whip Alan Cranston in mid-July showed a tilt toward Bork's chances for confirmation. By mid-August, the mobilization against him was accelerating. I helped it along by sending out briefing books on the nominee's positions to senators, and a personal letter to sixty-two hundred black elected officials across America alerting them to Bork's threat to civil rights. I telephoned many leaders of national civil rights organizations. I urged Archibald Cox himself to speak out on his views of the "Saturday Night Massacre."

The hearings began on September 15, led by Senate Judiciary Committee chairman Joe Biden. Fortified by preparation that was even more exhaustive than usual—I'd held mock hearing sessions with such constitutional experts as Laurence Tribe of the Harvard Law School—I was able to get the nominee to admit that at one time he saw no right of privacy in the Constitution, didn't think the equal protection clause of the Fourteenth Amendment applied to women, believed the states had the right to levy poll taxes, and that he'd once characterized the 1964 Civil Rights law requiring proprietors to serve African Americans in public places as "a principle of unsurpassed ugliness." These were words from his own testimony. The second two days were more of the same. On September 18, in fact, I played a tape that annihilated Bork's claim that as a justice he would give full weight to judicial precedent. The tape captured him telling a college audience in 1985, "I don't feel that in the field of constitutional law, precedent is all that important. . . . I think the importance is what the framers were driving at."

It was an onslaught of fact and damaging admission, and it worked dramatically. By late September, opinion polls were showing a 10 percent shift against Bork as a result of the hearings. On October 1, five previously uncommitted southern Democrats and the then Republican from Pennsylvania Arlen Specter announced their opposition to Bork. The full Judiciary Committee voted nine to five against recommending him five days later, and on October 23 his nomination was rejected by a vote of fifty-eight to forty-two, with seventeen Republicans in the majority—the largest margin of defeat in history for a Supreme Court nominee.

My final summation of Ronald Reagan is complicated. I recognize that millions of people will always remember him as a great president. It is too early to really know what history's verdict will be.

I believe that he failed to meet the ultimate criteria of greatness. His economic theories were certainly debatable, to say the least. But more than that was his complacency and even insensitivity regarding civil rights. He opposed the principles of the Voting Rights Act, for example, which he'd described during his campaign as "humiliating to the South," rather than focusing his comments on the practices that led to the need for such a law as humiliating to African Americans.

I feel that Ronald Reagan led the country in the wrong direction, sensing and playing to its worst impulses at a moment in history that called desperately for a higher vision. The term "government" was degraded into a working synonym for "ineptitude" or even "hostile entity." Nearly all the important imprints of his presidency bore features that rebuked or rolled back the hard-earned progress of African Americans dating to the Civil Rights Act of 1964. His choice of the Neshoba County Fair near Philadelphia, Mississippi, as the site for his first speech after being nominated was appalling: Philadelphia was the site of one of the most heinous racial crimes of the twentieth century, the murder of three young civil rights workers by white supremacists in 1964. He slashed education and social programs that protected the dispossessed, while scolding the phantom "welfare queens" who used their food stamps to buy steak and whiskey. He denounced the imprisoned Nelson Mandela as a terrorist and supported the apartheid government of South Africa. He vetoed a bill that would have authorized sanctions against that country's racist De Klerk regime. (Congress overrode the veto.)

And yet I cannot help affirming that Ronald Reagan deserves his special niche in the minds of the American people. As an optimist myself, I admire optimists. He made people feel upbeat about the country, a welcome mood shift after the Carter era.

As the nation moved rightward, many pundits suggested that—and many politicians acted as though—we were entering a sweeping and permanent new political climate. I never agreed with that view, harvested mainly from opinion polls and focus groups, nor the repositioning that it spawned. I recognized that some sort of shift was inevitable. My brother Jack used to say that ours was basically a conservative country, but that people wanted progress. So if you talked conservative and voted liberal, you'd win every time. I believe there's a lot to that bit of political wisdom.

While I haven't mastered the art of talking conservative, experience has convinced me that genuine, principled leadership can persuade our people that their enlightened self-interest lies to the left. The historic gains of the New Deal, the New Frontier, and the Great Society attest to that. I maintained my conviction that the working-class majority forged by Roosevelt remained our best hope for justice and progress.

CHAPTER TWENTY

The Family Business
1988–1990

As 1988 dawned and the Reagan administration entered its final year, I looked forward to a fascinating fall election season. Reagan's vice president, George H. W. Bush, was viewed as an early favorite in the crowded Republican primaries that also featured Congressman Jack Kemp of New York, Senator Bob Dole of Kansas, and former cabinet members Alexander Haig and Donald Rumsfeld. The Democratic primary field crackled with talent: Congressman Dick Gephardt of Missouri; Senator Paul Simon and the Reverend Jesse Jackson of Illinois; Governor Michael Dukakis of Massachusetts; Senators Al Gore of Tennessee and Joe Biden of Delaware; former senator Gary Hart of Colorado; and former governor Bruce Babbitt of Arizona. Hopes ran high among Democrats that one of these men would lead the nation past eight years of "Reaganomics" that had tripled the national debt, from $900 billion when he took office to more than $2.8 trillion at the end of his term.

I faced a reelection test of my own that year. But even as I prepared for it with the diligence that any campaign for the Senate deserves, my highest hopes were keyed to a race that involved neither the presidency nor the Congress, but a relatively obscure state-level district in Rhode Island, and a fellow just barely old enough to vote, let alone stand for office. In April, my son Patrick had decided to toss his hat into the political ring.

He was a sophomore at Providence College that spring. He would not turn twenty-one until July. Yet his call to politics was serious and mature, and his passion for it ran deep. And that passion was his own. Patrick was not a carbon copy of me, in his views or in his style. Though our beliefs are similar on most issues, I've never tried to tell him how to think. Nor has he needed me to. Patrick lived politics his whole young life. His friendly face beneath his shock of red hair instantly draws people to him. Patrick returns the warmth. Then too, he had and maintains a zest for campaigning, despite the fact that he had grown up reserved and rather shy. He quickly learned to love getting out there. He knew that people liked to see their representatives; needed to see them out there, working hard.

Patrick gave his political impulses a test run in early March, when he ran for and was elected a Rhode Island delegate to the Democratic convention, committed to Michael Dukakis. He liked the feel of that, and set his sights on the Rhode Island House of Representatives. A few months later, he threw himself into the fray like a veteran. Since no Republican was running, the Democratic primary would produce the overall winner. His opponent was the incumbent, Jack Skeffington, a veteran of the state's ward politics who, despite his good nature, was none too pleased to be going up against a youngster whom he considered no more than an upstart with a famous name who ought to be waiting his turn. Skeffington's fellow Rhode Island Democrats, an understandably close-knit group, felt the same way. And so my son found his welcome to electoral politics delivered with a bare knuckle or two.

Patrick fought back with energy and good cheer. He campaigned hard and shrewdly, but fairly, against Skeffington and his supporters. Patrick argued that Skeffington had grown out of touch with the people he represented. Still underweight and a little weakened from recent surgery on a benign spinal tumor, and packing an inhalator to combat his chronic asthma, Patrick bounded about the district, practicing retail politics in his neat blue blazer and white shirt with endless handshakes and knocks on doors. His strategy worked—reinforced somewhat by many voters' perception that Skeffington's people were coming down too hard on the young man. Patrick later admitted that he'd been anxious and nervous through much of the campaign. Yet he won in September with 1,324 votes, against 1,009 for his rival. He was off on a political career that six years later would take him to the United States House of Representatives.

One incident that has become part of our family lore is the one we call the "go back the way you came" story. When Patrick first became interested in running, I took him to meet the legendary pol John Pastore. John was eighty-one then and retired from political life. He'd served Rhode Island as both governor and senator, the first Italian American from the state to have held either office. He was a great Democrat. I remember those big soulful dark eyes of his, and the little mustache that he always kept trimmed. My brother Jack had thought the world of him and believed him the most electable figure in the history of Rhode Island. John had a great heart, and the people loved him.

Patrick and I drove to Pastore's house one day in the early spring. It was in a neighborhood that John had never left. He was a fellow who *literally* never forgot where he came from. No one else was at home, so it was just the retired senator, entertaining Patrick and me. John served us cookies and tea and talked politics. We were there for almost an hour. When we finally said goodbye and returned to the car, it was getting dark and we weren't sure how to get back to where we were going. Patrick got out, went back, and rang the bell. I could see him talking with Pastore, who was gesturing while Patrick nodded. Patrick returned and got back in the car, but didn't say anything. I asked, "What did he say?" And Patrick, in a perfect imitation of John Pastore, barked, "'Go back the way you came, Patrick, go back the way you came!'"

As I've noted, my son was challenging an incumbent, and within the close-knit Rhode Island Democratic establishment it was a rarity for anyone to support a challenger. Not long after his announcement, Patrick hosted a big kickoff breakfast, where lots of politicians made lots of speeches.

It had gone on for quite a while, and it was time to wind it up. Half the room had emptied and the rest were walking out.

Then Patrick spotted Senator Pell.

Claiborne Pell was one of the most splendid and civilized public servants I had ever been privileged to call a colleague. ("He was a gentleman and a gentle man," I said at his funeral in January 2009, after he died at age ninety.) He counted a political lineage that stretched well back into the nineteenth century. He'd served on a convoy in the treacherous North Atlantic in World War II after receiving a master's degree in history at Columbia University. Claiborne's self-effacing wit and his humane vision carried him through a thirty-six-year Senate career distinguished by his creation of the Pell grants for college students in 1973, his sponsorship of legislation for the National Endowment for the Arts and the Endowment for the Humanities, and his effective support for the environmentally critical United Nations Convention on the Law of the Sea.

I watched as Patrick walked over to Claiborne and asked him whether he would speak for just a minute. I thought: poor Claiborne! What an impossible situation for any politician. People want to go. They *are* going. And now he's supposed to keep their attention.

I should never have worried. The movement toward the doors ceased as Claiborne moved to the podium. He gave a talk I'll never forget. It was breathtakingly short, but he hit it out of the park. In his quiet voice, he said, "We're going to end, now, for this morning, but before we do I want to say why I'm here to support Patrick Kennedy. I believe that he shares the values of President Kennedy. And every night since we've lost President Kennedy, I've knelt down on my knees and prayed that this nation would live up to the promise of John Kennedy. I believe that Patrick Kennedy will, and that's why I support him."

His election victory made me feel so terribly proud of my son. After all these years, I finally understood how my dad must have felt.

I had won reelection and was in Hawaii with my sisters for a vacation that spanned the 1989 New Year when the representative-elect telephoned me. He wanted me present for his inauguration. He had earlier felt that I shouldn't be there, that he should be sworn in on his own, and I had accepted his judgment. I had seen my own father step into the background for his sons, and I was certainly prepared to do the same for mine. But if my son wanted me to be there after all, I was going to come through for him. So I flew fourteen hours from Honolulu to Providence for the swearing in. I arrived at his apartment late at night. It was cold and dark, and I was exhausted. Patrick greeted me with some interesting news. He said that he was so happy to see me, but his people thought it was best if I didn't go down for the swearing in. I said, "You must be kidding." He wasn't.

I didn't really mind. I was just so proud of him and so happy.

Patrick thus became the second member of the emerging generation of Kennedys to gain political office. Joseph Kennedy II, Bobby's eldest son, had been elected to Congress from Massachusetts the previous year, and would serve until 1999. Kathleen Townsend, Bobby's firstborn, would be elected lieutenant governor of Maryland in 1995. But Patrick became the youngest officeholder of us all.

Not all of the 1988 elections had gone so well. Incumbent vice president George H. W. Bush had defeated Michael Dukakis, the governor of Massachusetts, which meant another four years of Republican control of the executive branch.

I enjoyed a warm relationship with President Bush, and whenever the talk was about foreign policy, especially Russia, we had productive conversations. On domestic policy, however, he told me, "Relax." He had no plans for new social programs.

Nevertheless, my colleagues and I were able to get some things through Congress. On July 26, 1990, President Bush signed into law the Americans with Disabilities Act, which I'd co-advocated for many years and cosponsored with Senator Bob Dole. It brought some forty-three million disabled Americans into the mainstream via special services and protections, and has been called the most sweeping civil rights act since the original back in 1964.

At first, the administration had resisted our efforts. When I started discussing the legislation with John Sununu, Bush's chief of staff, he wanted to know how we were going to deal with a person in a wheelchair on a ski slope, or a blind person in a bookstore. He was looking for problems and putting up a lot of roadblocks. He was always available to talk to, but progress was slow.

Finally, after much negotiating, all of the important issues had been resolved. Key members attended a meeting in a Republican Senate conference room, with Dole presiding, to review everything—one last massage. Sununu was present, and once again, he became obstructive and said something aggressive to a Senate aide, Bobby Silverstein. I'd had it with Sununu's bullying and slammed my hand down on the table. I told him that if he had a problem, he could deal with me. I didn't want him yelling at our staff. At one point, Sununu said that all of the staff should leave so that the principals could finish negotiating. I said, fine, then he should leave, because he was staff. That seemed to quiet things down.

Everyone stayed and the rest of the meeting moved along smoothly.

Around this time, I had the privilege of meeting three great men. Our conversations weren't long, but their influences on me were profound.

In May 1987, at the Vatican, I was received by His Holiness, Pope John Paul II, in his "private workroom." He was sitting in a hard wooden chair near a plain wooden desk. I had just visited Poland, so I told him about an extraordinary religious experience I'd had in Gdansk with Lech Walesa. The pope said he'd been following Poland very closely and had been hearing many things from friends, not all of it good. He said he was concerned about the social and economic conditions, that young people might lose hope. "It's not good that they don't have a real sense of their future." Walesa provided great symbolism, he said. That Walesa continued to live in Poland could be a powerful example for people.

In February 1990, during a dinner at Katharine Graham's home, I met Vaclav Havel, the playwright and former dissident leader who, despite years of imprisonment and government intimidation, had led the 1989 Velvet Revolution against Czechoslovakia's communist regime. He had recently ascended to the presidency of his country and was hailed as a hero on his visit to Washington.

At the dinner table, he told me that when he was in prison, he was permitted to write for only one hour. Every three months, he was permitted a new pencil. He could write one letter, which could express no philosophy or poetry. It had to be factual.

When he mentioned that he hadn't been able to see much of America, because he was in his car constantly, I suggested that he visit the Lincoln Memorial. To my delight, he agreed, and together we made a late-night visit to the memorial, from which I read him the inscriptions on the wall from Lincoln's second inaugural and the Gettysburg Address. He said, "I am not able to understand the language, but I understand the poetry."

That same month, on February 15, I had my first conversation with Nelson Mandela, on the phone. He had been freed four days earlier, after twenty-seven years of imprisonment. While in South Africa in 1985, I had gone to Soweto and visited Bishop Desmond Tutu and Mandela's wife, Winnie. Mandela told me that he knew I'd been outside his prison on that day, and that it had given his friends hope and renewed power.

I invited him to visit the Kennedy Library, and four months later, on June 25, he attended a lunch in his honor, where I could not help but be impressed by his seriousness and honesty. He had not yet been elected president, but he expressed optimism about the integrity of South Africa's leader, F. W. de Klerk, and his intent to bring about substantive change.

I asked him what he thought was the most important thing the United States could do. He said it was very simple: jobs for the sixteen thousand exiled political activists who were returning to the country. Those people would need housing and job opportunities in order to be a source of stability for South Africa's future.

As inspiring as these men were, it would be a woman who changed the course of my life.

PART FOUR

Renewal

CHAPTER TWENTY-ONE

The Woman Who Changed My Life

1991

I have always believed that there are three stages of enjoying life: looking forward to something; experiencing it; and then having the memory of it.

There came a point in my own life when I had to admit that I'd stopped looking forward to things.

There had been so much loss. I understand that everyone suffers loss; it is hardly unique to me. Yet preparing myself to savor new experiences, and especially experiences that involved new personal commitments—I faced the fact that I no longer wanted to take that risk.

This is not to say I didn't enjoy life during those years. I am an enjoyer. I have enjoyed being a senator; I've enjoyed my children and my close friends; I've enjoyed books and music and well-prepared food, especially with a generous helping of cream sauce on the top. I have enjoyed the company of women. I have enjoyed a stiff drink or two or three, and I've relished the smooth taste of a good wine. At times, I've enjoyed these pleasures too much.

I've heard the tales about my exploits as a hell-raiser—some accurate, some with a wisp of truth to them, and some so outrageous that I can't imagine how anyone could really believe them. But I never tried to correct the record.

I decided long ago never to respond to tabloid gossip. Never. Once you respond to that kind of trash, you elevate it to something worth responding to. And anyway, once you begin refuting, you can never stop. Because then if you fail to deny even one such story, that might be taken as evidence that it is true. (The downside here, of course, is that rumors and fictions frequently enter the public consciousness as settled fact.)

Still, there was enough that I was doing to cause concern to those who cared about me. My friends didn't tell me that my drinking or my private life was getting out of control, but maybe that's because we were all having too much fun at the time. Certainly it didn't affect my Senate work. What was unspoken between me and my friends was my reason for excess. It was all part of my desire to escape, to keep moving, to avoid painful memories. And so I lived this string of years in the present tense, not despondently, because that is not my nature, but certainly with a sense of the void.

All of this began to change when I rang the doorbell of the home in Northwest D.C. where I had been invited to dinner on the evening of June 17, 1991, and found myself looking into the beautiful hazel eyes of Victoria Reggie.

The occasion was a dinner party to celebrate the fortieth anniversary of Vicki's parents, Judge Edmund and Doris Reggie. The Reggie and Kennedy families had been friends for many years, beginning with the judge's strong support for Jack as the presidential nominee in 1960. Inviting me had been the elder Reggies' idea, Vicki later told me. They'd said, "Oh, let's invite the Commander"—their nickname for me. Vicki and I were not strangers. Over the years, I'd seen her and her family a fair amount, usually on Nantucket where her family has a summer home, and I'd dined from time to time with them when the Reggies were in Washington. I was aware that Vicki and Grier Raclin had ended their nine-year marriage the previous summer.

When I walked up to Vicki's door that evening, I really wasn't expecting anything other than a pleasant evening with old friends. I got quite a bit more.

As Vicki ushered me into her home, she looked at me quizzically and then leaned over and looked behind me. And with a teasing half smile on her face, my future wife sort of looked me up and down and asked, "What's wrong? Couldn't you get a date?"

"I thought you'd be my date," I fired back. To which she responded, "Dream on, Kennedy."

I learned later that her mother had overheard the exchange and was horrified: "Oh, Vicki! You're just *never* going to find a man if you talk like that!" But I was enjoying the banter. Vicki was quick-witted, playful—and fun.

So, all right, perhaps it wasn't love at first sight. Vicki, in fact, charges me with not even remembering her from those '70s days, when she interned in my Senate office mailroom with her long hair pressed straight down below her shoulders, a charge to which I plead nolo contendere.

But as much as Vicki and I had seen each other at various events over the years, I think that anniversary dinner party night was the first time I really *saw* Vicki. I helped her as she took the place setting away for the date I didn't bring, and I hung out with her in the kitchen as she prepared dinner. We shared easy conversation about issues of the day and spent a lot of the evening laughing. I hadn't felt that relaxed or lighthearted in a long time.

Maybe that was what encouraged me to ask Vicki, as I left her house that night, "Well, can I call you? How about dinner tomorrow night?" Vicki said, "Sure." I've since learned that after the door closed, she went, "Did I just say *yes*? Have I lost my mind?"

Bear in mind that this was a woman who did not exactly have to worry much about whether she would ever "find a man." Vicki was then in the midst of a very fulfilling career in the law. She was a successful partner in a law firm in Washington, and she was rearing two young children. Her life was full and very busy.

We had dinner the next night, and in the weeks following I did everything I could think of to impress this amazing woman. I sent her bouquets of roses and fresh wildflowers. I telephoned her a lot. We went out to restaurants. We had dinner at my home. I met her friends.

She met mine. And we kept up the fun banter. As strange as it now seems, we didn't discuss any of the difficult things that were going on. One night at dinner, I did make reference to a poll that showed my approval rating plummeting to 48 percent, and Vicki comforted me by cracking, "That's a relief, because I never go out with anyone whose approval is less than 47." I developed instant friendships with her children: Curran, who was eight then, and Caroline, who was five. There is no question that I'd have been good pals with these two even if I hadn't been dating their mother. Curran was seriously into sports, so I found myself following football and baseball even more closely than usual; and I spent a lot of time coloring pictures on the living room rug with Caroline— who has blossomed into a very fine painter, incidentally. At night, I would read them to sleep.

One of our best adventures was trick-or-treating that first Halloween. I really enjoy Halloween with children, and used to make the neighborhood rounds with my own, along with my nieces, every October 31. On this night, Vicki and I walked with Curran and Caroline through their neighborhood. We received a lot of surprised looks from Vicki's neighbors that night, but none more than at the house occupied by the cultural attaché of China.

The children rang the doorbell and a gentleman opened the door to give them candy. As he looked up, he saw me and squealed, "Oooooooh, Kennedy!" I put out my hand to shake his and said, "How are you?" He asked us to come in and sit on the sofa. Actually, it was more like he ordered us to come in and sit on the sofa. Vicki and I looked at each other and the children kept asking why we weren't still trick-or-treating.

We could hear the gentleman who opened the door as he ran upstairs and knocked on what we assumed to be the cultural attaché's room. We heard them speaking in loud, rapid Chinese, which we could of course not understand, except for the periodic shouting out my name: "Ted Kennedy!" This back-and-forth went on for a few minutes. Vicki and I decided that the gentleman was trying to convince the attaché that it really was me and the attaché was telling him that it was just some person in a Ted Kennedy mask. Eventually we tiptoed out the door.

Ironically, given that we've spent so many happy hours together at sea, our first little falling-out was over a disagreement about sailing. (Vicki maintains that "falling-out" is too strong a term for it.) In mid-August, I sailed *Mya* over from Hyannis to Nantucket to pay a visit on the judge and Doris and, of course, Vicki, who was visiting them. I invited Vicki to sail back to Hyannis Port with me.

August was the beginning of the Atlantic hurricane season. The opening show, just then spiraling northeastward along the coast, was a doozie. Hurricane Bob had already bumped twice against Rhode Island, and according to news bulletins was now heading straight for Massachusetts. On Cape Cod, its peak winds would later be clocked at 125 miles an hour.

For some reason, Vicki was not terribly interested in sailing back with me. Her exact words, as I recall them, were, "There is no way." This hardly seemed like a flat refusal to me, and so I repeated the offer. "Come on," I said. "We're going to get ahead of the hurricane and sail back." Vicki said, "There is just no way." She was beginning to sound as though she might be serious.

(Full disclosure here: my wish to get *Mya* back to Hyannis Port before the hurricane hit was not frivolous. I knew that if I left her on the Nantucket side, where there was little protection, the high winds and waves would smash her to pieces. This in fact was the fate of many boats caught on that stretch of land. Far better shielding awaited her on the Hyannis side, and I had no doubt that I could beat the big winds—which I did.)

I won't say that I was hurt by Vicki's refusal to trust me at the helm of a fifty-foot boat sailing across open water in the path of a Category 2 hurricane. But I didn't call her for two weeks. I was back in my office after Labor Day thinking of what excuse I was going to come up with to end my radio silence, when the secretary in my Washington office buzzed me with the message that I had a call waiting from Vicki Reggie. I think it was the first time she had ever originated a call to me.

At the end of the conversation—I can't remember the exact topic; she'd called to wish me luck on something or other—I cleared my throat and said, "Well, listen, I was just thinking, uh—I know you don't want to go out a lot because of your children, so, uh—I thought I would come over to your house for dinner."

From then on, I began going to Vicki's house for dinner nearly every night—as often as my schedule would allow. Some evenings I arrived early and 'had the chance to spend fun time with Curran and Caroline before their mother got home from work. Sometimes I would bring friends of mine along with me, and Vicki would obligingly cook for them as well. She loves to cook. And with her southern roots and Lebanese heritage, she really turns out some delicious meals.

Vicki would put the children to bed around eight, and as she came back down the stairs we would often hear them calling, "Mommy, Mommy, Mommy!" The first time this happened, Vicki began to apologize for it, but I interrupted her. "Oh no," I said. "I think a child calling for his mother is the most beautiful sound in the world."

We really had an old-fashioned courtship, and I loved it that way. During those autumn evenings, Vicki and I would talk as she cooked. We talked during dinner. And then, after dinner, we'd talk some more. I usually headed back to my house by 10:30 or so—we both had work the next day and Vicki had to get the children off to school in the morning as well—but I knew we'd be together the next evening anyway.

We really took the time to know each other and we grew very close. As the months went on, I realized that I loved this woman very deeply and that my love for her was overcoming all the defenses I'd built up in myself against the potential heartbreak of marrying again. One night, as Vicki and I were listening to *La Bohème*—we both love opera—I asked whether she wanted to go to New York to hear it performed. She quickly agreed. But the date for the performance was two months away. I had decided to propose to Vicki at the opera, but I wanted to surprise her. So I waited—

for two months. And in the meantime, I made sure that we spent more time with my children and my sisters and sisters-in-law.

I asked Vicki to marry me—and she said yes—during the performance of *La Bohème* at the Metropolitan Opera in New York on January 14, 1992. We decided to keep our engagement quiet for a while, while we worked out the plans for our wedding. In mid-March, I felt the time had come to tell Kara, Teddy, and Patrick, and Vicki felt she should tell Curran and Caroline too. Everyone was asked to keep the wonderful news to themselves, but secrecy was too much to ask of then six-year-old Caroline. She told only "one person" in her kindergarten class, and he told his parents, who apparently worked for the *Washington Post*!

We announced our engagement in March and I gave Vicki an engagement ring in April when we were visiting my sister Pat, who had rented a house for Easter in St. Croix in the U.S. Virgin Islands. We were snorkeling at Buck Island Reef—named by President Kennedy to be part of the National Park system in 1961—where I had placed the ring for Vicki to find near a coral head. I'm just thankful that a big grouper didn't swim away with the ring before she saw it.

Our wedding, a private ceremony with our immediate families, took place at my McLean house on July 3, 1992. As a wedding gift to my bride, I did an oil painting of daffodils. The two of us had been reading William Wordsworth's poem "Daffodils" together several weeks earlier, and it was one of the readings we chose for our wedding. The poem begins, "I wander'd lonely as a cloud / That floats on high o'er vales and hills / When all at once I saw a crowd, / A host, of golden daffodils." The wildflowers lift the poet's spirits, and charm him by the way they seem to dance in the wind in a long line beside a bay. When later he lies in solitude on his couch, the image of the flowers returns to him: "And then my heart with pleasure fills / And dances with the daffodils."

CHAPTER TWENTY-TWO

Campaigning for Political Survival

1994

In 1994, after thirty-two years in the Senate, I found myself campaigning for my political survival.

I knew that this election was going to be more challenging than usual, so I had been laying the groundwork for more than two years, actively campaigning around the state for other candidates in the 1992 elections and reconnecting with voters who had not seen me for a while. After those elections, I continued to return to the Commonwealth as much as the Senate schedule allowed to meet with various constituency groups and visit more cities and towns.

But despite our hard work, there were red flags. When campaign workers were gathering signatures to qualify me for the ballot, they found the electorate to be less receptive than in other years. A changing world had transformed Massachusetts into a quite different state from the one I'd known as a boy, or even as a young senator.

Textiles and shoes had been the twin anchors of the Commonwealth's economic stability and working-class hopes back in Honey Fitz's day. But the redbrick factories and mills that once seemed as natural to the landscape as cranberry bogs had been declining even before World War II, and now were shuttered, losers to outsourcing and overseas competition. Mass production of shoes in America had begun in Lynn, Massachusetts, in

1885, but Ronald Reagan's favorite, the Bostonian, was being made in China and India now. Massachusetts textile mills had virtually ushered in the American industrial age, but Asian imports were rendering this industry uncompetitive as well.

As with any shrinkage of a job base, decline built on decline. Machine shops, mold makers, and electricians were drawn down into the spiral. Lower wages, unemployment, a shrinking tax base that supported fewer social services and funding for schools—it was enough to turn good people angry and cynical. And it had.

Massachusetts is a resilient state, and it wheeled about to stem the flow of lost jobs and revenues. Its network of higher learning centers began to draw in a new kind of worker, the white-collar professional in information, finance, biotech, and other high-tech jobs. Yet as welcome as they were, these "new economy" specialists could not fully compensate for the losses. New anxieties arose in the streets and neighborhoods, and were augmented by the rise of welfare and its perceived abuses. "What is Senator Kennedy doing about it?" ran the question in those neighborhoods. "Where is he? Why isn't he around here?" Reasonable questions, all of them; and to some, there were reasonable answers. But as Vicki and members of my staff tried to remind me from time to time, I was not in the habit of touting my accomplishments. (As a woman legislator urged Vicki during the campaign, "Honey, you've just got to tell him what my mama told me: 'If you don't toot your horn, nobody's gonna hear your tune.'") Well, I was taught not to toot my own horn. The last time I'd tried it, I'd gotten a letter from Dad telling me to stop mooing. But eventually I had to face up to the larger point in that criticism: I could no longer assume that the voters were closely monitoring my hard work on their behalf.

For one thing, I was not even especially well known to the newer, younger electorate, which had little investment in Boston's or the state's past. The name "Ted Kennedy" conveyed less information and less political connection to them than perhaps I would like to have thought.

For another, even my older base was perhaps starting to take me for granted. Or, if Vicki was to be believed, taking me for granite. "You've become like a building to them," she told me one day.

I soon grasped that my wife was handing me a hard and urgent truth. Her own conversations with people around the state had convinced her that to many, I'd become less a human being than a kind of monument. And that among those who did have strong opinions was a sizable percentage that didn't think I understood the problems and concerns of people like them.

I had also contributed to my political problems by persistent questions about my personal behavior, which were raised by the media during the Senate's confirmation hearings for Clarence Thomas and, more notoriously, in coverage of allegations of a date rape in Palm Beach. On March 30, 1991, my nephew William Smith was accused of the crime and I was named in tabloid stories because I had been with him earlier that evening. The episode interrupted what I'd hoped would be a quiet getaway from my Senate duties, a weekend at the house my father had purchased in 1933. My son Patrick and I joined my sister Jean, her four children, and other friends in Palm Beach for Easter.

William was thirty that spring, and a medical student at Georgetown University School of Medicine. He would go on to a productive career as an activist in the worldwide cause of finding and disabling military land mines. He founded the Center for International Rehabilitation, a network for supporting the disabled.

William, Patrick, and I had left the house and gone out for a late-evening drink at a popular Palm Beach watering hole. As I later told a jury, we had all spent much of the day and evening reminiscing about Steve Smith, who had recently died of cancer shortly before his sixty-third birthday. Steve had managed or helped manage the presidential campaigns of Jack, Bobby, and me. He had taken over the family finances after my father died, becoming chairman of our family business office in New York. He spearheaded the fund-raising for the John F. Kennedy Library in Boston, of which the Stephen E. Smith Center became a part. Beyond his accomplishments in the world, Steve was a gentle and humorous man beneath his façade of intensity. He was a good soul and I loved him very much.

My memories of Steve and other lost family members overwhelmed me as I tried to fall asleep. I invited Patrick and William to come with me to the club. William struck up a conversation with a woman, and he and she left the establishment. Out of that encounter came the woman's charge against William. Her claim, of course, made headlines and news broadcasts around the world. Ultimately, the jury wound up deliberating for only seventy-seven minutes before delivering a verdict of not guilty.

I could have avoided any involvement in the trial if I'd simply taken a walk on the beach by myself that night, instead of asking my son and nephew to accompany me to a bar.

Clarence Thomas, however, was another matter entirely. That was a controversy I could not avoid.

On July 1, 1991, President Bush nominated Thomas, a federal judge, to the Supreme Court to fill the seat of the great Thurgood Marshall. Marshall had been the first African American to serve as a Supreme Court justice. It seemed generally obvious that the president had been determined to select a black jurist to succeed Marshall, and a conservative black jurist at that.

The National Organization for Women objected to his nomination immediately. They focused on indications that he might vote to overturn *Roe v. Wade*, thus criminalizing abortion and denying women the right to make their own reproductive decisions. The NAACP and the Urban League objected sometime later. They pinpointed critical statements Thomas had made about affirmative action.

Worst of all, however, was Thomas's rating by the American Bar Association's fifteen-member evaluation committee for appointees. No member gave him the highest rating of "well-qualified." Two of them even pronounced him "unqualified." In stark contrast, every other sitting member of the Supreme Court has been determined to be "well-qualified" by the ABA. President Bush's earlier assertion that Thomas was the "best-qualified" nominee available hardly seemed credible.

I was a member of the Senate Judiciary Committee, chaired by Joe Biden, which began hearings on Thomas's appointment on September 10. The questioning went on for eight sessions spanning seventeen days, focusing on the nominee's opinions about issues such as the right to privacy, civil and minority rights, and his record as Equal Employment Opportunity Commission chairman, among other topics.

On September 27, the Judiciary Committee was evenly split on whether to recommend his confirmation: seven votes for his confirmation and seven against. In voting against confirmation, I said that "when ideology is the paramount consideration of the president in nominating a justice to the Supreme Court, the Senate is entitled to take that ideology into account in the confirmation process and to reject any nominee whose views are so extreme that they place him outside the mainstream." We sent the nomination to the Senate floor without a recommendation.

On October 6, as the full Senate body neared the end of its deliberations, two news outlets broke a story that threw the proceedings, and the nation, into an uproar: a tenured professor at the University of Oklahoma Law Center, Anita Hill, had submitted to our committee in September an affidavit stating that Thomas had sexually harassed her ten years earlier while she was employed as his personal assistant at the Office of Civil Rights in the Department of Education, which he then headed. Specifically, Ms. Hill charged, Thomas had discussed pornographic movies with her and had asked her several times for a date, even after she'd told him she did not wish to go out with him.

The Judiciary Committee reopened its hearings on October 11, and that is when the media and much of America suddenly developed a consuming interest in our deliberations. In defending himself, Thomas famously and furiously described his questioning as a circus and a national disgrace, "a high-tech lynching for uppity blacks who in any way deign to think for themselves."

On October 15, the full Senate confirmed Clarence Thomas as an associate justice of the Supreme Court by a vote of fifty-two to forty-eight, mostly but not entirely along party lines.

A sort of "urban legend" built up around my participation, or lack of participation, in the questioning of Clarence Thomas during the Anita Hill portion of the hearings. The idea took hold that I remained mostly silent— "muzzled myself," in the words of at least one journalist—because I was reluctant to interrogate the nominee on the question of his alleged sexual harassment of Hill: it would draw attention to my private life, especially in the wake of the Palm Beach incident.

The true reason why I did not ask many questions is less melodramatic and more procedural. Joe Biden had appointed Howell Heflin of Alabama and Patrick Leahy of Vermont, a former prosecutor, as the lead questioners of Thomas for this added-on stage of the hearings, which were out of the ordinary and subject to different rules. I had been a regular questioner in the main part of the hearings, and I don't think anyone doubted my performance then.

I was not at all reluctant to raise my voice. On day three of this phase, I angrily spoke up in protest of what I called the "character assassination" of Anita Hill. I made a strong statement at the end, as I voted in opposition to Thomas's confirmation. I worked to garner votes to turn down his nomination. I let it be known that I thought he was the wrong man for the job because of his narrow view of the Constitution and his judicial philosophy. But I also knew—and know—that perception is reality in politics. I had *appeared* to be silenced, and no amount of rational explanation about procedural mechanics was going to change that "reality." I also understood another hard truth: with all of the background noise about Palm Beach and my bachelor lifestyle, I would have been the wrong person to lead the questioning in the second phase of the Thomas hearing. And I know that many people were disappointed that I was unable to succeed in making a persuasive case against Thomas's confirmation.

That autumn was a time of soul-searching for me. The Palm Beach incident and the Clarence Thomas hearings, each in its own way, but really together, had stirred up public doubts about my past and my judgment. For the first time, my private life was viewed as impacting my public life. The high stakes of the Clarence Thomas nomination and the salacious allegations about *his* private life and its impact on his professional life certainly did not help that perception. My habitual reluctance to speak publicly about my personal life had intensified the doubting of many, and had allowed the latest tabloid frenzy to roll on unabated with rumor and innuendo.

I needed to reestablish good faith with my constituents. I began work on a speech to address the issues in a way I had never done before. It was not an easy one to write or give. I asked Vicki to accompany me to the speech and then to join me and my family at the Cape for the rest of the weekend. I told her that I was giving an important speech at Harvard, but I didn't tell her what I would say or why I wanted her to be there. Her presence was all I needed.

On October 25, with Vicki sitting amid the capacity audience, I took the microphone at the John F. Kennedy School of Government at Harvard. Television cameras focused their lenses on me from behind the packed auditorium. Late arrivals milled outside, unable to find seats. Many, I later gathered, had come because they expected me to announce a decision not to seek another term in the Senate.

I spoke of the nation's pressing policy issues for several minutes—national health insurance, gun control, civil rights. I alluded to the outrage of many progressive Americans at the confirmation of Thomas to the Supreme Court:

"Some of the anger of recent days reflects the pain of a new idea still being born—the idea of a society where sex discrimination is ended and sexual harassment is unacceptable—the idea of an America where the majority who are women are truly and finally equal citizens."

Then, shifting my focus to another source of recent public anger, I turned to the heart of what I'd come to say.

"I am painfully aware," I told my audience, "that the criticism directed at me in recent months involves far more than honest disagreements with my positions, or the usual criticism from the far right. It also involves the disappointment of friends and many others who rely on me to fight the good fight."

I looked around the auditorium and continued, in matter-of-fact tones:

"To them I say: I recognize my own shortcomings—the faults in the conduct of my private life. I realize that I alone am responsible for them, and I am the one who must confront them. I believe that each of us as individuals must not only struggle to make a better world, but to make ourselves better, too, and in this life those endeavors are never finished."

After the speech, I was relieved, but I knew it was only the beginning. I had work to do.

That evening, after a quiet dinner, I asked Vicki to take a walk with me. I wanted to show her some of the things that make Boston such a special place for me. We walked through the Public Garden and through the Common, jewels in Boston's Emerald Necklace, the magnificent park system created by Frederick Law Olmsted. We walked up Chestnut Street, where I showed her the buildings designed by Charles Bulfinch, the same architect who had designed the U.S. Capitol and the church, though I didn't know it at the time, at which my beloved mother eventually would be buried. I showed Vicki Louisburg Square, where citizens of Irish descent had gathered to challenge my grandfather when he appointed an Italian American to a post, shouting, "Remember your own, Honey Fitz. Remember your own!"

I always saw any campaign as an education, for me and for the voters. But I hadn't gone through especially competitive elections for a while, and the voters didn't know what I'd been doing in the Senate. They knew about all of the tabloid fodder, but not about the serious hard work of legislating and the many successes we had.

I faced some other troubling fires of discontent that burned in Massachusetts and the nation. There was increasing unhappiness with the status quo and a strong aversion to incumbency. "Term limits" was the cure-all of the moment. The Republicans' "Gingrich Revolution," which in 1994 would claim a net fifty-four House seats and eight in the Senate, was forming. Right-wing talk radio was on the rise, lending fury to the general discontent.

There were reasons enough for discontent. People were hurting in my state and all across the country. The rhetoric by political leaders was to demonize the poor as people getting something for nothing. Gingrich was calling America a welfare state. But the policies he was proposing were heartless.

And my likely Republican opponent was right out of central casting— young, tall, handsome, slender, with a beautiful wife and five attractive sons. Mitt Romney had a Harvard MBA and a fortune that he was prepared to spend.

The son of George W. Romney, the former Michigan governor and 1968 Republican presidential candidate, Mitt was forty-seven in 1994, and a legend in Boston financial circles. His private equity investment firm, Bain Capital, boasted a 113 percent average annual rate of return on investments. He'd never before won or even sought a political seat of any kind, but in 1994 this was held to be a good thing. In fact, one political analyst described him, for this very reason among others, as the ideal candidate: "a newcomer to politics, 45 to 50 years old, without any skeletons in his closet, a record of entrepreneurial success in the private sector, socially liberal, fiscally conservative." The analyst went on: "A critical mass of the voters are either like that themselves or aspire to that role. Mitt Romney at this point appears to fit that profile."

His TV ads cast me, by contrast, as old and tired. Time to retire old Ted. Say thank you, give him a gold watch, and let him spend his dotage on Cape Cod. At least that's how Romney started out. He also made a point of repeating that I had never held a real job. I had certainly heard that old saw before, but never from a candidate quite as eager and confident and charged up as Mitt.

Mitt ran as the man with a Mr. Clean image, whose hard work had blessed him with a fortune, and who was now going to "give something back" by bringing good honest business principles to the messy game of politics. I remember one newspaper profile of him that described him as singing only hymns and as having even his dog kneel down for nightly prayers.

I watched his media performance at a distance through the summer of 1994, getting ready as usual to transition into my own post–Labor Day campaigning after an unusually busy Senate year that ran through August. In May, after discussion with many Republicans, I'd proposed a compromise version of President Clinton's health care bill, a markup of existing legislation that would help assure coverage to workers who had lost or changed jobs. The effort had foundered in June after late partisan bickering undercut what had seemed a good chance for the bill's success. I had worked to draft the Goals 2000 legislation, which stimulated and supported local school reform efforts, including setting high standards for what students should learn. My efforts won broad bipartisan support. Working with the president, I'd led successful Senate efforts to pass the Family and Medical Leave Act and the School-to-Work Opportunities Act. I'd also spearheaded the Crime Act, which put ten thousand new policemen on America's streets and imposed tough new penalties for crimes involving gangs and firearms.

I ran ads in June and July, the earliest I had ever done so. It was a substantial buy. But I went dark in August. That was a mistake.

Mitt Romney's TV spots that summer were nominally geared to winning the September 20 primary against his fellow businessman John Lakian (whom he in fact defeated easily), but there was no mistaking the real target: me. Aggressive, slickly packaged, and frequent, they must have taken a good chunk out of his $7 million campaign budget, more spending than was usual for any campaign in Massachusetts. But were they getting him any traction? I doubted it. The ads boasted of Mitt's supposed success as a job-creating business executive, a success he promised to replicate as a senator. He was positioning himself as a moderate, almost an apolitical candidate. He was pro-choice, he declared. But efficiency was what he really had to sell: sleeves-rolled-up, businesslike efficiency, to replace the senior senator's outdated ways.

He called for an end to rewarding "children who have children" by terminating support for welfare mothers who give birth out of wedlock while on benefits.

This stand of his posed a sticky challenge to me, at least as some of my aides saw it. Romney was not alone in denouncing welfare. It was a convenient issue in 1994. People were hurting in my state and all across the country. Newt Gingrich was at the peak of his power, touting the Republicans' "Contract with America" and steering his party to a rout of Democrats in the midterm elections.

Thus the rhetoric of demonizing the poor as people getting something for nothing was especially effective this year, and some on my staff worried that my support of it could jeopardize my chances.

Just before Labor Day, my campaign manager and nephew Michael Kennedy called Vicki to say that the *Boston Herald* was going to publish a poll showing Mitt Romney and me virtually tied. Together they called our campaign pollster Tom Kiley to see what he thought of the poll, and he agreed that it was accurate. They then called me with the news: "You and Mitt are dead even."

That got my attention.

My Senate campaigns in the past had followed the timetable that Jack had formulated back in the 1950s. "Look," he used to tell me. "Everybody goes away in August. They're not paying much attention. They start caring after Labor Day, when vacation is over and the kids are back in school. And if the Red Sox are doing well, they're not going to focus on the election until after the pennant races. That's when they start making up their minds."

In 1994, the Senate business certainly did not go away in August. I divided my time between the critical legislative battles I've described above and getting the Kennedy campaign organization revved up for another go. We reactivated our trusty old troops and brought in promising newcomers. An effective political campaign force is a bit like an army: large, well trained, disciplined, with varying and complex missions, and overseen by a tight chain of command. As with my Senate staff, I have been lucky with the quality of my campaign personnel through the years.

This time around, they would be tested more intensely than usual. On Labor Day, polls showed that the race was even Steven.

I called a meeting at our Back Bay apartment on September 18 to discuss our strategy with Bob Shrum, John Sasso, Paul Kirk, Tom Kiley, Michael Kennedy, and other top campaign aides. Vicki and her father, Edmund Reggie (who had been so helpful in my brothers' campaigns), were also there. I listened as they made their presentations and recommendations.

Up until that point, for thirty-two years of public life, I had never mentioned my opponent in a campaign ad. But times had changed and my Republican opponents had been running ads against me while I remained silent. Those ads had obviously taken their toll. Shrum, pointing out that we could not attack my opponent's voting record because there was no record to attack, argued strongly that Romney's business practices were fair game. His business was to take over and invest in other companies, and it was in that arena where we should go searching for clues to the kind of judgments he would bring to bear in representing the people as their United States senator. Vicki strongly agreed with this, and I gave my go-ahead.

In addition, I was advised to take a position in favor of so-called welfare reform. Romney had made a point of being opposed to additional benefits being given to single mothers who had more children. None of us wanted to reward irresponsibility, but who were we punishing? It seemed to me that we would be hurting innocent babies who needed assistance. I told my staff that I was not going to try to win this election on the backs of poor women and children. Case closed.

After the meeting, I got on the phone and asked Ranny Cooper, my extremely capable former chief of staff, to take a leave of absence from her private-sector job to join the campaign. Ranny had run my office for many years. She knew me, knew how to get things done, and if she were there I knew I wouldn't have to worry about anything.

And then there was Dave Burke. Dave had also been my trusted chief of staff at an earlier time. When he wrote to offer to help in any way he could, I don't think he ever expected me to follow up in quite the way I did. Dave had been the president of CBS News and had had a very successful private-sector career. I doubt that he thought he was volunteering to leave his beautiful wife, Trixie, for six weeks to live out of a suitcase to be my "body man." But that's exactly what I asked him to do. I needed a peer to ride in the car with me, someone who knew me and had good judgment. There were press stakeouts at every campaign stop. There were constantly changing issues of the day. I needed a trusted aide to bounce ideas off of. Dave was the man. Vicki was usually campaigning on her own during the day, but she joined us for the evening events. And I have to say that with Dave and Vicki, my mood was lighter every day. I always enjoy campaigning, but we were really having fun.

Vicki, meanwhile, had been busy developing another new campaign avenue for me. We had decided actively and energetically to pursue the women's vote. Women had been brought into the political process by the Clinton campaign like never before, and Vicki wanted to harness that energy and enthusiasm for our campaign. And she did.

With trusted aide Lisa McBirney, Vicki began meeting with professional women in Massachusetts as early as 1993. She was a natural. As women in that group have since told me, she was one of them, swapping stories of working motherhood and even talking about how we met. While I have never been at ease discussing such things, Vicki apparently chatted about our courtship and the children and she listened to the stories of women who have since become her very good friends. My formerly "granite" exterior was falling away, as voters began to connect with me through Vicki's eyes.

For all of her natural ability and love of politics, Vicki had never been on the campaign trail before. But with the help of Angela Menino, the much-loved and politically savvy wife of Boston mayor Tom Menino, Vicki plunged in.

In the evenings, the two of us would laugh over the "war" stories we accumulated along the way. About being in a parade and seeing people give me the finger. Or even worse, young people with no expression at all—they had no idea who I was.

Vicki told me that many times Angela would introduce her to a woman and ask, "Would you like to meet Mrs. Kennedy?" and the woman would say, "No, thank you!" Vicki asked, "Angela, what do I *say*?" And Angela said, "You just ask them for their vote. Say you hope they'll be able to support your husband, and if they say no, say, 'Well, I hope you'll give it consideration.'"

But then there were wonderful little moments that gave both of us such joy. We were at a Lebanese festival in the northeast part of the state when an elderly Lebanese woman came up to Vicki, pulled her aside, and asked, "So, honey, is he good to you?" Vicki said yes, he is good to me. The woman asked, "Do you love him?" Vicki said she loved me. And then the most important question of all. "Does he eat Lebanese food?" Vicki said yes, I did, I loved Lebanese food. Then, in what Vicki described as the comforting tones of Arabic-accented English that reminded my wife of her beloved grandmother, and while making the sign of the cross, the old woman said, "Okay, honey, I'm gonna vote for him for the first time in my life." How we both loved that story.

Our campaign days were long. And I was still keeping a busy Senate schedule back in Washington. So Vicki and Michael Kennedy were surrogates for me at events around the state. And I had extraordinary assistance and support from my fellow Democrats in the congressional delegation and from local elected officials. The governor was a Republican, but the Senate president Bill Bulger and Speaker of the House Charlie Flaherty were in my corner, and they rallied their troops in a meaningful and effective way. Tom Menino was also tremendously helpful. I remember gathering in his basement one night in the spring of 1994, as he brought his organization together for pasta and a pep talk. When he finished, I was ready to go out and campaign for myself in the cold. The friendship and support of these dedicated elected officials is something I'll never forget. Tip O'Neill was right that all politics is local. And these political leaders had their fingers on the local pulse. Along with them and the state representatives and state senators and mayors all around the Commonwealth that welcomed us and encouraged their supporters to join our effort, we were able to rebuild a successful organization.

The Senate was in session for most of August that year, so I didn't have the month to hit the ground as usual. I was chairman of the committee that was churning out much of the important legislation, and I didn't want to be absent. I believed that my constituents would be pleased that I was doing the people's business, but the truth was that they were being bombarded with advertisements from the Republican Senate primary essentially aimed at me, and, other than weekends, I wasn't there to counteract the impact. So the local officials and the revitalized organization and surrogates were more important than ever that summer.

Vicki would come back from the campaign trail and regale me with tales of her adventures. She loved campaigning, and, as she said to me, she loved most of all sharing the stories with me at the end of the day. At a popular restaurant in Boston, where you had to shout to be heard above the din of the crowd, a campaign worker asked a woman diner, "HOW WOULD YOU LIKE TO MEET MRS. TED KENNEDY?" The woman looked up and said, without missing a beat, "NOT AS PRETTY AS THE FIRST ONE!" Vicki smiled and said, "THANK YOU SO MUCH! I HOPE YOU'LL SUPPORT MY HUSBAND!" Vicki loved that story and used it to tease me to no end about the sacrifices she made for me. And then she would dissolve into laughter. Yes, I love this woman. She told me about a man at another table who replied to her greeting with, "KENNEDY! I WOULDN'T VOTE FOR HIM IF YOU PAID ME

TO!" Then he remembered his manners. "BUT IT'S NICE TO MEET YOU, MA'AM!"

In Worcester a few days later, a fellow deflected her "I hope you'll support my husband" greeting with the off-center retort, "I only support people who are French." "Ah," Vicki said. "Then you'll want to support my husband, Ted Ken-a-*day!*" They both started laughing. She believes she won him over with that one.

When I was able to be there, I had my own interesting encounters that were a bit different from previous campaigns. The tenor of some of the questions fired at me at events left no doubt that the electorate was angry. People were hurting.

But there were still the fun times: singing Irish songs in senior centers; eating food at the ethnic festivals; walking in the parades. Those are the things that bring you close to the people and make politics fun. They're a long way from the more modern campaign staples of television advertising and the Internet, but they're every bit as important, at least for me. I wouldn't trade the people part of politics for anything in the world.

The Senate finally recessed on October 8, and I was able to be in Massachusetts full-time. Vicki's mother, Doris, basically relocated to our home in Virginia to help look after the children. Curran was eleven and Caroline was eight, and the separation was especially hard on them and on Vicki. But having Doris there helped ease the burden. We began to feel momentum as I was able to get around the state. As one state rep put it, "People just want to see your shoe leather hit the pavement." And hit the pavement we did.

I gained some impressive backup. My nephew John Kennedy, accompanied by his large German shepherd, Sam, joined the campaign and brought crowds to their feet with his infectious charm and witty but impassioned message. Another nephew, Chris Lawford, then playing a heartthrob in a popular daytime soap opera, created quite a stir wherever he went. Other nieces and nephews, and of course our own children, hit the trail. The actor Alec Baldwin went to college campuses to register new voters. President

Clinton and Hillary came to the state to stump for me. Both were enormously popular and great assets.

Meanwhile, we were matching Mitt Romney's sizable treasure chest with resources of our own, eventually spending upwards of $10 million. I mortgaged my house as part of the effort so I could spend more time campaigning and less time fund-raising in those important last weeks. That meant we would have an aggressive fund-raising schedule to retire debt after the election, but that was fine with me. It was money well and wisely spent: much of it supported the political TV spots created by Bob Shrum and his team.

Bob's and Vicki's intuition about probing Romney's corporate behavior proved brilliantly on target. It led to the most effective "negative" ad that we ran. The ad went directly to Romney's claim that he had created ten thousand jobs. From there, it went to the single word, "Ampad," which came to define his true record as a businessman.

Our campaign had received a call from a union representative, telling us about the takeover of an Indiana company by Ampad, Romney's Bain Capital subsidiary, and Ampad's subsequent firing or slashing of salary and benefits of most of the workers. Shrum's partner Tad Devine went out to Indiana to film the workers, and he threw away the script and just let them tell their stories. My dad always said that there's no substitute for sincerity, and these people, working people who were losing their health insurance and their jobs, spoke from the heart. One especially effective ad ended with a middle-aged female worker looking directly into the camera, saying, "I'd like to say to the people of Massachusetts, if you think it can't happen to you, think again, because we thought it couldn't happen here either."

Our first televised debate at Faneuil Hall was in the final week of October. With Romney's poll lead decreasing and the truth of his job creation record in deep question, Mitt had realigned himself a little. He'd moved away from his "businessman" strategy and begun to campaign almost as a liberal reformer. I had begun to joke at rallies that I had heard of flip and I had heard of flop. But with Mitt, it was flip-flop-flip. He'd changed positions so often that if we gave him a little more time he'd be voting for *me* on election day. Yes, I was having fun.

Still, I knew that a lot was riding on the outcome of the debate in Faneuil Hall. Romney was slipping, but things remained close. I was taking nothing for granted. This was a change year. People all over the country were itching for change, and Massachusetts was no exception. Term limits were in vogue. Mitt had talked about thanking me for my service and sending me home to Cape Cod to retire. He was young and slender and I was not. Would his message resonate in a face-to-face meeting? We were about to find out.

When the day arrived, Vicki and I went to the Kennedy Library and sat outside in the back. We ate sandwiches, and I pored over my briefing materials. We went back to our apartment, and I took a nap so I'd be at peak energy for the intensity of the give-and-take. By evening I was prepared, but nervous.

During the drive to Faneuil Hall, Dave Burke perceived that I was a little tense, and did his best to lighten me up. Dave is great—a superb mind, a loyal aide and friend over the decades, and a fellow who knows the value of laughter. From the time we got in the car, Dave and Vicki made fast patter to keep the mood light. Dave grilled us about the most important thing we had learned in the campaign, then provided the answer himself: that the Roy Rogers on the Mass Pike didn't serve fried chicken until 11 a.m. We laughed so much at that one, as it conjured up memories of long days crisscrossing the state and craving that chicken before the appointed hour. As we neared the hall, Dave tapped me on the shoulder: "I just want to know why Steve Breyer is sitting on the Supreme Court," he asked in mock seriousness, "and I'm sitting in this damn car with you."

I laughed and relaxed even more. But then I looked out of the window, and any remaining nervousness vanished. I saw a huge swell of people stretching for blocks. They carried Kennedy signs and chanted,

"Teddy! Teddy! Teddy!" It was like the old torchlight parades that Grampa used to tell me about, and that he loved so much. I rolled down the car window, leaned out, raised my arm, and pumped my fist. My adrenaline was flowing. These were my people. They were working people. They were the people I had been representing for thirty-two years, and we still had work to do.

As I stepped out of the car, onto the cobblestone street and into Faneuil Hall, I couldn't help but think of the history of the place: from meetings to plan the Revolutionary War to my brother Jack's last campaign speech in 1960 to more modern gatherings. This building, the Cradle of Liberty, was at the center of it all.

As Mitt and I took the stage, I noticed two exceptionally large podiums. For some reason, unlike every other election, I had been unable to lose weight this time, and I was at an all-time high. As I found out later, my dear friend Eddy Martin got into the hall and swapped the smaller podiums for two larger ones, masking my size and totally dwarfing poor Mitt. Eddy never told me what he did, and it was only years later, at the time of his death, that I learned the true story.

I remember the first question I was asked in the debate: "Why is this race even close?" My first thought was, *Good question. I'm wondering the same thing!* My next thought was, *I'd better start talking and hope I think of something pretty soon.* So I started talking and was relieved when my time was up.

Both Mitt and I were prepared. Both of us kept our composure, and both of us remained hyper-alert for an opening, any opening. I saw one when Mitt gave a long-winded, nuanced answer about supposedly being pro-choice (unlike his professed anti-choice stance as a candidate for the Republican nomination for president in 2008). I paused for a beat and said, "I am pro-choice. My opponent is multiple choice." The crowd laughed.

No one laughed, however, least of all me, when I was asked about how I coped with my personal failings. There it was. The unspoken was spoken. My personal life was on the table. And unlike other questions and answers that I had reviewed with my advisers during debate prep, this was an area that we did not cover. This one was all mine. I had thought about it, to be sure. I knew what I felt inside. But to have to say it in public was my challenge.

I decided to place my trust in the simple, unadorned truth. I paused a moment, and then began: "Every day of my life I try to be a better human being, a better father, a better son, a better husband. And since my life has changed with Vicki, I believe the people of this state understand that the kind of purpose and direction and new affection and confidence on personal matters has been enormously reinvigorating. And hopefully I am a better senator."

And then they asked Mitt Romney, and his unfortunate tone-deafness became evident to everyone. After making an ineffective attempt at humor—"I assume you mean *my* weakness"—he started to talk about how much he loved to volunteer and how his life had been about being able to give service to others. He went on in that way for so long that the moderator felt compelled to remind him that he was asked about his greatest *weakness*.

By the end of the evening, after I tried to pin Romney down on the specific costs of his health care proposals; after he became exasperated with me for asking for specifics and I shot back, "That's what you have to do as a legislator, Mr. Romney"; after he complained about my ads and I told him that we could discuss that after the debate because people were hurting and they wanted to hear about issues that affected their lives, I started to feel that things were going okay for me. And you could feel in the room that the crowd was feeling that way too.

My nephew Congressman Joe Kennedy told me that the next day people were crossing the street to shake his hand, congratulating him on the great debate. But, he said, he really knew we'd done well when they put their arm around his shoulders and whispered in his ear, "I've been with your uncle the whole time."

On election day, I won by a margin of 58 percent to Romney's 41 percent.

The next morning, Vicki and I woke up early to meet commuters coming in to Park Street Station in Boston. We just wanted to say thank you. The results around the country had not been so positive. Close friends and colleagues of mine had lost their seats in a Republican tsunami. But thanks to the people of Massachusetts, I was going back to Washington.

A lot of people have asked me since then whether the Romney race was my most difficult. It wasn't. It was competitive, clearly the most competitive since Eddie McCormack. But it wasn't *difficult* because I knew where I stood. I knew what I believed. I knew what I needed to do. And I was determined to do what I needed to do in terms of the hard campaigning, but not to trim down my positions and beliefs, even if they seemed out of favor that year. At the end of the day, I was running to do something I cared about that would make a difference in people's lives, not just to hold an office. And I was sharing the campaign with Vicki, the love of my life and my soul mate.

I also felt that I benefited from the good memories that many people in the state, particularly in Boston, still had of Grampa Fitzgerald and my mother. Both Grampa and my mother loved the personal side of politics, and their connections to the people ran deep. In 1994, my 104-year-old mother was still a presence, if not in the public square anymore, certainly in the public's heart. At the same time, the people of my state revered the memory of President Kennedy, their native son, and they remembered Bobby. I recognized that I stood on the shoulders of all of them, and that I had benefited from the goodwill that they enjoyed.

We had a joyful Thanksgiving celebration that year. As always, we gathered at our home in Hyannis Port. We had two wonderful new additions at the Thanksgiving table that year: Kiley Elizabeth Kennedy, the three-month-old daughter of my son Teddy and his wife, Kiki; and Grace Kennedy Allen, the two-month-old daughter of my daughter Kara and her husband, Michael. Joined by my mother, we were four generations of Kennedys gathered around the dinner table in the home that has always been such a refuge for me. I was a very happy man.

The next evening, the celebration continued, and in addition to our children, we were joined for dinner by Vicki's parents, Paul and Gail Kirk, and Eddy and Marge Martin. Vicki had prepared her usual post-Thanksgiving fare—turkey gumbo, in honor of her Louisiana roots, and turkey tetrazzini, which was a favorite of Michael Allen's—and wine was flowing as everyone was toasting me and congratulating me on the win. I don't like attention directed to me in that way, as loving as it was, so I stood up and began, "Well, this victory really isn't about me. It's about my family, and it's about the people of Massachusetts and their residual goodwill that goes all the way back to Grampa's day—"

Suddenly, Vicki was on her feet, cutting me off. *"Please excuse my language, but BULLSHIT!"*

That got everyone's attention. She went on, "This is just ridiculous!" She paused to let that sink in, and I stared back at her. Then she said, "You know, Teddy, if you had lost, it would've been *you* that lost. It wouldn't have been your family that lost. *You* would've lost.

"You *won*. *You* won! Not your family. *You*."

She sat down again.

Her outburst lingered in the air. It has lingered in my mind ever since. I'm grateful to her for it. Her message to me was one I needed to hear—perhaps one I'd yearned to hear.

CHAPTER TWENTY-THREE

The Clinton Years
1992–2000

Prior to his election to the presidency in 1992, I didn't really know Bill Clinton. I had met him briefly at the midterm convention in Memphis in 1978, and years later at the funeral of a mutual friend. He had that southern gift of storytelling that kept everyone around him engaged. He didn't forget a name. He loved people. He was a natural politician. After his victory, we established a warm personal relationship. I had longed for a return to a progressive national agenda and was thrilled to see a Democrat back in the White House.

A month after his victory, Vicki and I were invited to a dinner in honor of the Clintons at the home of Katharine Graham. It was a hopeful time and there was much talk of the new agenda. President-elect Clinton said that if he didn't get national health insurance through Congress, he should not be president. Hillary invoked the possibility of tax deductions for educational training programs. Senator Sam Nunn suggested we try a pilot program on national service.

Shortly before his inauguration, the president-elect endeared himself to my extended family when he asked us to accompany him to Arlington Cemetery to visit my brothers' gravesites. About a year later, President Clinton joined us at the rededication of the John F. Kennedy Library in Boston. I had heard and relished the story he often told of having been inspired to enter politics after meeting Jack at the White House in 1963, as a Boys Nation "senator." As we walked through the library together, he was fascinated and wanted to take his time on the tour. He seemed most moved by the Cuban Missile Crisis film, where he sat next to Jackie and asked questions about Jack's mood during that period. He was particularly interested in the civil rights exhibit, referring to the historic integration of Little Rock, Arkansas. We agreed about how slow progress had been, and how quickly both younger and older generations seemed to have forgotten the struggle that took place.

When we reached the exhibit on the Nixon-Kennedy debate, I asked him how he had felt during his first debate with President George H. W. Bush. Nervous at the start, he said, but then it was like an out-of-body experience: you had to respond to the question and answer it, but you also had to be thinking how it would stack up in terms of the total TV performance. He said he was sure President Kennedy had felt that way too.

I'll never forget one of my first meetings with Clinton at the White House. He had walked into a firestorm over the question of whether gays should be allowed to serve in the military. (I always thought that if he had laid the groundwork in the right way, he could have changed the policy with the support of the military, and all of the brouhaha would have died down. After all, no less a conservative icon than the retired senator Barry Goldwater fully supported the repeal of the ban on gays in the military at this juncture.) He'd invited all the Democratic members of the Armed Services Committee to this gathering. He went around the room, asking everyone's opinion about gays in the military. Some senators gave long answers. Some were terse. Some were flowery and revealing, and others held their cards close to their vest. It added up to a very lengthy meeting.

I remember it well partly because Vicki and I had tickets to the ballet that night. Baryshnikov was dancing at the Warner Theatre. I'd told Vicki to go ahead and that I'd meet her there when I could. But the meeting went on and on and on, for more than two hours—extraordinary by White House standards. Finally, my turn to speak came. I made a brief comment in support of allowing gays in the military, in which I mentioned that all the arguments against such a policy had already been made—in opposition to blacks, and then to women, serving in an integrated military.

Well, I was wrong about that. *Almost* all the arguments had been used before. The last senator to speak was Robert Byrd, and he came up with a new one on all of us. Senator Byrd stood up and declared to the president in emotional tones that except for his relationship with his wife, his most sacred possession and thought in this world was his grandson. And that he would never, never, never, ever, *ever* let his grandson go off to the military if we were going to have gays there. And then the senator went off into a long story about Tiberius.

He informed us, with many ornate flourishes, that there had been a terrible problem in ancient Rome with young military boys being turned into sex slaves. I don't remember the exact details, but I think the story involved Tiberius Julius Caesar being captured and abused and used as a sex slave. He escaped and then years later he sought vengeance and killed his captors. Anyway, it was something like that.

The room fell silent. The senator continued. (By this time, Baryshnikov was leaping and a lot of the Democratic senators were stealing glances at their wristwatches.) Then President Clinton stood up.

His response was short and sweet. "Well," he said, "Moses went up to the mountain, and he came back with the tablets and there were ten commandments on those tablets. I've read those commandments. I know what they say, just like I know you do. And nowhere in those ten commandments will you find anything about homosexuality. Thank y'all for coming." He ended the meeting and walked out of the room.

Vicki's foot was tapping when I finally rushed into our box and took my seat next to her at the ballet. "Tiberius. Tiberius. Tiberius," I whispered into her ear. "Write it down. I'll tell you more at intermission, but just remember *Tiberius*."

That incident was probably the beginning of Bill Clinton's education on Robert Byrd. He was the president of the United States, though he'd only been president less than a month, and here he was being lectured to like a student. But that was not what mattered to him. Clinton was watching us, and he could see that none of us was interrupting the senator, and no one was leaving. Everybody was sitting there, paying deference to Byrd.

That said something to Clinton. He realized then that Byrd had power. He was learning a lesson about how the Senate works. I think Clinton never forgot it, because when the most devastating crisis of his presidency erupted a few years later, Robert Byrd was among those whom Clinton thought of first.

The most important single promise that Bill Clinton brought with him to the White House, from my perspective at least, was that his administration would, once and for all, reform American health care. Clinton had campaigned on the critical need for national health insurance legislation, and Americans seemed to agree. Two-thirds of them supported the idea of major reforms in health care.

I looked forward to working with him, not only in solving the insurance imbalance, but in fundamentally overhauling the entire costly, inefficient, and unfair system: the massive amalgam of doctors, hospitals, drug companies, insurers, health maintenance organizations, and governmental agencies.

I'd remained active in as many health care initiatives as possible in the years leading up to Clinton's election, enjoying some successes and the usual run of disappointments. Getting the Americans with Disabilities Act pushed through under George H. W. Bush was an accomplishment to savor. Yet other good ideas remained non-starters after months of partisan infighting and exhaustive committee work. I was dismayed by the lack of support accorded the eminently simple and reasonable "play or pay" concept that came out of the Bipartisan Commission on Comprehensive Health Care. Under it, companies would have been required either to provide affordable health insurance to their workers or else pay into a federal fund for the uninsured. The Gulf War of 1990 siphoned off the attention being paid to that idea, and it failed to receive legislative action.

I recommended "play or pay" to President Clinton shortly after his inauguration. I'd hoped that the Democrats could combine it with the moderate Republican John Chafee's bill, which aimed at universal coverage via mandating uninsured individuals to buy insurance from private carriers. Tax deductions and subsidies would make it possible for them to do so. Bob Dole and several other prominent Republicans supported Chafee's bill. But Clinton did not immediately endorse a specific plan.

In January 1993, I began to understand the reason. Word spread through the Senate that the president intended to name Hillary as head of a task force charged with creating a sweeping health care reform bill in one hundred days, from within the purview of the White House. The idea at first seemed thrilling, perhaps even revolutionary. For the first time since the Truman administration, a president was going to battle against a cruelly broken system that perpetuated American suffering and poverty on a needlessly vast scale.

It would not be easy, of course, because all the familiar political enemies of reform were running up all the tattered flags of dissent: health reform would lead to socialized medicine; it would stunt medical research; it would add bureaucracy and limit patient choice. They were aligned with extremely powerful and dedicated groups—the pharmaceutical companies, the insurance companies, the American Medical Association—determined to protect their interests.

I offered the resources of my staff and myself to the First Lady and her people. Dan Rostenkowski, the House Ways and Means chairman from Illinois, was far more cautious, and more prescient, as he later recounted in a lengthy interview.

President Clinton telephoned the Democratic congressman to ask, "Danny, what do you think of me making Hillary the head of this group?" Rostenkowski reports that he shot back, "Bill, I didn't know you disliked her that much." Clinton asked what he meant. "You know, you're not in

Arkansas anymore," the congressman reminded him. "You're going against probably the most talented group of lobbyists and trade association people in the country. This is their *job*. You're not going to be able to tell them, 'Well, here's a job for your cousin and I want you to support me.' These people are here, and this is a lifestyle for them."

Rostenkowski (who favored health care reform) then raised another tough line of objection: "The people you're talking about putting together on this issue, Bill—did any of them ever run for sheriff? Did they ever get any dirt underneath their fingernails? Did they ever do anything in their communities for health care, or in the Washington area? You're getting academicians who like to sit back and smoke their pipes and say, Oh, this is the way it should be. That's not the way it is in real life. And you should know this, for God's sake. You're a politician!"

And Clinton, in Rostenkowski's accounting, came back with, "Well, you know, I would love to name Hillary."

He did, which I felt was a bold statement of commitment by the president. He would not have appointed his wife to head a task force if he weren't serious about the issue. In terms of vision, Hillary Clinton performed admirably. But the process clearly got bogged down—and became very complicated.

In March 1993 I tried to move things along by proposing that we include health care as part of the budget reconciliation process. There, it would need only fifty votes to pass, and would not be subject to a filibuster and thus a sixty-vote threshold for passage. With President Clinton's approval, I approached Bob Byrd, to see whether he would agree to waive the "Byrd rule" and allow the measure to go forward. The Byrd rule prohibits the Senate from considering extraneous matter as part of a reconciliation bill debate.

Byrd turned me down.

Public opinion was shifting against the administration's great undertaking. By the time the plan was formally presented in the fall, the task force had dissolved. President Clinton himself had read the signs of disaster and backed away from it, choosing to emphasize his economic program and, later, the North American Free Trade Agreement instead.

I was not ready to abandon the fight. I wanted to get a health reform bill, even a compromise bill, to Congress for a vote in September 1994. A few other Democrats, notably Tom Daschle, didn't want to give up either.

The road got rougher in early 1994. Republicans managed to exploit Whitewater, the overblown and eventually discredited real estate "scandal" laid at Hillary Clinton's doorstep, for its value in undercutting the public's trust in Hillary and her plan. The task force lost a powerful ally when Dan Rostenkowski was indicted on charges of conspiracy to defraud the federal government and was obliged to resign his position. Hard-line conservatives increased their pressure on moderate Republicans, such as Bob Dole, who had indicated an interest in a compromise bill. These moderates were branded by the far right in news interviews as not being "true believers." Dole himself was warned that his own presidential ambitions in 1994 rested on his willingness to abandon a compromise bill.

In June, I steered my Labor and Human Resources Committee to approval of a reform draft similar to the Clinton plan. It faced opposition not only from Republicans, but from members of my own party such as Daniel Moynihan, who'd succumbed to the belief that only strong Republican support would save the day. Moynihan introduced his own bill, whose centrist provisions he hoped he could merge with Dole's.

The air filled now with contending voices. Bill and Hillary exhorted top White House staffers to keep pressing congressmen for positive action; Hillary summoned leaders from groups that until recently had been allies and demanded that they reenergize themselves, stop their internal bickering, and unite behind the goal of universal coverage. Such groups were running short of money.

Well-intentioned alternative efforts began to fade. John Dingell gave up his efforts to get a bill out of his Energy and Commerce Committee. Dole, hearing the warnings from the right, outflanked his would-be Democratic partner Moynihan by introducing a bill made meaningless by its incrementalism: its silence, for instance, on such essentials as price controls, employer or individual mandates, and premium caps. Business lobbies and the Republican National Committee, naturally, loved it. Moynihan watched his own tepid effort get dismantled in committee.

George Mitchell, the Senate majority leader, made a "rescue" bid of his own in July for salvaging health care, and even turned down President Clinton's offer of a Supreme Court appointment to continue his fight. House majority leader Dick Gephardt at the same time started work on his own bill.

In late July the Republican right abandoned all pretense and acknowledged bluntly the real motive for its relentless crusade against a health care bill. Newt Gingrich, his power and ambitions on the rise, frankly told the *New York Times* that the House Republicans were going to use opposition to the bill as a springboard to win Republican control of the House in the November elections. Less than a month later, abetted by Phil Gramm of Texas, Gingrich made similar use of the president's crime bill, attacking it. His nakedly obvious purpose was to further tie up Congress in paralyzing debate and controversy before adjournment, and thus delay a vote on health care and the accountability such a vote would demand of each congressman before the fall elections.

I could see that we were running out of time. I remained stubbornly committed to persevering on to the end. I wanted that vote. I wanted to put every member of the Senate and the House on record as being for or against health reform, before we adjourned. Now committee jurisdictional battles raged, and further impeded the momentum necessary to salvage this most urgent of social reform causes.

By mid-August, defections from the ranks and gestures of defeat by Democrats were beginning to do the work of the Republicans for them. Many in my party conceded publicly that health care would be delayed indefinitely. Among those holding fast with me was Mitchell, who on August 15 threatened to keep the Senate in round-the-clock session until the Republicans agreed to vote. I was white-hot now for continuing the pushback against the obstructionists, and I let it show at a leadership luncheon on August 18, when I got into a shouting match with Bob Kerrey of Nebraska over whether the debate over health care should be continued. (There was never a problem between Bob and me. Emotions were just running high.)

But it was slipping away. I could feel it. The schedule was running against us. We lost on the schedule. We gave up, in fact. I recall my exasperation when Democrats were told on a Thursday afternoon that we wouldn't work through the weekend.

Well, you *have* to keep your people around if you want to win. The Senate is a chemical place. Something happens when senators are all in the room, debating an issue, especially when everyone understands that we are going to stay in and not adjourn until we get things done. I had talked to a number of my colleagues who agreed to stay. We had the headcount. We could have held the vote and at least put everybody on the public record as to whether or not they supported health care reform. But we didn't do that. If we'd stayed there, we'd have caught the attention and perhaps the conscience of other senators. If we'd stayed there, we'd have had all the newspapers in the country writing about it. If we'd stayed, we'd have had people all over the country asking why, why, *why* are they doing this? And then maybe we'd have had them thinking again about the whole issue, the whole value, of health care reform. Thinking about what it was that we senators believed in enough to be staying all night for.

In a private meeting, I told the Senate leadership that this was a complete abdication (along with some other less elevated words). I'm told that I was in what Vicki would call my "red-faced and full-throated" mode.

I left the meeting and closed the door. But I didn't slam it. I didn't close it all the way. Because I knew I would be back.

The 1994 midterm elections were as disastrous as any Democrat expected, if not worse. Many party stalwarts were turned out of office: Tom Foley, Jim Sasser, Jack Brooks, and New York governor Mario Cuomo. A conviction took hold that the electorate had embraced the conservative cause. This became a settled truth for many pundits, other opinion-makers, and, sadly, for many Democratic leaders as well.

I never accepted this. The Democratic *Party* may have lurched to the right in response to the elections. The Democratic Leadership Council and, I feared, President Clinton were moving in that direction. But I believed they were chasing a phantom. As I'd put it in remarks to the National Press Club on January 11, "If the Democrats run for cover, if we become pale carbon copies of the opposition, we will lose—and deserve to lose." Republicans had made gains by depressing voter turnout. They hadn't won a mandate. They'd gained control of Congress by the narrowest of margins.

I had a couple of telephone conversations with President Clinton after the midterm elections. He said he was "bone tired" from being on the campaign trail in the immediate aftermath of a demanding trip to the Middle East. He believed the National Rifle Association had murdered him in the South by making guns a cultural rather than a law enforcement issue. I mentioned that I thought we had more Democrats voting in the election nationwide, but President Clinton corrected me and said, "No—one percent more Republicans."

I made the case that he would be effective as an underdog and that we could still get some major legislation passed—on health care and student aid for education and job retraining and cuts in corporate subsidies. Then we made a bet on the upcoming basketball game between the University of Massachusetts and the University of Arkansas—a bushel of bay scallops to a bushel of barbecued chicken.

Meanwhile, I continued my advocacy for an increase in the minimum wage. To some extent, the president agreed, supporting the increase in his State of the Union address. But other persuasive voices also had access to the president's ear; people such as his adviser Dick Morris. It was thanks in large part to Morris and his concept of "triangulation," or gaining the large, safe middle ground by co-opting ideas from both the left and the right, that Clinton began his move toward the center.

While I did not agree with all of President Clinton's concessions, I found much to admire in his presidency. I am especially proud of the effort we shared in bringing peace to Northern Ireland.

This historic healing required the courage and cooperation of many men and women, of course—Irish, British, and American. Among those who distinguished themselves was my sister Jean Kennedy Smith, who in 1993 stepped gracefully from a life of quiet good works into the world of diplomacy.

My sister Jean and I have always had a special relationship. We are closest in age of all of my siblings. When we were growing up, she was my partner at the small table in the dining room for more years than she would have liked, and she was my companion during those winter school terms in Palm Beach. In later years, we spent much time together. I was extraordinarily close to her husband, Steve, as well, and we all took ski vacations together and enjoyed each other's company enormously.

In 1974, Jean had founded Very Special Arts, now VSA Arts, a non-profit organization that allowed people with disabilities to participate in and enjoy the arts. She has expanded the organization to include affiliates in more than sixty countries, including Ireland.

At my suggestion, President Clinton appointed Jean ambassador to Ireland not long after taking office. Jean's appointment was very well received by the Irish people. In addition to becoming steeped in issues relating to the Republic of Ireland, she had been a well-informed observer of the turmoil in Northern Ireland since the early 1970s, and had gained the respect both of the Irish people and political leaders, including my friend John Hume. She performed admirably in her confirmation hearings and took up her duties in Dublin. One of Jean's first and most significant accomplishments was to persuade me to support the issuance of a U.S. visa for Gerry Adams, the head of Sinn Fein, the political arm of the IRA.

Jean was convinced that Adams no longer believed that continuing the armed struggle was the way to achieve the IRA's objective of a united Ireland. He was in fact working to convince the IRA's more aggressive members to end the violence and pursue the political path. Most convincingly, Adams had held a series of conversations with John Hume that led Hume to believe a cease-fire and negotiations could soon be achieved.

The State Department refused Adams a visa in March 1993, but in mid-December that year the British prime minister John Major and the new taoiseach (head of state), Albert Reynolds, raised hopes significantly when they issued their joint declaration affirming Northern Ireland's right of self-determination.

Two weeks after the joint declaration, Vicki and I visited Jean in Dublin over the Christmas holidays. It took only a couple hours' conversation with Jean after we landed to discover what was really the most important thing on her mind: the opportunity for a breakthrough in the Northern Ireland stalemate, which she believed depended on a visa for Gerry Adams to visit the United States so that he could bring along those Irish Americans who had, for years, been sending guns and money to the IRA. When I met later on that trip with Albert Reynolds, he was passionate, thoughtful, and brilliantly informed, and quickly reinforced Jean's instinct that this was the right moment to act. He told me he was convinced to a moral certainty that Adams was now an advocate for a peaceful resolution. I returned to the United States primed to do all in my power to help move their hopes to diplomatic reality.

The occasion for commencing my efforts was a sad one: the funeral of Tip O'Neill. Tip had died on January 5 at age eighty-one. The retired Speaker of the House was unquestionably one of the towering American figures of his time, a generous and wise man, and a friend and a political ally.

Tip was an important force in the long struggle to spur the United States to involvement in Northern Ireland. His funeral was held at St. John the Evangelist's Church in what had been a working-class Irish neighborhood of North Cambridge in which Tip grew up. Among the seventeen hundred people present on the freezing day of January 10 were a few players in the peace process who'd flown over from Ireland to pay their last respects. It was almost as if Tip were calling down to us: "C'mon, fellas! I've done everything I could. Now finish the job!"

I had dinner that night with one of the best of them, John Hume. (I took John to a place that would appeal to his Irishman's sense of fine irony, Locke-Ober's, the elegant redoubt of the Protestant Brahmins for more than a century.) New York businessman Bill Flynn, chairman of the National Committee on American Foreign Policy, had already done his part to force the Gerry Adams issue by offering the Sinn Fein leader an invitation to speak in New York at the end of the month. Now Hume told me at dinner that the IRA had split over whether to accept the joint declaration, and that a visa for Adams would help him win that internal debate.

I drafted a letter to President Clinton that laid out a list of reasons in favor of granting the visa. Adams could be a critical player in the process, I told the president. The momentum of hope was increasing via the Hume-Adams dialogue and the joint declaration and the British government's activity in talking directly to IRA members. Even should Adams fail to deliver, the visa was a one-time proposition, and the prospect of peace made it well worth the risk. Clinton himself had just established a precedent of sorts: he had met with President Assad of Syria, who in 1982 had 20,000 of his own countrymen killed. Finally, if we refused granting the visa and the fragile peace effort should fall through, America would be blamed for not doing its share.

Even if Clinton went along with my request, I knew that resistance would be strong from both the State Department, which was locked into a view of Adams as a terrorist, and the British embassy, which resented U.S. involvement in what it considered its home affairs. To counter this opposition and bolster Clinton's resolve, my staff and I rounded up as many signatures from senators and congressmen as we could. Eventually more than fifty signed up with us, including such influential figures as Daniel Moynihan, Chris Dodd, George Mitchell, Claiborne Pell, and Bill Bradley. I personally contacted Vice President Gore, Secretary of State

Leaving the JFK Library in the snow
with Vicki, March 21, 1992.
George Rizer/Boston Globe/Landov

Wedding photo,
July 3, 1992.
Denis Reggie

With Nelson Mandela,
deputy president of the
African National Congress,
at a rally in his honor
at the Esplanade in Boston
before a crowd of more than
200,000 people, June 25, 1990.
AP Photo

With Sinn Fein leader Gerry Adams, center, and Sen. Christopher Dodd (D-Conn.), talking to reporters on Capitol Hill, September 3, 1997.
Dennis Cook /AP Photo

Waving to a crowd gathered in Menemsha Harbor aboard the yacht *Relemar* with President Bill Clinton, Vicki, Caroline Kennedy, Ed Schlossberg, First Lady Hillary Clinton, Vernon Jordan, and Chelsea Clinton, August 1993.
Win McNamee/Reuters

At the wedding of John Kennedy and Carolyn Bessette.
Denis Reggie

Little Teddy, winner of Most Improved Sailor award.

With grandkids Grace, Kiley, Ted and Max, Summer 2006.

The Daily Show with Jon Stewart, April 20, 2006.
Stuart Ramson/AP Photo

Dressed as The Grinch for the office Christmas party.

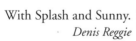

With Splash and Sunny.
Denis Reggie

"Daffodils," a painting I made for Vicki.

At the beach. BACK ROW: Caroline, Vicki, Grace, Kara, Patrick, me, Teddy Jr., and Curran. FRONT ROW: Max, Teddy, Kiki, and Kiley.
Tom Fitzsimmons

Surrounded by family at Massachusetts General Hospital in Boston, 2008: Patrick, Curran, Teddy Jr., Kara, Vicki, and Caroline.
AP Photo

The 2008 Democratic National Convention in Denver, Colorado, August 25, 2008.
Stephen Crowley/The New York Times/Redux

My birthday celebration at the Kennedy Center, March 8, 2009. President Obama
joins host Bill Cosby, Frederica von Stade, Lizz Wright, Denyce Graves, and
James Taylor onstage to sing "Happy Birthday."
Chris Usher/UPI/Landov

With Michelle Obama at the Kennedy Center birthday celebration.
Margot Schulman

The Figawi Race: Karl Anderson, EMK Jr., David Nunes, Patrick, me, John Strachan, Kiki, Sen. Chris Dodd, and Vicki.

Throwing out the
ceremonial first pitch
on Opening Day
at Fenway Park
in Boston,
April 7, 2009.
*Elise Amendola /AP
Photo*

Discussing the signing of the Edward M. Kennedy Serve America Act,
with President Obama, former President Bill Clinton,
and Vice President Joe Biden in the Oval Office, April 21, 2009.
Brooks Kraft/Corbis

On the grounds
of the White House,
April 21, 2009.
Pete Souza/MAI /Landov

Warren Christopher, and National Security Adviser Anthony Lake. Other allies telephoned still other White House figures.

We were going up against powerful institutions skilled in the many ways of derailing initiatives they didn't like. On January 26, the day after Chris Dodd and I narrowly averted a White House denial of the visa by personally speaking with chief of staff Mac MacLarty and foreign policy adviser Sandy Berger, the State Department sent a challenge to Gerry Adams in Belfast: a demand for two assurances that the department clearly believed Adams would reject. One was that Adams personally renounce violence and assure that he was committed to working toward that end. The other was that Sinn Fein and the IRA were committed to ending the conflict on the basis of the joint declaration.

And yet Adams did attempt to satisfy the spirit of these demands. Through a back channel that included my foreign policy adviser, Trina Vargo, and Irish-American newspaper publisher Niall O'Dowd, Adams replied that he *wanted* to see an end to all violence, and that it was his priority to forge an end to armed actions and build the peace process. As for Sinn Fein, Adams said, it had moved under his leadership toward the same direction, in the framework of the Hume-Adams initiative. He was prepared, he affirmed, to go the extra mile.

The next day I called Jean in Dublin. She told me that the Consul General in Belfast, Val Martinez, had just finished interviewing Adams, who'd consented to come there for the meeting, and that as the Sinn Fein leader was walking out the door, the diplomat said to him, "In my opinion, there is no way you will get the visa."

"Well, you know," I said to Jean in the most somber of tones, "if that is the decision, you will have to resign your ambassadorship."

She picked up on the joke at once. "No way," she shot back. "I'm having too much fun."

I called up Anthony Lake at the White House. Their conditions were ridiculous, I told him. I promised him that my alternative would be to add language to the State Department authorization bill, then being debated on the floor of the Senate, saying the Adams visa should be granted. Lake urged me not to do that. I told him that the visa was a hot-button issue, ten times more important than Irish immigration.

Then I worked the telephones one more time: Al Gore. Mac MacLarty again. Attorney General Janet Reno, whom I could not reach. I phoned up certain key allies and emphasized the need for them to keep up the pressure.

On the following day, January 29, just as the White House seemed on the verge of granting our wish, I learned, confidentially, that hand grenades had turned up in San Diego. Each one had a note affixed, demanding a visa for Adams.

The news would inevitably go public. The White House, aware of it, was preparing three new demands for Adams: denounce the grenades in San Diego, condemn attacks on innocent civilians, and also condemn a recent bombing on Oxford Street in London. I let the White House know that Adams was a serious man and a key to Northern Ireland peace, and it would embarrass and insult him if we went back to him yet again. The White House agreed, and Adams himself consented to condemn the violent incidents if asked by the press.

His visa was granted the next day. The easy work was over. Now we waited seven months until the IRA declared a full cease-fire, and the long negotiations toward peace finally began. On Good Friday, April 10, 1998, representatives from the British and Irish governments and the political leaders of Northern Ireland met in Belfast to sign what became known as the Belfast, or Good Friday, Agreement, which was soon approved in a referendum by the people of Ireland and Northern Ireland.

President Clinton, meanwhile, was finding himself progressively mired in a series of rumors, charges, and investigations that went on and on before yielding nothing.

Vicki and I were watching television on the morning in January 1998 when the Monica Lewinsky story broke. Vicki turned to me at that moment and said, "If this is true, they are going to try to impeach him." I don't think either of us really believed that would happen, but the mood was so poisonous, anything was possible. On August 15, Clinton testified to a grand jury called by the independent counsel Kenneth Starr. On that same evening, he went on television and admitted that he'd had "an inappropriate relationship" with Lewinsky. He called the affair "a personal failure on my part, for which I'm solely responsible." I telephoned the president immediately after his appearance to tell him he could count on my support; that I was standing by to help him through whatever may come. I wanted to support the president—and perhaps, even more, the presidency, which had been under assault almost from the moment he took office. I felt that this kind of attempt to delegitimize a president was dangerous for our democracy.

I should pause here a moment and make clear my feelings about the right to scrutinize public officials.

Do I think such inquiry is fair? Absolutely. But do I think it tells the whole story of character? No, I truly do not. Human beings are much more complex than that. Some people make mistakes and try to learn from them and do better. Our sins don't define the whole picture of who we are.

At any rate, the larger reason for my decision to support the president was this: impeachment talk was indeed in the air. And I could not accept that Clinton's involvement with Lewinsky, or even his doomed attempt at "cover-up," was sufficient reason for impeachment. I'd had lunch around that time with Samuel Beer, who'd been a teacher of mine at Harvard. Sam was an expert on the Constitution and on impeachment law, and how it had developed from the British system. He went all the way back into the twelfth century at that lunch, establishing the parameters of the law that the Founding Fathers had used as their model. Clearly, he declared to me, nothing in this tradition covered personal conduct. It dealt entirely with the abuse of public power in the presidential office. Sam reinforced my belief that this was not an impeachable offense—nor even one meriting censure.

On August 24, Clinton came up to Worcester for a political appearance, and Vicki and I met him there. I showed him a Lou Harris poll indicating that the public's attitude toward the Lewinsky matter had not changed since it first surfaced six months earlier. Fifty-five percent of those interviewed believed there had been an affair; 77 percent believed that Congress should stay focused on the country rather than the president's private life; but 35 percent said that if Clinton had lied about it, he should resign.

Vicki and I were impressed with Clinton's demeanor at Worcester. He was functioning on all cylinders, focused on policy, talking about getting things done. He discussed his recent meetings with Boris Yeltsin and analyzed various races coming up around the country. He had a great deal of support in Worcester, and he was feeding off the energy of the crowds, enjoying his rapport with the people, who obviously felt a deep connection to him. In fact, I remember thinking that the president may have been a bit in denial, not quite ready to deal yet with the depth of his problem and the direction in which things were moving. But his magnetism was still powerful, and its effect extended beyond ordinary voters. John Kerry joined us and several others for lunch, during which the president— after downing his submarine sandwich and fries—sort of polled us informally: "What do you guys want me to do? What do you think?" When he got to Kerry, John seemed that he might have something more to say. But he finally said something like, "Focus on a message and a limited number of issues."

When I asked the president at dinner what I could do to help him, he asked me to talk to Robert Byrd. It was a smart request. The president had indeed learned an important lesson or two while listening to Byrd's peculiar homily about Tiberius being a sex slave. He appreciated the extent of Byrd's influence and understood his strict, old-fashioned code of morality.

There was in fact a great deal of speculation about where Byrd stood on the question of impeaching Bill Clinton. The West Virginia senator was nearly eighty-one then, but still a powerful figure. In fact, some of his greatest days still lay ahead, with his eloquent and passionate stand against

George W. Bush's authorization of the Iraq war on the grounds that Bush ignored the constitutional role of the Senate in the matter. Byrd was recognized as the guardian of the Senate as an institution. If it turned out that he believed Clinton should resign or be impeached on constitutional grounds, that would make a huge difference in Clinton's fortunes. And Clinton knew it.

I went to see Byrd at his office in Washington and spoke with him at length about the role of the Senate in this constitutional challenge. I suggested that we needed to proceed in a way that would enhance the American people's view of the Senate, and that this might be done by our remaining above the battle; to concentrate more on establishing the framework for any possible action than on being out front with an opinion. I believe that Senator Byrd welcomed this discussion. He held his fire for the time being, which served everyone's interest.

Nevertheless, after the House Judiciary Committee made public the details of Ken Starr's report, the House voted 258 to 176, with thirty-one Democrats in favor, to authorize the Judiciary Committee to conduct an impeachment investigation.

The midterm elections on November 4 gave a boost to the president's prospects. Against expectations, Democrats gained five seats in the House, and Republican senators Al D'Amato of New York and Lauch Faircloth of North Carolina were defeated. The opinion polls showed that the Republicans' losses were tied to a growing disapproval among the public for impeachment. Two days later Newt Gingrich announced his retirement as Speaker of the House. He'd been among the most aggressive advocates for Clinton's removal.

On the same day of Newt's announcement, nearly nine hundred legal scholars and historians issued a statement declaring that the charges against Clinton did not rise to the level of impeachable offenses—a statement that powerfully buttressed my own efforts to head off this action. Even the influential Pennsylvania Republican Arlen Specter went on record saying the impeachment effort should stop, and that Clinton should answer instead to the criminal justice system at the end of his term. House Judiciary chairman Henry Hyde, reading the prevailing mood, quickly moved to scale back his hearings to one witness, Starr, as a concession to the public's wish for a quick resolution. At the end of November, President Clinton reluctantly let it be known that he would be receptive to the idea of censure and a large fine.

On December 4, Byrd rejected the idea of censure—but only to declare that if the House voted impeachment, the Senate must hold a trial, on pain of "shirking its duty" under the Constitution. Censure, Byrd said, should be considered only when impeachment had run its course.

Clinton's mood seemed privately to plummet during this period. But even as he finally accepted that his presidency was imperiled, he still didn't seem able to confront the ultimate cause. In telephone conversations with him, I sensed that this was not yet a place he could go: the awareness that his affair with Monica Lewinsky had deeply disturbed and disheartened people. And that perhaps they were even more disturbed that he had lied about it to his wife and the members of his cabinet and allowed them to be humiliated by publicly defending a falsehood. In his mind, it continued to be all about the Republicans, what they were doing to him, not what he had done.

I continued to be supportive. I met with him nearly every day as 1998 wound down. I was there for him in mid-December, when the Judiciary Committee rejected censure and voted for impeachment along party lines. I was there for him when the House Republican leaders called on him to resign and spare the country an ordeal. I spoke with him several times on the phone—he usually called late at night—as we pursued a plan developed by John Breaux of Louisiana to find thirty-five senators, one more than was necessary to acquit in a trial, to sign a letter saying they agreed with those legal scholars and historians who found the charges unimpeachable. Clinton brightened at this idea, saying that it would put him "back in the driver's seat" while a lesser punishment was worked out. In any event, I could find only fifteen or sixteen senators willing to sign, and learned from Tom Daschle that not even thirty-five would be enough to ward off a trial; at least fifty-one would be needed.

When Byrd learned about this proposed letter, he got angry. He went to the Senate floor and admonished, "Mr. President, do not tamper with this jury!"

Clinton did not seem to hear this. He remained fixated on getting the Democratic senators to sign a letter. "If we let Bob Byrd have his way on this procedure, they'll stay after it until my numbers go down," he told me. "Once that letter is out, from that time on, I can be president. I can't be president without that being out there." He talked about a lynch mob. He said, "I feel strongly about this. If they force me to resign, this is the end of the Democrats. Of course I'm not going to resign."

Then Bill Clinton asked me to say that the president must not resign. He had to deal with Iraq, he pointed out. "Every important decision I make will be second-guessed. They want to hound me out of office, drive my numbers down, and then go after the Democrats." He repeated, "This is a lynch mob, and it's out of control."

Less than a week before Christmas, President Clinton's private anguish was affecting his political optimism. Meeting with him at the White House to go over his legislative program for the coming Congress, I learned of a new fear: that Chief Justice Rehnquist, who would preside over the trial, would not give him "a fair shake," as he put it. At the same time, he was fitfully imagining scenarios of regaining his full power and prestige: "If we can get this over by the State of the Union, then I'll make a great State of the Union speech." This, the president believed, would change the mix, halt the drift of his presidency. But these hopeful ideas were interlaced with grim defiance: "We can drag this thing out with process and procedure. They're not going to get rid of me. I'll stay here. I'll never resign. They're never going to get rid of me."

On January 5, 1999, with the trial scheduled to begin in two days, the Senate found itself in the grip of partisanship and the fear of chaos. The future of President Clinton, momentous enough in itself, was now rivaled by an issue of perhaps even greater magnitude: the future of the United States Senate as an institution of unquestioned integrity and authority.

Specifically, the House impeachment managers wanted to call witnesses—as many as twelve of them, by implication including Monica Lewinsky. President Clinton's lawyers insisted on standard pretrial procedures for each witness to ensure preservation of their constitutional rights. This posed the danger of a drawn-out trial that could have paralyzed the government for months. Senators Joe Lieberman of Connecticut and Slade Gorton of Washington floated a compromise idea that would reduce the trial's duration to about a week, limited to presentations by the House managers and the president's lawyers, followed by a test vote to determine whether the sixty-seven votes needed for impeachment existed. Witnesses would be called only if the Senate decided to proceed with the trial. Majority Leader Trent Lott said he personally did not think witnesses necessary, but if the House managers considered them vital, the Senate would have to honor their opinion.

The day before the trial, Democratic senators caucused in the Lyndon Baines Johnson Room in the northeast corner of the Capitol, part of the extension that was built from 1851 to 1859. In that august space, Robert Byrd spoke of the historic nature of what lay immediately before the Senate and the need for all to adhere to the constitutional process so essential to the legitimacy of American tradition. Senator Daschle reported that although Trent Lott supported the Lieberman-Gorton plan, some twenty-two Republicans insisted on the longer proceeding.

After rising to speak, I argued that the entire process had been politicized, and that it was essential to try to restore bipartisanship. Tom Daschle was trying to do this, I pointed out; but if it became clear that the impeachment process was going to be a sham, then the Senate should move toward a test vote as quickly as possible so as not to dignify a partisan process. Then we should move on with the Senate's crowded legislative agenda. The caucus broke up without reaching a decision.

Opening day of Bill Clinton's impeachment trial on January 8 was filled with emotion, as senators, belatedly in some cases, tried to reconcile their partisan passions with an awareness that history had its eye on them. We met in closed session in the Old Supreme Court Chamber, a setting that virtually insisted on dignity and solemnity.

Robert Byrd pushed himself upright to speak first. His manner and words cast a spell that resonated with the surroundings. His heavy-lidded eyes swept over every one of us. With his shock of white hair parted fiercely over his high forehead, his dark suit showing not a wrinkle, and, above all, the bell-chimes of his West Virginia inflections, Byrd seemed to unite the past and the present of our institution.

"The White House has sullied itself," Byrd began. "The House has fallen into the black pit of partisan self-indulgence. The Senate is teetering on the brink." The senator implored his colleagues to "restore some order to the anger which has overtaken this country and the chaos which threatens this city."

Byrd's sense of the moment took hold among the senators. Chris Dodd arose to invoke a famous reminder of what can happen when things get out of control: the legendary Senate floor caning of the Massachusetts senator Charles Sumner by the South Carolina congressman Preston Brooks in 1856.

The next speaker was Phil Gramm of Texas. Gramm was no friend of mine, politically or personally. He had been an effective and destructive opponent of affordable health care and other causes I championed. But in this moment, I heard him quote Daniel Webster: "I wish to speak not as a Massachusetts man, but as an American. . . . I speak for the preservation of the Union. Hear me for my cause."

Gramm sought to close the partisan gap, especially on the critical question of calling witnesses to the impeachment trial. He pointed out that, with the exception of the witness question, there was no significant disagreement among the senators about using the rules of procedure laid down for the only other presidential impeachment trial in American history, that of

Andrew Johnson in 1868. As to witnesses, Gramm declared, it was not necessary to foreclose their use of them in advance: the rules required us to vote *later in the proceedings* on what witnesses, if any, to call.

I saw an opportunity here, and rose to grasp it. "Senator Gramm is right," I declared. "Both sides are willing to begin the trial with evidence based on the public record only, and defer the witness question until later. We're already agreed on how to get to first base and second base. We can see later on how we're going to get to third."

It worked. The novelty of me and Phil Gramm coming together on *any* issue cleared the air of partisanship, at least for a time. "Stranger things have happened in politics," John McCain remarked later, "but the Kennedy-Gramm alignment was one of the strangest." The caucus instructed Gramm and me and a handful of other senators to draw up a resolution on the initial procedure. The Senate approved our resolution unanimously.

Over four days beginning January 31, the Senate questioned Monica Lewinsky and Clinton advisers Vernon Jordan and Sidney Blumenthal in closed-door depositions. A day after those sessions ended, the Senate voted not to compel Lewinsky to testify in open hearings, but to allow House managers to use parts of her videotaped deposition.

On February 12, President Clinton was acquitted on each of the two articles of impeachment, perjury, and obstruction of justice.

As the Clinton administration entered its final years, the president and I continued to enjoy a good relationship. In the summer of 1997, we went sailing together near Martha's Vineyard. President Clinton took the helm of the boat, even though he'd never sailed before, and steered it into Menemsha Harbor under full sail, not knowing how tricky (and dangerous) it was. We were ready to drop the sails and start the engine if anything went wrong, but the president was a natural.

In 1998, Vicki and I joined the president on Air Force One on a trip to celebrate the seventy-fifth anniversary of *Time* magazine in New York City. The previous night, we'd all attended a benefit for the Kennedy

Library, which prompted Clinton to say to Vicki, "You've had two big nights in a row."

Vicki smiled and said jokingly, "Yes, Mr. President, and they've been with you."

The president laughed and said, "Well, you better be careful, you'll get subpoenaed."

The subject changed to movies. President Clinton had seen every movie nominated that year and offered a detailed opinion of each one. To our amusement, he interpreted *The Full Monty*, a comedy about a group of unemployed British working-class men who become strippers, as a sociological picture that Senator (and former Harvard University sociologist) Daniel Patrick Moynihan would enjoy because it showed how people suffer loss of self-esteem when they lose their jobs.

We fell short of our most ambitious goals during the Clinton years, but we accomplished a lot, including portable health insurance; the largest increase in health insurance for children since the creation of Medicaid; and an increase in the minimum wage.

On January 3, 2000, I met with Vice President Al Gore at his home to indicate my strong support for his candidacy. I was impressed by his positions on health and education and civil rights. I sought his support for a prescription drug benefit for catastrophic cases, which he had been resisting because of its cost. I asked him to advocate the minimum wage on the campaign trail and he agreed it was an important issue. I told him the lines that work best for me in describing it: This is a women's issue because the majority of minimum-wage workers are women. It's a children's issue. It's a civil rights issue. It's a fairness issue. He wrote it all down and, concerned about being accused of plagiarism, asked, "Can I use those?" I told him he was welcome to, and that I'd picked it all up from other sources myself.

He was optimistic about his chances and the future. The economy was benefiting from rapid reductions in the cost of transferring information and knowledge. This information revolution would be a golden opportunity to make progress in universal health and education and civil rights, the whole domestic agenda.

We talked for an hour. He was charming, relaxed, gracious, personable.

He told me, I believe I'm going to win this.

CHAPTER TWENTY-FOUR

The Living Rose
1994–1999

The nineties were a happy time for me, years in which my love for Vicki and my Senate work deepened. Yet it was also a time of loss. I've already described the devastation I felt when Steve Smith died, but we also mourned the passing of four other loves who captivated us and so many others.

On May 19, 1994, dear Jackie—Jacqueline Bouvier Kennedy Onassis—died of cancer, heartbreakingly young at sixty-four.

Jackie and I were always friends, always close. We enjoyed each other's company. I adored John Jr. and Caroline, and she loved and supported my relationship with them.

She always indulged me. I think that if Katie Lynch's Butter Crunch were still on the market, Jackie would have kept me supplied with it. I remember the summer that Vicki and I were reading David McCullough's biography of Harry Truman. I hadn't met David then (we have since become good friends), but I wanted to. I knew he and his wife, Rosalie, lived on the Vineyard, so I asked Jackie if she would invite them to dinner. She did. That's the kind of thing she would do, and she always made me feel that she was doing it joyfully. We all loved the evening, but I don't think anyone had more fun than Jackie.

In composing the eulogy that I offered at the funeral mass for her at the Church of St. Ignatius Loyola in New York four days later, I found myself replicating Jackie's own approach to beautiful things and profound ideas—with simple, unadorned truth:

"She was always there for our family in her special way. She was a blessing to us and to the nation—and a lesson to the world on how to do things right, how to be a mother, how to appreciate history, how to be courageous. No one else looked like her, spoke like her, wrote like her, or was so original in the way she did things. No one we knew ever had a better sense of self.

". . . No one ever gave more meaning to the title of 'First Lady.' The nation's capital city looks as it does because of her. She saved Lafayette Square and Pennsylvania Avenue. The National Cultural Center was her cause before it was the Kennedy Center. Jackie brought the greatest artists to the White House, and brought the arts to the center of national attention. Today, in large part because of her inspiration and vision, the arts are an abiding part of national policy."

I concluded, "She graced our history. And for those of us who knew and loved her—she graced our lives."

My mother's death on January 22, 1995, at home in Hyannis Port came as an even more heartbreaking blow than I could have anticipated. I felt that the legs had been knocked out from under me. She was eulogized at St. Stephen's Roman Catholic Church in Boston's North End, where she had been baptized 104 years earlier, just a little more than half the life span of the nation itself. Bernard Cardinal Law, the archbishop of Boston, celebrated the Mass of Resurrection.

It was not as though I hadn't understood for some time that this was going to happen. Mother had grown enfeebled (in body, but not in spirit) from a series of strokes even before she turned one hundred, and I had visited her at the Cape house nearly every weekend for years. During one of those visits, I pulled a tennis racket out of its cover and started to head out to the court for a few games with someone. Mother was watching me from across the room in her wheelchair. "Are you sure that is yours, Teddy?" she called out. "I've been looking all around the house for mine."

Nor was it that I disbelieved the words in my own eulogy at St. Stephen's: "Mother knew this day was coming, but she did not dread it. She accepted and even welcomed it, not as a leaving, but as a returning. She has gone to God. She is home. And at this moment she is happily presiding at a heavenly table with both of her Joes, with Jack and Kathleen, with Bobby and David." I fervently believed those words at the moment, and I believe them now.

On December 31, 1997, Vicki and I were ringing in the new year by having a quiet dinner at the Washington home of our dear friends Jean and Tim Hanan. Tim and I had gone to law school together and he continued to be among my closest lifelong friends. We received a call that night that my thirty-nine-year-old nephew Michael Kennedy had died in a skiing accident. He was with his three children and some of his siblings on a ski vacation in Aspen, Colorado, when he crashed into a tree.

I had become especially close to Michael during my 1994 campaign, and his death was almost incomprehensible to me. So young, so vital, so bright and talented. Michael was also the best athlete in the entire family, hands down. He could ski like the wind, and so the idea that he was taken from us in a skiing accident just added to my disbelief.

I worried about Ethel. She had already buried Bobby and then young David, whom Bobby had worried about before he was killed. And now Michael, who looked so much like Bobby. I remember being in the car with Michael in the mid-1980s or so, at dusk. The way the shadows fell, Michael's face was in the half-light, and for a few seconds it seemed as if I were looking at Bobby as he was when he was a young man. The resemblance was almost eerie. But Bobby was gone. And now Michael.

July 17, 1999, a Saturday, was marked on the calendar as a day of high celebration for the Kennedy clan. My wonderful niece Rory, an award-winning documentary filmmaker and social activist, and the youngest of

Bobby and Ethel's eleven children, was to marry the writer and editor Mark Bailey in Hyannis Port. On the evening of July 16, John Kennedy Jr., Rory's cousin and my nephew, took off in his small single-engine airplane from Fairfield, New Jersey, en route to the wedding. With him were his wife, Carolyn Bessette Kennedy, and Carolyn's sister Lauren Bessette. John, who had been flying for about a year, had planned to drop Lauren off at Martha's Vineyard and then fly the short hop to Hyannis.

Before the plane reached Martha's Vineyard, it crashed into the Atlantic Ocean, and all three young lives were lost. John was thirty-eight, Carolyn thirty-three, and Lauren thirty-four.

I spoke at John's funeral at the Church of St. Thomas More in Manhattan six days later. "From the first day of his life," I said, "John seemed to belong not only to our family, but to the American family. He had a legacy, and he learned to treasure it. He was part of a legend, and he learned to live with it."

A lot of people have wondered whether John ultimately would have sought public office. I think he might have, and that he would have excelled. John was really ahead of his time in understanding the link between pop culture and politics. He understood that there were different ways to get information to young people, and that the old ways wouldn't work. His easy way with people was already legendary, as was his gift for using language and images to get his message across.

Over the rest of that summer and into the autumn, I distilled my thoughts about my nephew, the meaning of his short life, the meaning of life, the weight of bereavement, and the obligations of the bereaved. On October 6, I shared those thoughts at a Senate prayer breakfast.

This was unusual for me for two reasons. I rarely speak in public on personal matters. It's something my generation was taught not to do.

I also was speaking in a quiet voice, which in itself is a challenge to me. My Republican Senate colleague John Chafee once told me I was "wrong at the top of my lungs." But I wanted to speak in a quiet voice because the louder our voices become, the more we grow strangers to each other and ourselves.

Here's what I told them:

"You know that my family and I have experienced our share of tragedy. We have tried to face that pain, when it has come, with a steadfast religious faith. It has not been a loud and boisterous faith, but it has been a faith of patience, pathos, endurance, and grace.

"I will not try to tell you that that faith has never, at least temporarily, been shaken. When my brother Joe died in World War II, my father sat on the porch in Hyannis Port night after night, looking out to the sea, while listening to classical music. I was young then and I thought he did that because he liked classical music. But of course, I know now that he did it to cope with his grief and to find solace. I know now that in the midst of the hurt, he was searching for God.

"Even my mother, who was the most devout and persistent believer I have ever known, experienced—only once to my knowledge but experienced nonetheless—a moment of what the Christian theologian Soren Kierkegaard called 'fear and trembling,' a moment of despair when, after her third son died, she cried out, 'But how could they have taken the father of ten children?' And what she meant, though she couldn't bring herself to say it aloud, was, 'How could God?'

"Every single one of us, if we are awake to the brokenness of the world and of our lives, wonders at some point, 'How could you allow this, O God? I believe, but help me in my unbelief!' And these questions, this wonder, this pain and this pleading know no bounds of faith—for the simple, hard fact is that God plays no favorites; that we all suffer; that we all die; that, at one time or another, we all shake our fists at God; and that, if we are lucky, we all come home to God in the end. Thomas Carlyle said, 'I had a lifelong quarrel with God, but we made up in the end.'

"The hardest thing for any human being to understand is that God loves even those who take what is most precious from us. The most awesome

thing about God is the width of His embrace. I think that in the end my
mother understood that too, for she never allowed her grief to cloud her joy,
never allowed that moment of despair to impede a lifetime of laughter.

"When I sit at a family gathering, with literally dozens of children and
grandchildren, nieces and nephews surrounding me, tears come to my
eyes. I marvel at their talents, their articulateness, their devotion to justice,
and their grace. I am reminded once again that family shapes us all, and
that to be held in the arms of a loving family redeems even the most
numbing pain.

"Relationships like that don't even require words. At the end of my
mother's life, when she could no longer speak, the smallest children in the
family used to love to spend time with her, exactly because there was no
expectation that they would have to talk to her, as they did with other
adults. We who sometimes drown in words could afford to learn that
sometimes the deepest relationships are built without them."

What binds us together across our differences in religion or politics or
economic theory is that when each one of us is cut, our blood flows red.
Mine does and yours does too. Those who would try to appropriate God
or family or country for their own narrow ends, who believe that religious
faith is the property of one particular ideology, forget the width of God's
embrace, the healing power of a family's arms, and the generosity of this
country's vision. God, family, and nation belong to us all.

And they belong to us all because of all that we share as human beings—the wonder that we experience when we look at the night sky; the
gratitude that we know when we feel the heat of the sun; the sense of humor in the face of the unbearable and the persistence of suffering. And
one thing more: the capacity to reach across our differences to offer a hand
of healing.

In 1958 my father wrote a letter to a friend whose son had died. Fourteen years earlier, my oldest brother Joe had been killed in World War II.
Ten years earlier, my oldest sister Kathleen had been killed in an airplane

crash in Europe. My father wrote to his grieving friend: "There are no words to dispel your feelings at this time, and there is no time that will ever dispel them. Nor is it any easier the second time than it was the first. And yet, I cannot share your grief, because no one could share mine. When one of your children goes out of your life, you think of what he might have done with a few more years, and you wonder what you are going to do with the rest of yours. Then one day, because there is a world to be lived in, you find yourself a part of it again, trying to accomplish something—something that he did not have time enough to do. And, perhaps, that is the reason for it all. I hope so."

I wish that life were simpler. I wish that loved ones didn't have to die too young. I wish that tragedy never haunted a single soul. But to wish all that is to ask for an end to our humanity. God, family, and country sustain us all.

Legend has it that in the ancient world, a poetry contest was held each year. The third-place winner received a rose made out of silver. The second-place winner received a rose made out of gold. But the first-place winner received a real rose, a beautiful living rose that soon wilted, dried up, and died. I ask you, is there a single one among us who would not choose the living rose?

CHAPTER TWENTY-FIVE

Senator
2000–2008

In 1947, shortly after Jack was sworn in to Congress for the first time, he gave me a tour of Capitol Hill. I was nearly fifteen, and right then was when I first felt a physical love of the place, the columns and corridors and canvases. At the end of our tour, Jack gave me advice that has stayed with me to this day:

"You've just seen all the buildings that symbolize what is important about this country. But remember that it isn't just the buildings. It's what happens inside the buildings that matters."

To say that I love the Senate does not begin to convey what that institution means to me. Let me put it this way: after nearly half a century, I still cannot be in a car, headed for the Capitol, especially in the evening, and glimpse it in the distance without the hair standing up on my arms. I've told Vicki: if ever that sight does not move me, I will know it is time to step aside.

That building symbolizes to me the benevolent power and the majesty of our government. It is awesome to me: not "awesome" in the reflexive way that young people use the word, but in its real sense, its older sense, as evoking reverence.

Being a senator changes a person. Something fundamental and profound happens to you when you arrive there, and it stays with you all the time that you are privileged to serve. I have seen the changes in people who have come into the Senate. It may take a year, or two years, or three years, but it always happens: it fills you with a heightened sense of purpose.

I'm not alone in those sentiments. I remember visiting Senator Russell Long in his cavernous office shortly after I heard he planned to retire. Like me, he had become a senator at age thirty, and he represented Louisiana for thirty-nine years. He told me that he had counted on his cousin Congressman Gillis Long to tell him when to quit, because he'd seen other senators who had hung on too long. But Gillis was dead, so he had decided on his own.

"Well, Russell," I said, "a few hours ago one of the real pillars that hold up that building over there disappeared from underneath the structure."

"Kennedy," he responded, "let me tell you how long it will take for another pillar to spring right up. It doesn't take long with these younger fellows." He added, "Once in a while around here, you do something that you believe in—that's right." For Long, it was supporting the Panama Canal Treaty against strong opposition.

That desire to do the right thing, to serve the national interest, is inspired by the surroundings. I've studied the great architecture of government buildings and memorials in France, in Germany, in Great Britain, and other nations. Our Capitol is unique in the world in its design. It is a presence at once historic and alive in the moment.

As a senator, you move past the impact of the building itself. But you never move very far past it. You cannot go from one room to another— and there are so many rooms—without expecting to see something new or different, even in the familiar.

Take the paintings, for example; the magnificent paintings. I paint a little myself, as I've mentioned, and so perhaps I am more moved, and humbled, by their richness. I think of those big, sweeping, elegant canvases of John Trumbull that hang in the Rotunda: *Declaration of Independence, Surrender of General Burgoyne, Surrender of Lord Cornwallis,* and *General George Washington Resigning His Commission.* Trumbull was a Harvard man and an aide to Washington in the Revolutionary War; he witnessed the Battle of Bunker Hill. Those oils are the most dramatic paintings in the Capitol. They have hung there since 1826. And of course there are those towering murals and frescoes and portraits by Constantino Brumidi. Brumidi was Italian, but when he arrived in the United States in 1852 at age forty-seven, he made himself one of us by declaring, "My ambition and my daily prayer is that I may live long enough to make beautiful the Capitol of the one country on earth in which there is liberty." Which he did, over twenty-seven years of constant work. His fresco *Apotheosis of George Washington* graces the Rotunda along with the Trumbulls, and his paintings flow through many rooms and hallways, most notably the famous "Brumidi corridor."

Even the Senate desks hold great meaning. A lot of these mahogany desks, forty-eight of them, I believe, date to 1819: the Senate bought them that year as part of the restoration after the British set the Capitol afire during the War of 1812. My desk is the one that Jack sat in when he was in the Senate. Barack Obama sat in Bobby's old desk when he was a senator. Daniel Webster's old desk is always reserved for the senior senator from New Hampshire, Webster's native state.

Then there's the tradition of scratching our names into the wood on the bottoms of our desk drawers, to chronicle which senator held which desk down through the years. This custom dates only to the early 1900s. Jack did this, and I did it, and Bobby did it.

Finally, we have the tradition of the "candy desk." In the late 1960s, Senator George Murphy of California had a desk on the back row on the Republican side of the chamber. We all knew that George had a sweet tooth and kept candy in his desk drawer. Senators had to pass by his desk to walk on and off the floor and would often reach into his desk drawer for candy. It quickly became a tradition that whoever occupied that desk inherited the responsibility of keeping its drawer well stocked with candy. As I write this, Senator Mel Martinez of Florida sits at the candy desk and maintains its supply of sweets.

Sometime later, Democratic senators began their own candy desk tradition. It's the Democratic Secretary's desk—a beautiful old rolltop desk in a corner of the Senate chamber. Senators contribute to a candy fund to keep that desk supplied, too.

I love spending time in the Russell Senate Office Building, known before 1972 as the Old Senate Office Building. It's a fine old Beaux-Arts structure that was finished in 1909. Being inside it gives you a marvelous sense of closeness to its history. You walk into that old building and it takes your breath away. You stand up straighter. The architecture is such that you can speak in its rotunda and hear your voice echoing back perfectly. In fact, in the Senate chamber, even if you haven't got a booming voice, you can still be heard just about all through that building.

Senators and their families used to have picnics on the grounds back in the 1960s and '70s. A number of us had young children at that time, and we'd sit out on the lawn with them and enjoy the evening. There's a lantern atop the dome of the Capitol that stays lit as long as either the House or Senate is in session. Also, the American flag stays raised over the Senate chamber as long as the Senate is in session. So we could always tell when the Senate was meeting. And there's a system of lights and bells throughout the Senate complex that told us what was happening on the floor at that moment. One light or one bell meant a vote was starting. Five lights or five bells told us that vote was ending soon and we'd better hurry over to cast our votes. Two lights or two bells were a "quorum call," which meant that we could safely continue picnicking with our families. We would leave the windows of the Russell Building open during our picnics so that we were sure to hear the bells and know when we needed to run off to a vote. It was a friendly, welcoming place back then, the Senate. That has not been lost: the sense that it is the people's building.

In my early years in the Senate, there were not nearly the number of votes that we have now. When the weather was good, the Old Bulls—the senior members who wielded all the power—would spend their mornings at the Congressional Country Club in Bethesda playing golf. They'd return to their offices around noon, just in time for lunch in the Senate Dining Room. After that, they would sign their mail, perhaps make a speech on the Senate floor; and by then it was time to gather for a little drink in some senator's office. Then they'd spend their evenings at various social events.

The events that changed all that were the civil rights era and the Vietnam War, both in the mid-1960s. This time marked the resurgence of the filibuster, and also of the five-day workweek. The Senate was suddenly in session virtually twelve months a year, with only the Fourth of July, Labor Day, and Thanksgiving off. I remember coming back to Washington to cast a vote between Christmas and New Year's when Bobby was in the Senate.

And yet this constant work under extreme social pressure gave the Senate a real sense of community. We were in session a good number of evenings, so everyone stayed around through the week. I can remember having my children at the office. Many senators did. In summer, the military bands used to play in front of the Senate steps on the east side of the Capitol. At intervals, senators might scurry away from outdoor family picnics and onto the floor to offer an amendment.

This camaraderie in the midst of hard work helped senators to listen to one another, and sometimes even to take action on matters they might have otherwise avoided. That's missing today. Now the Senate is basically in session from Tuesday through Thursday. Colleagues "speak" to each other via BlackBerry and telephone. This loss of face-to-face interaction certainly isn't unique to the Senate, but I do think it's a loss. I'm a big believer in going to a colleague's office if I have something I want to discuss or a request I want to make. I want to read their face, interact, laugh.

Ninety-five percent of the nitty-gritty work of drafting and even negotiating is now done by staff. That alone marks an enormous shift of responsibility over the past forty or fifty years. We have an extraordinarily capable, committed, and professional staff, themselves tremendous public servants. Most senators do. And we couldn't tackle the myriad issues without their essential work. But we walk a fine line. As senators, we need to be vigilant that we don't lose track of the whole essence of what the Senate *is*; of what our involvement in it signifies; of our relationship with people; and of what all of that should lead to, which is the unfettered and vital exchange of ideas.

I think of the withering away of collegiality and sense of collective mission as the corruption of the Senate. I don't mean corruption in a legal sense; rather I mean corruption in the sense that things are broken. This breakdown has been driven primarily by two factors. First, there are forces that actually do not want the Senate to meet and be active in the affairs of the nation. If the Senate is not active, legislation slows down, we don't deal with the hard issues, because dealing with them suggests change. And second is the distorted influence of money and the power of vested interests in the legislative process. I don't think any unbiased observer can deny that the way campaigns are financed has an unhealthy influence on the legislative process. I was an early supporter of public financing for House and Senate campaigns as well as presidential campaigns, but that isn't going to happen in my lifetime. Perhaps the advent of Internet fund-raising, which was so successful in President Obama's election, will undercut the disproportionate impact of money on the legislative process.

I was naturally dismayed by the ambiguities of the 2000 election, and disturbed by the Supreme Court's role and decision-making process in it. But I applauded Al Gore's grace and civility in handling the outcome, and prepared myself to deal with the realities. Alan Simpson, who'd been a political adversary and personal friend of mine when he was a Republican senator from Wyoming, assured me that George W. Bush was a fellow I could work with; his word counted; and he told the new president the same thing about me. I took Alan at his word, which I always knew I could count on.

Our first social invitation from the new president and First Lady was to a screening of *Thirteen Days*, the new movie about the Cuban Missile Crisis starring Kevin Costner as Jack's aide Kenny O'Donnell. The screening was held on Thursday night, February 1, 2001, the day the Senate voted to confirm John Ashcroft as attorney general by a vote of fifty-eight to forty-two.

I recognized this invitation as a gesture of respect and goodwill from the president and took it as a harbinger of cooperation in the months ahead. In that spirit, Vicki and I arrived at the White House with a gift to the Bushes, a framed memento of President Kennedy's historic *Resolute* desk. On my first meeting with Bush in the Oval Office a week or so earlier, he'd pointed out to me that he had chosen the desk Jack used in the Oval Office.

When the president and First Lady came down the stairs, I greeted him and said, "Congratulations on your day." He shot me a cool glance. I guessed that I couldn't blame him much. I'd been vocal in my opposition to the confirmation of John Ashcroft as attorney general, and in the debate that preceded the vote earlier in the day I'd repeated my charge that the nominee had used litigation and legislation "in creative and inappropriate ways" to advance his ideological goals. How could we have any confidence, I'd asked, that Ashcroft wouldn't do the same thing as attorney general? I had not thought this exceeded the bounds of legitimate debate, and I'd assumed the president would not take it personally. He did not.

He introduced Vicki and me to the First Lady, and we quickly found an upbeat topic—the quality of the singing at the prayer breakfast that morning. The East Room was quickly filling up with other guests. We repaired to the buffet for a distinctive dinner of hamburgers, hot dogs, and chili, and then we filed in for the screening. Vicki and I were invited to sit in the front row next to the Bushes.

I could tell that the president loved the movie. He was amused that the film didn't show Lyndon Johnson in any of the critical meetings on the crisis, and got a great kick out of the portrayal of Bobby, who was depicted as always rasping about straightening somebody out, or kicking tail, or loyalty. We were out of there by 9:40.

President Bush had signaled a willingness to tackle education reform, and I was certainly willing to work together to find agreement on something that would make a difference. He called his effort No Child Left Behind.

Republicans controlled the Senate and the House, and I was the ranking Democratic member of the Senate Health, Education, and Labor Committee, of which Jim Jeffords of Vermont was the chairman. I was pleased that the president was interested in education reform and assumed that time would tell just how serious he was.

But in the meantime, I felt it imperative to keep the lines of communication with the White House open. One reason was the opportunity to keep the federal government involved in education. Abolishing the Department of Education had been a popular cause among some Republicans, who preferred to see school policy reside entirely within the individual states. But some states are wealthier than others, and some are more under the sway of extra-educational forces that can affect the quality of learning. But I believed that federal resources could be effectively used as a helping hand in areas where there is an obvious need: as a partner, not a competitor, in improving education.

The other reason is that we were elected to do something. And, politics aside, if we had a shot at education reform, especially with a Republican president and a Republican Senate and Republican House, well, I was going to try to seize it. Several months of negotiation, frustration, and compromise led at last to the passage of No Child Left Behind late in 2001. Flawed but necessary, No Child was itself a child of bipartisanship.

My faith in No Child Left Behind was bolstered by the evaluation of Bush's blueprint by my counterpart in the House, George Miller of California. Miller was the new ranking Democrat on the House Education and Labor Committee. He was a powerhouse on many progressive issues, education foremost among them. He'd been impressed with Bush's grasp of educational matters. Miller and I would work closely together in crafting the "No Child" concept into legislation, along with two Republicans, Senator Judd Gregg of New Hampshire and Congressman John Boehner of Ohio.

No Child Left Behind was to be the title for Bush's proposed $46.7 billion reauthorization of the Elementary and Secondary Education Act, a leading feature of Lyndon Johnson's War on Poverty back in 1965. It had been set to expire in 1970, but had been reauthorized by Congress approximately every five years since. Partisan fighting in Congress had stunted the Education Act's effectiveness for many years, with Republicans demanding more emphasis on block grants and voucher programs, and Democrats pushing for reduced class size and teacher training. Its scheduled reauthorization in 1999–2000 was in fact lost in the ideological sparring of the presidential campaign.

The annual expenditure for Bush's plan was budgeted at $17.4 billion. Its tools of reform were to be standards and accountability, with a high emphasis on testing and with the federal government taking the dominant role in measuring the results. I had spent a good deal of time familiarizing myself with testing measures, and I found this approach full of promise. Accordingly, I expressed great public enthusiasm at the outset. I complimented Bush's personality and his intelligence. I emphasized to the press the areas in which Republicans and Democrats generally agreed on No Child. And I downplayed such thorny issues as the vouchers question.

By early April, things were looking rather good; enough compromise had been achieved that Senate debate on the bill could move forward. The Democrats agreed to use federal funds for private tutoring of students at failing schools and Republicans let go of the push for vouchers, at least for the time being. Our side even consented to a trial block-grant program involving seven states. To the consternation of some of my Senate colleagues, I announced "substantial progress" to the press and praised President Bush for keeping education reform as his top priority.

Full Senate debate on No Child began in May and continued for a rigorous and exhausting six weeks. Bipartisanship ruled the day in the early going; my Democratic colleagues and I were pleased to see several important agreements and concessions from the administration's side: targeting resources to children in the neediest schools, increased support for teachers, and stronger parent involvement in schools. These and other progressive measures were authorized in the bill that finally emerged. That was the good news.

But, as with all bills of this nature, we would still need the necessary appropriation of funds from the Congress. The president never fought for the funds he promised. When the Republican-controlled Congress announced its budget resolution in early May, appropriations for No Child Left Behind fell far short of what we needed. I was angry, and said so, yet my thoughts were focused not on accepting defeat but on finding ways to keep success within reach. I announced my hope of opening up funding by attacking the huge tax cuts then being debated in Congress, and by getting more money into the Labor, Health, and Human Services appropriations bill that was also headed for a vote.

My party had been adapting itself to survival without institutional power since the 2000 elections, but on May 24 an act of unusual political courage abruptly ended that situation. The Republican Jim Jeffords of Vermont announced that he was ending his affiliation with his party. The precipitating event was the president's and the Republican Party's lack of commitment to special education funding in the budget. Jeffords would become an independent, but would caucus from now on with the Democrats. Jeffords's decision had several immediate effects. It gave Democrats a de facto fifty-one-seat majority. It turned over committee chairmanships to Democrats, unseated Trent Lott as majority leader in favor of Tom Daschle, and on June 6 restored me to chairmanship of the Health, Education, Labor, and Pensions Committee.

On June 14, the Senate passed the bill to reauthorize the Elementary and Secondary Education Act, with ninety-one senators voting in favor. I was enormously heartened; I had done everything in my power to keep people from both parties together on this. I understood the apprehension of some on my side. "What is absolutely essential," I pointedly told the press, "is having the kind of funding levels to make sure children who need extra help get it." For now, what mattered to me was that education reform was still alive. The bill now would head for a conference committee that would try to bring it and the House's bill into alignment. Improving its weaker elements and fighting for funding, I believed, could be tackled once it became law.

Bush called for Congress to send him a bill to sign before recessing in early August. Easier said than done. George Miller and I, leading the Democrats, worked hard to find common ground with the Republicans John Boehner and Judd Gregg, but we stalled on several issues. July and August passed without an agreement.

On the morning of September 11, 2001, I sat in my Senate office with Senator Gregg, awaiting the arrival of Laura Bush, whom we were to escort across the hall to her testimony before our committee on the subject of early education. I had brought a painting of mine to give her as a memento. The First Lady's husband was at an elementary school in Sarasota, Florida, reading to a class of young pupils as part of his tour to publicize his administration's commitment to education reform. I was waiting for Mrs. Bush when someone from my office came to tell me that Vicki had just called: an airplane had crashed into one of the World Trade Center towers in New York. At this point, reports were that it was likely a small plane that veered off course, but Vicki raised the specter of terrorism.

I found the news bizarre, grotesque. Judd Gregg felt the same way. A few minutes later Vicki called again.

Aware now that something cataclysmic and deliberate had happened to the nation, we saw Mrs. Bush perhaps seventy-five yards down the corridor, walking toward me in front of her Secret Service detail. The rest of that day is part of the nation's history. Mrs. Bush, Judd Gregg, and I announced that we would postpone our hearing, but that we would not be defeated by terrorism. Senator Gregg and I then spent the next couple of hours on Capitol Hill with Mrs. Bush. We kept the television set off and simply talked for a while. I will always remember her composure and elegance, qualities that she drew upon in the hours that followed to help comfort a nation in shock.

A sense of patriotism and shared responsibility took hold in all of us. Getting the education bill enacted into law had become both an affirmation of America's values and a demonstration to all countries that this Congress would not allow terrorism to cripple its ability to continue the nation's essential work.

Huge differences remained, however, and as talks progressed through the fall, they centered more and more on the cost of the reforms. Those crafting the appropriations bill for 2002 had floated a figure of $4 billion in discretionary spending increases for education. That was far too little to do what needed to be done. I called for twice that amount. And House conservatives revealed their own preferred level of expenditure increases: none whatsoever.

Exhaustive negotiations regarding testing requirements and funding provisions (and many other issues) continued for almost two months among designated members in the House and Senate. Finally, on December 12, 2001, we agreed on the specifics of the legislation. It was the only bipartisan measure of any scope passed in that year. The following January, President Bush signed No Child Left Behind into law.

In several important ways, the Democrats had scored a major victory. Our negotiations had produced an appropriations agreement of $22.6 billion for education in fiscal 2002, a gigantic increase over Bush's original goal of just a $685 million increase over the previous year's $17.4 billion. And we had retained many of the policy principles that we'd considered essential from the start.

My remarks as the bill became law were conciliatory. "This is the president's signature issue," I said. "He can claim a big victory. But so can we, as well as the children." I genuinely believed this. No Child, as I saw it then, was the most significant advance in public education of the past quarter century.

In other important ways, however, our victory rested on shaky ground. Though the $22.6 billion represented a 20 percent increase over the previous education budget, Miller and I believed that it was still not enough to fulfill the standards that the act itself required.

That worry became sadly moot a few weeks later, when President Bush sent his new budget to Congress. It included none of the new money he had promised us. He blamed the costs of the military strike in Afghanistan, seeking the terrorists responsible for the 9/11 attacks, for the need to trim back.

No Child has struggled on through the ensuing years, effective in some ways, but never the transformative tool that it could have been: "underfunded, mismanaged, and poorly implemented," as I put it, "a spectacular broken promise of the Republican administration and Congress." I added that America's children deserved better.

All of America's people deserved better than the misuse of U.S. power in Iraq. As did the Iraqi people. The war's effects are still fresh as I write these words, and so I will attempt no detailed retelling of them here. Looking over my personal journals and the many speeches and briefing memos in my files, I am struck once again at how clear the march to disaster seemed to me at the time, and how brazenly the administration's justifications departed from reality.

That march began in the glow of Americans' support for President Bush immediately following the September 11 attacks by Al Qaeda, and for his sending troops to Afghanistan to hunt down the terrorists responsible. The president and his men lost no time exploiting that trust and goodwill. In what I have called an "extraordinary policy coup" led by Vice President Cheney, Secretary of Defense Donald Rumsfeld, and Rumsfeld's deputy Paul Wolfowitz, the administration succeeded in changing the subject to Iraq.

I had met Vice President Cheney years before, when he was a congressman, through our mutual friend Alan Simpson, who like Cheney was from Wyoming. Cheney seemed agreeable to me at first, affable and smart, even though we had different political views. His votes were ultra-conservative. Maybe we just didn't notice how extreme he was because his positions didn't carry the day. But when he became vice president, he had the power, but he lacked the good judgment to see beyond those extreme views.

I withheld my final judgment on the prudence of the Iraq war until I went back to the Senate in September 2002. There are no more important votes that a senator makes than on issues of war and peace, and I wanted to understand the issue fully before reaching a final decision. As a member of the Armed Services Committee, I listened carefully to the testimony of the witnesses.

I was struck by the consistent drumbeat of opposition to the rush to war by respected military leaders—General John Shalikashvili, former chairman of the Joint Chiefs of Staff; General Wesley Clark, former Supreme Allied Commander, Europe; marine general Joseph Hoar, former commander in chief of Central Command. I will never forget what General Hoar in particular said in response to my question about urban warfare. He said that Baghdad would look like the last fifteen minutes of the Spielberg movie *Saving Private Ryan*.

My views on war drew upon the teachings of Saint Augustine and Saint Thomas Aquinas. A distillation of their philosophies has yielded six principles that guide the determination of a "just" war, and these principles were my guiding arguments:

- A war must have a just cause, confronting a danger that is beyond question;
- It must be declared by a legitimate authority acting on behalf of the people;
- It must be driven by the right intention, not ulterior, self-interested motives;
- It must be a last resort;

- It must be proportional, so that the harm inflicted does not outweigh the good achieved; and
- It must have a reasonable chance of success.

There was no just cause for the invasion of Iraq, I declared time and again. Iraq posed no threat that justified immediate, preemptive war, and there was no convincing pattern of relationships between Saddam and Al Qaeda. The "legitimate authority," the Congress, indeed approved authorization for the use of force in Iraq in October 2002, but it acted in haste and under pressure from the White House, which intentionally politicized the vote by scheduling it before midterm elections. By contrast, in 1991, the administration of the first President Bush timed the vote on the use of military force against Iraq to occur *after* midterm elections, in order to de-politicize the decision.

As for "motives," those stated by the Bush administration itself were unacceptable on their face. "The Bush administration says we must take preemptive action against Iraq," I pointed out from the Senate floor in October 2002. "But what the administration is really calling for is preventive war, which flies in the face of international rules of acceptable behavior." I was far blunter less than two years later, when the loss of life among our young troops and the devastation to Iraqi society had grown grotesque. The war, I charged on the Senate floor in July 2004, was "a fraud, cooked up in Texas" to advance the president's political standing.

I said that the administration had told "lie after lie after lie after lie" to trigger and perpetuate "one of the worst blunders in the history of U.S. foreign policy." The war failed the "last resort" principle for reasons too obvious to dwell on here. On the question of proportionality—did the harm inflicted outweigh the good achieved?—I pointed, again, to the loss of American and Iraqi lives, the collapse of Iraqi civil society, the self-fulfilling prophecy of terrorists flooding into the ravaged country and using it as a base, the heightened tensions with the entire Islamic world, and our loss of international prestige generally. As for "a reasonable question of success," there never was a question that we would win the military phase of the Iraq war. The more significant success—ending terrorism, promoting regional stability, sustaining America's reputation as a just nation and a model for enlightenment—has yet to be achieved.

I'd first met John Kerry in the spring of 1971, when the Vietnam veterans protesting the war were bivouacked on the Mall in Washington. I was impressed by the forcefulness of this young man with the long, serious face and the great mop of dark hair as he articulated the case against the war, and also by his record of courage in combat.

I wasn't surprised when John decided to enter politics, and I campaigned for him in his first effort, a losing bid for Congress in 1972. He was elected lieutenant governor under Michael Dukakis ten years later, and in 1984 won election to the Senate, taking the seat of Paul Tsongas, who'd retired. He and I voted together on nearly all the issues.

I have enormous respect for John Kerry. He is not only my colleague; he is my friend. When John decided to run for president, I was convinced that a John Kerry presidency would be good for the country. He has courage and strength of character and a strong grasp of foreign policy. He is a certifiable, decorated war hero. I also knew that with Kerry in the White House, we would be able to advance health care for all Americans. I enthusiastically signed on to his team.

But in 2003, John's campaign was faltering. I noticed a sluggishness when I campaigned with him in Iowa. Howard Dean of Vermont was coming on strong as a fresh face. His passion and his fearless stance against the Iraq war were galvanizing Democrats, and he was amassing more money than John with his pioneering use of the Internet as a fund-raising tool. By late September, John's Boston and Washington advisers were at loggerheads, creating divisions that distracted from his campaign. My own chief of staff, the highly competent Mary Beth Cahill, joined him as campaign manager. A new energy soon swept through the Kerry ranks.

When I returned to Iowa with the candidate two weeks before the

January caucuses, I saw that he had been regenerated as well. I was seeing a "new" Kerry, whose speeches were shorter and punchier, and who was making a warm personal connection to the voters.

I was having great fun too, revving up the crowd, teasing them about not voting for me in '80, but saying all would be forgiven if they just voted for John. *Hello, Cedar Rapids. Are you glad to see me? Well I'm glad to see you!* And around the state we went. Jim Rassmann joined John on the trail too, to testify to John's character and heroism. John had saved Rassmann's life in Vietnam and hadn't seen him since, but the veteran found him because he wanted to share his story. Kerry won the Iowa caucuses, won New Hampshire, and rang up nine victories on Super Tuesday to clinch the Democratic nomination in Boston. He picked John Edwards as his running mate. We conferred frequently through the early summer, strategizing on his approaches to the economy and the Iraq war.

In August, not long after the Democratic convention, the so-called Swift Boat Veterans for Truth unleashed their $20 million television smear campaign against John, falsely impugning his stellar military record. They used gutterball tactics of the worst kind.

John had three outstanding debate performances, with the first being especially impressive. Vicki and I continued to campaign hard for him until the last moment.

On election morning, Vicki and I voted at the town hall in Hyannis. The lines were moderate, but we heard that earlier, around dawn, they'd been very long. I had a sense that the momentum was with John. We took a sail before noon, then traveled the seventy miles west to Providence to spend a little time with Patrick, who was headed toward an overwhelming victory in his reelection to Congress. Vicki and I spent the evening in Boston, where I did some television interviews and met with Democratic supporters. The news was reporting enormous turnouts, which all of us believed were to the Democrats' advantage. And the exit polls were showing big advantages for Kerry. "I've been proud to call John Kerry my friend," I told one group of boosters, "and I'm going to be even prouder to call him my president!" The crowd went wild. And then Vicki and I headed to our Boston apartment to watch the returns. Earlier in the evening, when I was doing television interviews, I learned that the networks couldn't get prominent Republicans to respond to the early trends because they were so decisively in John's favor. The White House was in hunker-down mode. Relatives and friends wandered in and out of the apartment as the evening wore on. Projections began to appear showing Bush winning the western states, but that was predictable. The producers were trying to inject drama into a race that they knew had been decided.

Not exactly. Later in the evening, we began to notice that some of the eastern states we'd expected to end up in our column were not going that way. Florida went for Bush, a disappointment but not a surprise. But the number of states showing up as red in the graphics was a surprise. The heavy Kerry votes we'd counted on—that the exit polls had told us were there—were just not coming in.

Suddenly, we noticed that Republicans were materializing onscreen for live interviews. They were no longer in the bunker. The terrible awareness of a turning tide crept in. Then Bush called reporters into the White House, where he was watching with his family. We tried to tell ourselves that this was just a bit of stagecraft, to give the illusion that he was winning.

Around 11 p.m., California came in with a big win for John, but the sea of red between California and Illinois was unbroken. And it started to become clear that the only path to a Democratic victory was through Ohio. James Carville on one of the channels was saying that John Kerry had to pull an inside straight; that it was time to recognize that this was George Bush's night, not Kerry's, unless something dramatic happened. The people in our apartment were rather distraught by James saying that. They thought perhaps it was sour grapes because he hadn't been invited to run the campaign. But I just thought he was being honest. I telephoned Tim Hagan, a friend of ours in Cleveland who said things still were fine, Cuyahoga County was looking good, we think we've got Ohio; the exit polls . . .

The night went on, and the numbers grew more disturbing. Vicki later said she'd felt the networks were not calling the election for Bush only for fear of repeating the Florida fiasco of four years earlier. I called Hagan again. Nick Littlefield, a top lawyer in Boston and former staff director of my committee, was there, and he talked to Hagan. Michael Myers, our friend and current committee staff director, talked to Hagan. And then I talked to Hagan again and Tim said quietly, "I think we've lost it."

Almost at the same moment, Fox News called the election for Bush.

In the silence that followed, people began to leave the apartment to go home to bed. Soon Vicki and I were alone. It was well after midnight. I made a decision. "We're going to Louisburg Square," I told my wife, "to see John and Teresa."

It was a drizzly, dreary, humid, cold night in Boston, and close to 2:30 a.m. when we arrived. Gabby, the Kerrys' household assistant, met us at the door and told us that John and Teresa had gone to bed. We offered to leave, but Gabby told us not to: "The senator will be upset if he knows you're here and he wasn't told." She went upstairs. A few minutes later, the defeated Democratic candidate for the presidency came down into the living room to greet us. Vicki spotted him first. "Gosh, Vicki, what a drag. This is a drag, isn't it?" he said as Vicki hugged him and said, "Boy, is it ever." I gave John a warm handshake and then an embrace. "My friend, how are you doing?" I asked him. He replied, "There are so many things I wanted to do for this country."

I was deeply moved by the reaction of this war hero who had fought so hard to win the election and who just hours earlier looked to all the world like he was going to be the next president of the United States. He wasn't bitter or angry. And he wasn't really focused on himself. He was down about the opportunities lost to move the country in a new, more progressive direction. I shared his disappointment. We had worked so hard, and come so close.

The reelection of President Bush meant that it would be another four years before there might be a great leader in the White House. In my nearly fifty years of public life, we have not had a president as successful as FDR. The closest we've come (family relations excluded) is Lyndon Johnson. Civil rights was the issue of our time. He picked up that unfinished work and ensured the passage of the Civil Rights Act and Voting Rights Act. If he hadn't, we certainly wouldn't be where we are today. We certainly wouldn't have the president we have today. Lyndon Johnson knew how to work Congress and move things forward to achieve his goal of a Great Society.

Tragically, the Vietnam War ended all that. Johnson got caught up in it and handled it miserably. The cold war was at its height, and we all had reasons for believing at first that our involvement was vital. But the continued escalation was a huge blunder. It needlessly took so many lives and sucked all of the air and energy out of our progressive ideals. We lost our way. It would take time for voters to endorse those values again.

I rejoice in having lived to see it happen.

CHAPTER TWENTY-SIX

Perseverance
2009

I have never dwelled on reversals: a defeated bill or a legislative cause that remains unrealized year after year; an election that goes the wrong way. There has been so much to be thankful for. There have been so many reasons for hope.

In the early months of 2008, out of a crowded field of talented Democratic primary candidates, there emerged a young man so compelling, so electric, his mind so alive with good ideas, that before I knew it, I was hopscotching around the western states for him like a fellow half my age, pumping my fist and telling wildly cheering crowds, "I smell *change* in the air!"

I had many longtime friends among the Democratic presidential contenders: Joe Biden, Hillary Clinton, Chris Dodd, John Edwards, Bill Richardson. And I had come to respect my new colleague Barack Obama. All of these candidates were more than qualified to be president and I would have enthusiastically supported any of them had they been the party's nominee. But I held back at first from getting involved in the primary. As I said many times, I was waiting to see who was capable of lifting up and inspiring our nation to move forward, toward our highest and best ideals, before I decided to endorse anyone. On the night of the Iowa caucuses, Vicki and I watched Barack Obama's victory speech and knew that he had the capacity to inspire. I was among the millions moved as well by Senator Clinton's powerful and uplifting appeal, but I came to believe that Obama was the candidate we needed now at this time in our history. As I talked with my niece Caroline, her children, and our children, I saw the impact that Obama's words were having on them. I felt more and more certain that history had handed us that rarest of figures, one who could truly carve out new frontiers. Or, as the candidate put it in a phrase that resounded everywhere: "Yes we can!"

At around eight o'clock on Thursday morning, January 24, 2008, two days before the critically important South Carolina primary, I spoke with Senator Obama from my home in Washington. "Listen, pal! Is there room on that train of yours for an old—" I couldn't get the rest of it out before the future president's delighted laughter interrupted me, and I laughed along with him. Then I told him, more seriously, "I'm really very strongly in your corner. At the beginning of this whole process I was looking for the person who was going to inspire. That's what the country needs, and I think you've got it."

The next day, Barack gained his breakout victory in South Carolina. Shortly after that, we were out campaigning like it was 1960.

New Mexico, California, New Jersey, Connecticut, Massachusetts— all on February 4, the eve of Super Tuesday. Barack picked up thirteen states to Hillary's ten the next day. A day later, I saw Hillary on the Senate floor and congratulated her on her strong showing. She was smiling and laughing. Despite my endorsement of Obama, my state of Massachusetts was one of those in her "win" column. Barack, who was nearby, caught the mood of the moment; he came over to us and joked, "Maybe, Hillary, I should have let him endorse you." Then I spotted John Kerry and said, "Well, I'm not too good on the endorsing. I endorsed Kerry, too, and look what happened to him!" It was a lighthearted and lively moment, which I think the Senate sometimes shows when it's at its best.

Then Vicki and I hit the trail again: Maine, Pennsylvania, Washington. Maine again. D.C., Maryland, Virginia, Ohio. Our packed schedule of flights and motorcades might have been exhausting, but we were constantly recharged by the prevailing mood of joy. The crowds were large and festive and welcoming, and they made it a pleasure for me to be back on the stump. It was fun, sheer fun.

Hillary fought on with extraordinary determination and skill, and kept the outcome in doubt until the late spring. By that time, of course, I was recovering from my successful surgery at Duke Medical Center, and hoping to be well enough by August to make that appearance at the Democratic convention in Denver. That hope came true, as did my promise to be in Washington for the inauguration of President Obama. He has the potential to be a great president.

And speaking of hope, I still recall that first evening I spent after my seizure in Massachusetts General Hospital: eating chowder from Legal Seafood with Vicki and my children and watching the Red Sox game on TV. But not even someone as hopeful as I would have imagined that on April 7, 2009, I would be standing on the mound at Fenway Park. Like Honey Fitz in 1912, I was ready to throw out the first pitch on Opening Day. I leaned in and peered down for the sign from Hall of Famer Jim Rice, who crouched a few feet away. The first pitch fell short of the target, but I was determined, so I threw a second one and hit my mark. As I later told my grandchildren, I was going to keep throwing until I got it right. Persistence matters.

As my story draws to a close, I am living with cancer. And I know that I will die with it and likely from it. But I don't dwell on that. I have good days and not-so-good days. But more than a year after my diagnosis, I have not yet spent a day in bed. With Vicki's constant help and encouragement, I follow a healthy diet and continue to do moderate exercise. I look forward to going outside every day, rain or shine, to breathe fresh air. I tire more easily than before and need extra rest, and I sometimes use one word when I mean to use another. Still, I continue to sail, as much as the weather allows. And I pray.

All of my life, the teachings of my faith have provided solace and hope, as have the wonders of nature, especially the sea, where religion and spirituality meet the physical. This faith has been as meaningful to me as breathing or loving my family. It's all intertwined.

My faith, and the love of following its rituals, has always been my foundation and my inspiration. Those foundations have been shaken at times by tragedy and misfortune, but faith remains fixed in my heart, as it has been since my childhood days. It is the most positive force in my life and the cause of my eternal optimism. I have fallen short in my life, but my faith has always brought me home.

For almost fifty years, I have represented people who are facing injustice or pain. Life can be violent and grim, but I think of the Resurrection and I feel a sense of hope. When I've started down a spiral of depression or negativism or loss, I've been lucky enough to be able to see another side that can catch me on the way. I believe that if you have a warm and embracing heart, faith can have a powerful impact on your outlook. Vicki has been a great source of strength and love because we share this underlying belief and faith.

Life is eternal. Work continues. It is a calling, an opportunity to do things about injustice or unfairness. It helps to have a goal. I've always tried to have one.

Even this disease has proved itself an impetus for hope. In my lifetime I have witnessed advances in medical understanding of malignancy and treatment for it that would have been unthinkable in my early years. Teddy Jr., then Kara, then myself—three "hopeless" victims of unusually deadly attacks—are among the millions who've enjoyed extended life thanks to these ongoing breakthroughs. Yet so much more is possible. I see how far we've come in my lifetime. When I first campaigned for Jack in the 1960 presidential primaries, Medicare didn't even exist. Now it is part of our national contract.

Even in these challenging times, there are daily reasons to rejoice. After years of work, we finally passed a national service bill that will triple the size of AmeriCorps and dramatically expand opportunities for service by all Americans.

And, of course, my work to improve health care, the great cause of my life, will continue to my last day (and beyond if, as I hope, these words inspire readers to take up the cause). One of the great lessons I've learned from a life in politics is that no reform is ever truly complete. We must constantly keep moving forward, seeking ways to create that more perfect union. In my personal life, I kept moving to avoid the tragedy behind me. As a senator, that same motivation has been a blessing.

These days, simple pleasures fill me with happiness. In my seventy-seven years I have never grown tired of sitting on my front porch and looking out over Nantucket Sound. The waters change texture and color with the light, the weather, the seasons, the time of day. I still pass many contented hours sitting in my green-cushioned wicker chair, with a hot mug of tea on the table beside me, gazing at the sea, the diving osprey, the gulls that can be suspended in midair as they fly against the wind. I love the reflection of the setting sun on the wooden masts of *Mya*; the rising moon; the beauty of a rainbow after a storm. I am seldom far from the company of my dogs, Splash, Sunny, and now our new pup Captains Courageous (Cappy). They love to retrieve tennis balls, and if a ball finds its way into the water, the dogs won't be far behind.

Sailing is still my favorite pastime. Being on the ocean has thrilled me and comforted me and protected me for all my life, and I love that time now, perhaps more than ever. I also take pleasure in knowing that the sea has formed a bond with our grandchildren as well.

One of my favorite stories is how Little Teddy in particular has developed into a sailor. I'm Big Teddy. Medium Teddy is my son. And Little Teddy is his son, Edward Moore Kennedy III, born in 1998.

In the summer of 2008, ten-year-old Little Teddy spent the summer in Hyannis Port, working hard on his sailing. As he told me one evening, his father passed sailing on to him just as I had passed it on to his father. It was a Kennedy tradition to sail. The problem was, though, that throughout July, nothing seemed to go right with Little Teddy's sailing and he wasn't having very much fun. He would race his boat and come in last or second to last. He would swamp his boat and spend his time bailing it out. He was often miserable and shed more than a few tears. But his father and I encouraged him. Keep sailing. Try this technique. Don't give up. I told Teddy of my being eighth string on the Harvard football team and how I was not the best athlete by far. But I stayed with it and didn't give up and by my senior year I was a starter and caught touchdown passes. His face seemed to light up a bit. "We might not be the best, Teddy, but we can work harder than anyone," I told him. "And that will make the difference."

Little Teddy stayed with it. He grew eager to learn. He got better. He got more than better; he started winning races. When they gave the sailing awards at the end of August, Teddy had won first place for the August series in his division. What a triumph. But what meant even more to him—and, I must say, more to me—is that he won the award for the Most Improved Sailor.

It was a great moment—a grand moment. You couldn't even button up Teddy's coat because his chest was so filled with pride and achievement.

This is the greatest lesson a child can learn. It is the greatest lesson anyone can learn. It has been the greatest lesson I have learned: if you persevere, stick with it, work at it, you have a real opportunity to achieve something. Sure, there will be storms along the way. And you might not reach your goal right away. But if you do your best and keep a true compass, you'll get there.

Acknowledgments

The greatest blessing to me of my more recent years has been my wife Vicki's presence in my life. Indeed, I would never have engaged in this endeavor had she not helped me to talk more openly about feelings that had long since been shut away. Our conversations are long, our banter is fast, and her humor keeps life fun. Words are very much a part of our lives, but it is also the quiet moments when, hand in hand, we invite the stillness in, which truly sustains my faith and touches my heart.

Vicki understood the story I wanted to tell before I did. She helped me address aspects of my life I'd never expressed to anyone before, and she gave me the guidance and confidence to proceed.

This project began in 2004 at the Miller Center of Public Affairs at the University of Virginia, where I have worked closely with James Sterling Young, the director of the Edward M. Kennedy Oral History Project. The oral history served as a basis for many additional conversations with my collaborator on this project, Ron Powers, and my editor, Jonathan Karp.

Ron's gifts as a prose stylist were immediately apparent to me from his acclaimed biography of Mark Twain. Over the past two years, he has infused my stories with his gift for language, his humor, his intelligence, and his compassion. It has been an honor to work with such a dedicated and talented writer.

The judgment and integrity of my attorney Robert Barnett is a matter of fact. He has been a consummate adviser and literary representative in every aspect of this process.

At the Hachette Book Group, we are especially grateful to Chief Executive Officer David Young for supporting this project. Jamie Raab, the publisher of Grand Central Publishing, has been an enthusiastic advocate from our first meeting, and we are deeply grateful for her passion and conviction throughout this process. My publisher and editor, Jonathan Karp, understood this book from the beginning and has been a wise counselor every step of the way. He has prodded me, questioned me, coaxed me, and helped me tell my story in a way that was honest and true to myself. Jon is brilliant and talented, and working with him has been a real gift.

Brendan O'Malley, PhD, and a true son of Boston's Irish community, provided masterful historic research and fact-checking; his talents added immeasurably to the work.

I'm deeply grateful to my friend and attorney Greg Craig who was also part of our team, providing, as always, superb advice and sound judgment.

Thanks as well to Deneen Howell for her outstanding legal work.

Judy Campbell and Caroline Gannon facilitated the many meetings and interviews that went into the writing of this book, and they kept my papers organized. I could not have completed the book on time without them.

Bob Shrum and Linda Semans Donovan joined together to interview me (Bob) and film me (Linda) about the book, and they produced a superb short film. I thank them both for their amazing talent, enormous contribution to the project, and most of all, for decades of friendship.

I am deeply grateful to Stephanie Cutter for all of her advice and assistance. She is the consummate professional and a master of communications.

Jim Young conducted the oral history interviews that formed the basis of much of the book. With his insight as an historian, he prodded me to think about aspects of my life and public service in new and deeper ways.

Kathy Kruse has been a liaison, organizer, facilitator and all around magician. In addition, she and Diane Pyles have been indispensable in gathering photographs from our home collection.

This book was enhanced and improved by the contributions of several outstanding public servants who are my former and present staff members, who worked on some of the issues and events covered in the book and took some of their private time to review relevant passages of the book to help confirm my recollection. I give a warm and sincere thanks to George Abrams, Jeff Blattner, David Burke, Phil Caper, James Flug, Larry Horowitz, Paul Kirk, Nick Littlefield, Michael Myers, David Nexon, Barbara Souliotis, Trina Vargo, and Sharon Waxman. I also thank Eric Mogilnicki for his help along the way and Carey Parker for the indispensable role he's played in every aspect of my public life since 1969.

Special thanks to: Twelve's superb director of publicity, Cary Goldstein; art director Anne Twomey; Denis Reggie, the extraordinary photographer (and my brother-in-law) who shot the cover photo; managing editor Bob Castillo; copy editor Roland Ottewell; interior designer Ellen Rosenblatt, production manager Tom Whatley; indexer Kay Banning; photo researcher Kristine Smith; chief operating officer Kenneth Michaels; production director Antoinette Marotta; advertising director Martha Otis; sales director Christine Barba; counselors Eric Rayman and Carol Ross; Joe Gargan; Twelve assistants Colin Shepherd and Laura Lee Timko; typist Meredith Fletcher of Castleton College; transcribers Connie Procaccini and Gary Girton; literary agent Jim Hornfischer (who represented Ron Powers); Ron's wife, Honoreé Fleming; and everyone else at Hachette and beyond who has contributed to bringing this book to you.

Bibliography

We consulted many books and magazine articles in our research, and we gratefully acknowledge the following works.

Bradlee, Ben. *Conversations with Kennedy.* New York: W.W. Norton & Co, 1975.

———. *A Good Life: Newspapering and Other Adventures.* New York: Simon & Schuster, 1995.

Branch, Taylor. *America in the King Years.* 3 vols. New York: Simon & Schuster, 1988–2006.

Bronner, Ethan. *Battle for Justice: How the Bork Nomination Shook America.* New York: W. W. Norton, 1989.

Burns, James MacGregor. *Edward Kennedy and the Camelot Legacy.* New York: W. W. Norton, 1976.

Cameron, Gail. *Rose: A Biography of Rose Fitzgerald Kennedy.* New York: Putnam, 1971.

Canellos, Peter S., ed. *The Last Lion: The Fall and Rise of Ted Kennedy.* New York: Simon & Schuster, 2009.

Clarke, Thurston. *The Last Campaign: Robert F. Kennedy and 82 Days That Inspired America.* New York: Henry Holt, 2008.

Clymer, Adam. *Edward M. Kennedy: A Biography.* New York: William Morrow, 1999.

Dallek, Robert. *An Unfinished Life: John F. Kennedy, 1917–1963.* Boston: Little, Brown, 2003.

Drew, Elizabeth. A Reporter at Large, "1980: Kennedy." *The New Yorker,* February 4, 1988, 42–95.

Fink, Gary. "Fragile Alliance: Jimmy Carter and the American Labor Movement." In *The Presidency and Domestic Policies of Jimmy Carter,* edited by Herbert D. Rosenbaum and Alexej Ugrinsky. Westport, CT: Greenwood Press, 1993.

Goodwin, Doris Kearns. *The Fitzgeralds and the Kennedys: An American Saga.* New York: Simon & Schuster, 1987.

Gordon, Colin. *Dead on Arrival: The Politics of Health Care in Twentieth-Century America.* Princeton, NJ: Princeton University Press, 2003.

Hersh, Burton. *The Shadow President: Ted Kennedy in Opposition.* South Royalton, VT: Steerforth Press, 1997.

Honan, William H. *Ted Kennedy: Profile of a Survivor.* New York: Quadrangle, 1972.

Kennedy, Edward M. *America Back on Track.* New York: Viking, 2006.

———. *In Critical Condition: The Crisis in America's Health Care.* New York: Simon & Schuster, 1972.

———. *The Fruitful Bough: A Tribute to Joseph P. Kennedy.* Halliday Lithograph Corporation, 1965. Printed for private distribution.

Kennedy, Rose Fitzgerald. *Times to Remember.* Garden City, NY: Doubleday, 1974.

Lippman, Theo, Jr. *Senator Ted Kennedy: The Career Behind the Image.* New York: Norton, 1976.

Lukas, J. Anthony. *Common Ground: A Turbulent Decade in the Lives of Three American Families.* New York: Knopf, 1985.

Mudd, Roger. *The Place to Be: Washington, CBS, and the Glory Days of Television News.* New York: PublicAffairs, 2008.

Nesi, Edward. "Lion in Winter: Edward M. Kennedy in the Bush Years; A Study in Senate Leadership." Honors thesis submitted to the political science department of Wheaton College, Norton, MA, May 19, 2007.

O'Brien, Michael. *John F. Kennedy: A Biography.* New York: St. Martin's Press, 2005.

Perlstein, Rick. *Nixonland: The Rise of a President and the Fracturing of America*. New York: Scribner, 2008.

Schlesinger, Arthur M., Jr. *Journals: 1952–2000*. New York: Penguin, 2007.

———. *Robert Kennedy and His Times*. Boston: Houghton Mifflin, 1978.

———. *A Thousand Days: John F. Kennedy in the White House*. Boston: Houghton Mifflin, 1965.

Sherrill, Robert. *The Last Kennedy*. New York: Dial, 1976.

Shrum, Robert. *No Excuses: Concessions of a Serial Campaigner*. New York: Simon & Schuster, 2007.

Smith, Amanda, ed. *Hostage to Fortune: The Letters of Joseph P. Kennedy*. New York: Viking, 2001.

Stevenson, James. A Reporter at Large, "Senator from Massachusetts." *The New Yorker*, August 25, 1975, 52–77.

Talbert, Jeffrey C., Bryan D. Jones, and Frank R. Baumgartner. "Non-legislative Hearings and Policy Changes in Congress." *American Journal of Political Science* 29, no. 2 (May 1995): 383–405.

Thomas, Evan. *Robert Kennedy: His Life*. Simon & Schuster, 2000.

Walsh, Elsa. A Reporter at Large, "Kennedy's Hidden Campaign." *The New Yorker*, March 31, 1997, 66–81.

Weiner, Tim. *Legacy of Ashes: The History of the CIA*. New York: Doubleday, 2007.

Young, Marilyn B. *The Vietnam Wars, 1945–1990.* New York: Harper-Collins, 1991.

Index

NOTE: The abbreviation EMK in subheadings refers to Edward Moore Kennedy. Italic page numbers refer to photographs.

For information about a signed,

leather-bound limited edition of

True Compass,

go to www.twelvebooks.com

ABOUT TWELVE

TWELVE

TWELVE was established in August 2005 with the objective of publishing no more than one book per month. We strive to publish the singular book, by authors who have a unique perspective and compelling authority. Works that explain our culture; that illuminate, inspire, provoke, and entertain. We seek to establish communities of conversation surrounding our books. Talented authors deserve attention not only from publishers, but from readers as well. To sell the book is only the beginning of our mission. To build avid audiences of readers who are enriched by these works—that is our ultimate purpose.

For more information about forthcoming TWELVE books, please go to www.twelvebooks.com.